·SOUTH-WESTERN·
CENTURY 21
ACCOUNTING

GENERAL JOURNAL
WRAPAROUND TEACHER'S EDITION
VOLUME 2   CHAPTERS 18-26

Kenton E. Ross, CPA
Professor Emeritus of Accounting
Texas A&M University–Commerce
Commerce, Texas

Mark W. Lehman, CPA
Associate Professor
School of Accountancy
Mississippi State University
Starkville, Mississippi

Claudia Bienias Gilbertson, CPA
Teaching Professor
North Hennepin Community College
Brooklyn Park, Minnesota

Robert D. Hanson
Late Associate Dean
College of Business Administration
Central Michigan University
Mount Pleasant, Michigan

THOMSON

SOUTH-WESTERN

Australia · Canada · Mexico · Singapore · Spain · United Kingdom · United States

THOMSON
SOUTH-WESTERN

Century 21 Accounting, Multicolumn Journal, Anniversary Edition
by Kenton E. Ross, Claudia Bienias Gilbertson, Mark W. Lehman, and Robert D. Hanson

Vice President/
Executive Publisher
Dave Shaut
Team Leader
Karen Schmohe
Acquisitions Editor
Marilyn Hornsby
Project Manager
Carol Sturzenberger
Sr. Marketing Manager
Nancy A. Long

Marketing Coordinator
Yvonne Patton-Beard
Production Manager
Patricia Matthews Boies
Manufacturing Coordinator
Kevin Kluck
Editorial Assistant
Stephanie White
Production Assistant
Nancy Stamper

Design Coordinator
Tippy McIntosh
Cycle Opener Artwork
Marti Shohet
Cover Design
Tom Nikosey
Composition/Prepress
Better Graphics
Printer
Von Hoffmann Press

For permission to use material from this text or product, contact us by
Tel (800) 730-2214
Fax (800) 730-2215
www.thomsonrights.com

For more information, contact South-Western, 5191 Natorp Boulevard, Mason, OH 45040; or find us on the World Wide Web at http://www.swep.com

About the Authors
Kenton E. Ross, Ed.D., C.P.A., is Professor Emeritus, Department of Accounting, at Texas A&M University—Commerce. He formerly served as Dean of the College of Business and Technology; Director of Business and Economic Research; and Head, Department of Accounting.

Claudia Bienias Gilbertson, M.B.A., C.P.A., is an experienced high school and community college instructor. She is currently a teaching professor at North Hennepin Community College.

Mark W. Lehman, Ph.D., C.P.A., is an Associate Professor in the School of Accountancy at Mississippi State University, where he teaches in the areas of microcomputers, accounting systems, and auditing. He regularly teaches continuing education classes on microcomputers and internal control.

The late **Robert D. Hanson,** Ph.D., was Professor of Business Education and Associate Dean of the College of Business Administration at Central Michigan University.

INSTRUCTIONAL STRATEGIES TABLE OF CONTENTS

INSTRUCTIONAL STRATEGIES

THE ACCOUNTING TEXTBOOK TEACHERS DESIGNED

We asked. You answered. South-Western Educational Publishing listened to extensive market research and your feedback. We have designed *Century 21 Accounting, Seventh Edition* to help you succeed in your accounting classroom.

Complete Accounting Coverage

Century 21 Accounting, Seventh Edition continues to provide complete coverage of three complete accounting cycles—**proprietorship, partnership,** and **corporation.** Instructors value the three-step process of moving from simple to complex business organizations.

Short, Accessible Lessons

Have you ever heard a student say, "Accounting is hard"? *Century 21 Accounting, Seventh Edition* has the answer. We divide chapters into **short, accessible lessons** that cover one or two concepts each. This Wraparound Teacher's Edition contains comprehensive lesson plans for each lesson, which allows you to plan your instructional time with greater efficiency.

Consistent Placement of Illustrations

Illustrations are consistently placed directly above the corresponding text. No more flipping pages back and forth to find an illustration that appears on a different page from the explanatory text!

Steps and call-outs are completely integrated into the illustrations. This makes it easy to understand and then apply the procedure being taught. Listed below an illustration are clear, concise, step-by-step instructions that are directly linked to the specific part of the illustration where the work is recorded.

Reinforcement for Every Lesson

Each lesson ends with an activity page that provides immediate reinforcement of the lesson material. Instructors can use the end-of-lesson page to make sure students fully understand all concepts and procedures before moving on to the next lesson.

Problems, Problems, Problems

Century 21 Accounting, Seventh Edition gives students **many short problems**. Students can now easily find and fix mistakes. Many of the problems can be completed using *Automated Accounting* software. And something new: most chapters contain one problem using real-life transaction statements.

Read on to learn more about the leading high school accounting textbook and family of products.

INNOVATIVE ENHANCEMENTS FOR STUDENTS

Many new enhancements have been made to the student text and student support materials.

A Bright and Colorful Accounting Textbook

Bright, interesting colors throughout the text draw students in and get them excited about accounting! Scattered throughout the accounting cycles are **eye-catching photos** that represent the businesses featured in the cycles.

Emphasis on Critical Thinking

Critical thinking activities are emphasized throughout the textbook and teacher's edition. A wealth of activities are provided in the student text and additional suggestions for enhancing these activities are provided in the lesson plans in the Teacher's Edition.

Special Features

Many of the special features provide opportunities for critical-thinking activities.

- Accounting in Your Career features appear on the second page of each chapter and include questions for critical thinking. Suggested answers are provided in the lesson plan in the margins as well as additional questions for Thinking about Careers, based on the feature.
- The Professional Business Ethics feature in Chapter 1 presents a method for determining whether specific actions are ethical or not. This first feature uses a set of three questions and an ethical decision-making matrix. Additional Professional Business Ethics features throughout the textbook require students to read a scenario and determine whether the actions described are ethical or not.
- Cultural Diversity, Technology for Business, Accounting at Work, and Global Perspective features in the student text provide additional information on a variety of subjects. Suggested questions and additional activities based on these features are presented in the lesson plans in the margins to add a critical-thinking dimension to the features.

End-of-Chapter Activities

- Explore Accounting activities at the end of each chapter also provide opportunities for critical thinking. Questions posed at the end of each Explore Accounting activity stretch students to explore additional, more advanced accounting topics. Suggested answers are provided in the margins of the Teacher's Edition.
- Challenge Problems require students to stretch their understanding of learned accounting procedures and apply them in a new way. Solutions are provided in the Teacher's Edition of the Working Papers.
- Cases for Critical Thinking require application and synthesis of accounting knowledge acquired in the chapter to new situations encountered by accounting professionals. Suggested answers are provided in the margins of the Teacher's Edition.
- Applied Communication activities require students to accurately communicate solutions to accounting and business problems using their own words and thoughts. Suggested solutions are provided in the margins of the Teacher's Edition.

Special Features

New special interest features have been added to this edition. These features may be used as part of the accounting instruction to add interest to the course.
- Accounting in Your Career
- Cultural Diversity
- Professional Business Ethics
- Small Business Spotlight
- Global Perspective
- Accounting at Work
- Technology for Business
- Legal Issues in Accounting
- Explore Accounting
- Automated Accounting

End-of-Lesson Activities

A new feature with this edition, each lesson within each chapter ends with activities and problems for reinforcing the lesson.
- Terms Review lists new accounting terms introduced in the lesson.
- Audit Your Understanding questions provide an informal review of comprehension. Answers are provided in Appendix D of the student text for self-checking.
- Work Together problems in each lesson provide the opportunity for the instructor and the students to work as a group to complete a problem based on the lesson before proceeding to independent work. Work Together fulfills the Guided Practice part of the lesson plan.
- On Your Own problems in each lesson provide the stu-

dent's first opportunity to work a short problem based on the content covered in the lesson. On Your Own fulfills the Independent Practice part of the lesson plan and is designed to mirror the concepts and procedures covered in Work Together.

End-of-Chapter Activities

- Application Problems are provided for each lesson within a chapter so that students can apply their learning to an extended problem.
- Mastery Problems are provided for each chapter to integrate the learning from all the lessons in the chapter into one problem and demonstrate mastery of the chapter content.
- Challenge Problems are provided for each chapter to stretch students to apply their learning to slightly different applications.
- Internet Activities in each chapter require accessing the Internet to work with another aspect of accounting.
- Applied Communication activities in each chapter require responding to a situation in writing or verbally.
- Cases for Critical Thinking describe an accounting situation students must resolve.

Integrated Technology

Technology has been integrated into this text through the use of software.
- Automated Accounting is a new technology feature. These topics appear at the end of every chapter and describe the procedures necessary to use *Automated Accounting 7.0* or higher to complete selected end-of-chapter problems.
- Accounting Connection provides an interactive study guide for each chapter. Students answer objective questions, complete accounting rulings, and receive immediate feedback on their understanding of concepts and procedures.
- Spreadsheet Accounting Templates provide practice in using spreadsheet software to complete selected end-of-chapter problems. Routine portions of the template are already keyed in so that students focus on writing the spreadsheet formulas that perform the necessary calculations, thus reinforcing the relationships between different kinds of accounting data.
- The Internet Activity in each chapter provides Internet access as an additional accounting activity.

STUDENT SUPPORT MATERIALS

Three major supplements exist outside the textbook to aid student understanding and reinforcement of skills.

Working Papers

Using the working papers is the most efficient method of assuring that students complete problems accurately and in the least time possible. Each workbook provides sufficient ruled paper for completing the Work Together problems, On Your Own problems, Application Problems, Mastery Problems, Challenge Problems, and Reinforcement Activities 1, 2, and 3. For the first time, the forms for each new problem begin on a new page. Students no longer have to wait for instructors to complete grading one problem before starting to work on the next problem.

Study Guide and Recycling Problem Working Papers

Study Guides present objective questions and matching exercises for terminology that cover the presentation of each chapter. Recycling Problems provide an additional problem for students who need more reinforcement after completing the Application and Mastery Problems. The narrative of the recycling problems is in Appendix C of the student text.

Simulations

The simulations available are:

Foreign Exchange Translation Service, a service business organized as a proprietorship, is recommended for use with Cycle 1. One month's transactions are recorded in the books of account. The narrative of transactions is provided in the simulation envelope.

Fitness Junction, a merchandising business organized as a partnership, is recommended for use with Cycle 2. One month's transactions are recorded in the books of account.

Putting Green Golf Supply, a merchandising business organized as a corporation, is recommended for use with Cycle 3. One month's transactions are recorded in the books of account.

All simulations are available in both manual and automated versions. Separate teacher's keys are needed for the manual and automated versions.

USING THE WRAPAROUND TEACHER'S EDITION

The wraparound teacher's edition has margin notes next to reduced student pages that contain lesson plans for each lesson of each chapter; teaching suggestion boxes that address relevant topics; answers to Accounting in Your Career, Explore Accounting, Internet Activity, Applied Communication, and Cases for Critical Thinking; as well as check figures for end-of-chapter problems.

Chapter Interleaf Pages

Preceding each chapter, interleaf pages feature grids to assist the instructor in planning the presentation of the chapter.

Lesson Plans

A complete lesson plan is printed in the margins of the wraparound teacher's edition for each lesson in each chap-

ter. In addition, modified lesson plans are provided for the beginning of each cycle and chapter, as well as for the end-of-chapter pages in each chapter. A typical plan for each chapter is as follows:

Introductory Pages

- **Overview.** The opener page for each of the three cycles describes the chapter content of all the chapters in that cycle, as well as the Automated Accounting features, simulation, and reinforcement activity that are appropriate for that cycle.
- **Chart of Accounts.** The chart of accounts page has a list of important points about the chart of accounts for that cycle.
- **Introduce the Chapter.** There are three sections in the Introduce the Chapter notes: (1) Preview Accounting Terms, (2) Preview Chapter Objectives, and (3) Introduction.
- **Software Focus.** A Software Focus box at the bottom of the chapter opening page details the software that is available for use with the chapter and the problems to be used with the software.
- **Accounting in Your Career.** The Accounting in Your Career page is the second page of each chapter. This section of the teaching suggestions lists ways to present the feature.
- **Thinking about Careers.** Questions to direct students' thinking toward accounting and business careers are suggested under this heading in the lesson plan.
- **Suggested Answers.** Suggested Answers are provided for the Critical Thinking questions posed in the Accounting in Your Career feature.

Lesson Plan for Each Lesson

Every lesson in every chapter has its own lesson plan. The following elements are included in each lesson plan:

- **Objectives.** The chapter learning objectives that apply to the lesson are listed.
- **Motivate.** The Motivate section suggests questions, examples, or group discussion topics. A **Preview** subheading suggests ways to encourage students to preview the lesson using good study habits.
- **Materials.** A list shows the transparencies, videos, software, working papers, and other materials needed.
- **Explain.** Items detailed are the points that should be emphasized in the presentation of the lesson.
- **Demonstrate.** This section describes how to demonstrate accounting procedures. Instructors may wish to vary the order of presentation of the Explain and Demonstrate sections to fit the needs of the classroom.
- **Ongoing Assessment.** The instructor notes facial expressions, responds to student questions, and re-presents concepts. A **Troubleshooting** section describes problems

students typically have with the content of the lesson.

- **Reteach.** The Reteach suggestions give specific means of reteaching the lesson.
- **Guided Practice.** The Terms Review, Audit Your Understanding questions, and Work Together problems are the means for providing guided practice. The instructor and students do the suggested guided practice activities together. The instructor's role is to demonstrate, monitor, observe, and answer questions.
- **Independent Practice.** Students perform suggested independent practice activities by themselves. The On Your Own and Application Problems (one per lesson) are the means for providing independent practice for the lesson.
- **Enrich.** Suggestions for extension and enrichment activities take students beyond the traditional assignments.
- **Close.** Closure suggestions describe ways to review and reinforce the lesson.

End-of-Chapter

The end-of-chapter pages also contain a lesson plan. Different activities are suggested for completing the chapter.

- **Putting It All Together.** This section suggests a summarizing activity, such as using a summary transparency.
- **Independent Practice.** Mastery and Challenge Problems bring together all lessons of the chapter.
- **Ongoing Assessment.** Solutions are reviewed and reteaching is conducted as needed.
- **Reteach.** Recycling Problems and Accounting Connection are available.
- **Enrich.** Included in this section are suggestions for activities to extend the chapter presentation.
- **Formal Evaluation.** Formal assessment instruments (tests) are suggested. In addition, the final page of each chapter suggests how a portfolio assessment program can be used in an accounting program.
- **Automated Accounting.** The Automated Accounting pages also have lesson plan suggestions.

Teaching Suggestions

In addition to the lesson plans, boxes in the side and bottom margins describe various teaching strategies or tips. These can be categorized in three general areas:

1. Suggestions Related to Building Student Skills: These boxes describe actions the instructor can take to build applied skills in the following areas:
   - Communications
   - Language Arts
   - Mathematics
   - Writing Across the Curriculum
   - Building Study Skills
2. Suggestions Related to Other Teaching Methodology: Boxes describe actions the instructor can take to reinforce concepts developed in the chapter. They can be categorized in the following areas:
   - Assessment by Portfolio
   - Different Learning Abilities
   - Different Learning Styles
   - Cooperative Learning
   - Expanding Beyond the Classroom
3. Suggestions Related to Student Features: Boxes highlight special student features and their benefits and or/solutions.
   - Accounting in Your Career
   - Software Focus
   - Professional Business Ethics
   - Cultural Diversity
   - Technology for Business
   - Small Business Spotlight
   - Accounting at Work
   - Legal Issues in Accounting
   - Global Perspective
   - Explore Accounting

Check Figures

Check figures are given for end-of-chapter activities and reinforcement activities. When student solutions match these check figures, it can be assumed that the student's solutions are significantly correct. A blackline master of check figures is provided in the TRG to use as a student handout if desired.

ORGANIZATION OF THE TEXT

The student text is organized in a logical manner. Learning progresses from the simple to the complex both within a given cycle and across cycles as similar topics are treated in progressively more detail in each succeeding cycle.

- **Cycle Opener Page** lists the chapter titles in the cycle.
- **Chart of Accounts** at the beginning of each cycle provides a point of reference to account titles and numbers.
- **Chapter Opener Page** shows a list of the learning objectives and a preview of the terms to be defined.
- **Accounting vocabulary terms** are carefully defined in complete sentences and highlighted in color.
- The chapters feature many **illustrations**. A new feature is the steps indicated within the illustrations.
- **End-of-Lesson Activities** include Terms Review, Audit Your Understanding, Work Together, and On Your Own.
- **End-of-Chapter Activities** include Explore Accounting; Application, Mastery, and Challenge Problems; Internet Activity; Applied Communication; and Cases for Critical Thinking.
- An **Automated Accounting** feature at the end of each chapter describes how the accounting cycle is automated.
- **Reinforcement Activities** in each accounting cycle synthesize all learning from the cycle.

- **Appendices** present Accounting Concepts, Using a Calculator and Computer Keypad, Recycling Problems, and Answers to Audit Your Understanding.

USING SOFTWARE AND TECHNOLOGY

After manual accounting procedures are mastered, computer software may be used as an enrichment activity to facilitate the processing of accounting data and experience the use of computers in accounting.

Three software packages are available to use with *Century 21 Accounting, First-Year Course* to augment teacher instruction: Accounting Connection; Spreadsheet Accounting Template; and *Automated Accounting 7.0* or higher, and the accompanying templates. Software applicable to individual chapters is noted in lesson plans and interleaf pages.

Each software package and its documentation is available from South-Western Educational Publishing.

Accounting Connection

Accounting Connection provides an interactive study guide for each chapter. Students answer objective questions, complete accounting rulings, and receive immediate feedback on their understanding of concepts and procedures.

Spreadsheet Accounting Template

The Spreadsheet Accounting Template may be used with selected end-of-chapter problems. Templates are available for a variety of popular spreadsheet programs.

Automated Accounting

Automated Accounting 7.0 or higher may be used to complete selected end-of-chapter problems, all three Reinforcement Activities, and all three simulations. The *Century 21 Accounting, Seventh Edition* Textbook/Simulation Template Disk, First-Year Course is also needed to complete the automated accounting activities.

Century 21 Accounting, Seventh Edition Textbook/ Simulation Template Disks are also available for use with *Automated Accounting 6.0, Windows* and *Automated Accounting 6.0, Macintosh*. However, a small number of end-of-chapter problems can be completed only with *Automated Accounting 7.0*—for example, Planning Tool problems.

End-of-chapter problems with corresponding template database files are marked with an icon. Instructions for using the template file are included in the Automated Accounting sections at the end of relevant chapters. Students should be careful to open the filename given in those instructions.

Teachers may choose to demonstrate the operation of *Automated Accounting* to their students. A good method would be to open a *Century 21 Accounting, Seventh Edition* template database file provided for the chapter being covered. The teacher can then enter sample transactions from the end-of-chapter problem corresponding to the template file.

It is suggested that the text that accompanies the relevant version of *Automated Accounting* be used as a reference for students who need complete information about the operation of the software. Students can also access Problem Instructions through the *Automated Accounting* Help menu.

The *Electronic Auditor* helps check students' work. The software will compare student data files (stored on data disks or a hard disk) with solution data files. In addition, a summary report of the results will be provided. There are certain template files that do not have a corresponding solution provided for *Electronic Auditor*. These template files are simply exercises in which students generate relevant reports using *Automated Accounting*.

Solutions may be added to the *Electronic Auditor* for problems created by teachers. Once added, these solutions will appear in the solutions directory and can be used to check students' solutions. A full explanation of how to use the *Electronic Auditor* is provided in the teacher's manual that accompanies *Automated Accounting*.

STRATEGIES FOR OPTIMIZING INDIVIDUAL LEARNING

The student population not only reflects the cultural diversity in American society as a whole, but it also consists of students with different abilities and different styles of learning. Many of these individual student differences require an adjustment in teaching style or presentation. This section describes teaching strategies for students with different learning abilities, students with different learning styles, and cooperative learning.

Teaching Strategies for Students with Different Learning Abilities

Classrooms typically contain students with a wide variation of ability, intelligence, and motivation. Although the instructor must direct a majority of the instruction to the "average" student, optimal learning will occur only when the curriculum is modified to meet the needs of each individual student.

The first and greatest challenge facing the instructor is identifying the special abilities of each student. Whereas physical disabilities are usually relatively easy to identify, learning disabilities can be very difficult to detect and classify. Classifying students solely on examination scores and prior classroom performance may be misleading and should be avoided. For example, poor subject examination scores and short attention spans may be the symptoms of either a student with a specific learning disability or a gifted student who is bored.

The correct assessment of students should be a combined effort of the instructor, the school counselor or special education instructor, and the student. Together, this team can design an individualized program that will challenge the student while providing adequate opportunity to achieve attainable goals.

Gifted Students

One objective of programs for gifted students should be the development of leadership skills. Current literature suggests that four skill areas are involved in the development of effective leadership.

1. Cognition—The ability to identify, research, and learn factual knowledge.
2. Problem Solving—The ability to identify problems and develop creative solutions.
3. Interpersonal Communication—The ability to work with other people.
4. Decision Making—The ability to develop and implement realistic goals, and evaluate performance of the goals.

Different hemispheres of the brain control these functions. Cognition and Problem Solving are typically associated with left-brain functions; Interpersonal Communication and Decision Making are associated with right-brain functions. Therefore, effective leadership training must target development of both hemispheres. Most students will enter the classroom with stronger development in some skill areas than in others. Thus, a student lacking interpersonal communication skills should undertake projects to develop those skills.

The Professional Business Ethics and Applied Communication activities in the student textbook provide opportunities for gifted students to develop these leadership skills. Encourage gifted students to extend these activities by developing related activities.

Gifted students may need to move through the accounting program at an accelerated pace. It may not be appropriate for gifted students to work every problem provided. For example, after a chapter has been reviewed, gifted students may demonstrate mastery by working only the Mastery or Recycling Problem. Others may need to work one or more of the Application Problems. The Challenge Problem should always be assigned to gifted students to provide the "stretch" for exploring alternatives to the chapter content.

Additional activities might include the following:

1. Gifted students should master transaction analysis quickly; therefore, challenge them to identify a special research project that interests them. The students should be encouraged to identify a project that requires interac-tion with a businessperson. For example, a student could contact a bank loan officer to learn how a proprietor would apply for a loan, research formats for a business plan, and develop a business plan for a hypothetical business. Finally, the student could invite the bank loan officer to class and use role-playing to demonstrate how communication skills can enhance an individual's chance of getting the loan.
2. Partnerships require effective communication and cooperation among partners. Gifted students can best learn about the opportunities, problems, and challenges of a partnership by forming a real partnership. Encourage gifted students to form a partnership to sell a service or product of their selection. The students should prepare the partnership agreement, operate the business, and report the results of operations. Suggest that the students consult businesspersons, such as lawyers and accountants, for assistance.
3. Using gifted students as tutors for other students can be an effective way of teaching the topics students find most difficult. Allow the gifted student to complete one of these chapters while the class completes the first two chapters of a cycle. The gifted students can then assist you in presenting the concepts and procedures on their chapter to the class. Encourage the students to use visual aids and develop methods to assess student learning.

Limited English Proficiency Students

Limited English Proficiency (LEP) students are individuals whose native or dominant language is a language other than English. Although these students may be involved in special English-as-a-Second-Language (ESL) classes, the instructor can significantly improve learning by adopting several strategies.

1. Provide students with translations of key terms prior to presenting each chapter. Encourage students to use dictionaries.
2. Create visual instructional methods, such as posters and bulletin boards, that reinforce accounting concepts in both English and the other dominant language(s).
3. At early levels, LEP students have limited comprehension of English and can respond with one or two word answers. Assess understanding by having students match, choose, move, draw, or point. Students at this level can respond to directions that require them to name, list, categorize, label, or reply with one or two words.
4. Allow for longer pauses when you ask questions. Non-native speakers need more time to formulate their answers.
5. Speak directly. Avoid negative constructions and passive verbs, such as "Don't forget that Cash is not debited in

this transaction." Instead say, "Remember to credit Cash in this transaction."

6. Rather than asking students whether they understand what you have said, ask them to restate what you have said in their own words.

7. Adjust the length of time allotted to complete assignments and tests. Remember that the primary objective is to assess knowledge of accounting rather than the ability to translate and comprehend the question or problem.

8. Be cautious if there are no interruptions or questions. It may mean that very little has been understood.

Additional activities might include the following:

1. Recruit businesspersons willing to act as mentors for LEP students. These mentors should be invited to speak to the class and periodically meet with LEP students to assist with assignments. The instructor should be actively involved in any meetings with LEP students to show support for both the mentor and the students.

2. Although LEP students may feel handicapped in the classroom, their knowledge of two languages provides them with excellent career opportunities in today's international business environment. LEP students should identify what unique career opportunities exist for them in various types of organizations, such as international businesses and government. Students could create a bulletin board to inform other students of these opportunities. Successful bulletin boards could also be used in the classrooms of younger students, or in elementary schools.

Specific Learning Disability (SLD) Students

Instructors need not be reminded that adolescence is a period of turmoil and adjustment. What many instructors often view as adolescent behavior may, however, be caused by a student's specific learning disability (SLD). The correct assessment of SLD students is difficult because adolescent behavior is similar to the typical characteristics of SLD students.

• **Passive Learners.** When faced with making a decision, SLD students avoid making a decision in favor of waiting for a teacher to provide specific direction.

• **Poor Self-Concept.** Years of failure cause SLD students to have low self-esteem, thus reducing their confidence that they can achieve academic success.

• **Inept Social Skills.** SLD students often have difficulty making and keeping friends.

• **Attention Deficits.** SLD students often lack the ability to concentrate on one topic for an extended period.

• **Lack of Motivation.** Years of failure have conditioned SLD students to doubt their abilities and therefore view their efforts as being futile.

Once an SLD student is correctly assessed, the instructor should work with the student to develop an individualized program. The basic objective of the program should be the development of functional (life) skills. The student should be counseled to establish challenging yet attainable goals and provide frequent feedback as to the attainment of these goals. The student's academic success should be measured on the demonstrated ability to learn as much as the mastery of a defined body of knowledge.

Several general instructional strategies are effective in teaching SLD students:

1. When asking questions during class, ask SLD students questions that they can likely answer successfully. Save more difficult or unstructured questions for better students.

2. Rotate instructional materials rather than trying to complete a single text. Supplemental instructional materials may include additional texts, business magazines, government publications, etc.

3. Encourage students to maintain a daily log or journal that describes their academic progress. Students can share this log, if they desire, with the instructor when updating their individual program.

4. When feasible, SLD students should become involved in work-study programs that are consistent with course content. When work-study opportunities are unavailable, simulations can be used to provide a simulated work environment. Field trips are an excellent method to expose students to the business world.

Additional activities might include the following:

1. The popular board game Monopoly is well known as an enjoyable way to practice mathematical skills. The game also provides students the opportunity to analyze and record their transactions. Playing Monopoly enables students to see how transaction analysis and the accounting equation provide information for business decisions. Students should use T accounts until they have completed the first cycle. The instructor may need to assist students with identifying accounts, such as plant assets, that are not presented in the first cycle.

2. Many students will ultimately work in inventory-related jobs. Simulating the inventory of a business will enable students to actively participate in the accounting for inventory. For example, students could establish a classroom store carrying school supplies, snacks, or other low-cost items. The students would record the purchase and sales transactions and update the perpetual inventory. Students would periodically take inventory and reconcile the periodic and perpetual inventory quantities.

At-Risk Students

Many environmental factors may negatively impact a student's ability and motivation to succeed academically. Any student who is a potential dropout may be classified as an at-risk student. At-risk students typically are deficient in mathematics, reading, and language skills. These students provide a unique challenge to the accounting instructor because the instructor has little, if any, power to correct problems in the home environment.

Effective instructional strategies for at-risk students should be based on the premise that all individuals have a need for achievement and social acceptance. Within the accounting classroom, these needs can be fulfilled by developing a curriculum that promotes academic success and acceptance by the instructor. Techniques for working with at-risk students include the following:

1. Develop a personal profile of the student. Avoid placing too much significance on past academic performance as this may represent a symptom rather than the underlying problem.
2. Together with the student, develop an individualized program that allows the student to attain both short-term and long-term goals. When identifying goals, consider the student's anticipated career goals.
3. Modify presentation strategies to include more visual displays, and supplement explanations with current, realistic examples.
4. Organize field trips and mentor programs to expose students to the business environment.

Additional activities might include the following:

1. Assist students to understand how accounting is a useful skill in careers that interest them. This could be accomplished in many ways. For example, a student who shows interest in auto mechanics could be introduced to the owner of a local auto repair business. The student could then report his/her observations to the instructor in oral or written form. If no mentor is available, trade magazines often present articles to assist their readers in managing their businesses.
2. Many at-risk students can become motivated to begin self-improvement only when they recognize that they have a need to improve. One method of promoting self-evaluation is to have students identify the qualities they would require of another individual. Have students imagine that they are partners in a business that is considering hiring employees for both service and office positions. Require the student to prepare a job description that includes both skill and personal characteristics that applicants should possess. This activity should enable students to compare their qualifications with the job descriptions they have developed.

Visually-Impaired Students

Students with mild visual impairments are typically mainstreamed and may elect to enroll in accounting. The nature and degree of students' visual impairments will vary. A student's visual impairment may include a difficulty in reading print, an inability to distinguish colors, a sensitivity to light, and a limited field of vision. The instructor must identify each student's exact impairment and adapt teaching strategies appropriately.

Many sources exist for providing alternative teaching materials. Most states have schools for the blind and rehabilitation service agencies that can enlarge the textbook and working papers. Consult these organizations to identify the latest technologies available for assisting the students.

The instructor and student should develop an individualized program that establishes a time frame for achieving specific learning objectives. The learning objectives should be consistent with the student's anticipated career goals. The time frame should consider the student's impairment and the availability of technical assistance, such as enlarged materials and closed circuit television. The use of software should not be overlooked for visually-impaired students, particularly if oversized monitors with larger displays are available.

Additional activities might include the following:

1. It is important for visually-impaired students to have confidence in their ability to participate fully within the business world. Require students to prepare an oral or written report that profiles a successful visually-impaired business professional.
2. New technologies are continually being developed that assist visually-impaired students to participate fully in both school and business. Students must be aware of these technologies and know how to continually learn of new technologies. Using government agencies as a resource, assist the students in preparing a report concerning anticipated technologies.

Teaching Strategies for Students with Different Learning Styles

There are many different learning styles. Some people learn best from reading material. Others need to see a demonstration or learn by feeling. Still others may learn best from auditory cues. It is important to remember, however, that no matter what learning style works best for any individual, learning style is not an indicator of intelligence. Two people of similar levels of intelligence may learn best in two different styles of learning. Learning style is also not necessarily a rigid behavior. Many individuals may have a dominant learning style; however, most also have the flexibility to adapt their learning styles to the demands of the material to be learned. Different learning styles include print, visual, auditory, tactile, and kinesthetic learning.

Print Learners

The print learner prefers to see the data in print—preferably printed in words.

1. When introducing the T account, a print learner would prefer to study the illustration in the textbook which shows a T account, labeled with the words *DEBIT* and *CREDIT.*
2. When covering journal entries, the instructor should discuss the entries, using the textbook examples and referring to the textbook. The print learner can later go back and study the entries.
3. When learning how to post, the print learner would prefer to see the process in print. This can be done by distributing a handout that explains the steps in the posting process. Allow the student to study the handout.

Visual Learners

The visual learner needs to *see* the concept. One way for the learner to see the concept is mental visualization. Illustrations and visual aids are important to the visual learner.

1. Ask the student (with eyes closed) to picture a T account. The student should be able to see both sides of the account. Next, the student should visualize the word *DEBIT* on the left side of the account. Finally, the student should visualize the word *CREDIT* on the right side of the account. Once this concept takes on a visual form, the student will be able to access it when needed.
2. When covering journal entries, the instructor should discuss the entries, using a transparency or the chalkboard to record the entry. In addition, the student should be asked to mentally picture each part of the entry before the instructor actually writes it on the transparency or chalkboard.
3. To teach posting, the instructor could use a transparency to assist in the lecture. The transparency could be (1) a blank transparency that the instructor completes or (2) a prepared transparency that uses arrows to trace the steps involved in posting.

Auditory Learners

The auditory learner will best learn by hearing. Auditory learners who read a textbook chapter benefit from hearing reinforcement of key concepts spoken out loud.

1. When introducing the T account, have the student say out loud that the "left side is the debit side of the account." Repeating this statement a few times will increase the chances of its being reinforced. Repeat the process with the statement the "right side is the credit

side of the account."
2. To reinforce the learning of journal entries, the auditory learner should verbally repeat the analysis of the transaction. The student should also verbally list the steps involved in making the entry.
3. When learning how to post, the auditory learner would prefer to hear the steps involved in posting. This can be done via a live lecture or a taped tutorial. To reinforce learning, the student could recite the posting steps to another student or group of students.

Tactile Learners

The tactile learner learns best by touching or handling objects.

1. Using play money, have the student touch the right side of the desk and place an amount of money on it to reinforce an amount in the right side or credit side of an account. Repeat the process for the left/debit side.
2. Tactile learners may benefit from using the computer to key journal entries and then print reports. The student should be encouraged to place a finger on each account title in the journal entries report and trace it over to the amount in the amount column of the report to check it for accuracy. Tactile learners should also be given the opportunity to journalize transactions from at least one simulation that contains source documents, which must be handled to analyze, journalize, and file.
3. The tactile learner can use a group of index cards to represent the general ledger. Each card should represent an account and should have three vertical lines to distinguish between the debit and credit columns, and balance columns. Have the tactile learner post each example of a journal entry to the appropriate cards (accounts).

Kinesthetic Learners

The kinesthetic learner learns best by taking an active part in the instruction. Motion is an important part of kinesthetic learning.

1. Have the student draw a T account in the air or use a finger to draw a T account on the back of the hand or arm. Next, have the student label the left side with the word *DEBIT* and the right side with the word *CREDIT.*
2. The kinesthetic learner would prefer to participate in the posting process. Use a transparency of the ledger account and have each student complete one or more steps of the posting process at the overhead projector. Other students can be completing the posting process individually on printed ledger accounts.
3. Provide the opportunity to perform the calculations to solve formulas. Calculators or computerized spreadsheet programs may be used.

COOPERATIVE LEARNING

Cooperative learning activities should be an integral part of accounting pedagogical strategies. Cooperative learning involves small heterogeneous groups of students who work together to share the responsibility for learning. Cooperative learning activities should be designed with the following goals in mind:

1. All students should be able to participate.
2. Groups should be heterogeneous.
3. Each student needs to be held accountable for his or her contribution to the group.

Cooperative learning is more successful with heterogeneous rather than homogeneous groups. Research further supports cooperative learning as a teaching strategy to increase students' motivation, achievement, and behavior. The teacher should select team members for a cooperative learning activity. Group composition should include a mixture of gender, ability level, cultural or ethnic background, and learning style. For example, placing a visual learner with an auditory learner enhances and strengthens the group's performance. Group members should be rotated frequently.

The time needed to complete an activity will vary among groups. Therefore, the teacher needs to provide additional activities to be completed by groups as they finish. These activities might include, for example, specific questions about the activity. These additional activities are often referred to as debriefing.

Cooperative learning promotes the development of higher-order thinking skills where brighter students explain concepts or principles to slower students. Using higher-order thinking skills to articulate ideas in accounting will normally result in the material being learned more effectively with improved retention rates.

To be successful, each student must be held accountable for his/her contribution to the cooperative learning activity. A variety of evaluation methods may be employed. These methods may include (1) a short quiz taken individually, (2) instructor observation of individual contributions to a group activity, or (3) bonus points assigned to individuals only if all group members do well individually. Performance on cooperative learning activities in accounting should range from no more than 5 to 10 percent of the final grade.

One of the goals of cooperative learning is to have students work out the roles of the group members themselves. Some groups will assign a role to an individual, such as when a representative of the group will need to record results and present them to the class, and sometimes individuals within a group will assume roles within the group without being asked to do so.

Some cooperative learning activities are as follows:

1. *Research project:* Assign students to groups of two. Each group researches the financial statements (through the annual report) of a company in which they are interested, perhaps because they are familiar with the product. Students look for a list of specific items such as what kinds of stock is the corporation authorized to issue, what categories of assets are listed on the balance sheet, what is the total of current liabilities, did net income increase/decrease from the previous period, and so on. The group must then plan and deliver a presentation of the data to the entire class. Additional time outside class is needed to complete research and prepare presentation. Time frame: 45 minutes.

2. *Explain what component percentages measure:* Assign students to groups of three. Each group is to plan, prepare, and deliver a presentation to non-accountants. The presentation should explain what component percentages are and how they are used to analyze financial statements. Time frame: 30 minutes over several class periods.

3. *Divide the class into groups of two or three students each.* Have each group discuss and prepare a list of service businesses found in the local community. Each group should appoint a leader who will present the list of businesses and services to the class. Time frame: 20 minutes.

4. *Divide the class into two groups.* Each group stands and faces each other. The instructor or a student moderator states an accounting term. The first student to raise a hand has the opportunity to give the correct definition. The group with the most correctly defined terms is declared the winner. As an alternative to this game, the instructor or moderator may read the definition of a term, such as "Anything of value that is owned," while the groups must identify the term. If you wish to imitate a popular television show, the answer should be given in a question format, such as "What is an asset?"

5. *Reinforcement Activities:* Assign reinforcement activities as homework. Divide the class into groups of two students each. Each pair of students exchange and evaluate each other's work in class. Students are permitted to correct their work, based on their partner's evaluation. Time frame: 15 minutes.

6. *Divide the class into groups of four or five students each.* Using Cases for Critical Thinking, each group analyzes the cases and arrives at agreed-upon solutions. One member of each group is appointed the recorder and presents the group's analysis to the class. Time frame: 20 minutes.

7. *Divide the class into groups of two or three students each.* Each group will discuss and prepare a list of merchandising businesses found in the local community. The group-appointed leader presents to the class the list and

merchandise being sold. Time frame: 25 minutes.

8. *Divide the class into auditing groups of three or four students per group.* Each auditing group is responsible for assisting other class members as well as correcting homework assignments. A lead auditor is appointed by the group and is responsible for turning in completed homework assignments for each group member to the instructor.

SUGGESTIONS FOR TEACHING PROFESSIONAL BUSINESS ETHICS

Businesses have recently become aware of the severe implications of the unethical behavior of employees. In response, many businesses have begun training their employees to make ethical decisions and establishing company codes of conduct. The message from businesses today is clear—employees must be capable of making ethical decisions to protect the business from legal liability and to maximize long-term profits.

Most students' principles of right and wrong are well established prior to their enrolling in high school accounting. Thus, the presentation of business ethics does not involve the teaching of right and wrong. Instead, students need to learn how to apply their principles of right and wrong to business situations.

Professional Business Ethics

There are seven Professional Business Ethics features in this text to give instructors an opportunity to teach ethics in the accounting class.

Causes of Unethical Behavior

Chapter 1 provides an introduction to business ethics. The major causes of unethical behavior are presented to assist students in recognizing the forces that can cause unethical behavior. Recognizing the causes of unethical behavior is the first step in making business decisions that prevent employees from being placed in compromising situations.

Steps for Analyzing Ethical Situations

A three-step checklist is presented to help students analyze the ethics of an action. This approach encourages students to collect pertinent information that will provide a basis for their decision. Ultimately, students' decisions are based on their personal ethics applied to the facts of the situation.

Assessment

Correct solutions are generally obvious if the action is either illegal or violates a business or professional standard. For example, most students will agree that it is unethical to dispose of hazardous waste into the water supply. However, students may challenge compliance with other laws and standards. A class discussion of whether the truck drivers of a business should be required to drive the speed limit and wear safety belts may demonstrate many students' willingness to disregard selected laws.

Many of the situations in the Professional Business Ethics activities provide situations where the line between right and wrong is unclear. As a result, students will likely differ in their decisions as to whether the action is ethical. Assessment of Professional Business Ethics activities should be based on the students' analysis of the facts and the objective support for their decisions. The students' decisions about whether a case demonstrates ethical behavior should not be assessed. Therefore, no conclusions are provided with the solutions.

Teachers can adopt several strategies to cover a Professional Business Ethics activity. The activity can be presented initially as a classroom discussion. Alternately, the activity can be assigned as an individual or group project. Whichever method is used, students should be given the opportunity to discuss the case in class. This exchange of ideas enables students to observe how other individuals make and support their decisions. When asking questions and making observations, the instructor should be careful not to reveal her or his personal bias.

Communication Skills

The Professional Business Ethics activities provide an opportunity for students to practice communication skills. For example, the Professional Business Ethics activity in Chapter 5 requires students to determine what action, if any, a manager should take when an employee obtained a position by falsifying a resume. Students could assume the position of manager and prepare the appropriate message to the employee. In this case, the students would also be required to identify the correct method of communication.

Solutions for Professional Business Ethics

Chapter 1: Introduction to Business Ethics

Chapter 1 presents the framework for analyzing ethical behavior that will be applied in subsequent Professional Business Ethics features.

Chapter 5: Can I Say This on My Resume?

Students are required to evaluate the ethical behavior of a person who overstated a resume. Students are instructed to use the three-step checklist to determine whether Kendra demonstrated ethical behavior in preparing her resume.

The textbook includes the solution to this Professional Business Ethics activity. The solution given illustrates the use of the three-step checklist.

The textbook will not provide answers for the ethics activities in future chapters.

Chapter 9: Is It Discrimination or Poor Judgment?

Step 1. Is the action illegal? No. The committee members have not done anything illegal by expressing their opinions. However, denying a candidate employment based solely on his or her age constitutes discrimination, and age discrimination in employment is illegal.

Step 2. Does the action violate company or professional standards? No.

Step 3. Who is affected, and how, by the action? (See Ethics Table 1.)

Ethics Table 1

People Affected	Negative	Positive
Candidate A	This person may be denied employment because of her age.	This candidate may be happier working at a different company where age and experience are welcomed.
Candidate B	A candidate who met the stated qualifications may be denied employment.	If the position does require more than two years experience, this candidate might be unsuccessful in the position if hired.
Candidate C	Other candidates might not get proper consideration if they have no connections.	This person may get the job because of his connections.
The Company	The company may miss hiring the best candidate in the case of Candidates A and B. If Candidate C is hired based on connections rather than qualifications, he may not be a useful resource to the company.	

Chapter 11: Is Anyone Listening?

Situation 1:

Step 1. Is the action illegal? No. Seamus Ryan is not violating any laws.

Step 2. Does the action violate company or professional standards? No. Company or professional standards do not apply.

Step 3. Who is affected, and how, by the action? (See Table 2.)

Ethics Table 2

People Affected	Negative	Positive
Seamus Ryan	Is seen as a gossip by some co-workers and managers.	Enjoys the popularity that comes with being "in the know."
Co-workers	Cannot assume that their workspace is private.	Enjoy learning the information that Seamus provides.

Situation 2:

Step 1. Is the action illegal? No. Ricki Bassett did nothing illegal.

Step 2. Does the action violate company or professional standards? No. Company or professional standards do not apply.

Step 3. Who is affected, and how, by the action? (See Table 3.)

Ethics Table 3

People Affected	Negative	Positive
Ricki Bassett	May receive poor ratings because she completes less work than expected.	Enjoys a break from her work.
Other employees	Might have to answer more calls because Ricki is not doing her job.	
Customers	Might not get prompt service because telephone lines are busy or customers are put on hold.	
Company	Might lose sales because customer calls are not answered promptly.	

Situation 3

Step 1. Is the action illegal? No. Employee e-mail is not considered a private communication. The company has the right to monitor e-mail.

Step 2. Does the action violate company or professional standards? No.

Step 3. Who is affected, and how, by the action? (See Table 4.)

Ethics Table 4

People Affected	Negative	Positive
Tillar and Rebold	Feel they do not have privacy.	
George Parton		Can effectively supervise his employees.

Situation 4:

Step 1. Is the action illegal? No. Kathy Martz did nothing illegal when she looked through Ann Xiao's computer files.

Step 2. Does the action violate company or professional standards? No.

Step 3. Who is affected, and how, by the action? (See Table 5.)

Ethics Table 5

People Affected	Negative	Positive
Ann Xiao	Might feel repercussions since her supervisor knows she is job hunting.	

Chapter 16: Technology Temptations

Situation 1:

Step 1. Is the action illegal? No.

Step 2. Does the action violate company or professional standards? Yes. Most credit card companies have company standards related to information about customers. Accessing information for fun is probably a violation of company policy.

Step 3. Who is affected, and how, by the action? (See Table 6.)

Ethics Table 6

People Affected	Negative	Positive
Customers	Unable to protect information about their financial transactions.	
Jack	Could be fired for violating company standards.	Increased popularity with his friends.
The company	Could be sued if a customer discovered the privacy invasion.	

Situation 2:

Step 1. Is the action illegal? No.

Step 2. Does the action violate company or professional standards? No.

Step 3. Who is affected, and how, by the action? (See Table 7.)

Ethics Table 7

People Affected	Negative	Positive
Other employees	Unable to protect mail files.	

Situation 3:

Step 1. Is the action illegal? No.

Step 2. Does the action violate company or professional standards? No.

Step 3. Who is affected, and how, by the action? (See Table 8.)

Ethics Table 8

People Affected	Negative	Positive
Customers	Are sometimes over-charged.	Are sometimes under-charged.
Company	Will not have accurate sales figures.	

Situation 4:

Step 1. Is the action illegal? No.

Step 2. Does the action violate company or professional standards? No.

Step 3. Who is affected, and how, by the action? (See Table 9.)

Ethics Table 9

People Affected	Negative	Positive
Andrew Kwan	Risks his job if someone finds out he is doing favors for friends on company time.	Helps his friend.
Mike Buckley		Gets the information he requested.
Company	Is paying for credit checks that have no business purpose.	

Chapter 19: Who Owns My Time?

Situation 1:

Step 1. Is the action illegal? No. The receptionist has no legal obligation to perform tasks not specifically assigned.

Step 2. Does the action violate company or professional standards? No. Unless the company has a policy that prohibits employees from using idle time for personal activities, no company standard has been violated.

Step 3. Who is affected, and how, by the action? (See Table 10.)

Ethics Table 10

People Affected	Negative	Positive
Gabriel Peña	Failure to spend time improving skills may lead to termination. May be resented by other employees.	Enjoys recreation.
Other employees	May resent Gabriel Peña's light workload.	
Company	Fails to fully utilize employee. Customers and vendors who observe receptionist might question the quality of company's management.	

Situation 2:

Step 1. Is the action illegal? No. Laws generally do not require businesses to provide employees with a minimum number of hours or health care benefits.

Step 2. Does the action violate company or professional standards? No. Company and professional standards do not apply.

Step 3. Who is affected, and how, by the action? (See Table 11.)

Ethics Table 11

People Affected	Negative	Positive
Customers		Reduced benefit costs may reduce the cost of merchandise.
Part-time employees	Part-time employees must buy their own health insurance policy.	Reducing total employee expenses provides more employment opportunities for typical part-time employees such as students.
Full-time employees		Benefits may be better than would be available if all employees were insured. Company can spend its benefit dollars to buy better coverage for fewer employees.
Backyard Gourmet	Employee morale and commitment to the firm may be low, resulting in poor production. Employee turnover may be high, resulting in higher training costs.	Reduces total employee expenses.
Local community		Provides a good source of employment for traditional part-time employees.

Chapter 26: Is This Really A Business Expense?

Situation 1:

Step 1. Is the action illegal? Yes. The government allows expenses to include only those items necessary to conduct business. Unless Mr. Duermit could prove a business purpose for the phone calls, reporting the cost of the personal calls on the tax return would be illegal.

Steps 2 and 3. Because the action is illegal, no evaluation of these questions is necessary.

Situation 2:

Step 1. Is the action illegal? Yes. The government allows expenses to include only those items necessary to conduct business. Unless Mr. Duermit could prove a business purpose for hiring Tyler, reporting the cost of paying Tyler on the tax return would be illegal.

Steps 2 and 3. Because the action is illegal, no evaluation of these questions is necessary.

SUGGESTIONS FOR TEACHING APPLIED COMMUNICATION

Several accounting organizations have emphasized that successful accounting professionals must possess good oral and written communication skills. Since effective communication is a skill developed with practice, this textbook has incorporated several opportunities for students to develop their skills. There is an Applied Communication activity at the end of every chapter. Suggested solutions are printed in the margin of this Wraparound Teacher's Edition.

Students' knowledge of communication and language arts skills will vary. You may consider asking an English or communications instructor to assist you in reviewing communication skills that students have learned previously in other classes.

Whether preparing an outline for an oral presentation or a letter for a written assignment, students should be encouraged to use word processing software to prepare their messages. Word processing software is now used extensively by both public and private accountants, and proficiency in its use is essential. By using word processing to complete Applied Communication activities, you will be able to emphasize the importance of computer skills from the first week of the semester.

Assessment

Since the activities allow students to prepare unique messages, there are no "correct" answers. Your students may create excellent solutions that differ significantly from the sample solution. Thus, evaluate each student's solution on its ability to transmit the message in an efficient, effective, and professional manner. The activities should be evaluated for both content and format. Each instructor must determine the importance of errors.

Revising Written Documents

A significant amount of learning occurs when students are provided the opportunity to correct mistakes in their original written documents. Require students to revise documents and incorporate your suggestions. The revised document should be assessed and, if necessary, revised again. Teachers should consider giving students credit for successful revisions.

Cases for Critical Thinking

Most of the Cases for Critical Thinking in this textbook require students to prepare a written answer. You can adapt these cases to further reinforce students' communication skills. Rather than simply answering the questions, require students to prepare an oral or written message to an individual or business mentioned in the case. Vary the requirements of each activity by requiring different types of oral and written messages.

ASSESSMENT BY PORTFOLIO

Assessment by portfolio is a popular tool for assessing student performance. A portfolio enables the instructor to assess student goals and accomplishments while providing the student with the opportunity to collect information that will help set and accomplish current and future goals.

A portfolio should be organized across the curriculum with each discipline making a contribution. A complete portfolio should include the following:

1. A resume.
2. Copies of personal information such as social security card and driver's license.
3. A completed job application to use as a guide.
4. Copies of awards and achievements.
5. Samples of letters of application, cover memos to attach with a resume, and thank-you letters for interviews.
6. Reference letters.
7. Copies of performance in skills, communications, and any other evaluation that would contribute to success in a job.

The accounting class can contribute as many of these items to the portfolio as the instructor desires. Most instructors will want to have accounting students complete a resume (number 1) and documentation of performance (number 7).

Writing a resume is an Applied Communication activity in Chapter 2, which provides the opportunity for Writing Across the Curriculum. This can be a positive writing experience for students and is a good way to start off the school year.

Documenting performance in accounting should include a variety of accounting material that is produced by the student. A portfolio might include items such as problems the student has completed, a personal journal describing references and procedures the student used to complete the problem, and a summary report on what was learned from the project. The portfolio should be based on the accounting cycle to produce the most desirable results. Each documentation of performance should have an evaluation sheet that the student completes to explain what activity has been accomplished. The instructor should review and sign this evaluation. A sample Portfolio Assessment sheet is in the Teacher's Resource Guide.

The portfolio should be an example of the student's best work that will reflect the skills and knowledge the student has learned. Each student should have a binder or folder so that the work may be organized and presented in an attractive manner. Suggested organization of the portfolio is as follows:

1. Table of contents.
2. Personal information (resume, job applications, etc.).
3. Documentation of performance (work samples, personal journals).

SPECIAL FEATURES GRID

Century 21 Accounting has been expanded to cover many contemporary special features. The following grid illustrates the features and their location.

Chapter	Automated Accounting	Accounting in Your Career	Professional Business Ethics	Cultural Diversity	Technology for Business	Accounting at Work	Legal Issues in Accounting	Global Perspective	Explore Accounting	Small Business Spotlight
1	Computer Safety Tips and Operation Basics	The Job Interview	Introduction to Business Ethics	Professional Organizations					What Is GAAP?	
2	Language and Skills for Automated Accounting	A Small-Business Opportunity		Cultural Values in the United States					When Is It Called "Revenue"?	
3	Setting Up the Automated Accounting Software Database	Adding Accounts		Ancient China	Dining Out with Computers				Owner Withdrawals	
4	Recording Transactions	High Standards for Journalizing				Mary Witherspoon	Forming and Dissolving a Proprietorship	Foreign Currency	Prenumbered Documents	Characteristics of Small Business Owners
5	Automated General Ledger Accounting	Time for Posting	Can I Say This on My Resume?	Accounting in Ancient Civilizations					Designing Charts of Accounts	
6	Automated Cash Control Systems	Managing Cash and the Checking Account			Electronic Spreadsheets and Bank Reconciliation				Cash Controls	Motivations for Starting a New Business
7	Manual Accounting Cycle vs. Automated Accounting Cycle	Networking on Work Sheets				Daryl Stanton		International Weights and Measures	Fiscal Periods	
8	Financial Statements Generated from Automated Accounting	Enhancing Financial Reporting		Feng Shui					Comparative and Interim Financial Statements	
9	Automated Adjusting and Closing Entries for Proprietorships	Replace Yourself with a Computer	Is It Discrimination or Poor Judgment?						Public Accounting Firms	
10	Automated Entries for Purchases and Cash Payments Using Special Journals	Untangling Cash Payments				John Chuang		Accountancy in Africa	Freight Charges	Business Plans

Chapter	Automated Accounting	Accounting in Your Career	Professional Business Ethics	Cultural Diversity	Technology for Business	Accounting at Work	Legal Issues in Accounting	Global Perspective	Explore Accounting	Small Business Spotlight
11	Automated Entries for Sales and Cash Receipts Using Special Journals	Growing the Business	Is Anyone Listening?				Forming a Partnership		Business Forms	
12	Correction of Errors	How to Keep Your Job		Timeless Tools	Communication Overload			The International Business Day	Categories of Internal Control	Ways of Starting a Small Business
13	Automated Payroll Accounting	Why Companies Offer Benefits					Dissolving a Partnership		Employee vs. Independent Contractor	
14	Payroll Taxes and Journal Entries	How Much Do Employees Really Cost?			How Smart Are Your Cards?			International Quality Standards	Net Income vs. Taxable Income	
15	Understanding Graphs	Discovering the Truth about Work Sheets				Glenda Cousins	Limited Liability Partnerships		Accounting Systems Design	
16	Generating Automated Financial Statements	Superstar Partnership	Technology Temptations	Business Culture and Accountancy in Russia					Alternative Fiscal Years	
17	End-of-Fiscal-Period Work for a Partnership	Frequent Financial Statements						International Business Transactions	The Perpetual Inventory Method	Franchises
18	Automated Entries for Purchases and Cash Payments Using Special Journals for a Corporation	Don't Lose Those Discounts			Who's in the Driver's Seat?	Pamela Aguirre	Piercing the Corporate Veil		Can Accounting Change the Course of History?	
19	Automated Entries for Sales and Cash Receipts Using Special Journals for a Corporation	12 Months Same as Cash	Who Owns My Time?		Computerized Accounting— Not Just for Corporations				How Credit Card Systems Work	
20	Automated Entries for Uncollectible Accounts and Write-Offs	Credit Problems				Tracy Stanhoff	Forming a Corporation		Accounting Estimates Use Interesting Assumptions	

Chapter	Automated Accounting	Accounting in Your Career	Professional Business Ethics	Cultural Diversity	Technology for Business	Accounting at Work	Legal Issues in Accounting	Global Perspective	Explore Accounting	Small Business Spotlight
21	Automated Accounting for Depreciation	Secrets of the Competition		Valuing Diversity in the Workplace			Dissolving a Corporation		Accounting for Leases	
22	Automated Inventory Systems	Inventory Time			Electronic Spreadsheets Answer "What If?" Questions				Costing a CD Can Make Your Head Spin	Small Business Development Centers
23	Calculating Notes and Interest Using Planning Tools	How to Choose a Loan				Arthur R. Velasquez			Low Interest or Cash Back?	
24	Automated Adjusting and Closing Entries for Accrued Revenues and Expenses	Notes Payable Spreadsheet				James W. Crawford, CPA			Annual Reports—Financial Information and More	
25	Using the Loan Planner	Taxes on Businesses			Spending More than Time on the Web				Audits Provide Stockholders with Positive Assurance	Outlook for Small Business
26	End-of-Fiscal-Period Work for a Corporation	Trying on a New Accounting System	Is This Really a Business Expense?						Statement of Cash Flows	

PLANNING THE YEAR'S WORK

A time schedule for a complete year should be planned before the year begins. Five steps for planning the year's work are given below.

1. Review what has been previous experience with the pace of work that students have maintained in past accounting classes.

2. Determine how many business simulations and reinforcement activities are to be used during the current year.

3. Decide how much allowance should be made for interruptions in the school day that occur on short notice.

4. Determine if computers will be used in the class. Learning how to use software may require additional class time. However, if computers are used to complete some problems, reinforcement activities, and simulations (rather than working them manually), time may be saved in the schedule.

5. Prepare a proposed schedule of work to be completed. Inspect the schedule to determine if typical breaks in the school year (vacations, special events, and scheduled reporting periods) come at a logical time.

A sample time schedule is given for planning the year's work.

SAMPLE TIME SCHEDULE (FOR THREE QUARTERS—180 DAYS TOTAL)

Week	First Quarter—12 Weeks (Chapters 1-9)	Second Quarter—12 Weeks (Chapters 10-17)	Third Quarter—12 Weeks (Chapters 18-26)
1	Chapter 1	Chapter 10	Chapter 18
2	Chapter 2	Chapter 11	Chapter 19
3	Chapter 3	Chapter 12	Reinforcement Activity 3—Part A
4	Chapter 4	Chapter 13	Chapter 20
5	Chapter 5	Chapter 14	Chapter 21
6	Chapter 6	Reinforcement Activity 2—Part A	Chapter 22
7	Reinforcement Activity 1—Part A	Chapter 15	Chapter 23
8	Chapter 7	Chapter 16	Chapter 24
9	Chapter 8	Chapter 17	Chapter 25
10	Chapter 9	Reinforcement Activity 2—Part B	Chapter 26
11	Reinforcement Activity 1—Part B	Begin Fitness Junction Simulation	Reinforcement Activity 3—Part B
12	Foreign Exchange Translation Service Simulation	Complete Fitness Junction Simulation	Putting Green Golf Supply Simulation

SOFTWARE CORRELATION

After manual accounting procedures are mastered, software may be used as an enrichment activity to facilitate the processing of accounting data and experience the use of computers in accounting.

Three software packages are available to use with *Century 21 Accounting, First-Year Course* to augment teacher instruction: Accounting Connection; Spreadsheet Accounting Template; and *Automated Accounting 7.0* or higher, and the accompanying templates. Each software package and its documentation is available from South-Western Educational Publishing.

Accounting Connection provides an interactive study guide for each chapter. Students answer objective questions, complete accounting rulings, and receive immediate feedback on their understanding of concepts and procedures. The Spreadsheet Accounting Template may be used with selected end-of-chapter problems. Templates are available for a variety of popular spreadsheet programs.

Automated Accounting 7.0 or higher may be used to complete selected end-of-chapter problems, all three

Reinforcement Activities, and all three simulations. The *Century 21 Accounting, Seventh Edition* Textbook/Simulation Template Disk, First-Year Course is also needed to complete the automated accounting activities. *Century 21 Accounting, Seventh Edition* Textbook/Simulation Template Disks are also available for use with *Automated Accounting 6.0, Windows* and *Automated Accounting 6.0, Macintosh.* However, a small number of end-of-chapter problems can be completed only with *Automated Accounting 7.0*—for example, Planning Tool problems.

End-of-chapter problems with corresponding template database files are marked with an icon. Instructions for using the template file are included in the Automated Accounting sections at the end of relevant chapters. Students should be careful to open the filename given in those instructions.

It is suggested that the text that accompanies the relevant version of *Automated Accounting* be used as a reference for students who need complete information about the operation of the software. Students can also access Problem Instructions through the *Automated Accounting* Help menu.

CENTURY 21 ACCOUNTING AUTOMATED ACCOUNTING AND SPREADSHEET ACCOUNTING PROBLEMS

Text Chapter	Automated Accounting Template	Spreadsheet Accounting Template
Chapter 4	**4-5 Application Problem:** Journalizing transactions **4-6 Mastery Problem:** Journalizing transactions	
Chapter 5	**5-1 Application Problem:** Preparing a chart of accounts and opening an account **5-4 Mastery Problem:** Journalizing transactions and posting to a general ledger	
Chapter 6	**6-2 Application Problem:** Reconciling a bank statement and recording a bank service charge **6-5 Mastery Problem:** Reconciling a bank statement; journalizing a bank service charge, a dishonored check, and petty cash transactions	**6-2 Application Problem:** Reconciling a bank statement and recording a bank service charge **6-5 Mastery Problem:** Reconciling a bank statement; journalizing a bank service charge, a dishonored check, and petty cash transactions
Reinforcement Activity 1—Part A	**Reinforcement Activity 1—Part A**	
Chapter 8	**8-3 Mastery Problem:** Preparing financial statements with a net loss **8-4 Challenge Problem:** Preparing financial statements with two sources of revenue and a net loss	**8-3 Mastery Problem:** Preparing financial statements with a net loss **8-4 Challenge Problem:** Preparing financial statements with two sources of revenue and a net loss

CURRICULUM AND INSTRUCTION THROUGH INTEGRATION OF SCANS

(The Secretary's Commission on Achieving Necessary Skills)

The Secretary's Commission on Achieving Necessary Skills (SCANS) was asked to examine the demands of the workplace and whether our young people are capable of meeting those demands.

Specifically, the commission was directed to advise the Secretary on the level of skills required to enter employment. SCANS research verifies that what we call workplace know-how defines effective job performance today. This know-how has two elements: competencies and a foundation. This report identifies five competencies (resources, interpersonal skills, information, systems, and technology) and a three-part foundation of skills and personal qualities (basic skills, thinking skills, and personal qualities) that lie at the heart of job performance. These eight requirements are essential preparation for all students, both those going directly to work and those planning further education. Thus, the competencies and the foundation should be taught and understood in an integrated fashion that reflects the workplace contexts in which they are applied.

Century 21 Accounting, Seventh Edition seamlessly integrates the SCANS competencies through the text and suggested activities.

NATIONAL BUSINESS EDUCATION ASSOCIATION STANDARDS FOR ACCOUNTING

The Role of Accounting in Business Education

The National Business Education Association has published a series of standards and expectations for business education. In addition to general attitudes and skills, specific expectations for content areas in business education have been developed. The content of the following correlation shows the expectations in the first and second years of high school accounting study. Most of the content expectations are covered in this first-year accounting textbook and then expanded in the advanced course text. However, some of the content expectations are considered to be more appropriate for a second year of study or even for post-high school education.

CENTURY 21 ACCOUNTING CORRELATION WITH NBEA ACCOUNTING STANDARDS

PROPRIETORSHIP, PARTNERSHIP, CORPORATE ACCOUNTING CYCLE

Accounting—define/purpose	p. 4
Accounting concepts	Chs. 1–26; Appendix A
Accounting equation	Chs. 1–3
Classifying items	Chs. 1–26
Owner's equity and revenue, expense, and drawing accounts	Chs. 2–3
Source documents	Chs. 4–26 and pp. 66–68, 86
Analyzing business transactions	Chs. 1–26
Double-entry accounting	Chs. 1–3 and p. 66
Journalizing	Chs. 4, 10, 11, 18, 19
Ledgers/posting	Chs. 5, 12, 18, 19
Trial balance	pp. 151–153, 374–375, 642
Adjustments	pp. 152–158, 192–196, 204–207, 374–385, 430–433, 528–532, 555–558, 618–619
Financial statements	Chs. 8, 16, 26
Closing entries	pp. 197–206, 434–444, 678–680

Post–closing trial balance	pp. 207, 445, 681
Automated/spreadsheet accounting	Automated Accounting feature at the end of every chapter (templates available) Spreadsheet Accounting software and templates And pp. 132, 586, 617

ACCOUNTING PROCESS—ASSETS FOR PROPRIETORSHIP, PARTNERSHIP, CORPORATION

Current assets/long-term assets	pp. 546
Cash controls including bank reconciliations, petty cash, cash control techniques, electronic fund transfers, ATM transactions, debit card	Ch. 6 and pp. 234, 305, 328, 470–471
File maintenance	pp. 31, 63, 96–99, 112, 116, 249, 270, 336, 487, 520
Subsidiary ledgers	Chs. 18, 19 and pp. 272, 274–292, 420
Credit card sales	pp. 261–262, 512
Uncollectible accounts	Ch. 20
Notes receivable/interest	pp. 594–599, 605, 608, 618–622
Inventory	Ch. 22 and pp. 377–378, 448
Depreciation	Ch. 21
Acquiring, depreciating, and disposing of assets	Ch. 21
Automated/spreadsheet accounting for short-term and long-term assets	Automated Accounting feature at the end of every chapter (templates available) Spreadsheet Accounting software and templates
Foreign currency	pp. 83, 428, 506–511
Depreciation methods	Ch. 21
Record repairs, improvements, and exchanges of plant and equipment	Ch. 21
Intangible assets and acquiring, amortizing, and disposing	Advanced Course Text
Natural resources and acquiring, amortizing, and disposing	Advanced Course Text
Short-term investments	Advanced Course Text
Long-term investments	Advanced Course Text

ACCOUNTING PROCESS—LIABILITIES FOR PROPRIETORSHIP, PARTNERSHIP, CORPORATION

Current liabilities	Ch. 24, and p. 671
Long-term liabilities	Ch. 24, and p. 671
Subsidiary ledgers/schedules	Chs. 18, 19 and pp. 272, 274–292, 420
Notes payable	pp. 594–604, 617, 623–628
Automated/spreadsheet accounting for liabilities	Automated Accounting feature at the end of every chapter (templates available); Spreadsheet Accounting software and templates; and p. 617

Foreign currency exchange rates	pp. 83, 428, 506–511
Bonds/mortgages	Advanced Course Text
Interest	pp. 594–604, 617, 623–628
Present value	Advanced Course Text
ACCOUNTING PROCESSES—OWNERS' EQUITY FOR PROPRIETORSHIP, PARTNERSHIP, CORPORATION	
Capital and drawing accounts	
Investments and withdrawals by owners	Chs. 2, 3, 4, and pp. 235, 242, 410–416, 462, 478, 536, 638–641, 668–670
Common stock	pp. 462, 638–641
Preferred stock	Advanced Course Text
Paid-in capital	pp. 638–641
Retained earnings	pp. 638–641, 668–670
Dividends	pp. 638–641
Investments by stockholders	pp. 462, 638–641
Declaration and payment of dividends	pp. 462, 638–641
FINANCIAL STATEMENTS—PROPRIETORSHIP, PARTNERSHIP, CORPORATION	
Income statement/component percentage	Chs. 8, 16, 26
Balance sheet	Chs. 8, 16, 26
Automated Accounting/spreadsheet	Automated Accounting feature at the end of every chapter (templates available) Spreadsheet Accounting software and templates
Ethics and financial statements	Professional Business Ethics, pp. 7, 99, 195, 265, 420, 493, 665
Business activities—operating, investing, financing	p. 684
Statement of cash flows	p. 684
Horizontal and vertical analysis	Chs. 8, 16, 26
Historical cost/financial statements	Chs. 8, 16, 26
Revenue and realization concept/financial statements	Chs. 8, 16, 26
Matching revenues and expenses/financial statements	Chs. 8, 16, 26
Realization of revenue/financial statements	Chs. 8, 16, 26
Cost of goods sold	pp. 223, 400–401, 580–588
Discontinued operations/income statement	p. 316

OWNERSHIP	
Three forms of ownership	Cycle 1, Cycle 2, Cycle 3
Formation, allocation of earnings, dissolution, and liquidation of a partnership	pp. 256, 316, 372
Government and not-for-profit accounting	Advanced Course Text
PAYROLL	
Payroll records	Chs. 13–14
Salary calculation	Ch. 13
Payroll deductions	Ch. 13
Employer's payroll taxes	Ch. 14
Payroll reports	Chs. 13–14
INCOME TAX	
Personal tax	pp. 316–321, 330, 536, 636
Business tax	pp. 330, 344–353, 360, 536, 549, 566, 636–637, 648–650
Income tax laws	pp. 316–321, 330, 344–360, 536, 636–637, 648–650
Generally accepted accounting principles/tax law	Chs. 1–26, Appendix A, and pp. 316–321, 330, 344–360, 636–637
MANAGERIAL ACCOUNTING	
Management process	Advanced Course Text
Manufacturing costs	Advanced Course Text
Statement of cost of goods manufactured	Advanced Course Text
Job order costing system	Advanced Course Text
Process costing system	Advanced Course Text
DATA	
Fixed, variable, mixed costs	Advanced Course Text
Cost-volume profit/contribution margin	Advanced Course Text
Budgets	Advanced Course Text
Automated Accounting/spreadsheet software for budgets	Advanced Course Text
Variable and absorption costing	Advanced Course Text
Master/flexible budgets	Advanced Course Text
Standard costing and variance analysis	Advanced Course Text
Responsibility accounting	Advanced Course Text

LOCATION OF ANSWERS AND SOLUTIONS

Due to the abundance of teacher support material available with this course, the table below is provided to guide you in locating solutions to student activities.

KEY TO LOCATION OF ANSWERS AND SOLUTIONS	
Item	**Found In**
Accounting in Your Career	Margins of Wraparound Teacher's Edition
Professional Business Ethics	Instructional Strategies section in front of Wraparound Teacher's Edition
Terms Review	Glossary in Student Text
Audit Your Understanding	Appendix D in Student Text
Work Together Problems	Teacher's Edition of Working Papers
On Your Own Problems	Teacher's Edition of Working Papers
Explore Accounting	Margins of Wraparound Teacher's Edition
Application Problems	Teacher's Edition of Working Papers
Mastery Problems	Teacher's Edition of Working Papers
Challenge Problems	Teacher's Edition of Working Papers
Recycling Problems	Teacher's Edition of Study Guide and Recycling Problem Working Papers
Reinforcement Activities	Teacher's Edition of Working Papers
Automated Accounting Problems	Teacher's Resource Guide and the Electronic Auditor
Study Guides	Teacher's Edition of Study Guide and Recycling Problem Working Papers
Tests	Assessment Binder
Manual Simulations	Keys for manual simulations
Automated Simulations	Keys for automated simulations
Supplemental Math Worksheets	Teacher's Resource Guide

PROFESSIONAL REFERENCES AND RESOURCES

Periodicals

Accountancy, International Edition, Institute of Chartered Accountants in England and Wales, London, UK. (International accounting)

Accounting Horizons, American Accounting Association, Sarasota, FL.

Accounting News, Warren, Gorham & Lamont, New York, NY.

Accounting, Organizations, and Society, Elsevier Science, Inc., New York, NY.

Accounting Review, American Accounting Association, Sarasota, FL.

Accounting Technology (formerly *Computers in Accounting*), Faulkner & Gray, Inc., New York, NY.

Accounting Today, Faulkner & Gray, Inc., New York, NY.

American Accounting Association Newsletter, Sarasota, FL.

Black Enterprise, Earl G. Graves Publishing Co., Inc., New York, NY. (multicultural awareness)

Business Ethics: Insider's Report on Responsible Business, Mavis Publications, Inc., Minneapolis, MN.

CPA Digest, Harcourt Brace Professional Publishing, Orlando, FL.

CPA Journal, New York State Society of CPAs, New York, NY.

Entrepreneur, Irvine, CA.

Forbes, Forbes Publishing, Inc., New York, NY. (business news)

Fortune, Time Publishing Ventures, Inc., New York, NY. (business news)

Hispanic, Hispanic Publishing Co, Austin, TX. (multicultural awareness)

Inc. Magazine, Goldhirsh Group, Boston, MA. (small business/entrepreneurship)

Internet Bulletin for CPAs, Kent Information Services, Inc., Kent, OH.

Journal of Accountancy, AICPA, Jersey City, NJ.

Journal of Accounting Education, Elsevier Science, Inc., New York, NY.

Journal of Business Ethics, Kluwer Academic Publishers, Norwell, MA.

Management Accounting, Institute of Management Accountants, Montvale, NJ.

Multicultural Education, Caddo Gap Press, San Francisco, CA. (multicultural awareness)

Multinational Business Review, University of Detroit–Mercy College of Business Administration, Detroit, MI. (global business)

Native Peoples, Media Concepts Group, Inc., Phoenix, AZ. (multicultural awareness)

Practical Accountant, Faulkner & Gray, Inc., New York, NY.

Transpacific, Transpacific Media, Inc., Malibu, CA. (multicultural awareness)

Wall Street Journal, New York, NY. (business newspaper)

Working Woman, MacDonald Communications, New York, NY. (multicultural awareness)

Books

Adams, Dennis. *Cooperative Learning; Critical Thinking and Collaboration Across the Curriculum.* Springfield: Charles C. Thomas Publisher, Limited, 1996.

AICPA. *A Survey of Perceptions, Knowledge and Attitudes Towards CPAs and the Accounting Profession*, 1986.

AICPA. *Accounting Trends and Techniques*, 1993.

AICPA. *FASB Accounting Standards.*

AICPA. *Upward Mobility of Women Special Committee: Report to the AICPA Board of Directors.*

Albrecht, Steve. *Ethical Workplace.* Menlo Park: Crisp Publications, Inc., 1998.

AT&T, International Telephone Guide.

Baldwin, Bruce. *The Financial Reporting Project*, Second Edition. Cincinnati: South-Western College Publishing, 1999.

Bieg, Bernard J. *Payroll Accounting*, Ninth Edition. Cincinnati: South-Western College Publishing, 1999.

Bloom, Benjamin S., ed., et. al. *Taxonomy of Educational Objectives: Handbook I, Cognitive Domain.* White Plains: Longman, Inc., 1984.

Cantlon, Teresa L. *Structuring the Classroom Successfully for Cooperative Team Learning.* Portland, OR: Prestige Publishers, 1989.

Champagne, Duane. *Native America: Portrait of a People.* Detroit: Visible Ink Press, 1994.

Chatfield, Michael. *The History of Accounting: An Encyclopedia.* New York: Garland Publishing, Inc., 1996.

Elashmawi, Farid, and Philip R. Harris. *Multicultural Management 2000.* Houston: Gulf Publishing Company, 1998.

Estell, Kenneth. *African America: Portrait of a People.* Detroit:

Visible Ink Press, 1994.

Estes, Ralph. *Dictionary of Accounting*. Second Edition. Cambridge: The MIT Press, 1985.

Fisher, Paul, William Taylor, and Rita Cheng. *Advanced Accounting*, Seventh Edition. Cincinnati: South-Western College Publishing, 1997.

Gelinas, Ulric J, Steve G. Sutton, and Allan E. Oram. *Accounting Information Systems*, Fourth Edition. Cincinnati: South-Western College Publishing, 1999.

Gibson, Charles H. *Financial Statement Analysis: Using Financial Accounting Information*, Seventh Edition. Cincinnati: South-Western College Publishing, 1998.

Gilbertson, Claudia. *Accounting: Learning and Instruction*. Second Edition. Cincinnati: South-Western Publishing Co., 1992.

Griseri, P. *In Search of Business Ethics*. New York: State Mutual Book and Periodical Service Limited, 1996.

Gronlund, Norman E. *Assessment of Student Achievement*. New York: Allyn and Bacon Computer Books, 1997.

Gronlund, Norman E. *Stating Objectives for Classroom Instruction*. 3d. ed. New York: Macmillan Publishing Co., Inc., 1985.

Hall, Georganna, and Gemmy S. Allen. *Internet Guide for Accounting & MSN CD-ROM*. Cincinnati: South-Western College Publishing, 1998.

Hall, James A. *Accounting Information Systems*, Second Edition. Cincinnati: South-Western College Publishing, 1998.

Harrell, Earl, and Cassandra Harrell. *Surviving in the Workplace: A Resource for Individuals, Educational Institutions, and Businesses for Promoting Safety and Awareness in the Workplace*. Milwaukee: E.T. Publishing Company, 1994.

Harris, Philip R. *Managing Cultural Differences*. Houston: Gulf Publishing Co., 1996.

Harris, Philip R., and Robert T. Moran. *Managing Cultural Differences*. Houston: Gulf Publishing Company, 1992.

Hartman, Bart, Robert Harper, James Knoblett, and Philip Reckers. *Intermediate Accounting,* Second Edition. Cincinnati: South-Western College Publishing, 1998.

Heintz, James A. and Robert Parry. *College Accounting,* Sixteenth Edition. Cincinnati: South-Western College Publishing, 1999.

Hughes, John. *Cases in Financial Accounting*. Cincinnati: South-Western College Publishing, 1994.

Ingram, Robert, Thomas Albright, Bruce Baldwin, and John Hill. *Accounting: Information for Decisions*. Cincinnati: South-Western College Publishing, 1999.

Iqbal, Zafar, Trini Melcher, and Amin Elmallah. *International Accounting: A Global Perspective*. Cincinnati: South-Western College Publishing, 1997.

Johnson, D. *Cooperation and Competition*. Edina: Interaction Book Company, 1989.

Johnson, David W. *Cooperative Learning in the Classroom*. Alexandria: Association for Supervision and Curriculum Development, 1994.

Johnson, David W. *The Nuts and Bolts of Cooperative Learning*. Edina: Interaction Book Company, 1994.

Knapp, Michael C. *Contemporary Auditing Issues and Cases,* Third Edition. Cincinnati: South-Western College Publishing, 1999.

Knechel, W. Robert. *Auditing: Text and Cases*. Cincinnati: South-Western College Publishing, 1998.

Konrath, Larry F. *Auditing Concepts and Applications: A Risk-Analysis Approach,* Fourth Edition. Cincinnati: South-Western College Publishing, 1999.

LaBonty, Dennis, ed. *Integrating the Internet into the Business Curriculum*. Reston: National Business Education Association, 1998.

Lawrence, Michael, and Joan Ryan. *Essentials of Accounting,* Ninth Edition. Cincinnati: South-Western College Publishing, 1999.

Lerner, Janet W. *Learning Disabilities.* Boston: Houghton Mifflin, 1992.

Mager, Robert F. *Preparing Instructional Objectives: A Critical Tool in the Development of Effective Instruction*. Atlanta: Center for Effective Performance, Inc., 1997.

Mamchur, Carolyn. *A Teacher's Guide to Cognitive Type Theory and Learning Style*. Alexandria: Association for Supervision and Curriculum Development, 1996.

Marzano, Robert J. *A Different Kind of Classroom: Teaching with Dimensions of Learning*. Association for Supervision and Curriculum Development, Alexandria, VA, 1992.

National Society of Public Accountants. *Portfolio of Accounting Systems for Small and Medium-Sized Businesses*. Revised. Paramus, NJ: Prentice Hall, 1992.

Nikolai, Loren, and John Bazley. *Intermediate Accounting,* Seventh Edition. Cincinnati: South-Western College Publishing, 1997.

Palepu, Krishna G., Victor L. Bernard, Paul M. Healy. *Business Analysis and Valuation Using Financial*

Statements. Cincinnati: South-Western College Publishing, 1996.

Palepu, Krishna, Victor Bernard, and Paul Healy. *Introduction to Business Analysis and Valuation.* Cincinnati: South-Western College Publishing, 1997.

Perry, James, and Gary P. Schneider. *Building Accounting Systems Using Access for Windows '95,* Second Edition. Cincinnati: South-Western College Publishing, 1998.

Pratt, Jamie, Krishnamoorthy Ramesh, and David Foster. *Interactive Cases in Financial Analysis.* Cincinnati: South-Western College Publishing, 1998.

Raiborn, Cecily A., Jesse T. Barfield, and Michael R. Kinney. *Managerial Accounting,* Third Edition. Cincinnati: South-Western College Publishing, 1999.

Ricchiute, David. *Auditing and Assurance Services,* Fifth Edition. Cincinnati: South-Western College Publishing, 1998.

Riding, Richard. *Cognitive Styles and Learning Strategies: Understanding Style Differences in Learning and Behavior.* Bristol: Taylor and Francis, Inc., 1998.

Schloss, Patrick J.. *Career-Vocational Education for Handicapped Youth.* Gaithersburg, MD: Aspen Publishers, Inc., 1982.

Scott, John L. *Vocational Special Needs.* Homewood: American Technical Publishers, 1995.

Secretary's Commission on Achieving Necessary Skills. *What Work Requires of Schools: A SCANS Report for America 2000.* Washington, DC: U.S. Department of Labor, 1991.

Shank, John K. *Cases in Cost Management: A Strategic Emphasis.* Cincinnati: South-Western College Publishing, 1996.

Shulman, Judith. *Groupwork in Diverse Classrooms: A Casebook for Educators.* New York: Teachers College Press, Teachers College, Columbia University, 1998.

Simons, George F., Carmen Vazquez, and Philip R. Harris. *Transcultural Leadership: Empowering the Diverse Work Force.* Houston: Gulf Publishing Company, 1993.

Skousen, Fred, James Stice, and Earl Kay Stice. *Intermediate Accounting,* Thirteenth Edition. Cincinnati: South-Western College Publishing, 1998.

Skousen, K. Fred, W. Steve Albrecht, James D. Stice, and Earl Kay Stice. *Accounting: Concepts and Applications,* Seventh Edition. Cincinnati: South-Western College Publishing, 1999.

Solomon, Ira, and Mark Peecher. *Assurance Services: An Introduction and Application.* Cincinnati: South-Western College Publishing, 1999.

Solomon, Robert C. *It's Good Business; Ethics and Free Enterprise for the New Millenium.* Lanham: Rowman and Littlefield, Publishers, Inc., 1997.

Stice, James, Steve Albrecht, and Fred Skousen. *Survey of Accounting.* Cincinnati: South-Western College Publishing, 1999.

Sunder, Shyan. *Theory of Accounting and Control.* Cincinnati: South-Western College Publishing, 1997.

U.S. Department of Commerce. *Basic Guide to Exporting.* 1986.

U.S. Department of Labor. *Dictionary of Occupational Titles.*

U.S. Department of Labor. *Occupational Outlook Handbook.*

Verdium, John R., Jr. *Helping Students Develop Investigative, Problem-Solving, and Thinking Skills in a Cooperative Setting: A Handbook for Teachers, Administrators, and Curriculum Workers.* Springfield: Charles C. Thomas Publisher, Limited, 1996.

Warren, Carl S., James Reeve, and Philip E. Fess. *Financial and Managerial Accounting,* Sixth Edition. Cincinnati: South-Western College Publishing, 1999.

Warren, Carl S., James M. Reeve, and Philip E. Fess. *Accounting,* Nineteenth Edition. Cincinnati: South-Western College Publishing, 1999.

Weirich, Thomas, and Alan Reinstein. *Accounting and Auditing Research: A Practical Guide,* Fourth Edition. Cincinnati: South-Western College Publishing, 1997.

Wolk, Harry, and Michael Tearney. *Accounting Theory,* Fourth Edition. Cincinnati: South-Western College Publishing, 1997.

Technology

AICPA. *The Bottom Line: Inside Accounting Today,* 1987. (Video)

AICPA. *It All Adds Up,* 1989. (Video)

AICPA. *A License to Succeed,* 1990. (Video)

AICPA. *Luca Pacioli: Unsung Hero of the Renaissance.* (Video)

AICPA. *Room Zoom: The CPA Source Disk™* (Interactive CD; CPAs and accounting careers)

AICPA. *Serving America: A Tradition of Excellence,* 1986. (Video)

AICPA. *Solving the Year 2000 Dilemma Videocourse* (Video)

Access (database software)

Paradox (database software)

Excel (spreadsheet software)

Lotus (spreadsheet software)

Pagemaker (desktop publishing software)

Quattro Pro (spreadsheet software)

Ventura Publisher (desktop publishing software)

Windows (operating system software)

WordPerfect (word processing software)

Works (integrated software)

·SOUTH-WESTERN·
CENTURY 21
ACCOUNTING
GENERAL JOURNAL

Kenton E. Ross, CPA
Professor Emeritus of Accounting
Texas A&M University–Commerce
Commerce, Texas

Mark W. Lehman, CPA
Associate Professor
School of Accountancy
Mississippi State University
Starkville, Mississippi

Claudia Bienias Gilbertson, CPA
Teaching Professor
North Hennepin Community College
Brooklyn Park, Minnesota

Robert D. Hanson
Late Associate Dean
College of Business Administration
Central Michigan University
Mount Pleasant, Michigan

THOMSON
✦
SOUTH-WESTERN

Australia · Canada · Mexico · Singapore · Spain · United Kingdom · United States

THOMSON

SOUTH-WESTERN

Century 21 Accounting, General Journal, Anniversary Edition
by Kenton E. Ross, Claudia Bienias Gilbertson, Mark W. Lehman, and Robert D. Hanson

Vice President/
Executive Publisher
Dave Shaut
Team Leader
Karen Schmohe
Acquisitions Editor
Marilyn Hornsby
Project Manager
Carol Sturzenberger
Sr. Marketing Manager
Nancy A. Long

Marketing Coordinator
Yvonne Patton-Beard
Production Manager
Patricia Matthews Boies
Manufacturing Coordinator
Kevin Kluck
Editorial Assistant
Stephanie White
Production Assistant
Nancy Stamper

Design Coordinator
Tippy McIntosh
Cycle Opener Artwork
Marti Shohet
Cover Design
Tom Nikosey
Composition/Prepress
Better Graphics
Printer
R. R. Donnelley/Willard

For permission to use material from this text or product, contact us by
Tel (800) 730-2214
Fax (800) 730-2215
www.thomsonrights.com

For more information, contact South-Western, 5191 Natorp Boulevard, Mason, OH 45040; or find us on the World Wide Web at http://www.swep.com

About the Authors

Kenton E. Ross, Ed.D., C.P.A., is Professor Emeritus, Department of Accounting, at Texas A&M University—Commerce. He formerly served as Dean of the College of Business and Technology; Director of Business and Economic Research; and Head, Department of Accounting.

Claudia Bienias Gilbertson, M.B.A., C.P.A., is an experienced high school and community college instructor. She is currently a teaching professor at North Hennepin Community College.

Mark W. Lehman, Ph.D., C.P.A., is an Associate Professor in the School of Accountancy at Mississippi State University, where he teaches in the areas of microcomputers, accounting systems, and auditing. He regularly teaches continuing education classes on microcomputers and internal control.

The late **Robert D. Hanson,** Ph.D., was Professor of Business Education and Associate Dean of the College of Business Administration at Central Michigan University.

REVIEWERS

SOUTH-WESTERN CENTURY 21 ACCOUNTING

SEVENTH EDITION

FAMILY OF PRODUCTS

South-Western Educational Publishing provides everything you and your students need to have a successful accounting classroom.

Wraparound Teacher's Edition provides

✳ **OVERVIEW** of each accounting cycle and each chapter within a cycle.

✳ **TEACHING STRATEGIES** loaded with hints, tips, and suggestions for reaching students with different learning styles—plus, a variety of instructional methods, such as cooperative learning, different media options, and more.

✳ **CHAPTER INTERLEAF CHARTS** that present concepts and skills covered in a chapter. Instructors can determine what will be new for students and what concepts and skills need reinforcement and emphasis. Also included is information about special features, technology and media, teaching strategies, and practice and assessment.

✳ **EFFECTIVE TEACHING MODEL LESSON PLANS** that provide step-by-step instructional support for every lesson. Each Lesson Plan includes the headings Motivate, Explain, Demonstrate, Guided Practice, Independent Practice, Reteach, Enrich, and Close.

✳ **CHECK FIGURES** that can be provided to students as guideposts as students complete their work or that can be used by instructors for quick and easy grading.

Working Papers contain accounting forms

and rulings for completing chapter problems and Reinforcement Activities. The *Working Papers* are carefully laid out so that forms for the next problem are available while the previous problem is being graded. Plenty of extra forms are provided for any necessary rework. The Teacher's Editions of the *Working Papers* provide solutions to the problems. A separate *Study Guide and Recycling Problem Working Papers* book is also available.

Transparency Packages

An extensive array of **transparency packages** includes full-color teaching transparencies, blank accounting rulings to be used for guided practice and demonstrations, and transparencies of the solutions in the Teacher's Edition of the *Working Papers*.

Simulations

A **new simulation** is available for each accounting cycle in both manual and automated versions.

❑ *FOREIGN EXCHANGE TRANSLATION SERVICE* is a language translation service business organized as a sole proprietorship.

❑ *FITNESS JUNCTION* is an exercise equipment merchandising business organized as a partnership.

❑ *PUTTING GREEN GOLF SUPPLY* is a golf equipment and supply merchandising business organized as a corporation.

Technology

✳ **TEMPLATE DISKS** are available for use with *Automated Accounting 7.0, Windows; Automated Accounting 6.0, Windows;* and *Automated Accounting 6.0, Macintosh.* Template files are available for many problems in the textbook, the comprehensive Reinforcement Activities in each cycle, plus the three simulations. *Electronic Auditors* are also available.

✳ **SPREADSHEET TEMPLATE DISKS** correspond to selected textbook problems.

Assessment Binder Package Includes

two separate versions of printed chapter and cycle tests, containing both objective questions and problems and a computerized testing program.

Other items available include

❑ **English and Spanish Dictionary**

❑ **Teacher's Resource Guide** in three-ring binder

❑ **Videotapes**

❑ **Multimedia CD-ROM**

CYCLE 1 ACCOUNTING FOR A SERVICE BUSINESS ORGANIZED AS A PROPRIETORSHIP

Contents

CYCLE 2 ACCOUNTING FOR A MERCHANDISING BUSINESS ORGANIZED AS A PARTNERSHIP

Contents

CYCLE 3 ACCOUNTING FOR A MERCHANDISING BUSINESS ORGANIZED AS A CORPORATION

Contents

INSTRUCTIONAL STRATEGIES

COMPLETE ACCOUNTING COVERAGE

Century 21 Accounting continues to provide complete coverage of three types of business—**proprietorship**, **partnership**, and **corporation**. Each type of business is presented in a complete accounting cycle covering analyzing transactions, journalizing, posting, petty cash, financial statements, and adjusting and closing entries. Accounting concepts are introduced using a modern business with owners that students can relate to in each cycle. In Cycle 1, students study Encore Music, a business that provides music lessons. Cycle 2 features Omni Import, a retail merchandising business that purchases and sells imported gift items. In Cycle 3, Winning Edge, Inc., sells sports equipment to school districts, colleges, and businesses and is organized as a corporation. Each accounting cycle opens with a two-page illustration connected to the business in the cycle.

South-Western Educational Publishing provides **two different approaches** to the study of first-year accounting. In its traditional blue cover, the Multicolumn Journal Approach lets students focus on analyzing transactions, knowing that all transactions will be entered in the same journal. Special journals are introduced in Cycle 3. In its familiar green cover, the General Journal Approach introduces special journals in Cycle 2. The earlier focus on special journals mirrors college accounting and automated accounting approaches.

COLORFUL, ATTRACTIVE PAGES

Bright, interesting colors throughout the text draw students in and get them excited about accounting! Imagine how eager students will be about reading a bright and colorful textbook.

Scattered throughout are **eye-catching photos** that represent the featured businesses. Encore Music in Cycle 1 is represented by photos of musical instruments such as drums, maracas, and a trumpet. Omni Import in Cycle 2 by photos of imported gift items such as an elephant bowl from Africa, a mask from Asia, a jaguar figurine from Latin America, and nesting dolls from Europe.

Winning Edge, Inc., in Cycle 3 by photos of athletic equipment such as a soccer ball, ice skates, and a baseball glove.

MANAGEABLE PEDAGOGY WITH SHORT, ACCESSIBLE LESSONS

Have you ever heard a student say, "Accounting is hard"? Century 21 Accounting, Seventh Edition has the answer. Chapters are divided into **short, accessible lessons** that cover one or two concepts.

The Wraparound Teacher's Edition contains comprehensive lesson plans for each lesson to help you plan your instructional time more easily.

❏ **Chart of Accounts** used throughout the cycle is provided on the cycle opening pages for easy reference.

❏ **Terms Preview** displays all the key words introduced in the chapter.

❏ **Objectives** are listed at the beginning of each chapter to highlight lesson concepts and preview what students will learn.

Illustrations are consistently placed directly above the corresponding text. No more flipping pages back and forth to find an illustration that appears on a different page from the explanatory text! Plus, students can quickly find the illustration they are looking for when reviewing or working problems.

Steps and call-outs are completely integrated into the illustrations. This makes it easy to understand and then apply the procedure being taught. Clear, concise, step-by-step instructions are directly linked to the specific part of the illustration where the work is recorded.

The **concentrated supporting text** covers one specific topic and motivates students to read each page. Students are not intimidated by pages of text, but are encouraged to investigate the illustration and get further information by reading.

Many students are visual learners. First-year accounting emphasizes learning step-by-step procedures. With the combination of consistently placed, easy-to-locate illustrations, call-outs and instructions placed inside the illustrations, and step-by-step instructions, students can see how to complete accounting procedures and can refer to **easy-to-read steps** for reinforcement and clarification.

LESSON PRACTICE

Each lesson ends with an activity page that provides immediate reinforcement of the lesson material. Instructors can use the end-of-lesson activities to make sure students fully understand all concepts and procedures before moving on to the next lesson.

❏ **Terms Review** lists all the important new words learned in the lesson in the order they appear in the text.

❏ **Audit Your Understanding** asks two or more conceptual questions about the material covered in the lesson. The answers appear in Appendix D so students can check their understanding.

❏ **Work Together** provides guided practice through the students' first hands-on application of chapter procedures and concepts. Forms to complete the exercise are given in the Working Papers. Performing this exercise together with the instructor gives students a basis for completing similar problems later.

❏ **On Your Own** mirrors and builds on the Work Together problem to give the student independent practice. Forms to complete the exercise are given in the Working Papers. Students work this problem to demonstrate proficiency, giving them a real sense of accomplishment. Instructors can informally assess whether students have mastered the basic concept covered in the lesson. Accounting isn't so hard after all!

❏ Students get further independent practice from an end-of-chapter **Application Problem** that mirrors the end-of-lesson problems.

WORK SHEET OVERLAY

The Work Sheet Overlay is an excellent visual summary of the steps taken to prepare a work sheet. Students can see how a work sheet is prepared one section at a time, simplifying the process. The Work Sheet Overlay appears in Chapter 7: Work Sheet for a Service Business.

CHAPTER PRACTICE

Century 21 Accounting, Seventh Edition gives students **many short problems**. Students can now easily find and fix mistakes.

The **Summary** is a quick, short list of the topics covered in each lesson. Students can use the Summary to review their understanding of the material presented in the chapter. Instructors can ask questions based on the Summary as a fast way to verify student comprehension.

End-of-chapter exercises contain

❏ **Application problems** at least one for each lesson.

❏ **Mastery problems** that test overall comprehension of the entire chapter.

❏ **Challenge problems** that test overall comprehension of the entire chapter.

Many end-of-chapter problems can be completed using Automated Accounting software.

❏ **Reinforcement Activities** in each cycle.

And something new, most chapters contain one problem using real-life transaction statements.

APPENDICES

❏ **Appendix A: Accounting Concepts** Lists in one place all of the accounting concepts that students encounter throughout the text.

❏ **Appendix B: Using a Calculator and Computer Keypad** Provides important instruction in business calculator use and the ten-key touch system.

❏ **Appendix C: Recycling Problems** Offers additional opportunities for student practice. There is one recycling problem for each chapter, and these problems mirror the end-of-chapter mastery problems. Working papers are provided in the Study Guide and Recycling Problem Working Papers.

❏ **Appendix D: Answers to Audit Your Understanding** Contains brief answers to Audit Your Understanding questions that appear at the end of each lesson. Students can use the questions and answers for self study.

FEATURES

Special features provide context for accounting learning and real-life information about business.
Features provide cross-curricular material for the accounting classroom.

LESSON FEATURES

❏ **Cultural Diversity** shows students that many different cultures around the world and throughout history have contributed to the development of accounting and financial record keeping.

❏ **Professional Business Ethics** presents dilemmas that can arise in day-to-day business operations.

❏ **Small Business Spotlight** features information about how to become a successful entrepreneur.

❏ **Accounting at Work** introduces real-life businesspeople who tell their stories about how accounting helps in their careers.

❏ **Technology for Business** covers the interplay between technology and business life. Topics covered include spreadsheets, the Internet, and commercial accounting software.

❏ **Global Perspective** provides insight into working with international suppliers and customers. Most students will have some global business experience in their careers. This feature introduces students to some of the issues involved in global business.

❏ **Legal Issues in Accounting** covers the legal issues involved in forming and dissolving the different forms of business organization and touches on other legal aspects of business life.

❏ **Applied Mathematics** boxes visually represent the intersection between accounting and mathematics and are strategically placed near relevant text to ensure optimum learning.

❏ **Remember** appears at the bottom of selected pages to reinforce critical accounting facts and procedures.

❏ **FYI** gives additional accounting and general business information related to the topics in a chapter.

CHAPTER FEATURES

❏ **Accounting in Your Career** features appear at the beginning of each chapter and entice students by showing how accounting is part of everyone's life. These scenarios answer the question, "Why should I learn this?" The Accounting in Your Career feature focuses your students' attention on the topics to be studied in the chapter.

❏ **Critical Thinking Questions** for Accounting in Your Career energize students with class discussions about accounting-related issues. The Critical Thinking Questions can even be used as an informal pretest and posttest to demonstrate how much students have learned after studying a chapter. Suggested answers to each question are provided in the Wraparound Teacher's Edition.

❏ **Internet Activity** provides the Web address and instructions for accessing the Internet activity for each chapter.

❏ **Applied Communication** offers exercises for strengthening communication skills, a must for all students. Employers are expecting their business and accounting new hires to be able to communicate effectively, so get started here.

❏ **Cases for Critical Thinking** require students to carefully consider one or more questions, based on the accounting scenario being presented. An excellent opportunity for in-class discussion or group work!

❏ **Explore Accounting** includes opportunities for higher-level learning with Discussion, Research, and Required exercises directly related to the material presented in the feature. Topics include GAAP, fiscal periods, cash controls, and more.

AUTOMATED ACCOUNTING

Automated Accounting sections conclude every chapter, and are a terrific opportunity for hands-on computer instruction with Automated Accounting. Now students see the connection between manual and automated accounting in every chapter.

INTRODUCTION

After studying this introduction, you will be able to:

1. Identify the many job opportunities available that require an accounting background.
2. Identify numerous careers in the accounting profession.
3. Identify the transferable skills an accounting class can strengthen.

On the first day of school, Kendra headed toward her fourth period class: accounting. She wondered what the class would be like. She had taken some other business classes, and enjoyed them. She was even thinking about pursuing a career in business. Last year, one of her teachers recommended that she take accounting. She hoped she would like it.

When she arrived at the classroom, Kendra was happy to find her friend Rob already there. "Hey, Rob, what are you doing here? I didn't know you were interested in business courses."

"Well, this is the first one I've taken. I really don't know what I want to do when I graduate in a couple of years, so I thought I should check out accounting. I'm really not sure it's for me, though."

The bell rang and the teacher came into the room. Everyone took a seat to get ready for class. Kendra sat next to Rob.

"Hi, everybody. I'm Mr. Perez, your accounting teacher for this year. And your first assignment is to come to the cafeteria with me."

Rob and Kendra looked at each other and at several of the other students. What was this?

Everyone followed Mr. Perez through the halls to the cafeteria. On the way there, Mr. Perez said, "I've assembled lots of people in the cafeteria. Professionals in all kinds of jobs. Feel free to talk to them about accounting fields, job opportunities, and more. You might be surprised at what you find out."

When they arrived at the cafeteria, they found a dozen people waiting to talk to them. They were from many companies, including accounting firms, entrepreneurial businesses, and governmental agencies. The class broke into smaller groups, and Rob and Kendra decided to walk around together. They chose to talk to an accountant first, because

When they arrived at the cafeteria, they found a dozen people waiting to talk to them. They were from many companies, including accounting firms, entrepreneurial businesses, and governmental agencies.

> **"I have a friend who has started her own floral shop, and she tells me she is very glad to have knowlege of accounting. It has really helped her ensure that the business succeeds."**

Kendra wanted to find out more about the different fields in accounting.

"Why, there are many different specialized jobs accountants can do," said Ms. Ikeda, an employee for a large accounting firm in town. "I am a financial accountant, which means I record a business's financial activities and prepare the financial reports for my business. What I do helps creditors, investors, bankers, and auditors know the financial stability of my firm.

"The managerial accountants I work with take the financial accounting information I prepare and then analyze, measure, and interpret the information for internal use. Managers then use these interpretations to help them make the right business decisions.

"Cost accountants analyze and control the costs of an organization. They provide information that aids in decision making concerning the costs of operating the business and the costs of manufacturing goods or services.

"And, of course, there are tax accountants. They prepare tax returns and also perform tax planning responsibilities. They must stay up-to-date with changes in the law to ensure a business complies with the law.

"Systems accountants design and adapt the accounting systems that create financial, manage-

rial, cost, and tax information reports for an organization. They also work hard to make these systems more efficient.

"An auditor's job is to review the reliability of a business's accounting records, and issue an opinion based on the information analyzed. An auditor's opinion enables those outside the business to feel confident about the stability of the business.

"Lastly, some accountants decide to become personal financial planners. They help individuals manage their personal investments, and they make suggestions about when and where money should be invested."

Rob and Kendra thanked Ms. Ikeda and then went to speak to some of the other professionals in the cafeteria. They found out about different types of employment opportunities available to people who have accounting backgrounds. Private accountants work for only one business; they may do all of the required summarizing, analyzing, and reporting, or they may specialize in one specific field of accounting. Public accountants can work independently or as a member of a public accounting firm, selling services such as preparing accounting reports or completing the tax forms for a business. Governmental/not-for-profit agencies also seem to have many opportunities for accountants. The Internal Revenue Service, hospitals, and churches all have needs for people to perform accounting duties.

Kendra thought all of the things she was learning were interesting. But Rob wasn't as excited as Kendra about possibly becoming an accountant. It just didn't seem to be for him, and he told Kendra he might decide to take a different class. He walked over to Mr. Perez and said, "Mr. Perez, maybe I shouldn't be taking this class. I don't think I want to be an accountant."

Mr. Perez smiled. "You don't have to want to be an accountant to benefit from taking this class. I'm not an accountant, but I have to know accounting to be your teacher. There are also many other accounting-related occupations that may interest you—travel agent, law clerk, manager, nurse, veterinarian. For these jobs, you'll need an understanding of accounting to make the right business decisions. I have a friend who has started her own floral shop, and she tells me she is very glad she has a knowledge of accounting. It has really helped her ensure that the business succeeds.

"Also, lots of small businesses need people to perform general accounting tasks. Businesses look for employees who can handle billing and collections, and payroll. But this is only part of the employee's job. They may also answer the phone, communicate with clients, and prepare annual reports or other documentation.

"What's more, there are many skills you will learn and strengthen by taking this class—skills that will help you regardless of what you decide you want to do. One of the most important skills you'll learn is how to communicate well, both when you write and when you speak. Accountants need to be able to communicate well because they often must relay information to people who have little or no accounting knowledge. But, being a good communicator is an invaluable tool for everyone to learn. Taking an accounting course will also help you learn to pay attention to details, improve your problem solving abilities, evaluate your own work, listen well, and interpret data. Those are all skills that will help you with any occupation you choose."

"Thanks Mr. Perez. I never realized I could learn so many important things by taking accounting," Rob said.

After finding out they could use accounting knowledge in so many different ways, Kendra, Rob, and all the other students were looking forward to studying accounting for the rest of the term.

Mr. Perez smiled. "You don't have to be an accountant to benefit from taking this class. I'm not an accountant, but I have to know accounting to be your teacher."

Accounting for a Merchandising

Cycle 3 presents the complete accounting cycle one more time, this time for a merchandising business organized as a corporation.

❏ Chapters 18 and 19 describe how the basic kinds of daily transactions for purchases, sales, cash payments, and cash receipts are recorded in special journals. In addition, Chapter 19 features a new lesson on the procedures for arranging and accounting for international sales.

❏ Chapter 20 covers the procedures for estimating uncollectible accounts expense at the end of a fiscal period.

❏ Chapter 21 describes a full range of concepts and procedures related to accounting for and reporting plant assets. Straight-line depreciation is emphasized, but declining-balance methods are also described. Disposal of plant assets is discussed, including the calculation and reporting of gains and losses on disposal. Property taxes are also covered.

❏ Chapter 22 focuses on merchandise inventory. Inventory is costed using the fifo, lifo, and weighted average methods. The gross profit method of estimating an inventory is also presented.

❏ Chapter 23 presents a range of topics related to notes payable and notes receivable.

❏ Chapter 25 continues the discussion of notes payable and receivable, focusing on end-of-fiscal-period adjusting, closing, and reversing entries for accrued revenue and expenses.

❏ Chapter 25 begins the end-of-fiscal-period work. Journal entries for distributing corporate earnings in the form of dividends are also illustrated.

❏ Chapter 26 concludes the presentation of end-of-fiscal-period work for a corporation with the preparation of a financial statement followed by adjusting, closing, and reversing entries.

❏ Chapters 18–26 model the accounting cycle for the third time. This time, the business is a merchandising business and a corporation and has more kinds of transactions than the merchandising business in Cycle 2. All accounting concepts and procedures are described within the context of the accounting cycle so students can see how each procedure contributes to the overall financial picture of the business.

CYCLE

3

458

AUTOMATED ACCOUNTING

❏ For those instructors who wish to fully integrate the accounting program, an Automated Accounting feature is provided at the end of each chapter.

REINFORCEMENT ACTIVITY

❏ Reinforcement Activity 3 is divided into Parts A and B. Part A may be completed after Chapter 19. Part B may be completed after Chapter 26. However, some instructors may wish to delay work on Part A until after Chapter 26 is completed. Then both Parts A and B can be completed as a single unit. The audit test is also divided into two parts.

SIMULATION

❏ Putting Green Golf Supply is the simulation for Cycle 3. Students can apply what they have learned in Cycle 3 to the realistic transactions completed during the accounting cycle of this merchandising business organized as a corporation.

WINNING EDGE, INC., CHART OF ACCOUNTS

General Ledger

Balance Sheet Accounts

(1000) ASSETS
1100   Current Assets
1105   Cash
1110   Petty Cash
1115   Notes Receivable
1120   Interest Receivable
1125   Accounts Receivable
1130   Allowance for Uncollectible
       Accounts
1135   Merchandise Inventory
1140   Supplies
1145   Prepaid Insurance
1200   Plant Assets
1205   Office Equipment
1210   Accumulated Depreciation—
       Office Equipment
1215   Store Equipment
1220   Accumulated Depreciation—
       Store Equipment

(2000) LIABILITIES
2100   Current Liabilities
2105   Notes Payable
2110   Interest Payable
2115   Accounts Payable
2120   Employee Income Tax Payable
2125   Federal Income Tax Payable
2130   Social Security Tax Payable
2135   Medicare Tax Payable
2140   Sales Tax Payable
2145   Unemployment Tax Payable—
       Federal
2150   Unemployment Tax Payable—
       State
2155   Health Insurance Premiums
       Payable
2160   Dividends Payable

(3000) STOCKHOLDERS' EQUITY
3105   Capital Stock
3110   Retained Earnings
3115   Dividends
3120   Income Summary

Income Statement Accounts

(4000) OPERATING REVENUE
4105   Sales
4110   Sales Discount
4115   Sales Returns and Allowances

(5000) COST OF MERCHANDISE
5105   Purchases
5110   Purchases Discount
5115   Purchases Returns and
       Allowances

(6000) OPERATING EXPENSES
6105   Advertising Expense
6110   Cash Short and Over
6115   Credit Card Fee Expense
6120   Depreciation Expense—Office
       Equipment
6125   Depreciation Expense—Store
       Equipment
6130   Insurance Expense
6135   Miscellaneous Expense
6140   Payroll Taxes Expense
6145   Rent Expense
6150   Repair Expense
6155   Salary Expense
6160   Supplies Expense
6165   Uncollectible Accounts Expense
6170   Utilities Expense

(7000) OTHER REVENUE
7105   Gain on Plant Assets
7110   Interest Income

(8000) OTHER EXPENSES
8105   Interest Expense
8110   Loss on Plant Assets

(9000) INCOME TAX EXPENSE
9105   Federal Income Tax Expense

The chart of accounts for Winning Edge, Inc., is illustrated above for ready reference as you study Cycle 3 of this textbook.

CHAPTER 18

	SCOPE AND SEQUENCE		ENHANCING	
	NEW	REVIEW/ EXTENSION	SPECIAL FEATURES	
INTRODUCE THE CHAPTER			Accounting in Your Career: Don't Lose Those Discounts Thinking about Careers	
Recording financial information		✓		
LESSSON 18-1 RECORDING PURCHASES ON ACCOUNT USING A PURCHASES JOURNAL			The Business—Winning Edge, Inc.	
Corporation accounting	✓			
Journalizing and posting using a purchases journal		✓		
Journalizing purchases of merchandise on account		✓		
Totaling and ruling a purchases journal		✓		
LESSSON 18-2 RECORDING PURCHASES TRANSACTIONS USING A CASH PAYMENTS JOURNAL			Math Work Sheet, Chapter 18, Part A Accounting at Work: Pamela Aguirre	
Journalizing using a cash payments journal		✓		
Journalizing cash payments for cash purchases of merchandise		✓		
Journalizing cash payments for purchases on account with purchases discounts	✓			
Journalizing cash payments for purchases on account without purchases discounts		✓		
LESSSON 18-3 JOURNALIZING PETTY CASH AND POSTING USING A CASH PAYMENTS JOURNAL			Math Work Sheet, Chapter 18, Part B	
Petty cash report	✓			
Cash short and over	✓			
Journalizing cash payments to replenish petty cash		✓		
Posting from a cash payments journal		✓		
Proving, totaling, and ruling a cash payments journal		✓		
LESSSON 18-4 RECORDING PURCHASES RETURNS AND ALLOWANCES			Legal Issues in Accounting: Piercing the Corporate Veil Technology for Business: Who's in the Driver's Seat?	
Debit memorandum	✓			
Journalizing purchases returns and allowances	✓			
Posting from a general journal		✓		
PUTTING IT ALL TOGETHER			Explore Accounting Internet Activity Applied Communication Cases for Critical Thinking 1 and 2	

RECORDING PURCHASES AND CASH PAYMENTS

INSTRUCTION		PRACTICE AND ASSESSMENT		
TECHNOLOGY AND MEDIA	TEACHING STRATEGIES	GUIDED PRACTICE	INDEPENDENT PRACTICE	RETEACHING AND ENRICHMENT
Internet Activity	Software Focus			

Transparency K	Building Study Skills	Terms Review
		Audit Your
		    Understanding
		Work Together
			On Your Own
			Application Problem
			    18-1
			Ongoing Assessment,
			    p. 464
				Reteach, p. 464
				Enrich, p. 465

South-Western
    Accounting Video:
    Ethics—Purchases
    and Returns
Transparency L
	Applied Skills:
	    Mathematics
	At-Risk Students
		Terms Review
		Audit Your
		    Understanding
		Work Together
			On Your Own
			Application Problem
			    18-2
			Ongoing Assessment,
			    p. 468
				Reteach, p. 468
				Enrich, p. 469

CNN Accounting Video
Transparency L
	Applied Skills:
	    Mathematics
	Applied Skills: Writing
	    Across the
	    Curriculum
		Terms Review
		Audit Your
		    Understanding
		Work Together
			On Your Own
			Application Problem
			    18-3
			Application Problem
			    18-4
			Ongoing Assessment,
			    p. 473
				Reteach, p. 473
				Enrich, p. 474

Transparency M	Print Learner
	Visual Learner
		Terms Review
		Audit Your
		    Understanding
		Work Together
			On Your Own
			Application Problem
			    18-5
			Ongoing Assessment,
			    p. 478
				Reteach, p. 478
				Enrich, p. 479

Transparency 18-1
Automated Accounting
Accounting Connection
	Specific Learning
	    Disability (SLD)
	    Students
	Expanding Beyond the
	    Classroom
	Cooperative Learning
	Tactile Learner
	Gifted Students
			Application Problem
			    18-6
			Mastery Problem 18-7
			Study Guide 18
			Chapter 18 Test
			ExamViewPro or
			    Westest, Chapter 18
			Portfolio Assessment
				Enrich, p. 480
				Challenge Problem
				    18-8
				Reteach, p. 480
				Recycling Problem
				    18-1
				Accounting Connection

460

INTRODUCE THE CHAPTER

PREVIEW ACCOUNTING TERMS

❑ Read each term out loud to verify pronunciation for students.

❑ Point out terms or parts of terms that should already be familiar to most students, such as corporation, stock, price, discount, and return.

❑ Point out that three kinds of discounts are defined and that it will be important to distinguish between them.

PREVIEW CHAPTER OBJECTIVES

❑ Point out that students have already learned how to journalize and post purchases on account, purchases, and petty cash in Cycle 2.

❑ Note that recording and posting purchases discounts and returns and allowances will be new transactions in this accounting cycle.

INTRODUCTION

❑ Have students read the two paragraphs under the heading "Recording Financial Information." You may ask a student to read the paragraphs out loud for the class.

❑ Ask students to describe different kinds of accounting information that may be important to the successful operation of a business.

❑ Point out that the kinds and details of information provided have a cost to the business and that the cost must be worth the benefit provided.

❑ This lesson explains why businesses use special journals.

INTERNET ACTIVITY

Point your browser to

http://accounting.swpco.com

Choose **First-Year Course**, choose **Activities**, and complete the activity for Chapter 18.

TERMS PREVIEW

corporation

share of stock

capital stock

list price

trade discount

cash discount

purchases discount

contra account

cash short

cash over

purchases return

purchases allowance

debit memorandum

460

18
Recording Purchases and Cash Payments

AFTER STUDYING CHAPTER 18, YOU WILL BE ABLE TO:

1. Define accounting terms related to purchases and cash payments.

2. Identify accounting concepts and practices related to purchases and cash payments.

3. Record purchases on account and post using a purchases journal.

4. Record purchases transactions using a cash payments journal.

5. Record petty cash and post using a cash payments journal.

6. Record purchases returns and allowances and post using a general journal.

RECORDING FINANCIAL INFORMATION

Reliable financial information is important for the successful operation of a business. However, the amount of information a business needs and can afford varies with the business's size and complexity. Several types of accounting systems may be used to record, summarize, and report a business's financial information. An accounting system may vary from a small manual system operated by one accounting employee to a large computerized system that requires hundreds of accountants and clerks. A business should use an accounting system that provides the desired financial information with the least amount of effort and cost.

A large business using a manual accounting system, for example, might use several different journals so that more than one employee could journalize transactions at the same time. However, the company would want to be sure the information provided was worth the cost of providing it.

SOFTWARE FOCUS

Software may be used for independent practice or enrichment as the instructor deems appropriate. For this chapter, the following software may be used: Automated Accounting 7.0 or higher with Application Problem 18-6 and Mastery Problem 18-7; and Accounting Connection, Chapter 18.

Instructors may wish to cover the Automated Accounting feature on pages 487–489, even if the Automated Accounting software is not being used in the classroom, so students get a sense of how the chapter's accounting procedures would be implemented in an automated environment.

ACCOUNTING IN YOUR CAREER

DON'T LOSE THOSE DISCOUNTS

MultiMedia, Inc., sells books, CDs, software, and the electronic equipment necessary to play the CDs and software. The company is only a year old, but it has been able to add several accounting specialists to handle the daily transactions and also do some planning and budgeting.

Audra Jackson is on the team that is conducting an internal audit of the company's books. As an internal auditor, Audra is responsible for analyzing all aspects of the purchases and cash payments system. In her review of payments to vendors, Audra discovers that payments on account are frequently 30 to 60 days past the due date and that none of the purchases discounts available are taken. The company does not usually have enough cash on hand to pay for purchases in a timely manner.

In their audit report, Audra's team recommends that cash be borrowed at a 12% annual interest rate to pay all invoices within the discount period. They further maintain that timely payments will improve relationships with vendors and other creditors. Audra makes sure that the report is well written, without technical jargon that could confuse the reader. The team's suggestions are sent to the company's management, which now plans to adopt the recommendations.

Critical Thinking:

1. If purchases of $1,000,000 per year qualify for 2% purchases discounts, what is the effect on net income if purchases discounts are not taken?
2. Why is it important to pay vendors on time?
3. What conclusions would you draw about the importance of good communication skills for accountants?

- ❏ This feature involves the concept of purchases discounts, which is introduced later in the chapter. Introduce the feature by explaining that purchases discounts are granted for early payments on account and that the discounts reduce the cost of merchandise.
- ❏ Ask students to read the feature or have one or more students read the feature out loud.
- ❏ Give students 5–10 minutes to jot down some ideas for answering the Critical Thinking questions, then discuss the answers in class.
- ❏ As an alternative, you can use brainstorming techniques to generate possible solutions to the questions. With this approach, you may also wish to record the suggestions and save them for additional discussion after the chapter is completed.

THINKING ABOUT CAREERS

- ❏ Use this feature to encourage additional thinking about accounting careers.
- ❏ Ask students what kind of education and experience Audra Jackson would need to be an internal auditor. (*Audra should have a college degree with an emphasis in accounting and realistic work experience under the supervision of an internal auditor. Her knowledge and credentials would be enhanced by having become a Certified Internal Auditor.*)
- ❏ Ask students what other categories of a company's workers might be included on a team that is conducting an internal audit. (*Individuals from other operating departments, such as management, finance, cash management, etc., can all bring different perspectives to a problem, thus improving the possibility of the group's identifying an effective solution.*)
- ❏ Ask students what kinds of personal qualities are desirable for employees who are working on a team. (*Answers might include: Interpersonal skills, leadership skills, patience, a team orientation*).

SUGGESTED ANSWERS

1. *Discounts of $20,000 are lost ($1,000,000 × 2%), and therefore net income is $20,000 less than it would be if the discounts had been taken.*
2. *Slow payments can jeopardize a company's credit rating. In addition, vendors may stop a company's credit and require cash payment in advance. If a company is unable to acquire inventory to sell, the company may fail. In addition, some discounts are based on early payment, and* these discounts will be lost if payments are slow.
3. *A common communications error is forgetting to write to the comprehension ability of the intended audience. In this scenario it was important for the company to accept the proposal; however, if the report had been written in highly technical terms, the management of the company would not have been able to understand it and might have rejected the proposal.*

462

THE BUSINESS—WINNING EDGE, INC.

WINNING EDGE, INC.
Sports Equipment for Physical Training Facilities at School or Work

1420 College Plaza
Atlanta, GA 30337-1726

(404) 555-8714
FAX (404) 555-6720
winning@email.web

Justin Cartwright and his sister, Regina Davis, were well-known track and field Olympic event winners in the 1980s. After they retired from amateur and professional athletics, they decided to take some earnings from their product endorsements and start a business.

During the 1990s physical fitness became a goal for many people. Many schools and businesses began adding facilities for physical training and they needed to purchase equipment for these facilities. Spotting the trend early, Justin and Regina started a sports equipment business and have been very successful.

Many businesses need amounts of capital that cannot be easily provided by a proprietorship or a partnership. An organization with the legal rights of a person and which may be owned by many persons is called a **corporation.** A corporation is formed by receiving approval from a state or federal agency. A corporation can own property, incur liabilities, and enter into contracts in its own name. A corporation may also sell ownership in itself. Each unit of ownership in a corporation is called a **share of stock.** Total shares of ownership in a corporation are called **capital stock.**

Winning Edge, Inc., is organized as a corporation. Winning Edge sells sports equipment to school districts, colleges, and businesses. Winning Edge was formed as a corporation because several owners can provide larger amounts of capital than one owner. The principal difference among the accounting records of proprietorships, partnerships, and corporations is in the capital accounts. Proprietorships and partnerships have a single capital and drawing account for each owner. A corporation has separate capital accounts for the stock issued and for the earnings kept in the business, which will be explained in more detail in Chapter 25. As in proprietorships and partnerships, information in a corporation's accounting system is kept separate from the personal records of the owners. *(CONCEPT: Business Entity)*

In Cycle 2, Omni Import used four special journals and a general journal to record transactions. In this cycle, Winning Edge also uses four special journals and a general journal. However, the amount columns of some of the special journals vary because of the needs of the business. Winning Edge uses the following special journals.

1. Purchases journal—for all purchases of merchandise on account
2. Cash payments journal—for all cash payments
3. Sales journal—for all sales of merchandise on account
4. Cash receipts journal—for all cash receipts

MATERIALS

JOURNALIZING PURCHASES ON ACCOUNT

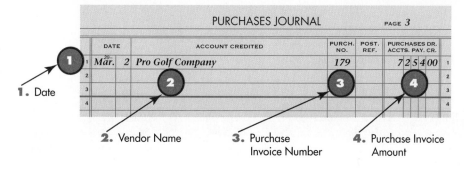

1. Date
2. Vendor Name
3. Purchase Invoice Number
4. Purchase Invoice Amount

A special journal used to journalize *only* purchases of merchandise on account is known as a purchases journal. When a purchase invoice is received from a vendor, Winning Edge's accounts payable clerk first verifies the mathematical accuracy of the purchase invoice. The date received and a number are then recorded on the purchase invoice. The purchase invoice is now ready to be recorded in the purchases journal.

March 2. Purchased merchandise on account from Pro Golf Company, $7,254.00. Purchase Invoice No. 179.

Purchases are recorded at their cost, including any related shipping costs and taxes. *(CONCEPT: Historical Cost)*

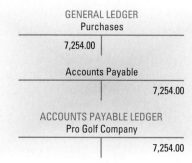

GENERAL LEDGER
Purchases
7,254.00

Accounts Payable
7,254.00

ACCOUNTS PAYABLE LEDGER
Pro Golf Company
7,254.00

Recording an entry in a purchases journal

1. Write the current year, *20—*, and the date, *Mar. 2,* in the Date column.
2. Write the vendor name, *Pro Golf Company,* in the Account Credited column.
3. Write the purchase invoice number recorded on the invoice, *179,* in the Purch. No. column.
4. Record the amount of the invoice, *$7,254.00,* in the amount column.

REMEMBER

Only purchases of merchandise on account are journalized in the purchases journal. A business buys many other goods and services in the course of its operations. For example, a company may buy office supplies on account. Office supplies are not merchandise for sale to customers, and therefore this transaction is not recorded in the purchases journal. A business may also purchase merchandise for cash. Because this is not an "on account" transaction, it is not recorded in the purchases journal.

F.Y.I

Many large businesses have a purchasing department that arranges the purchase of all goods and services. Buyers in the purchasing department identify vendors that can provide the best combination of quality, price, and service. The purchase invoice would be approved by a buyer in the purchasing department prior to being recorded in the purchases journal.

EXPLAIN

- Use Transparency K to illustrate the purchases journal or direct students to the illustration.
- Ask students what transactions are recorded in this journal.
- Ask students to describe other items a business might buy that are not recorded in the purchases journal.
- Describe how Winning Edge processes a purchase invoice. *(It is verified, and the date of receipt and purchase invoice number are recorded on it before the transaction is recorded.)*
- Ask students to read the Remember to reinforce what kinds of transactions are recorded in the purchases journal.
- Ask students to read the F.Y.I. for additional information about purchases.

DEMONSTRATE

Analyze the transaction
- Draw three blank T accounts on the board.
- Read the transaction statement.
- Ask students to analyze the transaction by answering: what accounts are affected, are they increased or decreased, and are they debited or credited? Complete the T accounts as the information is provided.
- Review the effect on the account for Pro Golf Company in the accounts payable ledger.

Record the transaction
- Use Transparency K to illustrate recording the transaction in the purchases journal or direct students to the illustration.
- Record each item in the journal, following the four steps shown.

TEACHING STRATEGIES — BUILDING STUDY SKILLS

Three new accounts—Purchases Discount, Purchases Returns and Allowances, and Cash Short and Over—are introduced in this chapter. Direct students to create a Quick Reference Guide (QRG) on a small card or sheet of paper to use as an aid in analyzing transactions. T accounts should be used to show normal balance sides.

- ❏ Direct students to the illustration to explain the posting procedure from a purchases journal to an accounts payable ledger.
- ❏ Describe each item in the accounts payable ledger, following the five steps shown.
- ❏ Describe how the journal's column total is posted to the two general ledger accounts at the end of the month.
- ❏ Remind students that the abbreviation for the purchases journal, *P*, and the page number are recorded in the Post. Ref. column of every ledger account affected, to furnish an audit trail.
- ❏ Remind students that the account number is recorded in the journal's Post. Ref. column or under the column total to show that posting has been completed and to furnish an audit trail.

ONGOING ASSESSMENT

- ❏ Assessment is an ongoing process. Circulate through the classroom or lab, observing which students have problems with the assignments.
- ❏ Troubleshooting: Diagnose what kinds of problems students have with this lesson. This lesson is largely a review of procedures from Chapter 10. However, students may have trouble (1) understanding the transaction statement or (2) omitting an item from a column in either the journal or the ledger.
- ❏ Assess student understanding by checking solutions to Independent Practice assignments.

POSTING FROM A PURCHASES JOURNAL

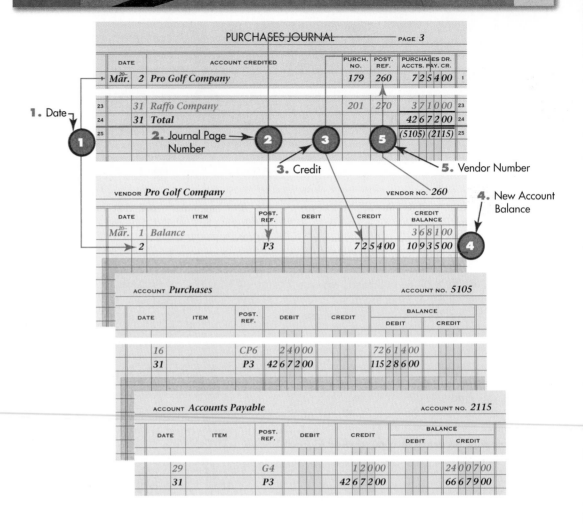

The amount on each line of a purchases journal is posted as a credit to the named vendor account in the accounts payable ledger. By posting frequently, each vendor account always shows an up-to-date balance.

After the purchases journal is totaled and ruled, the total amount is then posted, using the steps described in Chapter 12.

Posting from a purchases journal to an accounts payable ledger

1. Write the date, 2, in the Date column of the vendor account.
2. Write *P* and the page number of the journal, 3, in the Post. Ref. column of the account.
3. Write the amount, $7,254.00, in the Credit column of the vendor account.
4. Add the amount, $7,254.00, in the Credit column to the previous balance in the Credit Balance column. Write the new account balance, $10,935.00, in the Credit Balance column.
5. Write the vendor number, 260, in the Post. Ref. column of the purchases journal.

- ❏ Call on students to list the kinds of information needed to record a purchase on account transaction.
- ❏ Ask a student to make up an original purchase on account transaction statement that you write on the board or an overhead transparency.
- ❏ Ask another student to analyze the transaction using T accounts.

- ❏ Ask a student to name each column title in the purchases journal and describe what is recorded in it, both in general and specifically for the transaction.
- ❏ Ask a student to name each column title in the general and accounts payable ledgers and describe what is recorded in it, both in general and specifically for the transaction.

TERMS REVIEW

corporation

share of stock

capital stock

AUDIT YOUR UNDERSTANDING

1. What are some business transactions a corporation can conduct in its own name?

2. What is the principal difference between the accounting records of a corporation and those of a proprietorship or partnership?

3. What accounts are affected, and how, when the total amount of the purchases journal is posted?

WORK TOGETHER

Journalizing and posting purchase on account transactions

The general ledger and accounts payable ledger accounts for Magnolia Furniture are given in the *Working Papers*. Your instructor will guide you through the following examples.

4. Journalize the following purchases on account completed during April of the current year. Use page 4 of a purchases journal. The abbreviation for purchase invoice is P.
   Transactions:
   April 2. Purchased merchandise on account from Farris, Inc., $1,700.00. P45.
       5. Purchased merchandise on account from Delta Manufacturing, $3,265.00. P46.
       8. Purchased merchandise on account from Williams Company, $780.00. P47.

5. Post each amount in the purchases journal to the accounts payable ledger.

6. As shown in Chapter 12, total and rule the purchases journal. Post the total.

ON YOUR OWN

Journalizing and posting purchase on account transactions

The general ledger and accounts payable ledger accounts for Adamson Luggage are given in the *Working Papers*. Work these problems independently.

7. Journalize the following purchases on account completed during March of the current year. Use page 3 of a purchases journal. The abbreviation for purchase invoice is P.
   Transactions:
   March 1. Purchased merchandise on account from MJK, Inc., $3,200.00. P125.
       3. Purchased merchandise on account from Lambert Industries, $765.00. P126.
       6. Purchased merchandise on account from Taylor Imports, $1,964.00. P127.

8. Post each amount in the purchases journal to the accounts payable ledger.

9. As shown in Chapter 12, total and rule the purchases journal. Post the total.

JOURNALIZING CASH PAYMENTS FOR CASH PURCHASES

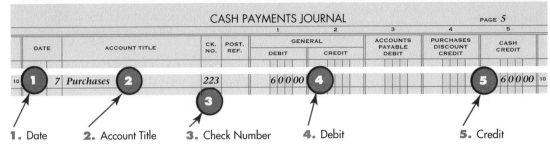

CASH PAYMENTS JOURNAL   PAGE 5

1. Date   2. Account Title   3. Check Number   4. Debit   5. Credit

Businesses usually purchase merchandise on account. However, vendors may not extend credit to all of their customers. Thus, these businesses must give the vendor a check before the merchandise is either shipped or delivered.

Trade Discount

Most manufacturers and wholesalers print price lists and catalogs to describe their products. Some businesses also make their products available in computer channels, such as Web sites on the Internet.

Generally, prices listed in catalogs are the manufacturers' suggested retail prices. A business's printed or catalog price is called a **list price.** When a merchandising business purchases a number of products from a manufacturer, the price frequently is quoted as "list price less trade discount." A reduction in the list price granted to customers is called a **trade discount.** Trade discounts are also used to quote different prices for different quantities purchased without changing catalog or list prices.

When a trade discount is granted, the seller's invoice shows the actual amount charged. This amount after the trade discount has been deducted from the list price is referred to as the invoice amount. Only the invoice amount is used in a journal entry. *(CONCEPT: Historical Cost)* No journal entry is made to show the amount of a trade discount.

Cash Purchases

Winning Edge pays cash for 30 tennis rackets with an invoice amount of $600.00, the list price less a trade discount.

March 7. Purchased merchandise for cash, $600.00. Check No. 223.

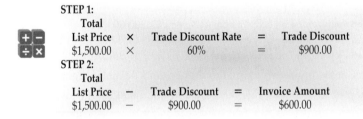

Purchases
| 600.00 |

Cash
| | 600.00 |

Winning Edge's list price for the 30 tennis rackets is $1,500.00, less 60% trade discount. The total invoice amount is calculated in two steps as follows.

STEP 1:

	Total List Price	×	Trade Discount Rate	=	Trade Discount
	$1,500.00	×	60%	=	$900.00

STEP 2:

	Total List Price	−	Trade Discount	=	Invoice Amount
	$1,500.00	−	$900.00	=	$600.00

466   CHAPTER 18   Recording Purchases and Cash Payments

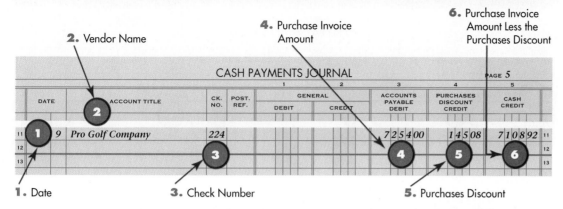

2. Vendor Name

4. Purchase Invoice Amount

6. Purchase Invoice Amount Less the Purchases Discount

CASH PAYMENTS JOURNAL PAGE 5

	DATE	ACCOUNT TITLE	CK. NO.	POST. REF.	GENERAL DEBIT	GENERAL CREDIT	ACCOUNTS PAYABLE DEBIT	PURCHASES DISCOUNT CREDIT	CASH CREDIT	
11	9	Pro Golf Company	224				7 2 5 4 00	1 4 5 08	7 1 0 8 92	11
12										12
13										13

1. Date

3. Check Number

5. Purchases Discount

Normally, the total amount shown on a purchase invoice is the amount that a customer is expected to pay. To encourage early payment, a vendor may allow a deduction from the invoice amount. A deduction that a vendor allows on the invoice amount to encourage prompt payment is called a **cash discount.** A cash discount on purchases taken by a customer is called a **purchases discount.** When a purchases discount is taken, the customer pays less than the invoice amount previously recorded in the purchases account. Taking purchases discounts reduces the customer's cost of merchandise purchased.

A cash discount is stated as a percentage deducted from the invoice amount. For example, 2/10, n/30 is a common term of sale, which is read *two ten, net thirty. Two ten* means 2% of the invoice amount may be deducted if the invoice is paid within 10 days of the invoice date. *Net thirty* means that the total invoice amount must be paid within 30 days.

Purchases discounts are recorded in a general ledger account titled Purchases Discount. An account that reduces a related account on a financial statement is called a **contra account.** Purchases Discount is a contra account to Purchases and is included in the cost of merchandise division of the general ledger. On an income statement, Purchases Discount is deducted from the balance of its related account, Purchases.

Since contra accounts are deductions from their related accounts, contra account normal balances are opposite the normal balances of their related accounts. The normal balance for Purchases is a debit. Therefore, the normal balance for Purchases Discount, a contra account to Purchases, is a credit. Trade discounts are not recorded; however, cash discounts are recorded as purchases discounts because they decrease the recorded invoice amount.

> *March 9. Paid cash on account to Pro Golf Company, $7,108.92, covering Purchase Invoice No. 179 for $7,254.00, less 2% discount, $145.08. Check No. 224.*

STEP 1:

Purchase Invoice Amount (P179)	×	Purchases Discount Rate	=	Purchases Discount
$7,254.00	×	2%	=	$145.08

STEP 2:

Purchase Invoice Amount (P179)	−	Purchases Discount	=	Cash Amount After Discount
$7,254.00	−	$145.08	=	$7,108.92

CHAPTER 18   Recording Purchases and Cash Payments   **467**

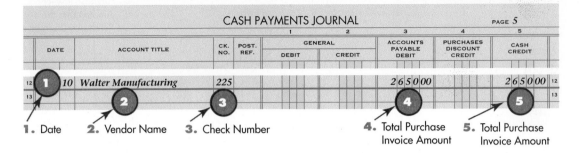

	CASH PAYMENTS JOURNAL				PAGE 5				
				1	2	3	4	5	
DATE	ACCOUNT TITLE	CK. NO.	POST. REF.	GENERAL		ACCOUNTS PAYABLE DEBIT	PURCHASES DISCOUNT CREDIT	CASH CREDIT	
				DEBIT	CREDIT				
10	Walter Manufacturing	225				2 6 5 0 00		2 6 5 0 00	

1. Date 2. Vendor Name 3. Check Number 4. Total Purchase Invoice Amount 5. Total Purchase Invoice Amount

- Ask students to identify two reasons why a business might not be able to use a purchases discount. *(The vendor does not offer a discount or the business does not have cash available.)*
- Ask students to identify the primary difference between the transaction illustrated on this page and the previous page. *(No amount is recorded in the purchases discount column.)*

DEMONSTRATE

Analyze the transaction
- Draw two blank T accounts on the board.
- Read the transaction statement.
- Ask students to analyze the transaction by answering: what accounts are affected, are they increased or decreased, and are they debited or credited? Complete the T accounts as the information is provided.

Record the transaction
- Use Transparency L to illustrate the cash payments journal or direct students to the illustration.
- Record each item in the cash payments journal, following the five steps shown in the illustration.

ACCOUNTING AT WORK
The Accounting at Work feature profiles people who are entrepreneurs or working in accounting-related fields. Ask students to read the feature and to write three words that summarize the Mexican Industries story *(e.g., opportunity, education, success)*. Ask students to discuss what role, if any, a corporation should have in providing educational opportunities to its employees.

ONGOING ASSESSMENT
- Assessment is an ongoing process. Circulate through the classroom or lab, observing which students have problems with the assignments.
- Troubleshooting: Students may have trouble (1) calculating the discounts or (2) understanding which discounts are (purchases discount) and are not (trade discount) recorded in the cash payments journal.
- Assess student understanding by checking solutions to Independent Practice assignments.

Some vendors do not offer purchases discounts. Sometimes a business does not have the cash available to take advantage of a purchases discount. In both cases, the full purchase invoice amount is paid.

Winning Edge purchased merchandise on account from Walter Manufacturing on February 25. Walter's credit terms are n/30. Therefore, Winning Edge will pay the full amount of the purchase invoice, $2,650.00, within 30 days of the invoice date, February 25.

March 10. Paid cash on account to Walter Manufacturing, $2,650.00, covering Purchase Invoice No. 192. Check No. 225.

PAMELA AGUIRRE

ACCOUNTING AT WORK

Pamela Aguirre is the Chairman of the Board and CEO of Mexican Industries in Detroit. The company manufactures and assembles airbags, head and arm rests, consoles, leather steering wheels, cruise control assemblies, and other automotive assemblies. The company was started by Pamela's father, Detroit Tigers pitcher Hank Aguirre, in 1979. Today Mexican Industries employs 1,500 workers in eight plants and enjoys sales of over $150 million.

Pamela once said, "My dad's dream was to give the Hispanic community the opportunity to help themselves." Of the 1,500 employees today, 86% are minorities. Most come to Mexican Industries from the inner city. The company provides a regular paycheck, benefits, training, and the life skills necessary to succeed in the working world.

Mexican Industries offers benefits such as health and life insurance and bonuses. But employees also enjoy company-paid college tuition, scholarships for children, English as a second language and G.E.D. classes, employee loans, and free cancer screening, among others.

Pamela says, "So many people in the world do not have the opportunity to learn and succeed. It hurts when I see students wasting the opportunities they are given today. They should work hard and take advantage of every educational opportunity that is offered because there might not be another chance later."

468

RETEACH

- Call on students to list the kinds of information needed to record a purchase with a trade discount.
- Ask a student to make up an original purchase with a trade discount transaction statement that you write on the board or an overhead transparency.
- Ask another student to analyze the transaction using T accounts.
- Ask a student to record the transaction in the cash payments journal.
- Repeat the steps above for a cash payment for a purchase on account, with and without a purchases discount.
- Assign Math Work Sheet, Chapter 18, Part A.

TERMS REVIEW

list price

trade discount

cash discount

purchases discount

contra account

AUDIT YOUR UNDERSTANDING

1. Why would a vendor grant a cash discount to a customer?
2. What is meant by terms of sale 2/10, n/30?
3. What accounts are affected, and how, when a check is issued as payment on account for a purchase with a purchases discount?

WORK TOGETHER

Recording cash payments for expenses and purchases using a cash payments journal

The cash payments journal for Preston Corporation is given in the *Working Papers*. Your instructor will guide you through the following example.

4. Record the following transactions completed during April of the current year. Use page 4 of a cash payments journal. The abbreviation for check is C.

Transactions:

April 4. Paid cash to Modern Radio for advertising, $275.00. C334.
    5. Paid cash to Maken Industries for merchandise with a list price of $1,978.00. Maken offers its customers a 60% trade discount. C335.
    16. Paid cash on account to Blanchard Company covering Purchase Invoice No. 156 for $4,346.00, less 2% discount. C336.

ON YOUR OWN

Recording cash payments for expenses and purchases using a cash payments journal

The cash payments journal for BackDoor Music is given in the *Working Papers*. Work this problem independently.

5. Record the following transactions completed during June of the current year. Use page 6 of a cash payments journal. The abbreviation for check is C.

Transactions:

June 6. Paid cash to Lisle Management for rent, $2,000.00. C476.
    9. Paid cash on account to MTX Company covering Purchase Invoice No. 267 for $1,709.60. MTX does not offer its customers a cash discount. C477.
    21. Paid cash on account to Northeast Manufacturing covering Purchase Invoice No. 286 for $1,565.00, less 2% discount. C478.

OBJECTIVES

❑ Define accounting terms related to cash payments.
❑ Identify accounting concepts and practices related to cash payments.
❑ Record petty cash and post using a cash payments journal.

MOTIVATE

Many students have jobs in retail businesses that require them to give customers change after a sale. Ask these students if they have ever made a mistake counting the cash. How should the business account for the mistakes in handling cash?

Preview
❑ Preview the accounting terms and definitions introduced in this lesson: cash short and cash over.
❑ Direct students to read the headings at the top of each page in this lesson and to examine the illustrations given.
❑ Point out that this lesson illustrates how to record mistakes made in working with the cash in a petty cash fund.

EXPLAIN

❑ Ask students what kind of cash payments should be made using a petty cash fund.
❑ Explain that Winning Edge uses a petty cash report form to account for any cash short or cash over.

DEMONSTRATE

Prepare a petty cash report
❑ Draw five columns on the board similar to the petty cash report.
❑ Using the amounts in the illustration, complete Steps 1–4 on the blackboard.
❑ Point out that students have performed Steps 1–4 in Cycle 2.
❑ Complete the petty cash report using Steps 5–8. These steps account for the cash short or cash over.
❑ Ask students why a business is more likely to have cash short than cash over. *(The person or business receiving the cash is more likely to call the petty cash custodian's attention to an underpayment than an overpayment.)*

PETTY CASH REPORT

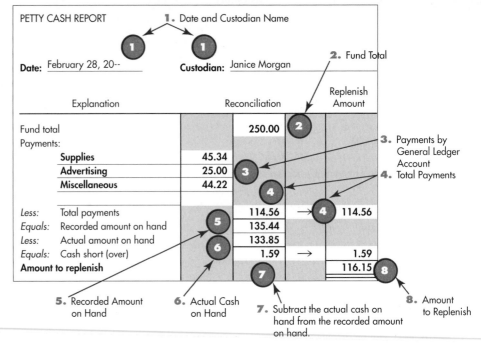

A petty cash fund enables a business to pay cash for small expenses where it is not practical to write a check. Establishing and replenishing a petty cash fund is described in Chapter 6.

Regardless of the care taken by the custodian, or person who maintains the petty cash records, errors may be made when making payments from a petty cash fund. These errors cause a difference between actual cash on hand and the record of the amount of cash that should be on hand. A petty cash on hand amount that is less than a recorded amount is called **cash short.** A petty cash on hand amount that is more than a recorded amount is called **cash over.**

The custodian prepares a petty cash report when the petty cash fund is to be replenished. The report provides a logical method for determining the amount to be replenished.

(S T E P S) Preparing a petty cash report

1. Write the date, *February 28, 20—,* and custodian name, *Janice Morgan,* in the report heading.
2. Write the fund total, *$250.00,* from the general ledger account.
3. Summarize petty cash payments by general ledger account and enter the totals for each account.
4. Calculate and write the total payments, *$114.56,* in the Reconciliation and Replenish Amount columns.
5. Calculate and write the recorded amount on hand, *$135.44 ($250.00 − $114.56).*
6. Count the actual cash on hand and write the amount, *$133.85,* in the Reconciliation column.
7. Subtract the actual amount on hand, $133.85, from the recorded amount on hand, $135.44, and write the amount, *$1.59,* in the Reconciliation and Replenish Amount columns.
8. Add the amounts in the Replenish Amount column and write the total, *$116.15,* as the amount to replenish.

470 CHAPTER 18 Recording Purchases and Cash Payments

MATERIALS

❑ Work Sheets:
 Math Work Sheet, Chapter 18, Part B
❑ Transparencies:
 L, Blank Cash Payments Journal (5-Column)

❑ Working Papers:
 Teacher's Edition of the Working Papers for Lesson 18-3
❑ Videos:
 CNN Accounting Video

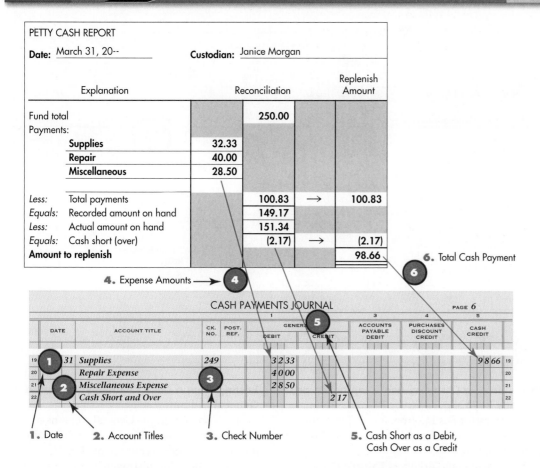

PETTY CASH REPORT

Date: March 31, 20--   Custodian: Janice Morgan

Explanation	Reconciliation		Replenish Amount
Fund total	250.00		
Payments:			
Supplies	32.33		
Repair	40.00		
Miscellaneous	28.50		
Less: Total payments	100.83	→	100.83
Equals: Recorded amount on hand	149.17		
Less: Actual amount on hand	151.34		
Equals: Cash short (over)	(2.17)	→	(2.17)
Amount to replenish			98.66

6. Total Cash Payment

4. Expense Amounts → **4**

				CASH PAYMENTS JOURNAL				PAGE 6	
				1	2	3	4	5	
DATE	ACCOUNT TITLE	CK. NO.	POST. REF.	GENERAL DEBIT	CREDIT	ACCOUNTS PAYABLE DEBIT	PURCHASES DISCOUNT CREDIT	CASH CREDIT	
31	Supplies	249		3 2 33				98 66	19
	Repair Expense			4 0 00					20
	Miscellaneous Expense			2 8 50					21
	Cash Short and Over				2 17				22

1. Date   **2.** Account Titles   **3.** Check Number   **5.** Cash Short as a Debit, Cash Over as a Credit

---

Petty cash short and petty cash over are recorded in an account titled Cash Short and Over. The account is a temporary account. At the end of the fiscal year, the cash short and over account is closed to Income Summary.

The balance of Cash Short and Over can be either a debit or credit. However, the balance is usually a debit because the petty cash fund is more likely to be short than over. A cash shortage adds to the cost of operating a business. Thus, the account is classified as an operating expense

Cash Short and Over	
Debit	Credit
Increase cash short	Increase cash over

March 31. Paid cash to replenish the petty cash fund, $98.66: supplies, $32.33; repairs, $40.00; miscellaneous, $28.50; cash over, $2.17. Check No. 249.

The petty cash fund is replenished for the amount paid out, $100.83, less cash over, $2.17. This total amount, $98.66, restores the fund's cash balance to its original amount, $250.00 ($100.83 − $2.17 + $151.34 cash on hand.)

EXPLAIN

❏ Use Transparency L to illustrate the cash payments journal or direct students to the illustration.
❏ Ask students why cash over reduces the replenish amount.

DEMONSTRATE

Analyze the transaction

❏ Draw five blank T accounts on the board.
❏ Read the transaction statement.
❏ Ask students to analyze the transaction by answering: what accounts are affected, are they increased or decreased, and are they debited or credited? Complete the T accounts as the information is provided.

Record the transaction

❏ Use Transparency L to illustrate the cash payments journal or direct students to the illustration.
❏ Record each item in the petty cash report, following the six steps shown in the illustration.
❏ Ask students how a petty cash report showing cash short would be recorded in a cash payments journal. (*Cash Short and Over would be debited.*)

APPLIED SKILLS

MATHEMATICS

Use the math work sheet in the Masters and Solutions to Enrichment/Application section of the Teacher's Resource Guide to integrate applied mathematics. In this work sheet, students will apply math concepts to reconcile petty cash and determine petty cash short or over.

EXPLAIN

- ❏ Direct students to the illustration.
- ❏ Point out that students have already learned how to post from the cash payments journal.
- ❏ Ask students to read the Remember to reinforce the posting of individual items from the cash payments journal.

DEMONSTRATE

Posting to the accounts payable ledger

- ❏ Ask students to describe each step represented by the five arrows in the illustration.
- ❏ Remind students that the accounts payable account number is written in the Post. Ref. column of the cash payments journal.

Posting to the general ledger

- ❏ Ask students to describe the steps required to post the Rent Expense transaction to the general ledger.
- ❏ Remind students that the general ledger account number is written in the Post. Ref. column of the cash payments journal.

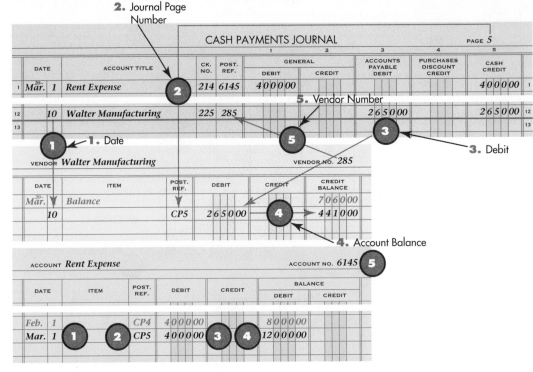

Posting from a Cash Payments Journal to an Accounts Payable Ledger

The steps for posting from a cash payments journal to an accounts payable ledger are shown in the illustration.

Each entry in the Accounts Payable Debit column of a cash payments journal affects the vendor named in the Account Title column.

Each amount listed in this column is posted separately to the proper vendor account in the accounts payable ledger. In this way, each vendor account shows an up-to-date balance.

The cash payments journal is identified in vendor accounts using the abbreviation *CP.*

Posting from a Cash Payments Journal to a General Ledger

Each amount in the General columns of a cash payments journal is posted individually to the general ledger account named in the Account Title column. Therefore, the totals of the general amount columns are not posted.

The steps for posting from a cash payments journal to a general ledger are similar to those described in Chapter 12 for posting from the general amount columns of a cash payments journal to a general ledger.

REMEMBER

Each entry in the Accounts Payable Debit column is posted individually to the vendor account in the accounts payable ledger. The total of the Accounts Payable Debit column will be posted to the controlling account, Accounts Payable, in the general ledger at the end of the month.

Each entry in the General Debit and General Credit columns is posted individually to the general ledger account named in the Account Title column.

472 CHAPTER 18 Recording Purchases and Cash Payments

APPLIED SKILLS

WRITING ACROSS THE CURRICULUM

Writing Paragraphs and Short Essays. The Cases for Critical Thinking are short, practical applications of the accounting principles developed in the chapter. Some cases are planned to present problems related to the chapter but not specifically discussed and answered in the chapter. These cases present an opportunity for critical thinking and decision making. These cases also require more than a short, objective-type response. Therefore, they provide ideal practice in writing paragraphs and short essays.

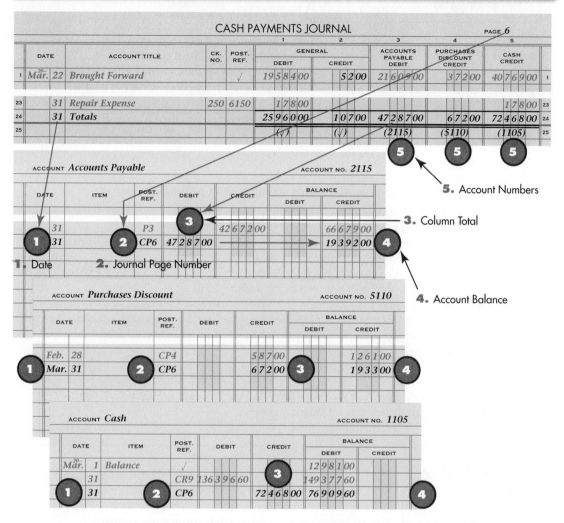

1. Date
2. Journal Page Number
3. Column Total
4. Account Balance
5. Account Numbers

EXPLAIN

❏ Point out that students have already learned how to post the special column totals of the cash payments journal to general ledger accounts.

❏ Note that the total of the Purchases Discount column is posted as a credit.

❏ Ask students to describe the five steps in posting a journal column total to the general ledger.

DEMONSTRATE

❏ Ask students to describe each of the five steps represented by the related arrows in the illustration.

❏ Remind students that the general ledger account number is written in parentheses below the column total to show that posting has been completed and to furnish an audit trail.

ONGOING ASSESSMENT

❏ Assessment is an ongoing process. Circulate through the classroom or lab, observing which students have problems with the assignments.

❏ Troubleshooting: Diagnose what kinds of problems students have with this lesson. Students may have trouble (1) calculating cash short and over, (2) understanding how a cash short or over impacts the replenish amount, or (3) journalizing cash short or over.

❏ Assess student understanding by checking solutions to Independent Practice assignments.

At the end of each month, equality of debits and credits is proved for a cash payments journal. Each column is totaled, and the total debits and total credits are compared. The cash payments journal is then ruled to show that the journal has been proved. The steps for proving and ruling the cash payments journal are not shown in the illustration. The steps are similar to those described in Chapter 10 for totaling, proving, and ruling a cash payments journal at the end of the month.

The steps for posting the totals of the special amount columns of a cash payments journal to a general ledger are shown in the illustration.

The total of each special column is posted to the account named in the journal's column headings. The total is entered in the appropriate amount column, and the new account balance is recorded. This procedure is followed until all special amount column totals are posted.

A check mark is placed in parentheses below each General column total to indicate that these totals are not to be posted. Each amount was posted individually to the general ledger.

RETEACH

❏ List the information required to complete a petty cash report.

❏ Call on students to identify whether cash short *(debit)* and cash over *(credit)* are recorded in the cash payments journal.

❏ Ask a student to explain why cash short and over is classified as an expense. *(Because cash short situations are more common than cash over situations, the account will usually have a debit balance.)*

❏ Assign Math Work Sheet, Chapter 18, Part B.

GUIDED PRACTICE

Terms Review
Call on students to define each term in the Terms Review. After each definition, ask the class if the definition is correct and whether the complete definition has been given or if anything needs to be added. Suggested definitions are given in the Glossary.

Audit Your Understanding
Call on students to answer the Audit Your Understanding questions. Ask the class if the answer is correct and/or complete. Answers are given in Appendix D of the textbook.

Work Together
Have students write the solutions to the Work Together problems as you guide the class through the examples.

❏ Direct students to record each amount in the petty cash report.

❏ Direct students to record each transaction in the cash payments journal as you elicit class participation in analyzing and recording each transaction.

❏ Call on students to describe each step in the process for posting separate amounts from the cash payments journal to the accounts payable ledger and the general ledger.

❏ Call on students to describe each step in the process for posting special column totals from the cash payments journal to the general ledger.

INDEPENDENT PRACTICE

On Your Own
❏ Assign the On Your Own problems to be worked independently.

❏ Use the Ongoing Assessment techniques to diagnose student understanding.

Application Problem
❏ Assign Application Problem 18-3: Preparing a petty cash report.

❏ Assign Application Problem 18-4: Journalizing and posting cash payment transactions using a cash payments journal.

474

cash short

cash over

1. How is a balance in the cash short and over account treated at the end of a fiscal period?
2. Why are the totals for the General Debit and Credit columns of a cash payments journal not posted?

Journalizing and posting cash payments using a cash payments journal

The cash payments journal and petty cash report for Preston Corporation are given in the *Working Papers*. Your instructor will guide you through the following examples.

3. Record the following transactions completed during May of the current year. Use page 5 of a cash payments journal. The abbreviation for check is C.

   May 4. Paid cash on account to Wilhelm, Inc. covering Purchase Invoice No. 297 for $3,590.00. Wilhelm does not offer its customers a cash discount. C520.

   31. Nancy Rackley is the custodian of a $200.00 petty cash fund. On May 31, she had receipts for the following total payments: supplies, $47.45; advertising, $37.00; and miscellaneous, $61.90. A cash count shows $54.85 in the petty cash box. Prepare the petty cash report. Record the replenishment of the fund on May 31. C521.

4. Post the amounts in the General columns of the cash payments journal to the general ledger accounts. Post the amounts in the Accounts Payable Debit column to the accounts payable ledger. Prove and rule the cash payments journal. Post the totals of the special amount columns to the appropriate general ledger accounts.

Journalizing and posting cash payments using a cash payments journal

The cash payments journal and petty cash report for BackDoor Music are given in the *Working Papers*. Work these problems independently.

5. Record the following transactions completed during July of the current year. Use page 7 of a cash payments journal. The abbreviation for check is C.

   July 9. Paid cash on account to Caliber Company covering Purchase Invoice No. 381 for $2,740.00, less 2% discount. C579.

   31. Patrick Simmons is the custodian of a $200.00 petty cash fund. On July 31, he had receipts for the following total payments: supplies, $35.48; repairs, $25.00; and miscellaneous, $32.45. A cash count shows $106.48 in the petty cash box. Prepare the petty cash report. Record the replenishment of the fund on July 31. C580.

6. Follow the posting instructions in Instruction 4 in Work Together.

ENRICH

❏ What amount of cash shortages are acceptable? Ask groups of students to develop a policy that a manager could use to evaluate a petty cash custodian's performance. What actions should be taken if cash shortages exceed the established limit?

❏ Show the CNN Accounting Video.

CLOSE

❏ Ask students to briefly summarize the procedure for journalizing cash payments for replenishing petty cash.

❏ Ask students to briefly summarize the posting of the cash payments journal to the accounts payable ledger and general ledger.

DEBIT MEMORANDUM FOR PURCHASES RETURNS AND ALLOWANCES

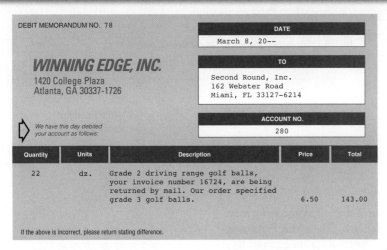

DEBIT MEMORANDUM NO. 78

WINNING EDGE, INC.
1420 College Plaza
Atlanta, GA 30337-1726

We have this day debited your account as follows:

	DATE
	March 8, 20--

	TO
	Second Round, Inc. 162 Webster Road Miami, FL 33127-6214

	ACCOUNT NO.
	280

Quantity	Units	Description	Price	Total
22	dz.	Grade 2 driving range golf balls, your invoice number 16724, are being returned by mail. Our order specified grade 3 golf balls.	6.50	143.00

If the above is incorrect, please return stating difference.

A customer may not want to keep merchandise that is inferior in quality or is damaged when received. A customer may be allowed to return part or all of the merchandise purchased. Credit allowed for the purchase price of returned merchandise, resulting in a decrease in the customer's accounts payable, is called a **purchases return.**

When merchandise is damaged but still usable or is of a different quality than that ordered, the vendor may let the customer keep the merchandise at a reduced price. Credit allowed for part of the purchase price of merchandise that is not returned, resulting in a decrease in the customer's accounts payable, is called a **purchases allowance.**

A purchases return or allowance should be confirmed in writing. A form prepared by the customer showing the price deduction taken by the customer for returns and allowances is called a **debit memorandum.** The form is called a debit memorandum because the customer records the amount as a debit (deduction) to the vendor account to show the decrease in the amount owed.

The customer may use a copy of the debit memorandum as the source document for journalizing purchases returns and allowances. However, the customer may wait for written confirmation from the vendor and use that confirmation as the source document. Winning Edge issues a debit memorandum for each purchases return or allowance. This debit memorandum is used as the source document for purchases returns and allowances transactions. *(CONCEPT: Objective Evidence)* The transaction can be recorded immediately without waiting for written confirmation from the vendor. The original of the debit memorandum is sent to the vendor. A copy is kept by Winning Edge.

Some businesses credit the purchases account for the amount of a purchases return or allowance. However, better information is provided if these amounts are credited to a separate account titled Purchases Returns and Allowances. A business can track the amount of purchases returns and allowances in a fiscal period if a separate account is used for recording them. The account enables a business to evaluate the effectiveness of its merchandise purchasing activities.

CHAPTER 18 Recording Purchases and Cash Payments **475**

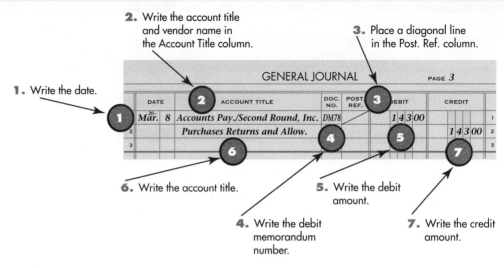

1. Write the date.

2. Write the account title and vendor name in the Account Title column.

3. Place a diagonal line in the Post. Ref. column.

6. Write the account title.

5. Write the debit amount.

4. Write the debit memorandum number.

7. Write the credit amount.

EXPLAIN

❏ Point out that students have already learned how to record transactions in a general journal.

❏ Draw a T account for Purchases Returns and Allowances and label the increase/decrease, debit/credit, and normal balance sides.

❏ Ask students to read the F.Y.I. for more information on how and when debit memorandums are prepared.

DEMONSTRATE

Analyze the transaction

❏ Draw three blank T accounts on the board.

❏ Read the transaction statement.

❏ Ask students to analyze the transaction by answering: what accounts are affected, are they increased or decreased, and are they debited or credited? Complete the T accounts as the information is provided.

Record the transaction

❏ Use Transparency M or direct students to the illustration.

❏ Record each item in the journal, following the seven steps shown.

❏ Remind students that the source document, a debit memorandum, is abbreviated as *DM*.

Purchases returns and allowances decrease the amount of purchases. Therefore, Purchases Returns and Allowances is a contra account to Purchases. Thus, the normal account balance of Purchases Returns and Allowances is a credit, the opposite of the normal account balance of Purchases, a debit.

The account is in the cost of merchandise division of Winning Edge's chart of accounts.

March 8. Returned merchandise to Second Round, Inc., $143.00, covering Purchase Invoice No. 230. Debit Memorandum No. 78.

GENERAL LEDGER
Accounts Payable

| 143.00 | |

Purchases Returns and Allowances

| | 143.00 |

ACCOUNTS PAYABLE LEDGER
Second Round, Inc.

| 143.00 | Bal.   820.00 |
| | (New Bal.   677.00) |

 Journalizing purchases returns and allowances

1. Write the date, *20—, Mar. 8,* in the Date column.

2. Write the account title and vendor name, *Accounts Payable/Second Round, Inc.,* in the Account Title column. A diagonal line is placed between the two accounts.

3. Place a diagonal line in the Post. Ref. column to show that the single debit amount is posted to two accounts.

4. Write the debit memorandum number, *DM78,* in the Doc. No. column.

5. Write the amount, *$143.00,* in the Debit column of the first line.

6. Write *Purchases Returns and Allowances* in the Account Title column on the next line, indented about 1 centimeter. Credit entries are indented in the general journal.

7. Write the amount, *$143.00,* in the Credit column of the second line.

F Y I

Using the debit memorandum as a source document is a proper accounting procedure only if the business is confident that the vendor will honor the request for the purchases return or allowance.

TEACHING STRATEGIES   DIFFERENT LEARNING STYLES

Print Learner. When covering journal entries with a print learner, the instructor should discuss the entries, using the textbook examples and referring to the textbook. The print learner can later go back and study the entries.

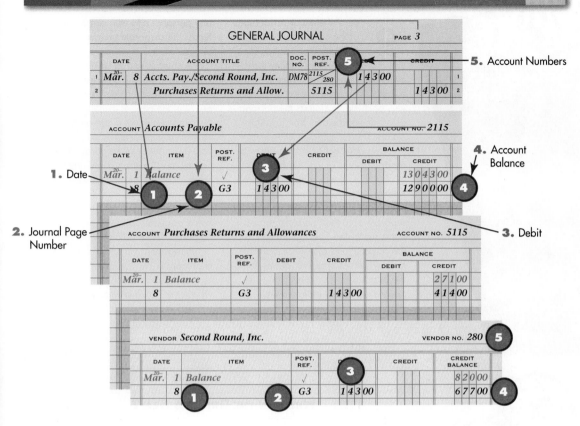

Each amount in the general journal Debit and Credit columns is posted separately to a general ledger account. The abbreviation for the general journal, G, is entered in the Post. Ref. column of the accounts. The steps for posting a debit entry from a general journal to a general ledger and an accounts payable ledger are shown. The steps for posting a credit entry from a general journal to a general ledger are not shown, but are similar to the steps described in Chapter 12 for posting a credit entry from a general journal to a general ledger.

S T E P S **Posting from a general journal**

1. Write the date, *8,* in the Date columns of the general ledger account and the vendor account.
2. Write *G* and the page number of the journal, *3,* in the Post. Ref. columns of the accounts.
3. Write the amount, *$143.00,* in the Debit column of Accounts Payable and of the vendor account.
4. Calculate and write the new account balance, *$12,900.00,* in the Balance Credit column of Accounts Payable. Calculate and write the new account balance, *$677.00,* in the Credit Balance column of the vendor account.
5. Write the account number for Accounts Payable, *2115,* to the left of the diagonal line in the Post. Ref. column of the general journal. Write the vendor number for Second Round, Inc., *280,* to the right of the diagonal line.

TEACHING STRATEGIES   DIFFERENT LEARNING STYLES

478

LEGAL ISSUES IN ACCOUNTING

PIERCING THE CORPORATE VEIL

One of the major advantages of the corporate form of business organization is that it provides limited liability for its owners. This protection from liability is sometimes referred to as a *corporate veil*, or shield. It protects the personal assets of stockholders from creditors' claims. This type of protection from creditors does not exist for owners of proprietorships or partnerships.

To enjoy the benefits of the corporate veil, stockholders must keep the affairs of the corporation completely separate from their personal affairs. If this separateness is maintained, only the corporation's assets are available for payment of creditors' claims if the business fails or owes money. If the owners do not maintain this separateness and, for example, pay personal bills with corporate funds, the corporate protection may be lost.

A court is said to "pierce the corporate veil" when it imposes personal liability on shareholders for corporate debts. In the case of owners active in the management of a corporation, a court may impose unlimited personal liability on them for corporate debts. For example, owners might pay themselves or family members excessive salaries or other benefits. If this type of abuse occurs and creditors are not being paid, the court will pierce the corporate veil and hold owners active in management personally liable to creditors.

Courts make decisions regarding whether or not to pierce the corporate veil on a case-by-case basis.

TECHNOLOGY FOR BUSINESS

WHO'S IN THE DRIVER'S SEAT?

Getting people and products from place to place is an important part of everyday business. Like so many other aspects of modern life, transportation is changing because of technology.

Driverless car projects are underway in the United States, Europe, and Japan. The various projects all use a computer to steer cars along existing roadways. One experimental minivan uses a global positioning system linked to satellites to chart its course. In addition, a video camera linked to an on-board computer follows existing line markers to keep the car in the proper lane.

Improved safety is another benefit of new technology. To let drivers know they have drifted off course, accident avoidance sensors will be available. These sensors will trigger alarms that emit tones and cause the steering wheel to vibrate. These options could be available on vehicles, particularly trucks, very soon.

It's not just vehicles that are getting smarter. Roads and highways are becoming more intelligent, too. The future includes sensors embedded in roadways and linked to computers. These systems will control traffic lights to reduce gridlock, warn motorists of congestion, and suggest other routes.

Automotive pioneers saw the automobile as simple transportation—getting from place to place. Imagine what they would have to say about the impact of technology on the industry they founded.

TERMS REVIEW

purchases return

purchases allowance

debit memorandum

AUDIT YOUR UNDERSTANDING

1. If purchases returns and allowances are a decrease in purchases, why are returns and allowances credited to a separate account?

2. What is a primary difference between a purchases return and a purchases allowance?

3. When is a debit memorandum a proper source document for a purchases return or allowance?

WORK TOGETHER

Journalizing and posting transactions using a general journal

The general journal and selected general ledger and accounts payable accounts for Tractor Enterprises are given in the *Working Papers*. Your instructor will guide you through the following examples.

4. Record the following transactions completed during March of the current year. Use page 3 of a general journal. Source documents are abbreviated as follows: memorandum, M; debit memorandum, DM.

Transactions:

March 3. Returned merchandise to Trainor Company, $238.00, from P134. DM18.
   5. Bought supplies on account from Hughes Supply, $152.00. M355.
   7. Bought store equipment on account from Retail Displays, Inc., $4,235.00. M356.

5. Post the general journal to the general and accounts payable ledgers.

ON YOUR OWN

Journalizing and posting transactions using a general journal

The general journal and selected general ledger and accounts payable accounts for McGinnis Stores, Inc., are given in the *Working Papers*. Work these problems independently.

6. Record the following transactions completed during May of the current year. Use page 5 of a general journal. Source documents are abbreviated as follows: memorandum, M; debit memorandum, DM.

Transactions:

May 6. Bought supplies on account from Pittman Supply Co., $472.00. M47.
   10. Returned merchandise to Best Industries, $671.00, from P326. DM19.
   14. Bought office equipment on account from Sanders Company, $2,109.00. M48.

7. Post the general journal to the general and accounts payable ledgers.

GUIDED PRACTICE

Terms Review
Call on students to define each term in the Terms Review. After each definition, ask the class if the definition is correct and whether the complete definition has been given or if anything needs to be added. Suggested definitions are given in the Glossary.

Audit Your Understanding
Call on students to answer the Audit Your Understanding questions. Ask the class if the answer is correct and/or complete. Answers are given in Appendix D of the textbook.

Work Together
Have students write the solutions to the Work Together problems as you guide the class through the examples.

❑ Direct students to record each transaction in the general journal as you elicit class participation in analyzing and recording each transaction.

❑ Call on students to describe each step in the process for posting amounts from the journal to the accounts payable ledger and the general ledger.

INDEPENDENT PRACTICE

On Your Own
❑ Assign the On Your Own problems to be worked independently.

❑ Use the Ongoing Assessment techniques to diagnose student understanding.

Application Problem
❑ Assign Application Problem 18-5: Journalizing and posting transactions using a general journal.

ENRICH

❑ Assign the Legal issues in Accounting feature on page 478.
❑ Assign the Technology for Business feature on page 478.
❑ How would a manager determine if purchases returns and allowances were excessive? What impact would excessive returns and allowances have on the business? Have students consider these questions and prepare a written statement that would assist a new manager in making these decisions.

CLOSE

❑ Ask students to briefly summarize the procedure for journalizing purchases returns and allowances.
❑ Ask students to briefly summarize the posting of the general journal to the accounts payable ledger and general ledger.

CHAPTER 18 SUMMARY

After completing this chapter, you can

1. Define accounting terms related to purchases and cash payments.
2. Identify accounting concepts and practices related to purchases and cash payments.
3. Record purchases on account and post using a purchases journal.
4. Record purchases transactions using a cash payments journal.
5. Record petty cash and post using a cash payments journal.
6. Record purchases returns and allowances and post using a general journal.

EXPLORE ACCOUNTING

CAN ACCOUNTING CHANGE THE COURSE OF HISTORY?

According to accounting historians, the start of the Industrial Revolution was delayed by nearly a century by restrictions on the use of the corporate form of organization. Events in Britain had a profound impact on the development of global commerce.

The scientific knowledge required to spur the Industrial Revolution began to emerge in the eighteenth century. The massive financial resources necessary to develop new industries could not be generated using partnerships, the traditional form of business organization. The British Parliament developed laws permitting the corporate form of organization, including limited liability for stockholders, as a means to

enable these new industries to generate financial resources.

The financial collapse of one corporation caused Parliament to reverse the corporation laws. Financial losses, mismanagement, and improper accounting caused the financial collapse of the South Sea Company. The ensuing personal financial losses of investors generated a public outcry against the corporation laws. The South Sea Bubble Act of 1720 eliminated limited liability, effectively restricting the formation of corporations. Only a limited number of businesses, granted special charters by the British Parliament, were able to form as corporations during the remainder of the century.

During the early nineteenth century a series of

court cases and law changes gradually loosened the rules governing the granting of limited liability. Finally, the 1862 Companies Act completely removed all restrictions, permitting the corporate form of organization used today. Accounting historians believe that the spread of the Industrial Revolution was helped by the growing acceptance of the corporate form of organization.

Required:

Research the start and growth of a major corporation in your state or region. Prepare a short report that discusses how the company generated the capital required to begin and expand the business. Would the company have been successful had it not been able to form as a corporation?

480 CHAPTER 18 Recording Purchases and Cash Payments

EXPLORE ACCOUNTING

Many of the largest corporations in the world were formed over 100 years ago. This fact may lead students to believe that they cannot be involved in the starting of a large corporation. However, there are many examples of large corporations that are fewer than 25 years old. Learning how these corporations began and expanded can inspire students to set starting their own business as a long-term career goal.

Many sources are available to identify how corporations were formed. For older, more established corporations, books and

encyclopedias should provide a good information source. Many corporations describe their history on their Internet sites.

Students' answers will vary, depending on the extent of available information. Students should be able to identify significant events in the corporation's life. Answers could include how the corporation was originally financed, as well as when additional capital was acquired through bonds and capital stock.

18-1 APPLICATION PROBLEM
Journalizing and posting purchase on account transactions

The general ledger and accounts payable ledger accounts for Wholesale Office Supply Company are given in the *Working Papers*. The balances are recorded as of June 1 of the current year.

Instructions:

1. Journalize the following purchases on account completed during June of the current year. Use page 6 of a purchases journal. The abbreviation for purchase invoice is P.

Transactions:

June 3. Purchased merchandise on account from Daniels Company, $276.00. P106.
      6. Purchased merchandise on account from Perkins Supply, $1,693.00. P107.
     12. Purchased merchandise on account from Tompson Mfg. Co., $870.00. P108.
     14. Purchased merchandise on account from Perkins Supply, $4,691.00. P109.
     21. Purchased merchandise on account from Tompson Mfg. Co., $713.00. P110.

2. Post each amount in the purchases journal to the accounts payable ledger.
3. Total and rule the purchases journal. Post the total.

18-2 APPLICATION PROBLEM
Recording cash payments for expenses and purchases using a cash payments journal

The cash payments journal for HiTech Company is given in the *Working Papers*.

Instructions:

Journalize the following cash payments completed during November of the current year. Use page 21 of a cash payments journal. The abbreviation for check is C.

Transactions:

Nov. 1. Paid cash for rent, $800.00. C871.
      8. Paid cash for supplies, $57.00. C872.
     13. Paid cash to Opticon Industries for merchandise with a list price of $1,925.50. Opticon offers its customers a 42% trade discount. C873.
     15. Paid cash on account to Miranda Company, $695.60, covering P706, no discount. C874.
     18. Paid cash on account to AdTech Company covering P707 for $3,023.00, less 1% discount. C875.
     22. Paid cash for repairs, $215.00. C876.
     25. Paid cash to Bear Lake Industries for merchandise with a list price of $2,772.50. Bear Lake offers its customers a 45% trade discount. C877.
     27. Paid cash on account to Technicraft Company covering P710 for $1,552.00, less 2% discount. C878.
     28. Paid cash on account to Kasongo Company, $1,164.00, covering P705, no discount. C879.
     30. Paid cash to replenish the petty cash fund: supplies, $37.00; advertising, $58.70; miscellaneous, $15.25; cash over, $1.22. C880.

FORMAL EVALUATION

Chapter 18 Test
ExamViewPro or Westest for Chapter 18
Assessment by Portfolio
❏ Review answers to all tests administered as a class activity. If time is limited, review only the items that were frequently incorrectly answered.
❏ Ask students if there are any questions about the chapter before proceeding to the next chapter.

CHECK FIGURES

✔ **Application Problem 18-1**
Purch. journal total, 8,243.00
Tompson Mfg. Co. balance, 2,055.00

✔ **Application Problem 18-2**
There are eight entries in the General Debit column.

See Teacher's Edition of the Working Papers for Chapter 18 for complete solutions.

TEACHING STRATEGIES   DIFFERENT LEARNING ABILITIES

Specific Learning Disability (SLD) Students. When feasible, SLD students should become involved in work-study programs that are consistent with course content. When work-study opportunities are unavailable, simulations can be used to provide a simulated work environment. Field trips are an excellent method to expose students to the business world.

✔ **Application Problem 18-3**
Amount to replenish, 70.38

APPLICATION PROBLEM
Preparing a petty cash report

Kevin Tomlinson is the custodian of a $200.00 petty cash fund. On January 31 he had receipts for the following payments:

Payee	Description	Amount
City Office Supply	Computer disks	$ 8.95
KEWQ Radio	Voice fee for radio advertisement	25.00
Rocket Computers	Fix laser printer	15.95
Hooksville PTA	Advertisement in monthly newsletter	10.00
John Simmons	Pick up recyclable materials	8.00
Myers Hardware	Nails to repair outdoor sign	2.50
Books and More	Mouse pad	3.15

Instructions:

1. Classify each expense into one of the general ledger accounts used by Winning Edge in this chapter.
2. Compute the total of expenses by account.
3. Prepare the petty cash report given in the *Working Papers*. A cash count shows $129.62 in the petty cash box.

✔ **Application Problem 18-4**
Cash payments journal totals:
2,574.05
4,867.60
35.03
7,406.62

APPLICATION PROBLEM
Journalizing and posting cash payment transactions using a cash payments journal

The general ledger and accounts payable ledger accounts for Jenson Company are given in the *Working Papers*. The balances are recorded as of July 1 of the current year.

Instructions:

1. Journalize the following cash payments completed during July of the current year. Use page 7 of a cash payments journal. The abbreviation for check is C.

Transactions:

July 1. Paid cash for rent, $600.00. C216.
    6. Paid cash on account to Argo Company covering P457 for $3,503.00, less 1% discount. C217.
    8. Paid cash for supplies, $128.00. C218.
    15. Paid cash on account to Catwell Company, $1,364.60, covering P463, no discount. C219.
    22. Paid cash for miscellaneous expense, $250.00. C220.
    25. Paid cash to Mober Industries for merchandise with a list price of $2,441.50. Mober offers its customers a 40% trade discount. C221.
    31. Paid cash to replenish the petty cash fund: supplies, $42.00; advertising, $62.60; miscellaneous, $25.25; cash short, $1.30. C222.

2. Post accounts payable amounts to the appropriate accounts in the accounts payable ledger.
3. Post the amounts in the general columns to the appropriate general ledger accounts.
4. Prove and rule the cash payments journal. Post the totals of the special columns to the appropriate general ledger accounts.

APPLICATION PROBLEM
Journalizing and posting transactions using a general journal

✔ **Application Problem 18-5**
Sched. A/P total, 7,289.00

The general ledger and accounts payable ledger accounts for Kinard Company are given in the *Working Papers*. The balances are recorded as of August 1 of the current year.

Instructions:

1. Journalize the following transactions completed during August of the current year. Use page 8 of a general journal. Source documents are abbreviated as follows: memorandum, M; debit memorandum, DM.

Transactions:

Aug.   2. Bought supplies on account from Cantrell Company, $462.00. M69.
      3. Returned merchandise to Flick, Inc., $128.00, from P434. DM26.
      7. Bought store equipment on account from Office Solutions, $576.00. M70.
   12. Returned merchandise to David Manufacturing, $93.00, from P428. DM27.
   14. Bought office equipment on account from Office Solutions, $1,208.00. M71.
   22. Bought supplies on account from Cantrell Company, $237.00. M72.

2. Post the general journal to the general and accounts payable ledgers.

3. Prepare a schedule of accounts payable similar to the one described in Chapter 12.

18-6

APPLICATION PROBLEM
Journalizing and posting purchases transactions

✔ **Application Problem 18-6**
Purchases journal total, 3,984.00
Cash payments journal totals:
3,709.00
74.18
3,634.82

The general ledger and accounts payable ledger accounts for Far East Company are given in the *Working Papers*. The balances are recorded as of September 1 of the current year.

Instructions:

1. Journalize the following transactions completed during September of the current year. Use page 9 of a purchases journal, page 17 of a cash payments journal, and page 9 of a general journal.

Transactions:

Sept.   3. Received an order of merchandise from Bell Supply costing $1,354.00 plus shipping charges of $45.00. Bell Supply offers its customers 2/10, n/30 credit terms. The purchase invoice number 252 was stamped on the vendor's invoice.

      4. An order of merchandise from Brandon Company was received. The total cost was $2,354.00 plus $231.00 of shipping costs. Brandon offers 2/10, n/30 credit terms. The purchase invoice number 253 was stamped on the vendor's invoice.

      6. One box of merchandise costing $275.00 from the Brandon Company order (P253) was found to be defective. The goods were returned to Brandon, with Brandon paying for the shipping charges. The accounting clerk sent a copy of debit memorandum 34 with the returned goods.

   12. Issued check number 534 to pay for the Bell Supply shipment of September 3 (P252), taking advantage of the 2% discount.

   14. Prepared and mailed check number 535 to pay the remaining payable resulting from the Brandon Company purchase on September 4. The check reflected a reduction for the 2% discount on the remaining account balance.

2. Total and post the journals to the general ledger and accounts payable ledger.

TEACHING STRATEGIES   EXPANDING BEYOND THE CLASSROOM

Invite a local attorney who practices corporate law to speak to the class. The corporate form of business organization is rich territory for exploring legal issues with an attorney. At this point in learning about corporations, the speaker might address issues relating to forming a corporation and the organizational structure of a corporation.

18-7 MASTERY PROBLEM
Journalizing and posting purchases and cash payment transactions

The general ledger and accounts payable ledger accounts of City Plumbing Supply are given in the *Working Papers*. The balances are recorded as of November 1 of the current year. Use the following account titles.

Partial General Ledger	**Accounts Payable Ledger**
1105 Cash	210 Bennett Supply
1110 Petty Cash	220 Black, Inc.
1140 Supplies	230 Ford Supply
2115 Accounts Payable	240 Riddell Pipe Company
5105 Purchases	250 Wells Company
5110 Purchases Discount	
5115 Purchases Returns and Allowances	
6105 Advertising Expense	
6110 Cash Short and Over	
6135 Miscellaneous Expense	
6145 Rent Expense	

Instructions:

1. Journalize the following transactions affecting purchases and cash payments completed during November of the current year. Use page 11 of a purchases journal, page 21 of a cash payments journal, and page 11 of a general journal. Source documents are abbreviated as follows: check, C; debit memorandum, DM; memorandum, M; purchase invoice, P.

Transactions:

Nov. 1. Paid cash for rent, $500.00. C516.
  2. Purchased merchandise on account from Black, Inc., $3,520.00. P135.
  3. Paid cash on account to Bennett Supply covering P127 for $1,269.00, less 2% discount. C517.
  5. Bought supplies on account from Ford Supply, $152.00. M235.
  8. Purchased merchandise on account from Bennett Supply, $1,154.00. P136.
  8. Paid cash on account to Wells Company covering P129 for $2,503.00, less 2% discount. C518.
  9. Paid cash for supplies, $438.00. C519.
  15. Purchased merchandise on account from Riddell Pipe Company, $362.00. P137.
  15. Paid cash on account to Bennett Supply, covering P136, 2% discount. C520.

   Posting. Post the items that are to be posted individually. Post from the journals in the following order: purchases, general, cash payments. Some transactions will not be in order by date in the accounts.

  16. Returned merchandise to Black, Inc., $526.00, from P135. DM58.
  17. Paid cash to Stafford Company for merchandise with a list price of $192.25. Stafford offers its customers a 60% trade discount. C521.
  22. Purchased merchandise on account from Ford Supply, $378.00. P138.
  23. Paid cash on account to Black, Inc., $2,994.00, covering P135, no discount. C522.
  23. Paid cash for miscellaneous expense, $70.00. C523.
  24. Bought supplies on account from Wells Company, $350.00. M236.
  25. Returned merchandise to Riddell Pipe Company, $65.00, from P137. DM59.

Nov. 29. Purchased merchandise on account from Wells Company, $763.00. P139.
30. Purchased merchandise on account from Bennett Supply, $500.00. P140.
30. Paid cash to replenish the petty cash fund: supplies, $23.10; advertising, $42.20; miscellaneous, $16.75; cash short, $0.45. C524.

Posting. Post the items that are to be posted individually.

2. Total and rule the purchases journal. Post the total.
3. Prove and rule the cash payments journal. Post the totals of the special columns.
4. Prepare a schedule of accounts payable similar to the one described in Chapter 12. Compare the schedule total with the balance of the accounts payable account in the general ledger. The total and balance should be the same.

18-8 CHALLENGE PROBLEM
Journalizing transactions in a combined purchases-cash payments journal

The accountant for City Plumbing Supply has suggested that time could be saved if the purchases journal and the cash payments journal were combined into one journal. The accountant suggests using a journal such as the following.

				Purchases—Cash Payments Journal						
				1	2	3	4	5	6	7
Date	Account Title	Doc. No.	Post. Ref.	General		Purchases Debit	Accounts Payable		Purchases Discount Credit	Cash Credit
				Debit	Credit		Debit	Credit		

Christopher Howard, manager, has asked the accountant to show him how the journal would appear after transactions have been recorded. A purchases-cash payments journal and a general journal are given in the *Working Papers*.

Instructions:

1. Use page 21 of a purchases-cash payments journal and page 11 of a general journal. Journalize the transactions given in Mastery Problem 18-7. Do not post.
2. Prove and rule the combined purchases-cash payments journal.
3. Do you agree with the accountant that the combined purchases-cash payments journal used in this problem saves time in journalizing and posting? Why?

486

Because Internet sites can change frequently, the requirements of the Internet Activity are posted on a South-Western site where they can be updated as needed. Direct students to follow the directions given on their student page.

APPLIED COMMUNICATION

Students' solutions will vary. The letter will have very little content and, therefore, should be graded primarily on mechanics (grammar, spelling, punctuation, and sentence structure).

CASES FOR CRITICAL THINKING

CASE 1 Use the cash payments journal recommended by Mr. Ramundo. Special columns should be provided for entries that will occur frequently. Since the company is a merchandising company, probably many cash payments on account with purchases discounts will be made each month. Therefore, the special columns for Accounts Payable Debit and Purchases Discount Credit are justified.

CASE 2 Ms. Benson's treatment of cash shortages is not recommended. An important control feature is to establish a fund at a fixed amount. When this control feature is followed, the accuracy of the amount in the petty cash fund can be verified at any time. The amount of cash on hand plus the total of petty cash slips should always equal the original fund amount. Whenever a shortage occurs that is not replenished, the fund balance will change. With a changing balance, it will be difficult to verify the correct amount of the fund because there is no control amount for purposes of comparison.

INTERNET ACTIVITY

Point your browser to
http://accounting.swpco.com
Choose **First-Year Course**, choose
Activities, and complete the activity
for Chapter 18.

Applied Communication

The common stock of many corporations is traded on national stock exchanges. These corporations are required by the government to publish their financial statements in an annual report. The annual report also includes management's analysis of the year's operations and its projection of future financial activity. Annual reports are used by bankers, stockholders, and investment advisers for making business and investment decisions.

Instructions: Write a letter to a corporation requesting a copy of its annual report. Your letter should include your return address, inside address, and request for the report.

Cases for Critical Thinking

Case 1 Dessert Designs, Inc., has employed an accounting firm to install a new accounting system using special journals. You and two other accountants are designing the special journals. Patti Edwards, one of the accountants, recommends a cash payments journal with one special column—Cash Credit. Jose Ramundo, the other accountant, recommends a cash payments journal with three special columns—Accounts Payable Debit, Purchases Discount Credit, and Cash Credit. You have been asked to decide which cash payments journal should be used. Give your decision and the reason for that decision.

Case 2 Ashford Company has established a $300.00 petty cash fund. During a routine review of the petty cash records, you discover that small shortages totaling $20.00 have occurred over the past four months. The fund custodian, Kim Benson, has not listed cash short or over on any of the reports prepared for replenishment. When asked about this practice, Ms. Benson said that she always waits until the amount of the shortage is significant—approximately $50.00. Then she requests replenishment for the amount of the shortage. What is your opinion of this practice? What action do you recommend?

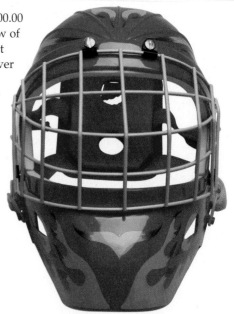

PORTFOLIO ASSESSMENT

Analyzing transactions and journalizing and posting are the first steps in the accounting cycle and critical to the accuracy of information in an accounting information system. Students should select an example of these activities that have been successfully completed to include in their portfolio. A copy of the Portfolio Assessment form (blackline master in the Teacher's Resource Guide) should be completed by the student, and the Description section should include any comments regarding how the student mastered these concepts and procedures. Alternatively, students might include in their portfolios the solutions to the Automated Accounting feature that follows this chapter.

AUTOMATED ACCOUNTING

AUTOMATED ENTRIES FOR PURCHASES AND CASH PAYMENTS USING SPECIAL JOURNALS FOR A CORPORATION

Corporations are owned by shareholders. These shareholders purchase interest in the corporation by buying shares of stock. The total of all shares held by shareholders is known as capital stock. Shareholders elect a board of directors to manage the corporation. The board of directors may declare a dividend that is paid from the earnings of the corporation. Because corporations are legal entities, they pay federal income taxes. The payment of dividends

and federal income taxes will be discussed in a later chapter.

Corporations typically have thousands of purchases and cash payments transactions each month. Computerized accounting systems allow faster processing of these transactions. For example, when a cash payment is entered in the cash payments journal, a check for the payment can be automatically generated by the accounting software.

Purchases of Merchandise

Merchandising businesses purchase from their vendors the goods they sell to customers. All purchases of merchandise on account are recorded in the purchases journal. To record a purchase, enter the date, invoice number, debit to Purchases, and the name of the vendor. The credit to Accounts Payable will be automatically generated by the accounting system.

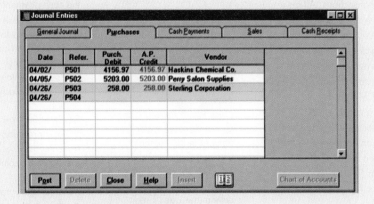

Merchandising businesses maintain a complete list of vendors. *Automated Accounting* maintains a vendor list using a procedure similar to maintaining the chart of accounts. To maintain the vendor list:
1. Click the Accounts toolbar button.

2. Click the Vendors tab.
3. Perform the maintenance:
   a. To add a vendor, enter the vendor name and click the Add Vendor button.
   b. To change an existing vendor, highlight the vendor's name, enter the correct name, and click

the Change Vendor button.
   c. To delete a vendor, highlight the vendor's name and click the Delete button. (A vendor with a balance cannot be deleted.)
4. Click the Close button.

EXPLAIN

❏ Preview the terms used or introduced in this feature: corporations, shareholders, shares of stock, capital stock, board of directors, dividend, and purchases discount.

❏ Explain that corporations typically have thousands of purchases and cash payments transactions each month and that computerized accounting systems facilitate processing.

❏ Explain that purchases on account are entered in the Purchases tab of the Journal Entries screen. Remind students that this is exactly the same process learned in Cycle 2.

❏ Explain that vendor accounts are maintained the same way as learned in Cycle 2.

❏ Explain that cash payments are entered in the Cash Payments tab of the Journal Entries screen. Remind students that this is exactly the same process learned in Cycle 2, except that a field for purchases discounts is added.

❏ Explain that two kinds of cash payments are entered in the cash payments journal: (1) cash payments on account, with and without purchases discounts, and (2) cash payments for other transactions that do not affect Accounts Payable.

DEMONSTRATE

Journalizing purchases of merchandise on account

❏ Demonstrate how to record a purchase in the Purchases Journal screen.

❏ State that to enter a transaction in the Purchases Journal screen, students would first select Journal, then the Purchases tab.

❏ Direct students to point to each field as you describe what to enter in each field.

❏ Explain that the A.P. Credit amount is entered automatically by the software.

❏ Explain that after the Tab key is pressed from the Purch. Debit field, the cursor is placed in the Vendor field for selecting the appropriate vendor from the pull-down list.

❏ Explain that after a transaction is entered, the Post button must be pressed to allow an additional transaction to be entered.

487

DEMONSTRATE

Maintaining the vendor list

❏ Remind students that maintaining the vendor list was learned in Chapter 10.

❏ Demonstrate clicking the Accounts toolbar button and clicking the Vendors tab.

❏ Demonstrate adding a vendor by entering a new vendor name and clicking the Add Vendor button.

❏ Demonstrate changing an existing vendor by highlighting the Vendor's name, entering the change, and clicking the Change Vendor button.

❏ Demonstrate deleting a vendor by highlighting the vendor's name and clicking the Delete button.

❏ Remind students that a vendor with an account balance cannot be deleted.

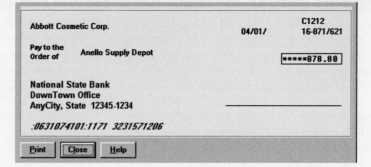

Cash Payment for a Purchase

The cash payments journal is used to enter all cash payments transactions. All merchandise purchases made on account should be paid within the terms granted by the vendor. If a vendor name is entered in the Vendor column and the Computer Check option is turned on, a check will be displayed for these transactions.

To turn on the Computer Check option in *Automated Accounting*:

1. Click the Custom toolbar button.
2. Click the Company Info. tab.
3. Click the Accounts Payable Checks check box.
4. Choose OK.

To process cash payments transactions for a purchase:

1. Choose the Journal Entries menu item from the Data menu or click the Journal toolbar button.
2. Click the Cash Payments tab.
3. Enter the transaction date and press Tab.
4. Enter the check number in the Refer. column and press Tab until the curser appears in the A.P. Debit column.
5. Enter the amount of the accounts payable debit and press Tab. If there is a purchases discount, enter the amount in the Purchase Discount Cr field and press Tab. The amount of the cash credit will appear automatically in the Cash Credit field.
6. Choose a vendor name from the Vendor drop-down list.
7. Click the Post button.

Other Cash Payments

Businesses have many cash payments that do not involve the purchase of merchandise. Payments for such items as utilities, rent, office supplies, and dividends are also recorded in the cash payments journal. To record these cash payments:

1. Choose the Journal Entries menu item from the Data menu or click the Journal toolbar button.
2. Click the Cash Payments tab.
3. Enter the transaction date and press Tab.
4. Enter the check number in the Refer. column and press Tab.
5. Enter the account number of the account to be debited and press Tab.
6. Enter the amount of the debit in the Debit column. The amount of the cash credit will appear automatically in the Cash Credit field.
7. Click the Post button.

AUTOMATED ACCOUNTING

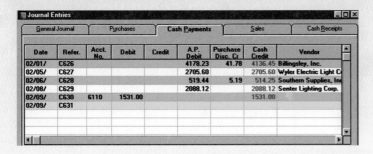

Date	Refer.	Acct. No.	Debit	Credit	A.P. Debit	Purchase Disc. Cr	Cash Credit	Vendor
02/01/	C626				4178.23	41.78	4136.45	Billingsley, Inc.
02/05/	C627				2705.60		2705.60	Wyler Electric Light C
02/06/	C628				519.44	5.19	514.25	Southern Supplies, Inc
02/08/	C629				2088.12		2088.12	Senter Lighting Corp.
02/09/	C630	6110	1531.00				1531.00	
02/09/	C631							

AUTOMATING APPLICATION PROBLEM 18-6: Journalizing and posting purchases transactions

Instructions:

1. Load *Automated Accounting* 7.0 or higher software.
2. Select database F18-1 from the appropriate directory/folder.
3. Select File from the menu bar and choose the Save As menu command. Key the path to the drive and directory that contains your data files. Save the database with a file name of XXX181 (where XXX are your initials).
4. Access Problem Instructions through the Help menu. Read the Problem Instructions screen.
5. Key the data listed on page 483.
6. Exit the *Automated Accounting* software.

AUTOMATING MASTERY PROBLEM 18-7: Journalizing and posting purchases and cash payment transactions

Instructions:

1. Load *Automated Accounting* 7.0 or higher software.
2. Select database F18-2 from the appropriate directory/folder.
3. Select File from the menu bar and choose the Save As menu command. Key the path to the drive and directory that contains your data files. Save the database with a file name of XXX182 (where XXX are your initials).
4. Access Problem Instructions through the Help menu. Read the Problem Instructions screen.
5. Key the data listed on pages 484–485.
6. Exit the *Automated Accounting* software.

PORTFOLIO ASSESSMENT

Students should be encouraged to print at least one report from one of the *Automated Accounting* problems to include in their portfolio to demonstrate mastery of automated accounting systems. A copy of the Portfolio Assessment form (blackline master in the Teacher's Resource Guide) should be completed by the student, and the Description section should include any comments regarding how the student mastered these concepts and procedures.

DEMONSTRATE

Journalizing cash payments on account

❏ Explain that cash payments on account are journalized in the Cash Payments Journal screen.

❏ Demonstrate how to record a cash payment on account

❏ State that to enter a transaction in the Cash Payments Journal screen, students would first select Journal, then the Cash Payments tab.

❏ Direct students to point to each field as you describe what to enter in each field.

❏ Explain that the debit amount is entered in the A.P. Debit column and the discount amount is entered in the Purchase Disc. Cr. column.

❏ Explain that the Cash Credit amount is entered automatically by the software.

❏ Explain that after the Tab key is pressed from the Purchase Disc. Cr. field, the cursor is placed in the Vendor field for selecting the appropriate vendor from the pull-down list.

❏ Explain that a cash payment on account without a discount is entered the same way except, of course, that there is no entry in the Purchase Disc. Cr. column.

Journalizing other cash payments

❏ Explain that account number and debit and credit amounts are entered in the usual way.

❏ Explain that the credit to Cash is automatically calculated.

PRACTICE

❏ Assign Automating Application Problem 18-6: Journalizing and posting purchases transactions.

❏ Assign Automating Mastery Problem 18-7: Journalizing and posting purchases and cash payment transactions.

ASSESSMENT

❏ Use the Electronic Auditor to assess student understanding.

CHAPTER 19

	SCOPE AND SEQUENCE		ENHANCING	
	NEW	REVIEW/ EXTENSION	SPECIAL FEATURES	
INTRODUCE THE CHAPTER			Accounting in Your Career: 12 Months Same As Cash Thinking about Careers	
Special journals improve efficiency	✓			
LESSSON 19-1 RECORDING SALES ON ACCOUNT USING A SALES JOURNAL			Professional Business Ethics: Who Owns My Time?	
Journalizing and posting using a sales journal		✓		
Journalizing sales on account		✓		
Proving and ruling a sales journal		✓		
LESSSON 19-2 RECORDING CASH RECEIPTS USING A CASH RECEIPTS JOURNAL			Math Work Sheet, Chapter 19, Part A Math Work Sheet, Chapter 19, Part B	
Journalizing and posting using a cash receipts journal		✓		
Calculating cash receipts on account with sales discount	✓			
Journalizing cash receipts on account with sales discounts	✓			
Proving and ruling a cash receipts journal		✓		
LESSSON 19-3 RECORDING TRANSACTIONS USING A GENERAL JOURNAL			Math Work Sheet, Chapter 19, Part C Technology for Business: Computerized Accounting—Not Just for Corporations	
Credit memorandum	✓			
Journalizing sales returns and allowances	✓			
Journalizing correcting entries affecting customer accounts	✓			
Order of posting from special journals		✓		
LESSSON 19-4 RECORDING INTERNATIONAL SALES				
Processing an international sale	✓			
Journalizing an international sale	✓			
Journalizing time drafts	✓			
Journalizing cash receipts from time drafts	✓			
PUTTING IT ALL TOGETHER			Explore Accounting Internet Activity Applied Communication Cases for Critical Thinking 1 and 2	

RECORDING SALES AND CASH RECEIPTS

INSTRUCTION		PRACTICE AND ASSESSMENT		
TECHNOLOGY AND MEDIA	TEACHING STRATEGIES	GUIDED PRACTICE	INDEPENDENT PRACTICE	RETEACHING AND ENRICHMENT
Internet Activity	Software Focus			
Transparency N	Auditory Learner	Audit Your Understanding Work Together	On Your Own Application Problem 19-1 Ongoing Assessment, p. 494	Reteach, p. 494 Enrich, p. 495
Transparency O	Applied Skills: Mathematics Cooperative Learning	Term Review Audit Your Understanding Work Together	On Your Own Application Problem 19-2 Ongoing Assessment, p. 499	Reteach, p. 499 Enrich, p. 500
CNN Accounting Video Transparency M	Kinesthetic Learner Print Learner	Terms Review Audit Your Understanding Work Together	On Your Own Application Problem 19-3 Ongoing Assessment, p. 504	Reteach, p. 504 Enrich, p. 505
Transparencies M and O	Gifted Students Print Learner Cooperative Learning	Terms Review Audit Your Understanding Work Together	On Your Own Application Problem 19-4 Ongoing Assessment, p. 510	Reteach, p. 510 Enrich, p. 511
Transparency 19-1 Automated Accounting Accounting Connection	Applied Skills: Language Arts Tactile Learner Tactile Learner Visual Learner Applied Skills: Writing Across the Curriculum Visual Learner Applied Skills: Word Processing Reinforcement Activity		Application Problem 19-5 Mastery Problem 19-6 Study Guide 19 Chapter 19 Test ExamViewPro or Westest, Chapter 19 Portfolio Assessment	Enrich, p. 512 Challenge Problem 19-7 Reteach, p. 512 Recycling Problem 19-1 Accounting Connection

PREVIEW ACCOUNTING TERMS

❏ Read each term out loud to verify pronunciation for students.

❏ Point out terms or parts of terms that
should already be familiar to most students, such as discount, sales return,
exports, and imports.

❏ Point out that students have already
learned about discounts and
allowances from the buyer's point of
view. This chapter presents them from
a vendor's point of view.

PREVIEW CHAPTER OBJECTIVES

❏ Point out that students have already
learned how to journalize sales on
account and cash receipts transactions
in an extended journal in Cycle 2.

❏ Note that sales returns and allowances
will be new transactions in this
accounting cycle.

❏ Note that recording international sales
will also be new in this chapter.

INTRODUCTION

❏ Have students read this page. Having a
student read the page out loud for the
class can help develop the student's
public speaking skills.

❏ This lesson explains why businesses
use special journals.

❏ Point out that the kinds and details of
information provided have a cost to the
business and that the cost must be
worth the benefit provided.

❏ Ask students to identify the sales tax
rates in their community. *(Some communities have different tax rates for
different products and services, such
as food, lodging, and clothing.)*

TERMS PREVIEW

sales discount
sales return
sales allowance
credit
   memorandum
exports
imports
contract of sale
letter of credit
bill of lading
commercial
   invoice
draft
sight draft
time draft
trade acceptance

490

19
Recording Sales and Cash Receipts

AFTER STUDYING CHAPTER 19, YOU WILL BE ABLE TO:

1. Define accounting terms related to sales and cash receipts.

2. Identify accounting concepts and practices related to sales and cash receipts.

3. Record sales on account and post, using a sales journal.

4. Record cash receipts and post, using a cash receipts journal.

5. Record transactions and post, using a general journal.

6. Record transactions for international sales.

SPECIAL JOURNALS IMPROVE EFFICIENCY

As the volume of business and the number of transactions increase for a business, efficiency of operation becomes more important in completing work accurately and on time. Winning Edge has sales of about $2,000,000.00 annually and has numerous transactions to record each day. Because of the size and the numerous transactions of the business, Winning Edge uses a system of special journals. Using special journals improves the efficiency of recording transactions and permits more than one accounting clerk to record transactions at the same time. Winning Edge uses four special journals and a general journal. A sales journal, a cash receipts journal, and selected uses of a general journal are described in this chapter. A purchases journal, a cash payments journal, and other selected uses of a general journal are described in Chapter 18.

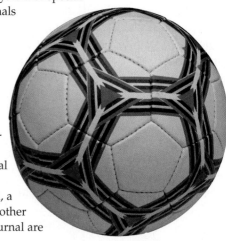

INTERNET ACTIVITY

Point your browser to

http://accounting.swpco.com

Choose **First-Year Course**, choose **Activities**, and complete the activity for Chapter 19.

SOFTWARE FOCUS

Software may be used for independent practice or enrichment as the instructor deems appropriate. For this chapter, the following software may be used: Automated Accounting 7.0 or higher with Application Problem 19-5 and Mastery Problem 19-6; and Accounting Connection, Chapter 19.

Instructors may wish to cover the Automated Accounting feature on pages 520–521, even if the Automated Accounting software is not being used in the classroom, so students get a sense of how the chapter's accounting procedures would be implemented in an automated environment.

ACCOUNTING IN YOUR CAREER

12 MONTHS SAME AS CASH

A-V Warehouse sells consumer audio and video equipment. The market is crowded with stores selling these same products. To compete effectively A-V Warehouse offers credit terms of no money down, 12 months same as cash.

The business is booming and is considering expanding by opening another store in the nearest large city. The morale among the sales associates is high, and they are making as much as 20% more than their regular salaries in commissions on the increased sales. However, the accounting department is having trouble managing the payment of vendors. To support the rapidly expanding sales, larger quantities of inventory are ordered. The commissions to sales associates are straining the payroll costs. Vendors have begun to refuse orders until payments are made for previous sales.

The bank has been lending money to meet immediate cash needs but has just denied the latest loan request. A-V Warehouse's board of directors has hired a consulting firm to analyze the problem and make recommendations. The preliminary report from Doris Jones, an experienced financial analyst with the consultants, makes the following points: (1) Accounts Receivable has become the largest asset on the balance sheet and is "non-productive." (2) The credit terms are the cause of the current cash crisis. (3) If vendor relationships are not quickly improved, there soon will not be enough cash to replenish the inventory.

Critical Thinking:

1. What does Doris Jones mean by referring to Accounts Receivable as "non-productive"?
2. How is it possible that sales are better than ever but the company does not have enough cash to pay its vendors?
3. How could the company begin to generate enough cash to meet current cash needs?

JOURNALIZING SALES ON ACCOUNT

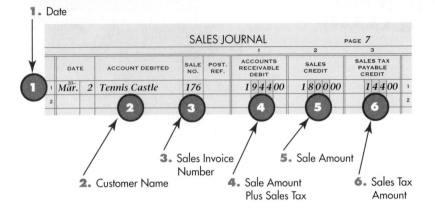

1. Date
2. Customer Name
3. Sales Invoice Number
4. Sale Amount Plus Sales Tax
5. Sale Amount
6. Sales Tax Amount

To encourage sales, Winning Edge sells on account to customers with approved credit. Regardless of when cash is received, revenue should be recorded when merchandise is sold. *(CONCEPT: Realization of Revenue)* Winning Edge uses a special journal to record only sales on account transactions. A special journal used to record *only* sales of merchandise on account is known as a sales journal.

Sales tax rates vary from state to state and may even vary within a state. An 8% sales tax is collected on items sold at retail in the city in which Winning Edge is located.

Winning Edge prepares a sales invoice in duplicate for each sale on account. The original copy is given to the customer. The copy of the sales invoice is the source document for journalizing a sales on account transaction. *(CONCEPT: Objective Evidence)*

March 2. Sold merchandise on account to Tennis Castle, $1,800.00, plus sales tax, $144.00; total, $1,944.00. Sales Invoice No. 176.

Winning Edge owes the sales tax to the state government. Therefore, the amount of sales tax charged each customer is a liability.

Some states exempt schools and other organizations from paying sales tax. A sale to a tax-exempt organization would be recorded using the same amount in the Sales Credit and Accounts Receivable Debit columns. No amount would be entered in the Sales Tax Payable Credit column.

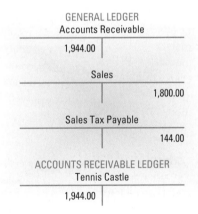

GENERAL LEDGER
Accounts Receivable
1,944.00 |

Sales
| 1,800.00

Sales Tax Payable
| 144.00

ACCOUNTS RECEIVABLE LEDGER
Tennis Castle
1,944.00 |

POSTING FROM A SALES JOURNAL TO AN ACCOUNTS RECEIVABLE LEDGER

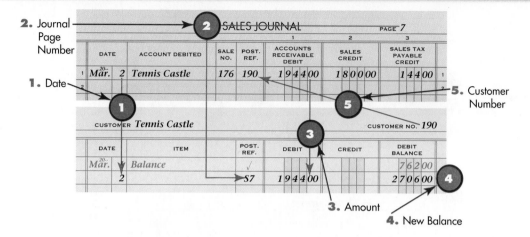

2. Journal Page Number

1. Date

3. Amount

4. New Balance

5. Customer Number

Explain that separate amounts are posted from the sales journal to the accounts receivable ledger frequently so that customer accounts are up to date.

DEMONSTRATE

❑ Direct students to the illustration to explain the posting procedure from a sales journal to an accounts receivable ledger.

❑ As you read each step, ask students to point to the related arrows in the illustration.

❑ Remind students that the abbreviation for the sales journal, *S*, and the page number are recorded in the Post. Ref. column of every ledger account affected, to furnish an audit trail.

❑ Remind students that the accounts receivable account number is recorded in the sales journal's Post. Ref. column to show that posting has been completed and to furnish an audit trail.

❑ Explain that the sales journal's column totals are posted to the three general ledger accounts at the end of the month.

S T E P S

Posting from a sales journal to an accounts receivable ledger

1. Write the date, *2*, in the Date column of the account.
2. Write the abbreviation for the sales journal and the page number, *S7*, in the Post. Ref. column.
3. Enter the amount, *$1,944.00*, in the Debit column of the customer account.
4. Add the amount in the Debit column of the customer account to the previous balance and record the new balance, *$2,706.00*.
5. Record the customer number for Tennis Castle, *190*, in the Post. Ref. column of the journal.

PROFESSIONAL BUSINESS ETHICS

PROFESSIONAL BUSINESS ETHICS

- Explain the importance of professional business ethics to the effective operation of a business.
- Review the three-step checklist to evaluate the ethical behavior of individuals. (1. Is the action legal? 2. Does the action violate company or professional standards? 3. Who is affected, and how, by the action?)
- Divide the class into two groups. Assign a situation to each group. Ask each group to discuss their situation for five minutes and be prepared to report their conclusion to the class.
- Suggested solutions are given in the Instructional Strategies section in the front of this book.

WHO OWNS MY TIME?

Employers and employees have a unique relationship. The employee agrees to provide the employer with a fair day's work. In return, the employer agrees to provide a fair day's wage.

Instructions

Use the three-step checklist to determine whether or not the following situations demonstrate ethical behavior.

Situation 1. Gabriel Peña is a receptionist for Traylor Technologies. After the company installed voice mail, Gabriel's workload became lighter, so his supervisor assigned additional responsibilities, including some accounting tasks. Even with these assignments, Gabriel is not always busy. To fill the time, he plays computer games.

Situation 2. At the Backyard Gourmet, most employees work less than 40 hours per week. However, only employees who work a minimum of 40 hours per week are eligible for health insurance.

493

TEACHING STRATEGIES   DIFFERENT LEARNING STYLES

Auditory Learner. When learning how to post, the auditory learner would prefer to hear the steps involved in posting. This can be done via a live lecture or a taped tutorial. To reinforce learning, the student could recite the posting steps to another student or group of students.

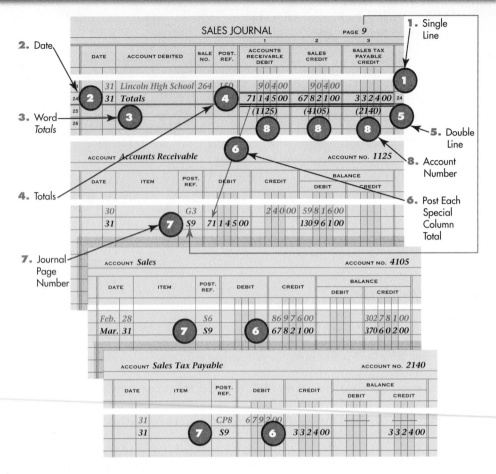

- ❑ Point out that students have already learned how to rule and prove a sales journal.
- ❑ Point out that students have already learned how to post the special column totals of other journals to general ledger accounts.
- ❑ Note that the total of the Sales Tax Payable column is a credit.

DEMONSTRATE

- ❑ Direct students to the illustration. As you read each step, ask students to point to the related arrows in the illustration.
- ❑ Remind students that the abbreviation for the sales journal, *S*, and the page number are recorded in the Post. Ref. column of every ledger account affected, to furnish an audit trail.
- ❑ Remind students that the general ledger account number is recorded in parentheses under the column total to show that posting has been completed and to furnish an audit trail.

ONGOING ASSESSMENT

- ❑ Assessment is an ongoing process. Circulate through the classroom or lab, observing which students have problems with the assignments.
- ❑ Troubleshooting: Diagnose what kinds of problems students have with this lesson. This lesson is largely a review of procedures from Chapter 11. Students may have trouble (1) recording the right information in the correct columns or (2) recording transactions involving a tax-exempt organization.
- ❑ Assess student understanding by checking solutions to Independent Practice assignments.

Equality of debits and credits is proved for a sales journal at the end of each month. The sales journal is then ruled, and the totals of special columns are posted.

Proving and ruling a sales journal and posting a sales journal to a general ledger

1. Rule a single line across the amount columns of the sales journal under the last amounts recorded.
2. Write the date of the last day of the month, *31*, in the Date column.
3. Write the word *Totals* in the Account Debited column.
4. To prove the journal, calculate the total of each column and record the totals below the single line. Determine that the totals of the debit and credit columns are equal.
5. Rule double lines across the amount columns under the totals.
6. Post the total of each special amount column by recording the date, amount, and new account balance in the related general ledger account.
7. Write the abbreviation for sales journal and the page number, *S9*, in the Post. Ref. column of each account.
8. Write each account number in parentheses under the amount column total in the sales journal.

494 CHAPTER 19 Recording Sales and Cash Receipts

RETEACH

- ❑ Call on students to list the kinds of information needed to record a sale on account transaction.
- ❑ Ask a student to make up an original sale on account transaction statement that you write on the board or an overhead transparency.
- ❑ Ask another student to analyze the transaction using T accounts.

- ❑ Ask a student to name each column title in the sales journal and describe what is recorded in it, both in general and specifically for the transaction.
- ❑ Repeat for a sale on account to a tax-exempt organization.
- ❑ Ask a student to name each column title in the general and accounts receivable ledgers and describe what is recorded in it, both in general and specifically for the transaction.

AUDIT YOUR UNDERSTANDING

1. To whom does a business owe the sales taxes collected?
2. Why does Winning Edge post frequently to customer accounts?

WORK TOGETHER

Journalizing and posting sales on account transactions

The ledger accounts for Nesbitt Company are given in the *Working Papers.* Your instructor will guide you through the following examples.

3. Journalize the following transactions completed during April of the current year. Use page 4 of a sales journal. The sales tax rate is 8%. The abbreviation for sales invoice is S.

Transactions:

April 2. Sold merchandise on account to Northland Hospital, $352.00, plus sales tax. S138.
4. Sold merchandise on account to Blanton College, $486.75. Blanton College is exempt from paying sales tax. S139.
9. Sold merchandise on account to Belmont Water Association, $245.00, plus sales tax. S140.
14. Sold merchandise on account to Tess & Sons, $623.00, plus sales tax. S141.

4. Post each amount in the Accounts Receivable Debit column of the sales journal to the accounts receivable ledger.
5. Prove and rule the sales journal.
6. Post the totals of the special columns of the sales journal to the general ledger.

ON YOUR OWN

Journalizing and posting sales on account transactions

The ledger accounts for Jenson Industries are given in the *Working Papers.* Work these problems independently.

7. Journalize the following transactions completed during June of the current year. Use page 6 of a sales journal. The sales tax rate is 8%. The abbreviation for sales invoice is S.

Transactions:

June 1. Sold merchandise on account to Lincoln Designs, $623.00, plus sales tax. S248.
6. Sold merchandise on account to Gulf High School, $2,374.45. Gulf High School is exempt from paying sales tax. S249.
12. Sold merchandise on account to King Services, $259.00, plus sales tax. S250.
18. Sold merchandise on account to Lynch Interiors, $722.00, plus sales tax. S251.

8. Post each amount in the Accounts Receivable Debit column of the sales journal to the accounts receivable ledger.
9. Prove and rule the sales journal.
10. Post the totals of the special columns of the sales journal to the general ledger.

GUIDED PRACTICE

Audit Your Understanding
Call on students to answer the Audit Your Understanding questions. Ask the class if the answer is correct and/or complete. Answers are given in Appendix D of the textbook.

Work Together
Have students write the solutions to the Work Together problems as you guide the class through the examples.

❏ Direct students to record each transaction in the sales journal as you elicit class participation in analyzing and recording each transaction.

❏ Call on students to describe each step in the process for posting separate amounts from the sales journal to the accounts receivable ledger.

❏ Ask a student to describe how to total and rule the sales journal.

❏ Ask another student to describe the steps for posting the sales journal totals to the general ledger.

INDEPENDENT PRACTICE

On Your Own
❏ Assign the On Your Own problems to be worked independently.

❏ Use the Ongoing Assessment techniques to diagnose student understanding.

Application Problem
❏ Assign Application Problem 19-1: Journalizing and posting sales on account transactions.

ENRICH

❏ Assign the Professional Business Ethics feature on page 493.

❏ Ask students to research how a new business registers with the state government to collect sales taxes. Officials in city government or the chamber of commerce can typically provide this information.

CLOSE

❏ Ask students to briefly summarize the procedure for journalizing and posting sales on account using a sales journal.

CALCULATING CASH RECEIPTS ON ACCOUNT WITH SALES DISCOUNT

To encourage early payment for a sale on account, a deduction on the invoice amount may be allowed. A deduction that a vendor allows on the invoice amount to encourage prompt payment is known as a cash discount. A cash discount on sales is called a **sales discount.** When a sales discount is taken, a customer pays less cash than the invoice amount previously recorded in the sales account.

To encourage prompt payment, Winning Edge gives credit terms of 1/10, n/30. When a customer pays the amount owed within 10 days, the sales invoice amount is reduced 1%.

In the state where Winning Edge is located, state regulations require that sales taxes be paid only on actual sales realized. When an invoice for a sale on account is prepared, Winning Edge does not know whether the customer will pay within the sales discount period. Therefore, the customer is invoiced for the full sales amount plus sales tax on that amount.

On March 2, Winning Edge sold merchandise on account to Tennis Castle for $1,800.00 plus 8% sales tax, $144.00, for a total invoice amount of $1,944.00. On March 11, Winning Edge received payment for this sale on account within the discount period. Because the payment is received within the discount period, the sales amount is reduced by the amount of the sales discount. The amount of sales tax is also reduced because the amount of the sale is reduced.

(1) *Sales Discount:*

Sales Invoice Amount	×	Sales Discount Rate	=	Sales Discount
$1,800.00	×	1%	=	$18.00

(2) *Sales Tax Reduction:*

Sales Discount	×	Sales Tax Rate	=	Sales Tax Reduction
$18.00	×	8%	=	$1.44

(3) *Cash Received:*

Total Invoiced Amount	−	Sales Discount	−	Sales Tax Reduction	=	Cash Received
$1,944.00	−	$18.00	−	$1.44	=	$1,924.56

F.Y.I.

In some states, sales taxes must be paid on the original invoice amount of sale. In these states a sales discount would not result in a reduction in the sales tax liability. It is critically important for accounting employees to be familiar with sales tax laws in the states in which their companies do business.

496 CHAPTER 19 Recording Sales and Cash Receipts

JOURNALIZING CASH RECEIPTS ON ACCOUNT WITH SALES DISCOUNTS

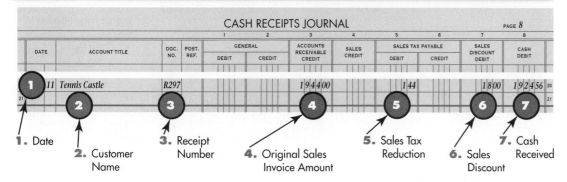

CASH RECEIPTS JOURNAL PAGE 8

1. Date
2. Customer Name
3. Receipt Number
4. Original Sales Invoice Amount
5. Sales Tax Reduction
6. Sales Discount
7. Cash Received

Sales discounts are recorded in a general ledger account titled Sales Discount. Since sales discounts decrease sales, the account Sales Discount is a contra account to Sales.

A business could debit Sales for the amount of the sales discount. However, better information is provided if these amounts are debited to Sales Discount. A separate account provides business managers with more information to evaluate whether a sales discount is a cost effective method of encouraging early payments of sales on account.

March 11. Received cash on account from Tennis Castle, $1,924.56, covering Sales Invoice No. 176 for $1,944.00 ($1,800.00 plus sales tax, $144.00), less 1% discount, $18.00, and less sales tax, $1.44. Receipt No. 297.

If a customer does not pay the amount owed within the sales discount period, the full invoice amount is due. If Tennis Castle had not taken the sales discount, the journal entry would be a debit to Cash, $1,944.00, and a credit to Accounts Receivable, $1,944.00. The same amount, $1,944.00, would also be credited to the account of Tennis Castle in the accounts receivable ledger.

GENERAL LEDGER
Cash
Mar. 11	1,924.56	

Sales Discount
Mar. 11	18.00	

Sales Tax Payable
Mar. 11	1.44	Mar. 2	144.00

Accounts Receivable
Mar. 2	1,944.00	Mar. 11	1,944.00

ACCOUNTS RECEIVABLE LEDGER
Tennis Castle
Mar. 2	1,944.00	Mar. 11	1,944.00

S T E P S

Journalizing cash receipts on account with sales discounts

1. Write the date, *11*, in the Date column.
2. Write the customer name, *Tennis Castle*, in the Account Title column.
3. Write the receipt number, *R297*, in the Doc. No. column.
4. Write the original invoice amount, *$1,944.00*, in the Accounts Receivable Credit column.
5. Write the reduction in sales tax, *$1.44*, in the Sales Tax Payable Debit column.
6. Write the amount of sales discount, *$18.00*, in the Sales Discount Debit column.
7. Write the debit to Cash, *$1,924.56*, in the Cash Debit column. The total of the three debits ($1.44 + $18.00 + $1,924.56) is $1,944.00 and is equal to the one credit of $1,944.00.

---

2. Journal Page Number

CASH RECEIPTS JOURNAL   PAGE *8*

				GENERAL		ACCOUNTS RECEIVABLE CREDIT	SALES CREDIT	SALES TAX PAYABLE		SALES DISCOUNT DEBIT	CASH DEBIT
DATE	ACCOUNT TITLE	DOC. NO.	POST. REF.	DEBIT	CREDIT			DEBIT	CREDIT		
11	Tennis Castle	R297	190			1 9 4 4 00			1 44	18 00	1 9 2 4 56

5. Customer Number

CUSTOMER *Tennis Castle*   CUSTOMER NO. *190*

3. Amount Posted

DATE	ITEM	POST. REF.	DEBIT	CREDIT	DEBIT BALANCE
2		S7	1 9 4 4 00		2 5 2 0 00
4		CR8		5 7 6 00	1 9 4 4 00
11		CR8		1 9 4 4 00	—

1. Date

4. New Balance

Each entry in the Accounts Receivable Credit column affects the account of the customer named in the Account Title column. Each amount listed in the Accounts Receivable Credit column is posted individually to the proper customer account in the accounts receivable ledger.

S T E P S Posting from a cash receipts journal to an accounts receivable ledger

1. Write the date, *11,* in the Date column of the customer account.

2. Write the abbreviation and page number of the cash receipts journal, *CR8,* in the Post. Ref. column of the customer account.

3. Write the amount, *$1,944.00,* in the Credit column of the customer account.

4. Subtract the amount of $1,944.00 in the Credit column from the previous balance in the Debit Balance column. Write the amount or draw a horizontal line to indicate a new balance of zero.

5. Write the customer number for Tennis Castle, *190,* in the Post. Ref. column of the cash receipts journal.

R E M E M B E R

The abbreviation *CR* is used when posting from the cash receipts journal. The abbreviation provides a reference back to the cash receipts journal in case the original entry needs to be examined.

498   CHAPTER 19   Recording Sales and Cash Receipts

POSTING TOTALS OF THE SPECIAL AMOUNT COLUMNS OF A CASH RECEIPTS JOURNAL TO A GENERAL LEDGER

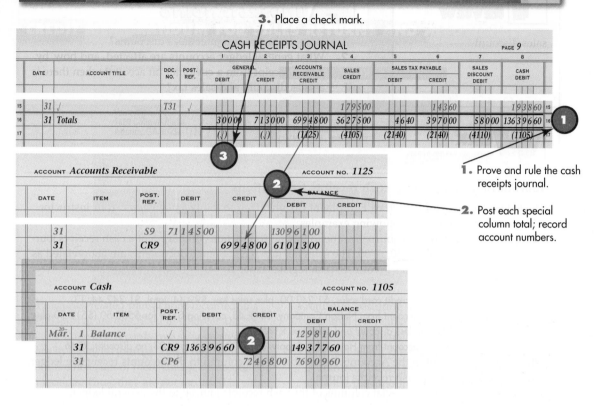

3. Place a check mark.

1. Prove and rule the cash receipts journal.

2. Post each special column total; record account numbers.

EXPLAIN

❑ This illustration reduces the steps that describe the process of proving and ruling a journal and posting the journal's special columns from eight steps (as shown for the sales journal) to three steps. Ask students to identify the steps that are not specifically identified in this illustration.

DEMONSTRATE

❑ As you read each step, ask students to point to the related arrows in the illustration.

❑ Point out that only two of the five general ledger accounts are shown in this illustration but that the other totals are posted the same way as those shown.

❑ Remind students that the abbreviation for the cash receipts journal, *CR*, and the page number are recorded in the Post. Ref. column of every ledger account affected, to furnish an audit trail.

❑ Remind students that the general ledger account number is written in parentheses under the related special column of the cash receipts journal to furnish an audit trail and indicate that the posting process is complete.

❑ Remind students that the totals of all special amount columns are posted to the general ledger the same way as the totals illustrated.

❑ Remind students that amounts in the General Debit and General Credit columns are posted individually to the accounts named in the Account Title column; therefore, check marks are placed under the column totals to indicate that the totals are not posted.

ONGOING ASSESSMENT

❑ Assessment is an ongoing process. Circulate through the classroom or lab, observing which students have problems with the assignments.

❑ Troubleshooting: Diagnose what kinds of problems students have with this lesson. Students may have trouble (1) calculating the sales discount and related reduction in sales tax payable, (2) journalizing a cash receipt on account with sales discount, or (3) confusing the two Sales Tax Payable columns.

❑ Assess student understanding by checking solutions to Independent Practice assignments.

At the end of each month, equality of debits and credits is proved for a cash receipts journal. The steps for proving and ruling the cash receipts journal are not shown in the illustration, but are similar to those described in Chapter 11 for totaling, proving, and ruling a cash receipts journal.

The steps for posting the totals of the special amount columns of a cash receipts journal to a general ledger are shown in the illustration.

Each amount in the General columns is posted individually to the general ledger account named in the Account Title column. The totals of the General amount columns are not posted. To indicate that these totals are not posted, a check mark is placed in parentheses below each column total.

Each special amount column total is posted to the account named in the cash receipts journal column heading.

Posting from a cash receipts journal to a general ledger

S **T** **E** **P** **S**

1. Prove and rule the cash receipts journal.
2. Post the total of each special account column by recording the date, Post. Ref., amount, and new account balance in the related general ledger account. Write the account number in parentheses below the column total in the cash receipts journal.
3. Place a check mark in parentheses below each General column total.

RETEACH

❑ Assign Math Work Sheet, Chapter 19, Parts A and B.

❑ Call on students to list the kinds of information needed to record a cash receipt on account with a sales discount.

❑ Ask a student to make up an original cash receipt with a sales discount transaction statement that you write on the board or an overhead transparency.

❑ Ask another student to analyze the transaction using

T accounts.

❑ Ask a student to record the transaction in the cash receipts journal.

❑ Ask a student to describe what is recorded in the Sales Tax Payable Debit column. Ask another student to describe what is recorded in the Sales Tax Payable Credit column.

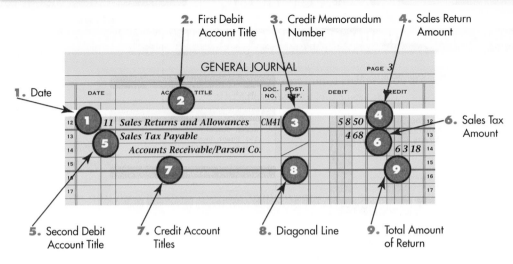

2. First Debit Account Title **3.** Credit Memorandum Number **4.** Sales Return Amount **1.** Date **5.** Second Debit Account Title **7.** Credit Account Titles **8.** Diagonal Line **6.** Sales Tax Amount **9.** Total Amount of Return

On March 8, Winning Edge sold merchandise on account to Parson Company for $475.00. Parson's account was debited for $513.00 ($475.00 sales and $38.00 sales tax). Later, Parson returned part of the merchandise. A customer is entitled to credit for the amount of a sales return or allowance. The credit must include the sales tax on the return or allowance.

March 11. Granted credit to Parson Company for merchandise returned, $58.50, plus sales tax, $4.68, from S160; total, $63.18. Credit Memorandum No. 41.

Parson is entitled to a $58.50 credit for the merchandise returned and a $4.68 credit for sales tax. Accounts Receivable is credited for the total

amount of the return, $63.18. The same amount is also credited to Parson's account in the accounts receivable ledger.

GENERAL LEDGER
Sales Returns and Allowances

Mar. 11	58.50

Sales Tax Payable

Mar. 11	4.68	Mar. 8	38.00

Accounts Receivable

Mar. 8	513.00	Mar. 11	63.18

ACCOUNTS RECEIVABLE LEDGER
Parson Company

Mar. 8	513.00	Mar. 11	63.18

 Journalizing sales returns and allowances

S T E P S

1. Write the date, 11, in the Date column.
2. Write Sales Returns and Allowances in the Account Title column.
3. Write CM and the credit memorandum number, 41, in the Doc. No. column.
4. Write the amount of the sales return, $58.50, in the Debit column.
5. Write Sales Tax Payable on the next line in the Account Title column.
6. Write the sales tax amount, $4.68, in the Debit column.
7. Indent and write the accounts to be credited, Accounts Receivable/Parson Company, on the next line in the Account Title column.
8. Draw a diagonal line in the Post. Ref. column.
9. Write the total accounts receivable amount, $63.18, in the Credit column.

502 CHAPTER 19 Recording Sales and Cash Receipts

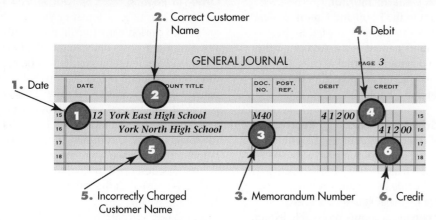

2. Correct Customer Name
4. Debit
1. Date
5. Incorrectly Charged Customer Name
3. Memorandum Number
6. Credit

Errors may be made in recording amounts in subsidiary ledgers that do not affect the general ledger controlling account. For example, a sale on account may be recorded to the wrong customer in the sales journal. The column total posted from the sales journal to the general ledger is correct. The accounts receivable account shows the correct balance. However, two of the customer accounts in the accounts receivable ledger show incorrect balances. To correct this error, only the subsidiary ledger accounts need to be corrected.

March 12. Discovered that a sale on account to York East High School on February 26, S133, was incorrectly charged to the account of York North High School, $412.00. Memorandum No. 40.

On February 28, the total of the Accounts Receivable Debit column in the sales journal was posted correctly. Accounts Receivable was debited

for the amount of the column total that included the $412.00 involved in this transaction. No correction is needed for this amount.

The account of York North High School was debited for $412.00 when the account of York East High School should have been debited. The correcting entry involves only subsidiary ledger accounts. York East High School's account is debited for $412.00 to record the charge sale in the correct account. York North High School's account is credited for $412.00 to cancel the incorrect entry.

ACCOUNTS RECEIVABLE LEDGER
York East High School

Mar. 12	412.00	

York North High School

Feb. 26	412.00	Mar. 12	412.00

Journalizing correcting entries affecting customer accounts

1. Write the date, *12,* in the Date column.

2. Write the name of the correct customer, *York East High School,* in the Account Title column.

3. Write *M* and the memorandum number, *40,* in the Doc. No. column.

4. Write the amount, *$412.00,* in the Debit column.

5. Indent and write the name of the incorrectly charged customer, *York North High School,* on the next line in the Account Title column.

6. Write the amount, *$412.00,* in the Credit column.

EXPLAIN

❑ Explain that accounting procedures must be established to correct the errors that occur in an accounting system.

❑ Ask students to identify the effect on the financial statements resulting from a sale on account being recorded to the wrong customer account. *(There is no effect on total accounts receivable on the financial statements; however, the affected accounts in the accounts receivable ledger are incorrect.)*

❑ Point out that students have already learned how to journalize transactions in a general journal.

❑ Ask students how this transaction recorded in the general journal differs from all other general journal transactions they have recorded. *(There is no general ledger account involved.)*

DEMONSTRATE

Analyze the transaction

❑ Draw two blank T accounts on the board.

❑ Read the transaction statement.

❑ Ask students to analyze the transaction by answering: what accounts are affected, are they increased or decreased, and are they debited or credited? Complete the T accounts as the information is provided.

Record the transaction

❑ Use Transparency M to illustrate the general journal or direct students to the illustration.

❑ Record each item in the journal, following the six steps shown.

❑ Remind students that the source document, a memorandum, is abbreviated as *M.*

TEACHING STRATEGIES   DIFFERENT LEARNING STYLES

Print Learner. When learning how to post, the print learner would prefer to see the process in print. This can be done by distributing a handout that explains the steps in the posting process. Allow the student to study the handout.

Posting from a General Journal

Each amount in the Debit and Credit columns of a general journal is posted to the account or accounts named in the Account Title column. The two general journal entries discussed in this chapter are posted in the same way as described in Chapter 18.

Preparing a Schedule of Accounts Receivable

A listing of customer accounts, account balances, and total amount due from all customers is known as a schedule of accounts receivable. A schedule of accounts receivable is prepared before financial statements are prepared to prove the accounts receivable ledger. If the total amount shown on a schedule of accounts receivable equals the accounts receivable controlling account balance in the general ledger, the accounts receivable ledger is proved. Preparation of a schedule of accounts receivable is described in Chapter 12.

Order of Posting from Special Journals

Items affecting customer or vendor accounts are posted periodically during the month. Winning Edge posts daily so that the balances of the subsidiary ledger accounts will be up to date. Since general ledger account balances are needed only when financial statements are prepared, the general ledger accounts are posted less often during the month. All items, including the totals of special columns, must be posted before a trial balance is prepared.

As was described in Chapter 12, journals should be posted in the following order:
1. Sales journal.
2. Purchases journal.
3. General journal.
4. Cash receipts journal.
5. Cash payments journal.

This order of posting usually puts the debits and credits in the accounts in the order the transactions occurred.

TECHNOLOGY FOR BUSINESS

COMPUTERIZED ACCOUNTING—NOT JUST FOR CORPORATIONS

For many years only large corporations could afford to computerize their accounting functions. Today a variety of computer software programs are available to handle the record keeping and accounting needs of small and not-so-small businesses. Examples include Peachtree, QuickBooks, and MYOB.

Depending on the needs of the business, there is a software program available to complete all or some accounting functions using a personal computer. These functions include the general ledger, accounts payable, accounts receivable, financial statements, and inventory. The software programs can print checks and main-tain a check register, as well as reconcile bank statements. Some programs can help prepare payroll, calculate taxes, and prepare tax forms. Other programs allow transfer of data to payroll and tax preparation software.

Record keeping or accounting software provides significant benefits. The software allows a business to improve the accuracy and completeness of financial records. Safeguards within the software alert the user to mistakes, problems, and inconsistencies. In addition, the software can create graphs and charts to complement financial reports and statements. Organization of records is an added benefit.

504

 **TERMS REVIEW**

sales return
sales allowance
credit memorandum

 **AUDIT YOUR UNDERSTANDING**

1. What general ledger accounts are affected, and how, by a sales returns and allowances transaction?
2. What is the best order in which to post journals?

 **WORK TOGETHER**

Journalizing and posting transactions using a general journal

The ledger accounts for Cline Interiors are given in the *Working Papers*. Your instructor will guide you through the following examples.

3. Using the current year, journalize the following transactions on page 6 of a general journal. Source documents: credit memorandum, CM; memorandum, M; sales invoice, S.

Transactions:

June 3. Granted credit to Wilbanks and Associates for merchandise returned, $457.00, plus sales tax, $36.56, from S356; total, $493.56. CM41.

6. Granted credit to Westfall High School for damaged merchandise, $67.00 (no sales tax), from S345. CM42.

9. Discovered that a sale on account to D. Howell, MD, on May 25, S346, was incorrectly charged to the account of Howsley Dance Studio, $414.99 ($384.25 plus sales tax, $30.74). M17.

4. Post the items to the general and accounts receivable ledgers.

5. Prepare a schedule of accounts receivable, similar to the one described in Chapter 12, as of June 30.

 **ON YOUR OWN**

Journalizing and posting transactions using a general journal

The ledger accounts for Batson Hardware are given in the *Working Papers*. Work these problems independently.

6. Using the current year, journalize the following transactions on page 7 of a general journal. Source documents: credit memorandum, CM; memorandum, M; sales invoice, S.

Transactions:

July 4. Granted credit to Ulman Builders for merchandise returned, $246.00, plus sales tax, $19.68, from S423; total, $265.68. CM54.

8. Granted credit to Brooksville High School for damaged merchandise, $156.00 (no sales tax), from S426. CM55.

12. Discovered that a sale on account to Naper Paper Co. on June 15, S435, was incorrectly charged to the account of Naper Glass Co., $372.60 ($345.00 plus sales tax, $27.60). M21.

7. Post the items to the general and accounts receivable ledgers.

8. Prepare a schedule of accounts receivable as of July 31.

GUIDED PRACTICE

Terms Review
Call on students to define each term in the Terms Review. After each definition, ask the class if the definition is correct and whether the complete definition has been given or if anything needs to be added. Suggested definitions are given in the Glossary.

Audit Your Understanding
Call on students to answer the Audit Your Understanding questions. Ask the class if the answer is correct and/or complete. Answers are given in Appendix D of the textbook.

Work Together
Have students write the solutions to the Work Together problems as you guide the class through the examples.

❏ Direct students to record each transaction in the general journal as you elicit class participation in analyzing and recording each transaction.

❏ Call on students to describe each step in the process for posting the amounts from the general journal to the general ledger.

INDEPENDENT PRACTICE

On Your Own
❏ Assign the On Your Own problems to be worked independently.
❏ Use the Ongoing Assessment techniques to diagnose student understanding.

Application Problem
❏ Assign Application Problem 19-3: Journalizing and posting transactions using a general journal.

ENRICH

❏ Assign the Technology for Business feature on page 504. Ask students to discuss whether knowledge of accounting is needed to use computerized accounting software.
❏ Ask students to identify and compare the return policies of some local merchandising businesses. Students should evaluate whether these policies are effective.
❏ Show the CNN Accounting Video.

CLOSE

❏ Ask students to identify the steps for calculating the reduction in sales tax for a sales return or allowance.
❏ Ask students to briefly summarize the procedure for journalizing sales returns and allowances.
❏ Ask students to briefly summarize the procedures for correcting a sale on account transaction posted to the wrong customer's account.

505

INTERNATIONAL SALES

Sales in the international market have become a major source of revenue for both small and large businesses. Businesses throughout the world are finding it necessary to buy and sell products and services from and to businesses in foreign countries.

Goods or services shipped out of a seller's home country to a foreign country are called **exports.** Goods or services bought from a foreign country and brought into a buyer's home country are called **imports.**

Businesses may be able to import materials or services that are not available or are less expensive than within their own country. Thus, many companies have entered into the export and import markets to maintain their competitiveness and provide the products and services to meet customer demand.

Selling merchandise to individuals or other businesses within one's own country, generally referred to as domestic sales, is much simpler than international sales.

Most domestic sales are sold for cash or on account after reviewing and approving a customer's credit. Because all transactions in the U. S. are covered by the same universal commercial laws and the same accounting standards, many transactions are based on trust. A customer with approved credit orders merchandise. The merchandise is shipped and an invoice is sent by the vendor. After receiving the merchandise and invoice, the customer pays the vendor.

However, because of the increased complexities of international sales, several issues must be considered. The lack of uniform commercial laws among countries makes settlement of disputes more difficult. Greater distances and sometimes more complex transportation methods increase the time to complete the transaction. The reduced ability to determine a customer's financial condition and ability to take legal action if a customer does not pay increases the risk of uncollected amounts. Unstable political conditions in some countries may affect the ability to receive payments from those countries. Therefore, most businesses dealing in exports and/or imports follow a general process in international trade that ensures the vendor receives payment for merchandise sold and the customer receives the merchandise ordered.

> **F.Y.I.**
> *The International Chamber of Commerce publishes Incoterms to attempt to coordinate international sales. This set of international rules interprets common sales terms used in foreign trade that are adopted by most international trade associations.*

A document that details all the terms agreed to by seller and buyer for a sales transaction is called a **contract of sale.** The contract includes a description and quantity of merchandise, price, point of delivery, packing and marking instructions, shipping information, insurance provisions, and method of payment.

Southwest Exports, Inc., located in San Diego, California, contracts to sell merchandise to Santiago Company in Mexico City, Mexico. The contract price is $25,000.00 in U.S. dollars, and merchandise is to be delivered to Mexico City. The Santiago Company is to pay transportation charges.

A letter issued by a bank guaranteeing that a named individual or business will be paid a specified amount provided stated conditions are met is called a **letter of credit.** The contract of sale specified a letter of credit as the method of payment.

Santiago prepared an application with its bank, Banco Nacional de Mexico, to issue a letter of credit. Banco Nacional de Mexico approved Santiago's application and issued the letter of credit. Banco Nacional de Mexico forwarded the letter of credit to Southwest's bank, First Bank in San Diego.

First Bank delivered the letter of credit to Southwest. Southwest reviewed the letter of credit to ensure that the provisions in the letter agreed with the contract of sale. Southwest then shipped the merchandise.

In order for Southwest to collect payment, three documents specified in the letter of credit must be submitted to First Bank: (1) a bill of lading, (2) a commercial invoice, and (3) a draft. A receipt signed by the authorized agent of a transportation company for merchandise received that also serves as a contract for the delivery of the merchandise is called a **bill of lading.** The transportation company sends the bill of lading to Southwest when the merchandise is shipped. Southwest then prepares the other two documents. A statement prepared by the seller of merchandise addressed to the buyer showing a detailed listing and description of merchandise sold, including prices and terms, is called a **commercial invoice.** A written, signed, and dated order from one party ordering another party, usually a bank, to pay money to a third party is called a **draft.** A draft is sometimes referred to as a bill of exchange. A draft payable on sight when the holder presents it for payment is called a **sight draft.**

First Bank examines the documents submitted by Southwest to ensure that all terms of sale are in compliance with the letter of credit. First Bank then forwards the documents to Santiago's bank, Banco Nacional de Mexico. Banco Nacional de Mexico examines the documents to ensure they are in compliance with the terms and conditions of the letter of credit. When Banco Nacional de Mexico determines all documents are in compliance, it deducts the amount of the sight draft from Santiago's account and sends that amount, $25,000.00, to Southwest's bank, First Bank.

Banco Nacional de Mexico then forwards the documents to Santiago Company. By presenting the bill of lading and letter of credit to the transportation company, Santiago can receive the merchandise.

- Ask students to describe the process for selling merchandise to an international customer.
- Explain that the bill of lading is a document that controls the transportation process of both national and international shipments of merchandise.
- Ask students to provide the definition for each term introduced.
- Ask students to read the F.Y.I. for more information regarding sales taxes in other countries.

The United States federal government does not collect a sales tax. However, many countries of the world, including most of the major industrial powers, do collect what is referred to as a "value added tax" or VAT. A value added tax is basically a national sales tax.

TEACHING STRATEGIES   DIFFERENT LEARNING ABILITIES

Gifted Students. This cycle presents a variety of accounting concepts, such as accounts receivable, plant assets, and inventory. Using gifted students as tutors for other students can be an effective way of teaching the topics students find most difficult. Allow the gifted student to complete one of these chapters while the class completes the first two chapters of the cycle. The gifted students can then assist you in presenting the concepts and procedures on their chapter to the class. Encourage the students to use visual aids and develop methods to assess student learning.

- ❏ Point out that students have already learned how to journalize transactions using a cash receipts journal.
- ❏ Point out that an international sale for cash is recorded the same as any other cash sale, except that the source document is a memorandum rather than a receipt.
- ❏ Ask students to identify why the source document for this transaction is a memorandum rather than a receipt.
- ❏ Point out to students that sales taxes are not included in this transaction only because the sale is not to the final customer.
- ❏ Ask students to read the F.Y.I. for more information regarding sales taxes in other countries.

DEMONSTRATE

Analyze the transaction

- ❏ Draw two blank T accounts on the board.
- ❏ Read the transaction statement.
- ❏ Ask students to analyze the transaction by answering: what accounts are affected, are they increased or decreased, and are they debited or credited? Complete the T accounts as the information is provided.

Record the transaction

- ❏ Use Transparency 0 to illustrate the cash receipts journal or direct students to the illustration.
- ❏ Record each item in the journal, following the six steps shown.
- ❏ Remind students that the source document, a memorandum, is abbreviated as *M*.

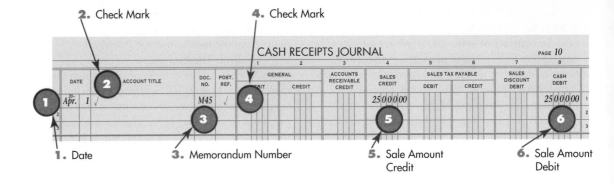

2. Check Mark   **4.** Check Mark

1. Date   **3.** Memorandum Number   **5.** Sale Amount Credit   **6.** Sale Amount Debit

After receiving payment from Banco Nacional de Mexico, First Bank deposits the payment for the sale in Southwest's account and sends Southwest a deposit slip for the amount deposited. After receiving the deposit slip from First Bank, Southwest prepares a memorandum as a source document for the cash received. The sale is then recorded as a cash sale.

April 1. Recorded international cash sale, $25,000.00. Memorandum 45.

Sales taxes are normally paid only on sales to the final consumer. Southwest's sale is to Santiago Company, a manufacturing company. Therefore, sales tax is not collected.

The sales and collection process Southwest followed assured Southwest of receiving payment for its sale and Santiago Company of receiving the merchandise it ordered.

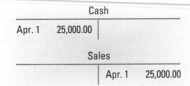

Cash	
Apr. 1 25,000.00	

Sales	
	Apr. 1 25,000.00

Visitors to foreign countries with a value added tax (VAT) typically are required to pay the VAT. However, if items purchased exceed a specified amount, a refund of a portion of the VAT can be requested.

S T E P S

Recording an entry for an international sale

1. Write the date, 20—, Apr. 1, in the Date column.
2. Place a check mark in the Account Title column to indicate that no account title needs to be entered.
3. Write M and the memorandum number, 45, in the Doc. No. column.
4. Place a check mark in the Post. Ref. column to indicate that the amounts on this line are not posted individually.
5. Write the sale amount, $25,000.00, in the Sales Credit column.
6. Write the sale amount, $25,000.00, in the Cash Debit column.

TEACHING STRATEGIES   DIFFERENT LEARNING STYLES

Print Learner. When covering journal entries with a print learner, the instructor should discuss the entries, using the textbook examples and referring to the textbook. The print learner can later go back and study the entries.

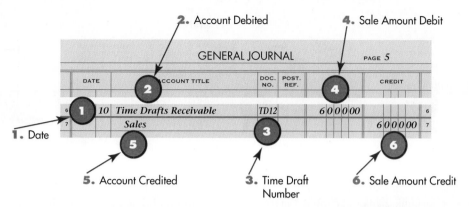

2. Account Debited

4. Sale Amount Debit

GENERAL JOURNAL   PAGE 5

DATE	ACCOUNT TITLE	DOC. NO.	POST. REF.		CREDIT
6	**1** 10	*Time Drafts Receivable*	**2**	TD12	**4** 6 0 0 0 00		6
7		*Sales*	**3**			**6** 6 0 0 0 00	7

1. Date

5. Account Credited

3. Time Draft Number

6. Sale Amount Credit

Southwest Exports, Inc. sold $6,000.00 of merchandise to Simov Co., located in Istanbul, Turkey. The contract of sale with Simov was similar to the contract with Santiago Company, with one exception. Southwest agreed to delay receipt of payment 60 days. A draft that is payable at a fixed or determinable future time after it is accepted is called a **time draft.**

The sales process with Simov is the same as with Santiago except Southwest submits with the documentation a time draft due 60 days from the date the draft is accepted. On May 10, all documentation for the Simov sale is verified to be correct by the seller's and buyer's banks, and Southwest's time draft is accepted.

After verifying the documentation, Simov's bank, Bank of Istanbul, returns the accepted time draft to Southwest and forwards the other documents to Simov Co. Simov can receive the merchandise by presenting the bill of lading and letter of credit to the transportation company.

S T E P S

Journalizing a time draft

1. Write the date, *10,* in the Date column.
2. Write *Time Drafts Receivable* in the Account Title column.
3. Write *TD* and the time draft number, *12,* in the Doc. No. column.
4. Write the sale amount, *$6,000.00,* in the Debit column.
5. On the next line, indent and write *Sales* in the Account Title column.
6. Write the sale amount, *$6,000.00,* in the Credit column.

May 10. Received a 60-day, time draft from Simov Co. for an international sale, $6,000.00. Time Draft No. 12.

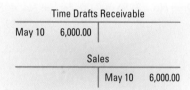

Time Drafts Receivable

| May 10 | 6,000.00 | |

Sales

| | May 10 | 6,000.00 |

F.Y.I.

The minimum value added tax (VAT) in the European Community is 15%; however, there is no additional local sales tax. The Philippines has a 10% VAT that applies to the sale, barter, or exchange of goods, properties, or services. Thailand applies a 7% VAT to selected beverages.

EXPLAIN

- ❑ Point out that students have already learned how to record a transaction in a general journal.
- ❑ Ask students to identify the purpose of time drafts.
- ❑ Point out that the time drafts receivable account is an asset having a normal debit balance. It is similar to Accounts Receivable.
- ❑ Ask students to read the F.Y.I. for more information regarding sales taxes in other countries.

DEMONSTRATE

Analyze the transaction

- ❑ Draw two blank T accounts on the board.
- ❑ Read the transaction statement.
- ❑ Ask students to analyze the transaction by answering: what accounts are affected, are they increased or decreased, and are they debited or credited? Complete the T accounts as the information is provided.

Record the transaction

- ❑ Use Transparency M to illustrate the general journal or direct students to the illustration.
- ❑ Record each item in the journal, following the six steps shown.
- ❑ Point out to students that the source document, a time draft, is abbreviated as *TD*.

TEACHING STRATEGIES   COOPERATIVE LEARNING

Divide the class into groups of two students each. Using Application Problem 19-5, have students orally analyze the transactions to each other, alternating transactions. This cooperative learning activity should not take more than 10 to 15 minutes of class time.

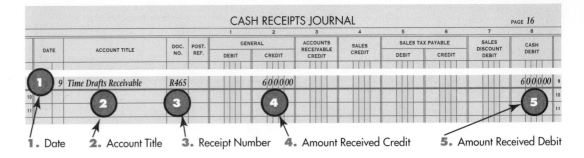

1. Date   **2.** Account Title   **3.** Receipt Number   **4.** Amount Received Credit   **5.** Amount Received Debit

When Simov's time draft is due and presented to its bank, Bank of Istanbul, the bank pays the draft. The payment process is the same as the payment of Santiago Company's sight draft.

July 9. Received cash for the value of Time Draft No. 12, $6,000.00. Receipt No. 465.

Cash	
July 9 6,000.00	

Time Drafts Receivable	
May 10 6,000.00	July 9 6,000.00

The process used by Southwest Exports, Inc. for international sales relies upon letters of credit from banks to assure receipt of payment for those sales. Occasionally, Southwest grants an extension of time for payment to long-time international customers by submitting a time draft.

Trade Acceptances

A form signed by a buyer at the time of a sale of merchandise in which the buyer promises to pay the seller a specified sum of money, usually at a stated time in the future, is called a **trade acceptance.**

A trade acceptance is similar to a draft except a draft is generally paid by a bank and a trade acceptance by the buyer. A seller generally has much more assurance of receiving payment from a bank than from a buyer. Because of the many complexities, few businesses use trade acceptances in international sales. Some businesses, however, use trade acceptances for domestic sales to very reliable customers.

S T E P S

Journalizing cash received from a time draft

1. Write the date, *9,* in the Date column.

2. Write *Time Drafts Receivable* in the Account Title column.

3. Write *R* and the receipt number, *465,* in the Doc. No. column.

4. Write the amount received, *$6,000.00,* in the General Credit column.

5. Write the same amount, *$6,000.00,* in the Cash Debit column.

REMEMBER

A sight draft and a time draft are similar. Both methods of international sales require the buyer's bank to guarantee the cash payment for the sale. The primary difference between a sight draft and a time draft is the timing of the payment; cash payment of a time draft is delayed for a period of time after the delivery of the goods to the buyer.

TERMS REVIEW

exports · draft

imports · sight draft

contract of sale · time draft

letter of credit · trade

bill of lading · acceptance

commercial
invoice

AUDIT YOUR UNDERSTANDING

1. What are some of the issues that must be considered before making international sales?

2. What two purposes does a bill of lading serve?

3. How does a sight draft differ from a time draft?

4. Why do many companies dealing in international sales rely upon letters of credit from banks?

5. How does a trade acceptance differ from a draft?

tions. Ask the class if the answer is correct and/or complete. Answers are given in Appendix D of the textbook.

Work Together

Have students write the solutions to the Work Together problems as you guide the class through the examples.

❏ Direct students to record each transaction in the cash receipts and general journals as you elicit class participation in analyzing and recording each transaction.

❏ Call on students to describe the process of proving a cash receipts journal.

INDEPENDENT PRACTICE

On Your Own

❏ Assign the On Your Own problems to be worked independently.

❏ Use the Ongoing Assessment techniques to diagnose student understanding.

Application Problem

❏ Assign Application Problem 19-4: Journalizing international sales transactions.

WORK TOGETHER

Journalizing international sales transactions

The cash receipts and general journals for Marlon Exports, Ltd. are given in the *Working Papers*. Your instructor will guide you through the following examples.

6. Using the current year, journalize the following international sales on page 9 of a cash receipts journal and page 5 of a general journal. Sales tax is not charged on these sales. Source documents are abbreviated as follows: memorandum, M; time draft, TD; receipt, R.

May 1. Recorded an international cash sale, $14,000.00. M323.

5. Received a 30-day time draft from Ying Shen for an international sale, $18,000.00. TD32.

9. Received cash for the value of Time Draft No. 10, $21,000.00. R221.

7. Prove and rule the cash receipts journal.

ON YOUR OWN

Journalizing international sales transactions

The cash receipts and general journals for Kazsumori Gallery are given in the *Working Papers*. Work these problems independently.

8. Using the current year, journalize the following international sales on page 3 of a cash receipts journal and page 2 of a general journal. Sales tax is not charged on these sales. Source documents are abbreviated as follows: memorandum, M; time draft, TD; receipt, R.

Feb. 1. Recorded an international cash sale, $12,000.00. M132.

4. Received a 60-day time draft from Danjiro Mori for an international sale, $5,000.00. TD22.

8. Received cash for the value of Time Draft No. 6, $13,500.00. R102.

9. Prove and rule the cash receipts journal.

ENRICH

❏ Selling merchandise to individuals or businesses in other countries requires that a business must understand its customers and the culture in which they live. Ask students to research a cultural difference in one country that a business person should know before attempting to sell merchandise in that country. *(For example, the proper method of making an introduction, including the exchange of business cards, can differ between countries.)*

CLOSE

❏ Ask students to identify the source documents involved in international sales.

❏ Ask students to briefly summarize the procedure for journalizing international sales.

PUTTING IT ALL TOGETHER

❏ Review the Chapter Summary.
❏ Use Transparency 19-1 to review the transactions presented in this chapter.
❏ Ask students to prepare a list of the new concepts introduced in this chapter.
❏ Discuss that the journalizing and posting procedures learned in this chapter could also be used for a merchandising business organized as a partnership.

INDEPENDENT PRACTICE

❏ Assign **Mastery Problem 19-6** to students who need the reinforcement of a problem that combines all transactions from the chapter in one problem; this will be most students.
❏ Assign **Application Problem 19-5**. This problem will emphasize transaction analysis skills because transactions are stated in a variety of different ways.
❏ Assign **Challenge Problem 19-7** to accelerated students who do not require the reinforcement of the mastery problem.
❏ Assign **Study Guide 19**.

ONGOING ASSESSMENT

Review solutions to the assigned problems in class, diagnosing troublespots.

RETEACH

❏ Call on students to describe how they avoid the troublespots diagnosed.
❏ Use reteaching suggestions from lesson plans as required.
❏ Assign Recycling Problem 19-1 if needed.
❏ Assign Accounting Connection, Chapter 19.

ENRICH

❏ Assign the Explore Accounting feature. Ask students to share the information they have gathered in a report to the class.
❏ Assign the Internet Activity.
❏ Assign the Applied Communication activity.
❏ Assign Cases 1 and 2 of Cases for Critical Thinking.
❏ Assign the Automated Accounting feature on pages 520–521 to automate Application Problem 19-5 and Mastery Problem 19-6.

CHAPTER 19 SUMMARY

After completing this chapter, you can

1. Define accounting terms related to sales and cash receipts.
2. Identify accounting concepts and practices related to sales and cash receipts.
3. Record sales on account and post, using a sales journal.
4. Record cash receipts and post, using a cash receipts journal.
5. Record transactions and post, using a general journal.
6. Record transactions for international sales.

EXPLORE ACCOUNTING

HOW CREDIT CARD SYSTEMS WORK

To promote sales, Chimes Music Store accepts major credit cards, such as VISA, MasterCard, American Express, and Discover. To process these sales, Chimes Music contracted with a processing center to install and maintain its credit card system.

When a customer presents Chimes with a credit card, the card is scanned and the amount of purchase is entered in a credit card reader. The reader uses phone lines to contact the processing center. If the processing center determines that the customer has an adequate amount of unused credit, the transaction is approved and a sales receipt is printed. At the same time,

the transaction is added to daily totals maintained by the processing center. After the customer signs the credit card receipt, both the customer and business keep a copy.

At the end of the day, Chimes enters a command to instruct the system to close its account. The credit card reader prints a summary receipt that lists the total number and amount of sales by credit card company. The processing center notifies each credit card company of its daily total. The credit card companies then make electronic funds transfers to Chimes Music's bank account. This process often requires several days to complete.

Both the processing center and the credit card companies charge Chimes with a fee for processing credit card sales. These charges are accumulated and a monthly fee is charged directly to Chimes Music's bank account.

Research:
Credit card processing companies can use different equipment and procedures to process credit card sales. Ask a local retailer to describe its credit card processing system. Prepare a report that describes the equipment and procedures used as well as the fees charged. Contrast the system you observed with Chimes Music's system. Which system is better? How could the system you researched be improved?

EXPLORE ACCOUNTING

Students may need assistance identifying a business to contact. Consider contacting a civic organization to seek the participation of its members, many of whom manage or own merchandising businesses.

Students' answers will vary depending on the nature and size of the merchandising business. Students' reports should include information concerning (1) the processing center, (2) forms, (3) end-of-the-day closing procedures, and (4) cash collections.

19-1 APPLICATION PROBLEM
Journalizing and posting sales on account transactions

The general ledger and accounts receivable ledger accounts for Yasunari Company are given in the *Working Papers*. The balances are recorded as of March 1 of the current year.

Instructions:

1. Journalize the following sales on account transactions completed during March of the current year. Use page 3 of a sales journal. The sales tax rate is 8%. The abbreviation for sales invoice is S.

Transactions:

March   3. Sold merchandise on account to Maitland Supply, $523.00, plus sales tax. S78.

         5. Sold merchandise on account to Hampton University, $745.40. Hampton University is exempt from paying sales tax. S79.

         6. Sold merchandise on account to Cruz and Diaz, $1,635.00, plus sales tax. S80.

         8. Sold merchandise on account to Valdez and Associates, $723.00, plus sales tax. S81.

      12. Sold merchandise on account to Maitland Supply, $816.00, plus sales tax. S82.

2. Post each amount in the Accounts Receivable Debit column of the sales journal to the accounts receivable ledger.
3. Prove and rule the sales journal.
4. Post the totals of the special columns of the sales journal to the general ledger.

19-2 APPLICATION PROBLEM
Journalizing and posting cash receipts transactions

The general ledger and accounts receivable ledger accounts for Gandy Stores are given in the *Working Papers*. The balances are recorded as of April 1 of the current year.

Instructions:

1. Journalize the following cash receipts transactions completed during April of the current year. Use page 5 of a cash receipts journal. Gandy Stores offers terms of 2/10, n/30. The sales tax rate is 8%. Source documents are abbreviated as follows: receipt, R; sales invoice, S; cash register tape, T.

Transactions:

April   4. Recorded cash and credit card sales, $3,623.00, plus sales tax, $289.84, total, $3,912.84. T4.

         5. Received cash on account from Lambert Company, $489.51, covering S81 for $499.50 ($462.50 plus sales tax, $37.00), less discount and sales tax. R65.

         7. Received cash on account from Fulton Supply, $315.00, covering S82; no discount. R66.

      10. Recorded cash and credit card sales, $2,493.00, plus sales tax, $199.44, total, $2,692.44. T10.

      14. Received cash on account from Westbrook Company, $723.00, covering S83; no discount. R67.

      22. Received cash on account from Okora Industries, $449.82, covering S82 for $459.00 ($425.00 plus sales tax, $34.00), less discount and sales tax. R68.

2. Post each amount in the Accounts Receivable Credit column of the cash receipts journal to the accounts receivable ledger.
3. Prove and rule the cash receipts journal.
4. Post the totals of the special columns of the cash receipts journal to the general ledger.

CHECK FIGURES

✔ **Application Problem 19-1**
Sales journal totals:
4,738.16
4,442.40
295.76

✔ **Application Problem 19-2**
Cash receipts journal totals:
1,996.50
6,116.00
1.42
489.28
17.75
8,582.61

See Teacher's Edition of the Working Papers for Chapter 19 for complete solutions.

LANGUAGE ARTS

Practicing Punctuation Skills. Special handouts for practicing punctuation skills can be created easily, using word processing software. Key in some text, either something that you have written yourself or that has appeared in a newspaper or magazine. After checking to be sure you have keyed it correctly, use the change feature of the word processor to change all punctuation to an underline. This will create an answer space for students to supply the correct punctuation. Student solutions can then be compared with the original copy for correctness. For additional challenge, the answer blanks can be omitted.

Apr. 9. Recorded cash and credit card sales, $1,820.00, plus sales tax. T9.

Posting. Post the items that are to be posted individually.

12. Merchandise was purchased on account from Grath Electric Co., $1,675.00. P177.

13. Wrote a check for money owed to Walters, Inc., covering P175 for $3,010.00, less DM9, $468.32, and less 2% discount. C127.

14. Jenkins Co. bought merchandise on credit, $546.00, plus sales tax. S86.

14. Paid for advertising, $450.00. C128.

14. Issued a check on account to Drake Supplies, $1,413.00, covering M14; no discount. C129.

15. Bird Company returned merchandise for credit, $226.00, plus sales tax, from S85. CM18.

16. Sold merchandise on account to Altman & Baird, $642.00, plus sales tax. S87.

16. Received a check on account from Bird Company, $128.07, covering S85 for $374.76 ($347.00 plus sales tax, $27.76), less CM18 ($226.00 plus sales tax), less discount and less sales tax on discount. R29.

16. Recorded cash and credit card sales, $2,246.00, plus sales tax. T16.

Posting. Post the items that are to be posted individually.

19. Cash was received on account from Hawbecker Company, $697.40, covering S60; no discount. R30.

20. Merchandise was purchased on account from Randle Company, $216.00. P178.

21. Sold merchandise on credit to Parker Supply, $723.00, plus sales tax. S88.

23. Wrote a check for miscellaneous expense, $205.00. C130.

23. Received on account from Jenkins Co., $577.89, covering S86 for $589.68 ($546.00 plus sales tax, $43.68), less discount and less sales tax on discount. R31.

23. Recorded cash and credit card sales, $2,152.00, plus sales tax. T23.

Posting. Post the items that are to be posted individually.

26. Sold merchandise on account to Bird Company, $1,015.00, plus sales tax. S89.

26. Merchandise was purchased on account from Grath Electric Co., $1,975.00. P179.

29. Paid cash on account to Randle Company, covering P178 for $216.00, less 1% discount. C131.

29. Purchased merchandise on account from Walters, Inc., $985.00. P180.

30. Recorded cash and credit card sales, $1,847.00, plus sales tax. T30.

30. Issued a check to replenish the petty cash fund, $130.25: supplies, $45.15; advertising, $60.00; miscellaneous, $22.50; cash short, $2.60. C132.

Posting. Post the items that are to be posted individually.

2. Prove and rule the sales journal and post the totals of the special columns.

3. Total the purchases journal and post the column total.

4. Prove and rule the cash receipts journal and post the totals of the special columns.

5. Prove and rule the cash payments journal and post the totals of the special columns.

6. Prepare a schedule of accounts payable and a schedule of accounts receivable as of April 30 of the current year. Compare each schedule total with the balance of the controlling account in the general ledger. The total and balance should be the same.

TEACHING STRATEGIES — REINFORCEMENT ACTIVITY

Reinforcement Activity 3 begins with Part A after this chapter and continues with Part B after Chapter 26. Reinforcement Activity 3 presents the whole accounting cycle for a merchandising business organized as a corporation. You may prefer to have your students begin Part A at the end of this chapter and continue with Part B later. Or you may reserve Part A to be completed with Part B after Chapter 26. Blackline masters for audit tests for Reinforcement Activity 3 are available in the Teacher's Resource Guide in three options: Part A only, Part B only, and Parts A and B combined. In addition, Automated Accounting 7.0 or higher can be used to automate Reinforcement Activity 3.

Applied Communication

The following letter, dated January 14, 20—, was received from John Westmore, Accounts Payable Clerk, Nettles Ceramics, P.O. Box 142, Chicago, IL 60024:

"On a recent shipment, your sales invoice #3253, 12 bags of mixing compound, costing $12.50 each plus tax, were water damaged. Please notify us on how to process a claim on this invoice."

Instructions on your sales invoice clearly state that damaged goods should be shipped collect on delivery to your company with a letter explaining the nature of the damage. Nettles Ceramics is a new customer and obviously did not read these instructions. Write a letter to the customer that (1) provides the requested information and (2) politely alerts the customer to the information provided on your sales invoice.

Cases for Critical Thinking

Case 1 Jenson Drilling Supply uses a 3-column sales journal with special amount columns similar to the one in this chapter. The company records sales tax payable at the time a sale on account is made. Patrick Hillcrest, the office manager, questions this practice. He suggests that sales tax payable not be recorded until cash is actually collected for a sale. Which procedure is preferable? Why?

Case 2 Eupora Store Center sells retail store displays to many businesses on account. In order to encourage prompt payment, Eupora offers a sales discount for those who pay within the discount period. Eupora is considering changing its payroll policy for sales personnel from a salary plan to a commission-on-sales plan in order to encourage sales personnel to increase their sales efforts. Commissions would be 5% of sales. Various sales personnel have asked you, the manager, whether commissions would be based on gross sales or on sales after sales discounts and returns and allowances. What should your response be? Explain.

PORTFOLIO ASSESSMENT

Analyzing transactions and journalizing and posting are the first steps in the accounting cycle and critical to the accuracy of information in an accounting information system. If you assign Reinforcement Activity 3—Part A at the end of this chapter and intend to use it as part of an assessment by portfolio evaluation, advise students that their work on this activity will be included in their portfolio. A copy of the Portfolio Assessment form (blackline master in the Teacher's Resource Guide) should be completed by the student, and the Description section should include any comments regarding how the student mastered these concepts and procedures. Alternatively, students might include in their portfolios the solutions to the Automated Accounting feature that follows this chapter.

EXPLAIN

- ❏ Explain that sales on account are entered in the Sales Journal and cash receipts in the Cash Receipts Journal of the Journal Entries screen. Remind students that this is the same process learned in Cycle 2.
- ❏ Explain that customer accounts are maintained the same way as learned in Cycle 2.
- ❏ Explain that two kinds of cash receipts are entered in the cash receipts journal: (1) cash receipts on account, with and without sales discounts, and (2) cash receipts for other transactions that do not affect Accounts Receivable.

DEMONSTRATE

Maintaining the customer list

- ❏ Remind students that maintaining the customer list was learned in Chapter 11.
- ❏ Demonstrate adding a customer by entering a new customer name and clicking the Add Customer button.
- ❏ Demonstrate changing an existing customer by highlighting the Customer's name, entering the change, and clicking the Change Customer button.
- ❏ Demonstrate deleting a customer by highlighting the customer's name and clicking the Delete button. Remind students that a customer with an account balance cannot be deleted.

Journalizing sales of merchandise on account

- ❏ State that to enter a transaction in the Sales Journal screen, students would first select Journal, then the Sales tab.
- ❏ Explain that after the transaction date is entered, the Tab key is pressed.
- ❏ Explain that after the invoice amount is entered, the Tab key is pressed.
- ❏ Explain that if the transaction involves sales tax, the amount is entered in the Sales Tax Credit text box and Tab is pressed. Otherwise, Tab is pressed to bypass the text box.
- ❏ State that the Accounts Receivable debit amount is calculated and displayed automatically.
- ❏ Explain that a customer name is chosen from the Customer drop-down list.
- ❏ Explain that after a transaction is entered, the Post button must be pressed to allow an additional transaction to be entered.

520

AUTOMATED ENTRIES FOR SALES AND CASH RECEIPTS USING SPECIAL JOURNALS FOR A CORPORATION

Many corporations are merchandising businesses that purchase and resell goods. All transactions involving the receipt of cash are recorded in a special journal known as the *cash receipts journal*. The sale of merchandise on account is recorded in the sales journal.

Sales

Corporations maintain a list of their customers. The total owed by all customers listed in the customer file is summarized in Accounts Receivable. Customer accounts may be added, changed, or deleted from the accounting system. To maintain the customer list:

1. Click the Accounts toolbar button.
2. Click the Customers tab.
3. Perform the maintenance:
   a. To add a customer, enter the customer name and click the Add Customer button.
   b. To change an existing customer, highlight the customer's name, enter the correct name, and click the Change Customer button.
   c. To delete a customer, highlight the customer's name and click the Delete button. (A customer with a balance cannot be deleted.)
4. Click the Close button.

The sales journal is used to enter all sales of merchandise on account transactions. To record a sale on account, enter the date, sales invoice number, credit to Sales, credit to Sales Tax, and the name of the customer. The debit to Accounts Receivable will be automatically generated by the accounting system.

To record transactions in the sales journal:

1. Click the Journal toolbar button.
2. Click the Sales tab.
3. Enter the transaction date and press Tab.
4. Enter the invoice number in the Refer. text box and press Tab.
5. Enter the amount of the invoice in the Sales Credit text box and press Tab.
6. If the transaction involves sales tax, enter the amount in the Sales Tax Credit text box and press Tab. Otherwise, press Tab to bypass this text box.
7. The Accounts Receivable debit amount is calculated and displayed automatically.

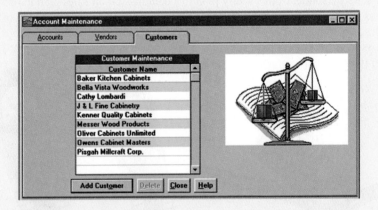

AUTOMATED ACCOUNTING

8. Choose a customer name from the Customer drop-down list.
9. Click the Post button.

Cash Receipts

The cash receipts journal is used to enter all cash receipt transactions. The debit to Cash is automatically calculated and displayed by the computer. There are two types of cash receipts:

1. Direct receipts are cash receipts that do not affect Accounts Receivable, such as a cash sale or cash received from a bank loan.
2. Receipts on account are amounts received from the payment of accounts receivable by customers.

To record transactions in the cash receipts journal:

1. Click the Journal toolbar button.
2. Click the Cash Receipts tab.
3. Enter the transaction date and press Tab.
4. Enter the transaction reference and press Tab.
5. If recording a direct receipt, enter the account numbers and amounts for each of the accounts to debit or credit and press Tab. For example, a direct receipt of cash sales would involve a credit to Sales and a credit to Sales Tax Payable. The cash debit is automatically calculated

and displayed by the computer. The Customer text box is left blank.

6. If recording a receipt on account, press Tab to move to the A.R. Credit text box. Enter the amount of the payment received. The cash debit is automatically calculated and displayed. Press Tab to move to the Customer text box, and choose the customer from the Customer drop-down list.
7. Click the Post button.

Other Transactions

When a corporation needs to record a sales return, or to correct an entry affecting a customer account, the general journal is used. The procedure is similar to other general journal entries.

AUTOMATING APPLICATION PROBLEM 19-5: Journalizing sales transactions

Instructions:

1. Load *Automated Accounting* 7.0 or higher software.
2. Select database F19-1 from the appropriate directory/folder.
3. Select File from the menu bar and choose the Save As menu command. Key the path to the drive and directory that contains your data files. Save the database

with a file name of XXX191 (where XXX are your initials).

4. Access Problem Instructions through the Help menu. Read the Problem Instructions screen.
5. Key the data listed on page 515.
6. Exit the *Automated Accounting* software.

AUTOMATING MASTERY PROBLEM 19-6: Journalizing and posting sales transactions

Instructions:

1. Load *Automated Accounting* 7.0 or higher software.
2. Select database F19-2 from the appropriate directory/folder.
3. Select File from the menu bar and choose the Save As menu command. Key the path to the drive and directory that contains your data files. Save the database with a file name of XXX192 (where XXX are your initials).
4. Access Problem Instructions through the Help menu. Read the Problem Instructions screen.
5. Key the data listed on pages 515–516.
6. Exit the *Automated Accounting* software.

DEMONSTRATE

Journalizing cash receipts on account

❏ State that to enter a transaction in the Cash Receipts Journal screen, students would first select Journal, then the Cash Receipts tab.
❏ Explain that the credit amount is entered in the A.R. Credit text box and the discount amount is entered in the Sales Disc. Dr. text box.
❏ Explain that the Cash Debit amount is entered automatically by the software.
❏ Explain that after the Tab key is pressed from the Sales Disc. Dr. field, the cursor is placed in the Customer field for selecting the appropriate customer from the pull-down list.
❏ Explain that a cash receipt on account without a discount is entered the same way except, of course, that there is no entry in the Sales Disc. Dr. column.

Journalizing other cash receipts

❏ Explain that account number and debit and credit amounts are entered in the usual way.
❏ Explain that the debit to Cash is automatically calculated.

PRACTICE

❏ Assign Automating Application Problem 19-5: Journalizing sales transactions.
❏ Assign Automating Mastery Problem 19-6: Journalizing and posting sales transactions.

ASSESSMENT

❏ Use the Electronic Auditor to assess student understanding.

PORTFOLIO ASSESSMENT

Students should be encouraged to print at least one report from one of the *Automated Accounting* problems to include in their portfolio to demonstrate mastery of automated accounting systems. A copy of the Portfolio Assessment form (blackline master in the Teacher's Resource Guide) should be completed by the student, and the Description section should include any comments regarding how the student mastered these concepts and procedures.

INTRODUCE THE ACTIVITY

❏ Reinforcement Activity 3 begins with Part A and continues with Part B after Chapter 26.

❏ Reinforcement Activity 3 presents the whole accounting cycle for a merchandising business organized as a corporation.

ASSIGN THE ACTIVITY

❏ You may prefer to have your students begin Part A and continue with Part B later. Or, you may reserve Part A to be completed with Part B after Chapter 26.

AUTOMATING THE ACTIVITY

❏ *Automated Accounting 7.0* or higher may be used to automate Reinforcement Activity 3.

❏ Direct students to read the Help screens for specific requirements for automating Reinforcement Activity 3.

ASSESSMENT

❏ Blackline masters for audit tests for Reinforcement Activity 3 are available in the Teacher's Resource Guide in three options: Part A only, Part B only, and Parts A and B combined.

❏ Use the Electronic Auditor to assess performance on automating Reinforcement Activity 3.

PORTFOLIO ASSESSMENT

A reinforcement activity that covers the whole accounting cycle is an ideal exhibit to demonstrate mastery in a portfolio. A copy of the Portfolio Assessment form (blackline master in the Teacher's Resource Guide) should be completed by the student, and the Description section should include any comments regarding how the student mastered these concepts and procedures.

An Accounting Cycle for a Corporation: Journalizing and Posting Transactions

Reinforcement Activity 3 reinforces learnings from Cycle 3, Chapters 18 through 26, and covers a complete accounting cycle for a merchandising business organized as a corporation. Part A reinforces learnings from Chapters 18 and 19. Part B reinforces learnings from Chapters 20 through 26. The general ledger account balances summarize transactions for the first eleven months of a fiscal year. The transactions given for December of the current year are for the last month of the fiscal year.

SUNSHINE GARDENS

Reinforcement Activity 3 includes accounting records for Sunshine Gardens, which is a corporation that sells plants and gardening supplies. The business is located near the city's industrial park and is open Monday through Saturday. Although the building is rented, the corporation owns its office and store equipment.

CHART OF ACCOUNTS

Sunshine Gardens uses the chart of accounts shown on the next page.

JOURNALS AND LEDGERS

Sunshine Gardens uses the following journals and ledgers. Models of the journals and ledgers are shown in the textbook chapters indicated.

Journals and Ledgers	Chapter
Sales journal	19
Purchases journal	18
General journal	18
Cash receipts journal	19
Cash payments journal	18
Accounts receivable ledger	19
Accounts payable ledger	18
General ledger	18

RECORDING TRANSACTIONS

The account balances for the general and subsidiary ledgers are given in the *Working Papers.*

Instructions:

1. Journalize the following transactions completed during December of the current year. Use page 12 of a sales journal, a purchases journal, a general journal, and a cash receipts journal. Use pages 23 and 24 of a cash payments journal. Sunshine Gardens offers its customers terms of 1/10, n/30. The sales tax rate is 8%. Source documents are abbreviated as follows: check, C; credit memorandum, CM; debit memorandum, DM; memorandum, M; purchase invoice, P; receipt, R; sales invoice, S; cash register tape, T.

MATERIALS

❏ Manual Accounting:
Working Papers for Reinforcement Activity 3—Part A
Teacher's Edition of the Working Papers for Reinforcement Activity 3—Part A
Blackline Master of Audit Test

❏ Automated Accounting:
Automated Accounting 7.0 or higher
The Electronic Auditor

SUNSHINE GARDENS CHART OF ACCOUNTS

Balance Sheet Accounts

(1000) ASSETS
1100 Current Assets
1105 Cash
1110 Petty Cash
1115 Notes Receivable
1120 Interest Receivable
1125 Accounts Receivable
1130 Allowance for Uncollectible Accounts
1135 Merchandise Inventory
1140 Supplies
1145 Prepaid Insurance
1200 Plant Assets
1205 Office Equipment
1210 Accumulated Depreciation—
     Office Equipment
1215 Store Equipment
1220 Accumulated Depreciation—
     Store Equipment

(2000) LIABILITIES
2100 Current Liabilities
2105 Notes Payable
2110 Interest Payable
2115 Accounts Payable
2120 Employee Income Tax Payable
2125 Federal Income Tax Payable
2130 Social Security Tax Payable
2135 Medicare Tax Payable
2140 Sales Tax Payable
2145 Unemployment Tax Payable—Federal
2150 Unemployment Tax Payable—State
2155 Health Insurance Premiums Payable
2160 Dividends Payable

(3000) STOCKHOLDERS' EQUITY
3105 Capital Stock
3110 Retained Earnings
3115 Dividends
3120 Income Summary

Income Statement Accounts

(4000) OPERATING REVENUE
4105 Sales
4110 Sales Discount
4115 Sales Returns and Allowances

(5000) COST OF MERCHANDISE
5105 Purchases
5110 Purchases Discount
5115 Purchases Returns and Allowances

(6000) OPERATING EXPENSES
6105 Advertising Expense
6110 Cash Short and Over
6115 Credit Card Fee Expense
6120 Depreciation Expense—Office Equipment
6125 Depreciation Expense—Store Equipment
6130 Insurance Expense
6135 Miscellaneous Expense
6140 Payroll Taxes Expense
6145 Rent Expense
6150 Repair Expense
6155 Salary Expense
6160 Supplies Expense
6165 Uncollectible Accounts Expense
6170 Utilities Expense

(7000) OTHER REVENUE
7105 Gain on Plant Assets
7110 Interest Income

(8000) OTHER EXPENSES
8105 Interest Expense
8110 Loss on Plant Assets

(9000) INCOME TAX EXPENSE
9105 Federal Income Tax Expense

Dec. 1. Paid cash for rent, $1,750.00. C621.
1. Received cash on account from Jenni Baker, $1,336.50, covering S81 for $1,350.00 ($1,250.00 plus sales tax, $100.00), less discount and sales tax. R92.
2. Purchased merchandise on account from Glenson Company, $4,658.00. P125.
2. Granted credit to Patrick Felton for merchandise returned, $126.00, plus sales tax, from S73. CM18.
2. Received cash on account from Patrick Felton, $1,543.40 (covering S73 less CM18), no discount. R93.
2. Sold merchandise on account to Pam Ruocco, $2,475.00, plus sales tax. S86.
3. Paid cash on account to Buntin Supply Company covering P92 for $4,260.00, less 2% discount. C622.
3. Recorded cash and credit card sales, $8,364.30, plus sales tax, $669.14; total, $9,033.44. T3.

TEACHING STRATEGIES   DIFFERENT LEARNING ABILITIES

Divide the class into groups of two students each. After completing the recording of transactions as a homework assignment, students evaluate each other's work in class. Students are permitted to correct their work based on their partner's evaluation. This cooperative learning activity should not take more than 15 to 20 minutes of class time.

Posting. Post the items that are to be posted individually. Post the journals in this order: sales journal, purchases journal, general journal, cash receipts journal, and cash payments journal.

5. Returned merchandise to Glenson Company, $420.00, from P90. DM21.
5. Paid cash on account to SHF Corp., covering P93 for $4,255.80, less 2% discount. C623.
6. Received cash on account from Samuel Horton, $3,341.25, covering S82 for $3,375.00 ($3,125.00 plus sales tax, $250.00), less discount and sales tax. R94.
7. Purchased merchandise on account from Walbash Manufacturing, $6,230.00. P126.
8. Sold merchandise on account to Hilldale Middle School, $645.00, no sales tax. S87.
8. Paid cash on account to Walbash Manufacturing, covering P94 for $3,354.60, less 1% discount. C624.
9. Paid cash for liability for November health insurance premiums, $725.00. C625.
10. Recorded cash and credit card sales, $12,632.20, plus sales tax, $1,010.58; total, $13,642.78. T10.
   Posting. Post the items that are to be posted individually.
12. Purchased merchandise on account from SHF Corp., $8,326.00. P127.
12. Paid cash for miscellaneous expense, $153.30. C626.
12. Received cash on account from Pam Ruocco, $2,646.27, covering S86 for $2,673.00 ($2,475.00 plus sales tax, $198.00), less discount and sales tax. R95.
13. Paid cash for supplies, $63.30. C627.
14. Sold merchandise on account to Camille Nelson for $2,875.00, plus sales tax. S88.
14. Paid cash for advertising, $634.30. C628.
15. Paid cash for semimonthly payroll, $3,319.00 (total payroll, $4,650.00, less deductions: employee income tax, $634.00; social security tax, $302.25; Medicare tax, $69.75; health insurance premiums, $325.00). C629.
15. Recorded employer payroll taxes expense, $426.65 (social security tax, $302.25; Medicare tax, $69.75; federal unemployment tax, $7.05; state unemployment tax, $47.60). M75.
15. Paid cash for liability for employee income tax, $2,125.00; social security tax, $1,150.00; Medicare tax, $265.40. C630.
15. Paid cash for quarterly estimated federal income tax, $3,000.00. C631. (Debit Federal Income Tax Expense; credit Cash.)
15. Paid cash to replenish the petty cash fund, $176.50: supplies, $25.75; advertising, $45.00; miscellaneous, $108.75; cash over, $3.00. C632.
16. Paid cash on account to Walbash Manufacturing, covering P126 for $6,230.00, less 1% discount. C633.
16. Received cash on account from Camille Nelson, $2,103.34, covering S83; no discount. R96.
16. Received cash on account from Hilldale Middle School, covering S87 for $645.00, less discount. R97.
17. Purchased merchandise for cash, $512.60. C634.
17. Paid cash for miscellaneous expense, $82.60. C635.
17. Recorded cash and credit card sales, $18,463.00, plus sales tax, $1,477.04; total, $19,940.04. T17.
   Posting. Post the items that are to be posted individually.

2. Prove and rule page 23 of the cash payments journal.
3. Forward the totals from page 23 to page 24 of the cash payments journal.
4. Continue recording the following transactions.

SOFTWARE FOCUS

Automated Accounting 7.0 or higher can be used to complete Reinforcement Activity 3. Students should read the Help screens for specific instructions on automating this reinforcement activity.

Dec. 19. Sold merchandise on account to Patrick Felton for $1,850.00, plus sales tax. S89.
20. Paid cash on account to Glenson Company, $2,364.70, covering P90 for $2,784.70, less DM21, $420.00; no discount. C636.
21. Paid cash on account to Draper Company, $2,643.50, covering P91; no discount. C637.
22. Purchased merchandise on account from Buntin Supply Company, $7,165.00. P128.
22. Paid cash on account to SHF Corp. covering P127 for $8,326.00, less 2% discount. C638.
23. Sold merchandise on account to Samuel Horton for $672.00, plus sales tax. S90.
24. Recorded cash and credit card sales, $12,543.60, plus sales tax, $1,003.49; total, $13,547.09. T24.
   Posting. Post the items that are to be posted individually.
26. Bought supplies on account from Hinsdale Supply Co., $533.00. M76.
27. Sold merchandise on account to Jenni Baker, $1,454.00, plus sales tax. S91.
27. Paid cash for repairs, $153.20. C639.
28. Purchased merchandise on account from Walbash Manufacturing, $12,734.00. P129.
28. Received cash on account from Patrick Felton, $1,978.02, covering S89 for $1,998.00 ($1,850.00 plus sales tax, $148.00), less discount and sales tax. R98.
29. Paid cash on account to Glenson Company, $4,658.00, covering P125; no discount. C640.
29. Sold merchandise on account to Pam Ruocco, $975.00, plus sales tax. S92.
30. Paid cash for liability for sales tax, $4,932.60. C641. (Debit Sales Tax Payable; credit Cash.)
31. Paid cash for semimonthly payroll, $3,284.00 (total payroll, $4,600.00, less deductions: employee income tax, $623.00; social security tax, $299.00; Medicare tax, $69.00; health insurance premiums, $325.00). C642.
31. Recorded employer payroll taxes expense, $421.50 (social security tax, $299.00; Medicare tax, $69.00; federal unemployment tax, $6.90; state unemployment tax, $46.60). M77.
31. Recorded credit card fee expense for December, $846.60. M78. (Debit Credit Card Fee Expense; credit Cash.)
31. Paid cash to replenish the petty cash fund, $109.20: supplies, $34.80; advertising, $22.00; miscellaneous, $46.40; cash short, $6.00. C643.
31. Recorded cash and credit card sales, $5,472.00, plus sales tax, $437.76; total, $5,909.76. T31.
   Posting. Post the items that are to be posted individually.

5. Prove and rule the sales journal. Post the totals of the special columns.
6. Total and rule the purchases journal. Post the total.
7. Prove the equality of debits and credits for the cash receipts and cash payments journals.
8. Prove cash. The balance on the next unused check stub on December 31 is $21,796.26.
9. Rule the cash receipts journal. Post the totals of the special columns.
10. Rule the cash payments journal. Post the totals of the special columns.
11. Prepare a schedule of accounts receivable and a schedule of accounts payable. Compare each schedule total with the balance of the controlling account in the general ledger. The total and balance should be the same.

The ledgers used in Reinforcement Activity 3—Part A are needed to complete Reinforcement Activity 3—Part B.

REINFORCEMENT ACTIVITY 3—PART A **525**

	SCOPE AND SEQUENCE		ENHANCING	
	NEW	REVIEW/ EXTENSION	SPECIAL FEATURES	
INTRODUCE THE CHAPTER			Accounting in Your Career: Credit Problems Thinking about Careers	
Uncollectible accounts	✓			
LESSSON 20-1 ESTIMATING AND RECORDING UNCOLLECTIBLE ACCOUNTS EXPENSE			Math Work Sheet, Chapter 20, Part A Math Work Sheet, Chapter 20, Part B Accounting at Work: Tracy Stanhoff	
Allowance method of recording losses from uncollectible accounts	✓			
Calculating estimated uncollectible accounts expense	✓			
Journalizing an adjustment for uncollectible accounts expense	✓			
Posting an adjusting entry for uncollectible accounts expense	✓			
LESSSON 20-2 WRITING OFF AND COLLECTING UNCOLLECTIBLE ACCOUNTS RECEIVABLE			Legal Issues in Accounting: Forming a Corporation	
Journalizing writing off an uncollectible account receivable	✓			
Posting an entry to write off an uncollectible account receivable		✓		
Reopening an account previously written off	✓			
Recording cash received for an account previously written off	✓			
Posting entries for collecting a written-off account receivable		✓		
PUTTING IT ALL TOGETHER			Explore Accounting Internet Activity Applied Communication Cases for Critical Thinking 1, 2 and 3	

UNCOLLECTIBLE ACCOUNTS RECEIVABLE

	INSTRUCTION		PRACTICE AND ASSESSMENT		
	TECHNOLOGY AND MEDIA	TEACHING STRATEGIES	GUIDED PRACTICE	INDEPENDENT PRACTICE	RETEACHING AND ENRICHMENT
	Internet Activity	Software Focus			
	South-Western Accounting Video: Computerized Accounting— Uncollectible Accounts Transparency M	Limited English Proficiency (LEP) Students Applied Skills: Mathematics	Terms Review Audit Your Understanding Work Together	On Your Own Application Problem 20-1 Ongoing Assessment, p. 531	Reteach, p. 531 Enrich, p. 532
	CNN Accounting Video Transparencies M and O	Expanding Beyond the Classroom Building Study Skills Applied Skills: Language Arts	Term Review Audit Your Understanding Work Together	On Your Own Application Problem 20-2 Ongoing Assessment, p. 537	Reteach, p. 537 Enrich, p. 538
	Transparency 20-1 Automated Accounting Accounting Connection	Applied Skills: Word Processing Applied Skills: Writing Across the Curriculum		Application Problem 20-3 Mastery Problem 20-4 Study Guide 20 Chapter 20 Test ExamViewPro or Westest, Chapter 20 Portfolio Assessment	Enrich, p. 539 Challenge Problem 20-5 Reteach, p. 539 Recycling Problem 20-1 Accounting Connection

OBJECTIVES

❑ Define accounting terms related to uncollectible accounts.

❑ Identify accounting concepts and practices related to uncollectible accounts.

❑ Calculate, journalize, and post estimated uncollectible accounts expense.

MOTIVATE

Ask students how the expenses incurred to create revenue can be recorded if those expenses are not known at the fiscal year end. When the exact amount of an expense is unknown, accountants estimate the expense. Estimating expenses based on objective information assures that financial statements are prepared using the *Matching Expenses with Revenue* concept.

Preview

❑ Preview the accounting terms and definitions introduced in this lesson: uncollectible accounts, allowance method of recording losses from uncollectible accounts, book value, and book value of accounts receivable.

❑ Direct students to read the headings at the top of each page in this lesson and to examine the illustrations given.

❑ Explain that this lesson presents how to calculate and record an estimate of uncollectible accounts expense.

EXPLAIN

❑ Ask students to discuss the *Matching Expenses with Revenue* concept.

❑ Review the purpose of a contra account.

❑ Explain why a contra account is used to record the estimated future uncollectible accounts.

❑ Ask students to identify the two objectives of using the allowance method.

❑ Ask students to describe how to calculate the book value of accounts receivable.

❑ Ask students to read the F.Y.I. to learn other titles used to record uncollectible accounts.

ALLOWANCE METHOD OF RECORDING LOSSES FROM UNCOLLECTIBLE ACCOUNTS

Uncollectible Accounts Expense		Accounts Receivable		Allowance for Uncollectible Accounts	
Debit	Credit	Debit	Credit	Debit	Credit
↑	↓	↑	↓	↓	↑

With each sale on account, a business takes a risk that customers will not pay their accounts. This risk is a cost of doing business that should be recorded as an expense in the same accounting period that the revenue is earned. Accurate financial reporting requires that expenses be recorded in the fiscal period in which the expenses contribute to earning revenue. (CONCEPT: *Matching Expenses with Revenue*)

At the end of a fiscal year, a business does not know which customer accounts will become uncollectible. If a business knew exactly which accounts would become uncollectible, it could credit Accounts Receivable and each customer account for the uncollectible amounts and debit Uncollectible Accounts Expense for the same amounts.

To solve this accounting problem, a business can calculate and record an *estimated* amount of uncollectible accounts expense. Estimating uncollectible accounts expense at the end of a fiscal period accomplishes two objectives:

(1) Reports a balance sheet amount for Accounts Receivable that reflects the amount the business expects to collect in the future.

(2) Recognizes the expense of uncollectible accounts in the same period in which the related revenue is recorded.

To record estimated uncollectible accounts, an adjusting entry is made affecting two accounts. The estimated amount of uncollectible accounts is debited to Uncollectible Accounts Expense and credited to an account titled Allowance for Uncollectible Accounts.

An account that reduces a related account is known as a contra account. Allowance for Uncollectible Accounts is a contra account to its related asset account, Accounts Receivable.

Crediting the estimated value of uncollectible accounts to a contra account is called the **allowance method of recording losses from uncollectible accounts.** The difference between an asset's account balance and its related contra account balance is called **book value.** The difference between the balance of Accounts Receivable and its contra account, Allowance for Uncollectible Accounts, is called the **book value of accounts receivable.** The book value of accounts receivable, reported on the balance sheet, represents the total amount of accounts receivable the business expects to collect in the future.

A contra account is usually assigned the next number of the account number sequence after its related account in the chart of accounts. Winning Edge's accounts receivable account is numbered 1125. Because Winning Edge numbers its accounts in sequences of five, Allowance for Uncollectible Accounts is numbered 1130.

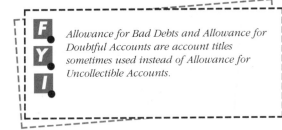

F.Y.I. *Allowance for Bad Debts and Allowance for Doubtful Accounts are account titles sometimes used instead of Allowance for Uncollectible Accounts.*

MATERIALS

❑ Transparencies:
M, Blank General Journal

❑ Working Papers:
Teacher's Edition of the Working Papers for Lesson 20-1

❑ Work Sheets:
Math Work Sheet, Chapter 20, Part A
Math Work Sheet, Chapter 20, Part B

❑ Videos:
South-Western Accounting Video

ESTIMATING UNCOLLECTIBLE ACCOUNTS EXPENSE

Total Sales on Account	×	Percentage	=	Estimated Uncollectible Accounts Expense
$982,800.00	×	1%	=	$9,828.00

Many businesses use a percentage of total sales on account to estimate uncollectible accounts expense. Each sale on account represents a risk of loss from an uncollectible account. Therefore, if the estimated percentage of loss is accurate, the amount of uncollectible accounts expense will be accurate regardless of when the actual losses occur.

Since a sale on account creates a risk of loss, estimating the percentage of uncollectible accounts expense for the same period matches sales revenue with the related uncollectible accounts expense. (CONCEPT: *Matching Expenses with Revenue*)

Winning Edge estimates uncollectible accounts expense by calculating a percentage of total sales on account. A review of Winning Edge's previous experience in collecting sales on account shows that actual uncollectible accounts expense has been about 1% of total sales on account. The company's total sales on account for the year is $982,800.00. Thus, Winning Edge estimates that $9,828.00 of the current fiscal period's sales on account will eventually be uncollectible.

ACCOUNTING AT WORK

TRACY STANHOFF

I n 1988 Tracy Stanhoff founded AdPro, located in Huntington Beach, California, which offers full-service advertising and public relations. The company will perform any or all functions including marketing plans, display booths, advertising, graphic design, and in-house printing services.

Tracy holds a bachelor's degree in journalism, with minors in marketing, economics, and art. She also studied enough accounting to be able to read financial statements and understand the importance of accounting to a business.

As a member of the Potawatomi Tribe, Tracy was able to get some help from the National Center for American Indian Enterprise in locating clients for her new business. The Center helps connect new businesses with leading Fortune 500 companies and federal agencies. Today Tracy's company provides services for both small, start-up businesses and for multinational corporations.

She firmly believes in the value of a liberal education for providing a wide and varied background. Communication skills include speaking and writing clearly. "Listening skills," says Tracy, "are very important too—you have to hear what people are really saying."

529

529

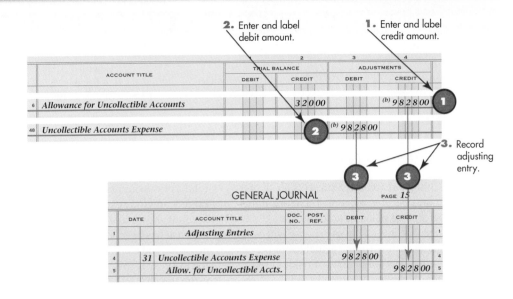

2. Enter and label debit amount.

1. Enter and label credit amount.

3. Record adjusting entry.

The percentage of total sales on account method of estimating uncollectible accounts expense assumes that a portion of every sale on account dollar will become uncollectible. Winning Edge has estimated that 1% of its $982,800.00 sales on account, or $9,828.00, will eventually become uncollectible.

At the end of a fiscal period, an adjustment for uncollectible accounts expense is planned on a work sheet.

The Allowance for Uncollectible Accounts balance in the Trial Balance Credit column, $320.00, is the allowance estimate from the previous fiscal period that has not yet been identified as uncollectible.

When the allowance account has a previous credit balance, the amount of the adjustment is added to the previous balance. This new balance of the allowance account is the estimated amount of accounts receivable that will eventually become uncollectible.

The adjustment planned on the work sheet must be recorded in a general journal and posted to the general ledger accounts.

Uncollectible Accounts Expense	
Dec. 31 Adj. 9,828.00	

Allowance for Uncollectible Accounts	
	Bal. 320.00
	Dec. 31 Adj. 9,828.00
	(New Bal. 10,148.00)

 Analyzing and journalizing an adjustment for uncollectible accounts expense

STEPS

1. Enter the estimated uncollectible amount, *$9,828.00*, in the Adjustments Credit column on the Allowance for Uncollectible Accounts line of the work sheet. Label the adjustment *(b)* with a small letter in parentheses.

2. Enter the same amount, *$9,828.00*, in the Adjustments Credit column on the Uncollectible Accounts Expense line of the work sheet. Label the adjustment using the same letter, *(b)*.

3. Use the debit and credit amounts on the work sheet to record an adjusting entry in a general journal.

APPLIED SKILLS

MATHEMATICS

Use the math work sheet in the Masters and Solutions to Enrichment/Application section of the Teacher's Resource Guide to integrate applied mathematics. In this work sheet, students will apply math concepts to calculate estimated uncollectible accounts expense using a percentage of total sales on account and calculate book value of accounts receivable.

POSTING AN ADJUSTING ENTRY FOR UNCOLLECTIBLE ACCOUNTS EXPENSE

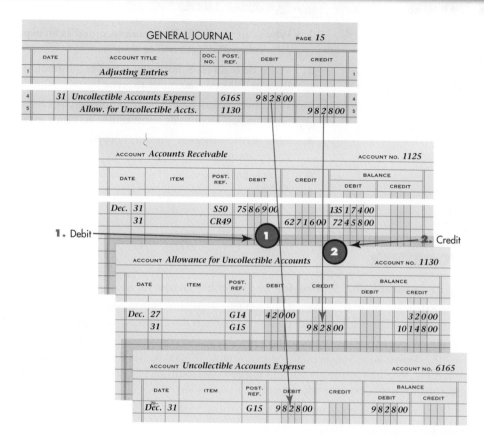

GENERAL JOURNAL — PAGE 15

	DATE	ACCOUNT TITLE	DOC. NO.	POST. REF.	DEBIT	CREDIT	
1		*Adjusting Entries*					1
4	31	Uncollectible Accounts Expense		6165	9 8 2 8 00		4
5		Allow. for Uncollectible Accts.		1130		9 8 2 8 00	5

ACCOUNT *Accounts Receivable*   ACCOUNT NO. *1125*

DATE	ITEM	POST. REF.	DEBIT	CREDIT	BALANCE DEBIT	BALANCE CREDIT
Dec. 31		S50	75 86 9 00		135 17 4 00	
31		CR49		62 71 6 00	72 45 8 00	

1. Debit

ACCOUNT *Allowance for Uncollectible Accounts*   ACCOUNT NO. *1130*

DATE	ITEM	POST. REF.	DEBIT	CREDIT	BALANCE DEBIT	BALANCE CREDIT
Dec. 27		G14	4 2 0 00			3 2 0 00
31		G15		9 8 2 8 00		10 1 4 8 00

2. Credit

ACCOUNT *Uncollectible Accounts Expense*   ACCOUNT NO. *6165*

DATE	ITEM	POST. REF.	DEBIT	CREDIT	BALANCE DEBIT	BALANCE CREDIT
Dec. 31		G15	9 8 2 8 00		9 8 2 8 00	

The adjustment for uncollectible accounts expense planned on the work sheet is recorded as an adjusting entry in the general journal. The adjusting entry is then posted to the general ledger.

The adjusting entry impacts two of the three accounts related to accounts receivable. After the adjustment, Allowance for Uncollectible Accounts has a credit balance of $10,148.00. The balance of this contra account is an estimate of outstanding accounts receivable that will become uncollectible during the next fiscal period.

The debit balance of Uncollectible Accounts Expense, $9,828.00, is the estimated uncollectible accounts resulting from sales on account during the current fiscal year.

The adjusting entry does *not* impact the balance of Accounts Receivable. Accounts Receivable has a debit balance of $72,458.00 before and after the adjusting entry is posted.

The book value of accounts receivable on December 31, $62,310.00, is an estimate of the amount of accounts receivable Winning Edge expects to collect during the next fiscal year.

Accounts Receivable	−	Balance of Allowance for Uncollectible Accounts	=	Book Value of Accounts Receivable
$72,458.00	−	$10,148.00	=	$62,310.00

CHAPTER 20   Accounting for Uncollectible Accounts Receivable   **531**

Terms Review

Call on students to define the terms in the Terms Review. Ask the class if the definitions are correct and whether the complete definitions have been given or if anything needs to be added. The suggested definition is given in the Glossary.

Audit Your Understanding

Call on students to answer the Audit Your Understanding questions. Ask the class if the answer is correct and/or complete. Answers are given in Appendix D of the textbook.

Work Together

Have students write the solutions to the Work Together problems as you guide the class through the examples.

❑ Call on students to write the calculation of the estimated uncollectible accounts expense on the board.

❑ Ask one student to explain the work sheet adjustment as another student analyzes the adjusting entry in T accounts on the board.

❑ Direct students to post the adjusting entry to the general ledger.

On Your Own

❑ Assign the On Your Own problems to be worked independently.

❑ Use the Ongoing Assessment techniques to diagnose student understanding.

Application Problem

❑ Assign Application Problem 20-1: Estimating and journalizing entries for uncollectible accounts expense.

TERMS REVIEW

uncollectible accounts

allowance method of recording losses from uncollectible accounts

book value

book value of accounts receivable

AUDIT YOUR UNDERSTANDING

1. Why is an uncollectible account recorded as an expense rather than a reduction in revenue?

2. When do businesses normally estimate the amount of their uncollectible accounts expense?

3. What two objectives will be accomplished by recording an estimated amount of uncollectible accounts expense?

4. Why is Allowance for Uncollectible Accounts called a contra account?

5. How is the book value of accounts receivable calculated?

WORK TOGETHER

Estimating and journalizing entries for uncollectible accounts expense

A general journal, work sheet, and selected general ledger accounts for Velson Company are given in the *Working Papers*. Your instructor will guide you through the following examples.

6. Velson Company estimates uncollectible accounts expense as 0.3% of its total sales on account. During the current year, Velson had credit sales of $2,152,000.00. The balance in Allowance for Uncollectible Accounts before adjustment is a $853.00 credit. As of December 31, record the uncollectible accounts expense adjustment on a work sheet.

7. Journalize the adjusting entry on page 13 of a general journal.

8. Post the adjusting entry to the general ledger.

ON YOUR OWN

Estimating and journalizing entries for uncollectible accounts expense

A general journal, work sheet, and selected general ledger accounts for McCain Company are given in the *Working Papers*. Work independently to complete these problems.

9. The McCain Company estimates uncollectible accounts expense as 0.8% of its total sales on account. During the current year, McCain had credit sales of $876,000.00. The balance in Allowance for Uncollectible Accounts before adjustment is a $145.00 credit. As of December 31, record the uncollectible accounts expense adjustment on a work sheet.

10. Journalize the adjusting entry on page 18 of a general journal.

11. Post the adjusting entry to the general ledger.

ENRICH

❑ Assign the Accounting at Work feature on page 529.

❑ Show the South-Western Accounting Video: Computerized Accounting—Uncollectible Accounts.

CLOSE

❑ Ask students to briefly summarize the procedures for recording uncollectible accounts expense.

OBJECTIVES

❏ Define accounting terms related to uncollectible accounts.
❏ Identify accounting concepts and practices related to uncollectible accounts.
❏ Journalize and post entries related to writing off and collecting uncollectible accounts receivable.

JOURNALIZING WRITING OFF AN UNCOLLECTIBLE ACCOUNT RECEIVABLE

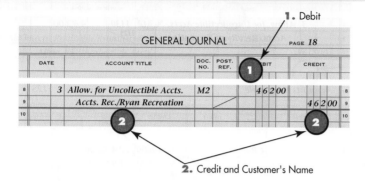

1. Debit

	DATE	ACCOUNT TITLE	DOC. NO.	POST. REF.	DEBIT	CREDIT	
8	3	Allow. for Uncollectible Accts.	M2		4 6 2 00		8
9		Accts. Rec./Ryan Recreation				4 6 2 00	9
10							10

GENERAL JOURNAL   PAGE 18

2. Credit and Customer's Name

When a customer account is determined to be uncollectible, a journal entry is made to cancel the uncollectible account. This entry cancels the uncollectible amount from the general ledger account Accounts Receivable as well as the customer account in the accounts receivable subsidiary ledger. Canceling the balance of a customer account because the customer does not pay is called **writing off an account.**

After months of unsuccessful collection efforts, Winning Edge decides that the past-due account of Ryan Recreation is uncollectible.

January 3. Wrote off Ryan Recreation's past-due account as uncollectible, $462.00. Memorandum No. 2.

Because the account of Ryan Recreation has been determined to be uncollectible, the $462.00 is now an *actual* uncollectible amount. Therefore, the amount of the uncollectible account is deducted from the allowance account.

Accounts Receivable is credited to reduce the balance due from customers. Ryan Recreation's account is also credited to cancel the debit balance of the account. Ryan Recreation's account is written off.

The book value of accounts receivable is the same both before and after writing off an uncollectible account. This is true because the same amount is deducted from the accounts receivable and the allowance accounts.

GENERAL LEDGER
Allowance for Uncollectible Accounts

Jan. 3	462.00	Bal.	10,148.00
		(New Bal.	9,686.00)

Accounts Receivable

Bal.	72,458.00	Jan. 3	462.00
(New Bal.	71,996.00)		

ACCOUNTS RECEIVABLE LEDGER
Ryan Recreation

Bal.	462.00	Jan. 3	462.00
(New Bal.	zero)		

	Before Account Written Off	After Account Written Off
Accounts Receivable	$ 72,458.00	$ 71,996.00
Allowance for Uncollectible Accounts	−10,148.00	−9,686.00
Book Value	$ 62,310.00	$ 62,310.00

CHAPTER 20   Accounting for Uncollectible Accounts Receivable   **533**

MOTIVATE

At the end of a fiscal year, a business does not know which customer accounts will become uncollectible. In this lesson, students learn what to do when they learn that a customer's account becomes uncollectible.

Preview

❏ Preview the accounting term "writing off an account" and its definition, introduced in this lesson.
❏ Direct students to read the headings at the top of each page in this lesson and to examine the illustrations given.

EXPLAIN

❏ Ask students to identify reasons why a customer (individual or business) may be unable to pay its account.
❏ Explain that efforts should continue to collect the account even though the account has been written off.
❏ Ask students to explain why the book value of accounts receivable is the same before and after the account is written off.

DEMONSTRATE

Analyze the transaction

❏ Draw three T accounts on the board.
❏ Read the transaction statement.
❏ Ask students to analyze the transaction by answering: what accounts are affected, are they increased or decreased, and are they debited or credited? Complete the T accounts as the information is provided.
❏ Review the effect on the account for Ryan Recreation in the accounts receivable ledger.

Record the transaction

❏ Use Transparency M to illustrate recording the transaction in the general journal or direct students to the illustration.
❏ Direct students to journalize the transaction, following the two steps illustrated.

MATERIALS

❏ Transparencies:
20-1, Chapter Summary
M, Blank General Journal
O, Blank Cash Receipts Journal (8-Column)
❏ Working Papers:
Teacher's Edition of the Working Papers for Lesson 20-2

❏ Software:
Accounting Connection, Chapter 20
Automated Accounting 7.0 or higher and Accounting Textbook Template
❏ Videos:
CNN Accounting Video

533

536

CASH RECEIPTS JOURNAL											PAGE 51
				1	2	3	4	5	6	7	8
				GENERAL		ACCOUNTS RECEIVABLE CREDIT	SALES CREDIT	SALES TAX PAYABLE		SALES DISCOUNT DEBIT	CASH DEBIT
DATE	ACCOUNT TITLE	DOC. NO.	POST. REF.	DEBIT	CREDIT			DEBIT	CREDIT		
29	Ryan Recreation	R8				462 00					462 00

After the entry to reopen Ryan Recreation's account is recorded, an entry is made to record the cash received on Ryan Recreation's account.

January 29. Received cash in full payment of Ryan Recreation's account, previously written off as uncollectible, $462.00. Memorandum No. 3 and Receipt No. 8.

The entry in the cash receipts journal is the same as for any other collection of accounts receivable.

GENERAL LEDGER
Cash

Jan. 29	462.00	

Accounts Receivable

| Bal. | 72,458.00 | Jan. 3 | 462.00 |
| Jan. 29 | 462.00 | Jan. 29 | 462.00 |

ACCOUNTS RECEIVABLE LEDGER
Ryan Recreation

Bal.	462.00	Jan. 3	462.00
Jan. 29	462.00	Jan. 29	462.00
		(New Bal.	zero)

LEGAL ISSUES IN ACCOUNTING

FORMING A CORPORATION

A corporation is a business organization that has the legal rights of a person. A corporation's legal rights exist separately from the legal rights of its owners. A person becomes an owner of a corporation by purchasing shares of stock. Thus, owners of corporations are called *stockholders*.

The corporate form of business organization offers the following advantages: (1) *Expanded resources.* By selling stock, the corporation has access to more capital than as a proprietorship or partnership. (2) *Limited liability.* Stockholders will not be held personally responsible for the company's liabilities. (3) *Ease of ownership transfer.* Ownership is transferred when a share of stock is

536

sold. Selling stock does not affect the continuation of the corporation. (4) *Legal rights.* Because a corporation has the legal rights of a person, the corporation may buy, own, and sell property in its corporate name.

The disadvantages of corporations include: (1) *High organization cost.* A corporation is the most complex and expensive form of business to establish. (2) *Extensive government regulation.* Corporations must comply with numerous government regulations. (3) *Double taxation.* As separate legal entities, the earnings of corporations are subject to taxation. The profits distributed to stockholders also are subject to taxation as stockholders' personal income.

APPLIED SKILLS

LANGUAGE ARTS

Paraphrasing, Writing Complete Sentences, and Identifying Subjects. For additional practice in language arts skills, direct students to write answers to Audit Your Understanding questions in their own words and in complete sentences. To further practice language arts skills, ask students to underline the subject(s) in each sentence of their answers.

POSTING ENTRIES FOR COLLECTING A WRITTEN-OFF ACCOUNT RECEIVABLE

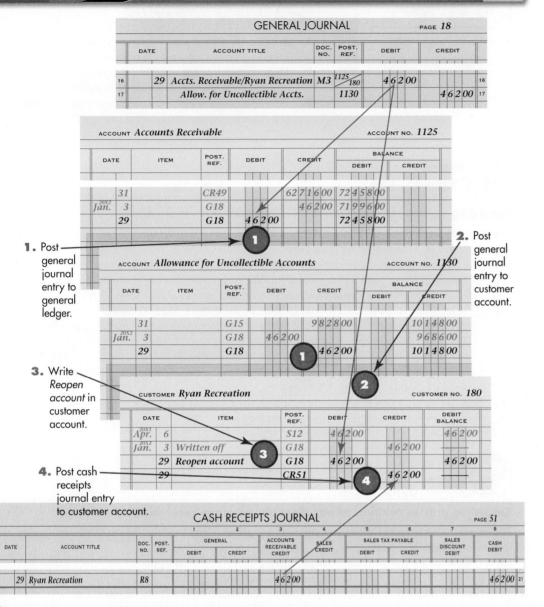

1. Post general journal entry to general ledger.

2. Post general journal entry to customer account.

3. Write *Reopen account* in customer account.

4. Post cash receipts journal entry to customer account.

Posting entries for collecting a written-off account receivable

1. Post the general journal entry to the general ledger.
2. Post the debit portion of the general journal entry to the customer account.
3. Write the words *Reopen account* in the Item column of the customer account.
4. Post the cash receipts journal entry to the customer account.

❏ Remind students that they have already learned how to post from the general journal and cash receipts journal to general and accounts receivable ledger accounts.

❏ Ask students to summarize the two entries required to record cash received from a previously written-off account.

❏ Ask students to explain why the words "Reopen account" are written in the customer's account.

DEMONSTRATE

❏ Post the entries to the general ledger and accounts receivable ledger, using the four steps shown.

❏ Point out that "Reopen account" is recorded in the Item column of the customer's account to provide a history for that customer.

❏ Remind students that the posting process includes recording both the amount in the ledger accounts and the posting references in both the accounts and journals.

ONGOING ASSESSMENT

❏ Assessment is an ongoing process. Circulate through the classroom or lab, observing which students have problems with the assignments.

❏ Troubleshooting: Diagnose what kinds of problems students have with this lesson. Students may have trouble understanding why two entries are recorded for a single event (collecting a previously written-off account).

❏ Assess student understanding by checking solutions to Independent Practice assignments.

RETEACH

❏ Ask a student to make up original transactions to write off and subsequently collect an uncollectible account; write the transactions on the board or an overhead transparency.

❏ Ask another student to analyze the transactions using T accounts.

❏ Ask a student to record the transactions in the journals.

Call on students to define the term in the Term Review. Ask the class if the definition is correct and whether the complete definition has been given or if anything needs to be added. The suggested definition is given in the Glossary.

Audit Your Understanding
Call on students to answer the Audit Your Understanding questions. Ask the class if the answer is correct and/or complete. Answers are given in Appendix D of the textbook.

Work Together
Have students write the solutions to the Work Together problems as you guide the class through the examples.

❏ Direct students to record each transaction in the journal as you elicit class participation in analyzing and recording each transaction.

❏ Direct students to post the transactions to the accounts receivable accounts and the general ledger.

INDEPENDENT PRACTICE

On Your Own
❏ Assign the On Your Own problems to be worked independently.

❏ Use the Ongoing Assessment techniques to diagnose student understanding.

Application Problem
❏ Assign Application Problem 20-2: Recording entries related to uncollectible accounts receivable.

TERM REVIEW

writing off an account

AUDIT YOUR UNDERSTANDING

1. Why is Allowance for Uncollectible Accounts debited when a customer account is written off?
2. Does the book value of accounts receivable differ before and after writing off an account? Explain.
3. Why is a customer account reopened when the account is paid after being previously written off?

WORK TOGETHER

Recording entries relating to uncollectible accounts receivable

The journals and ledgers for Spartan Company are given in the *Working Papers*. Your instructor will guide you through the following examples.

4. The following transactions occurred during June of the current year. Journalize the transactions using page 6 of a general journal and page 9 of a cash receipts journal.

    June   3. Wrote off Kelton Corporation's past-due account as uncollectible, $396.00. M14.
        12. Wrote off Matlin Co.'s past-due account as uncollectible, $575.00. M18.
        13. Received cash in full payment of Marris Inc.'s account, previously written off as uncollectible, $571.00. M19 and R134.
        25. Wrote off Johnston, Inc.'s past-due account as uncollectible, $819.00. M23.
        30. Received cash in full payment of Kelton Corporation's account, previously written off as uncollectible, $396.00. M27 and R152.

5. Post each entry to the customer accounts in the accounts receivable ledger.
6. Post general journal entries to the general ledger.

ON YOUR OWN

Recording entries relating to uncollectible accounts receivable

The journals and ledgers for Potera Company are given in the *Working Papers*. Work independently to complete these problems.

7. The following transactions occurred during November of the current year. Journalize the transactions using page 11 of a general journal and page 15 of a cash receipts journal.

    Nov.   5. Wrote off Angela White's past-due account as uncollectible, $159.00. M45.
        8. Wrote off Peter Ewing's past-due account as uncollectible, $612.00. M47.
        12. Received cash in full payment of Mike Novak's account, previously written off as uncollectible, $853.00. M51 and R313.
        16. Wrote off Tim Haley's past-due account as uncollectible, $238.00. M58.
        29. Received cash in full payment of Peter Ewing's account, previously written off as uncollectible, $612.00. M61 and R345.

8. Post each entry to the customer accounts in the accounts receivable ledger.
9. Post general journal entries to the general ledger.

538 CHAPTER 20   Accounting for Uncollectible Accounts Receivable

---

ENRICH

❏ Assign the Legal Issues in Accounting feature on page 536.
❏ Assign the Automated Accounting feature on pages 544–545 to automate Application Problem 20-3.
❏ Show the CNN Accounting Video.

CLOSE

Ask students to briefly summarize the procedures for accounting for uncollectible accounts.

After completing this chapter, you can

1. Define accounting terms related to uncollectible accounts.
2. Identify accounting concepts and practices related to uncollectible accounts.
3. Calculate, journalize, and post estimated uncollectible accounts expense.
4. Journalize and post entries related to writing off and collecting uncollectible accounts receivable.

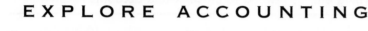

EXPLORE ACCOUNTING

ACCOUNTING ESTIMATES USE INTERESTING ASSUMPTIONS

Accountants use many accounting estimates to adjust the historical cost of certain transactions to better reflect the company's financial condition.

One of the most interesting accounting estimates concerns a payroll-related expense known as post retirement benefits other than pensions. Some companies offer their employees free services, such as health care, during their retirement. For many years companies have expensed these costs when the services were actually provided and paid for in cash. Accounting rules recently changed to require that these costs be recognized as an expense over the employee's

years of work. The promise of free health care during retirement is part of the total benefits that the company provides an employee in exchange for the employee's services.

For example, Hass Industries has promised free health care to its retired employees and their family members under 21 years of age. Bob Atkinson is expected to work for Hass Industries for 30 years. Health care costs for Bob, his wife, and any future children during his retirement are currently estimated to be $30,000. Rather than expense the $30,000 when the bills are paid during Bob's retirement, the new accounting rule requires that the $30,000 be expensed over Bob's 30 years of service. Therefore, $1,000 will be expensed each year.

To estimate the projected benefit, assumptions must be made regarding the following items: (1) percentage annual growth rate in health care costs, (2) life expectancy, (3) retirement age, (4) number of children, and (5) interest costs.

Management's assumptions can dramatically impact accounting estimates. Companies that prepare public financial statements have independent auditors examine the assumptions used to compute accounting estimates to assure that these assumptions are reasonable.

Research: Research the annual growth rate of health care costs. Do you believe this growth rate will continue? Identify factors that might cause further increases or decreases in growth rate.

PUTTING IT ALL TOGETHER

❏ Review the Chapter Summary.
❏ Ask students to prepare a list of the new concepts introduced in this chapter.
❏ Use Transparency 20-1 to review the transactions covered in this chapter.
❏ Discuss that the journalizing and posting procedures learned in this chapter could also be used for any business that sells its product or service on account.

INDEPENDENT PRACTICE

❏ Assign **Mastery Problem 20-4** to students who need the reinforcement of a problem that combines all concepts and transactions from the chapter in one problem; this will be most students.
❏ Assign **Application Problem 20-3.** This problem will emphasize transaction analysis skills because transactions are stated in a variety of different ways.
❏ Assign **Challenge Problem 20-5** to accelerated students who do not require the reinforcement of the mastery problem.
❏ Assign **Study Guide 20**.

ONGOING ASSESSMENT

Review solutions to the assigned problems in class, diagnosing troublespots.

RETEACH

❏ Call on students to describe how they avoid the troublespots diagnosed.
❏ Use reteaching suggestions from lesson plans as required.
❏ Assign Recycling Problem 20-1 if needed.
❏ Assign Accounting Connection, Chapter 20.

ENRICH

❏ Assign the Explore Accounting feature. Ask students to share the information they have gathered in a report to the class.
❏ Assign the Internet Activity.
❏ Assign the Applied Communication activity.
❏ Assign Cases 1, 2, and 3 of Cases for Critical Thinking.
❏ Assign the Automated Accounting feature on pages 544–545 to automate Mastery Problem 20-4.

EXPLORE ACCOUNTING

If needed, give students direction on resources for researching the requirements of this feature. You might suggest that the students begin their search in the *Business Periodicals Index* or other periodical indexes or various search engines on the Internet.

There is likely to be a wide distribution in the annual health care growth rates cited in various periodicals. Numerous organizations and government agencies attempt to estimate the annual

growth rate in health care. The many assumptions regarding what activities constitute health care and the methods used to collect the data can have a significant impact on the resultant growth rate estimates. The variety of growth rates demonstrates the difficulty accountants face in their goal to calculate a reasonably accurate estimate of future health care costs.

20-1 APPLICATION PROBLEM
Estimating and journalizing entries for uncollectible accounts expense

A general journal, work sheet, and selected general ledger accounts for Kellogg, Inc., are given in the
Working Papers.

Instructions:

1. Kellogg, Inc., estimates uncollectible accounts expense as 1.0% of its total sales on account. During the
current year, Kellogg had credit sales of $3,426,000.00. The balance in Allowance for Uncollectible
Accounts before adjustment is a $534.00 credit. Record the uncollectible accounts expense adjustment
on a work sheet.
2. Journalize the adjusting entry on page 25 of a general journal.
3. Post the adjusting entry to the general ledger.

20-2 APPLICATION PROBLEM
Recording entries related to uncollectible accounts receivable

The journals and ledgers for Waldron Company are given in the *Working Papers.*

Instructions:

1. The following transactions related to accounts receivable occurred during July of the current year.
Journalize the transactions using page 7 of a general journal and page 9 of a cash receipts journal.

Transactions:

July   4.   Wrote off Annie Jamison's past-due account as uncollectible, $102.00. M56.
     6.   Received cash in full payment of David Dowdle's account, previously written off as uncollectible,
$157.00. M58 and R214.
   13.   Wrote off Jeanne Lewis's past-due account as uncollectible, $97.00. M61.
   18.   Wrote off Rebecca Snow's past-due account as uncollectible, $310.00. M67.
   28.   Received cash in full payment of Annie Jamison's account, previously written off as uncollectible,
$102.00. M71 and R226.

2. Post each entry to the customer accounts in the accounts receivable ledger.
3. Post each entry in the general journal to the general ledger.

20-3 APPLICATION PROBLEM
Recording entries related to uncollectible accounts receivable

The journals and ledgers for Wister Co. are given in the *Working Papers.*

Instructions:

1. The following transactions related to accounts receivable occurred during February of the current year.
Journalize the transactions using page 4 of a general journal and page 2 of a cash receipts journal.

Transactions:

Feb.   3.   Received a $1,458.00 check from Bearden Co. in full payment of its account. The account was
written off in the previous month based on a newspaper story that indicated the company was
about to close. M24 and R134.
    7.   Michelle Pearce, controller of Hampton Industries, just called stating that the company had seri-
ous cash flow problems and would not be able to pay its $2,584.00 account balance. M25.
   10.   Received a letter from Rankin Co.'s legal counsel stating that the company was in the process of
filing bankruptcy. The letter gave little hope that Wister would collect Rankin's $948.00 account.
M28.

Feb. 12. Received a check from Camden Enterprises in full payment of its $1,784.00 account. The account was written off in January after months of efforts to collect the account. M31 and R142.

     21. A letter from Wilmont Co.'s receiving department supervisor stated that Wilmont refuses to pay for a prior year shipment of product for $548.00. The supervisor contends that the products were spoiled on arrival and were discarded. M34.

     27. Received a letter and check in the mail from Michelle Pearce of Hampton Industries. Two weeks ago the company was purchased by another company and, therefore, has access to cash to pay its debt. M35 and R159.

2. Post each entry to the customer accounts in the accounts receivable ledger.

3. Post each entry in the general journal to the general ledger.

20-4   MASTERY PROBLEM
Recording entries for uncollectible accounts

The accounts receivable and general ledger accounts for Lepanto Industries are given in the *Working Papers*. The following transactions relating to uncollectible accounts receivable occurred during the final quarter of the current fiscal year.

Instructions:

1. Journalize the following transactions completed during October using page 10 of a general journal. Post the transactions to the customer accounts and general ledger accounts.

Transactions:

Oct.   7. Wrote off Kingston Corporation's past-due account as uncollectible, $247.60. M202.
    18. Wrote off Gentry Corporation's past-due account as uncollectible, $482.50. M206.

2. Journalize the following transactions completed during November using page 11 of a general journal and page 11 of a cash receipts journal. Prove the cash receipts journal. Post the transactions to the customer accounts and general ledger accounts.

Transactions:

Nov.   8. Wrote off Burrell Company's past-due account as uncollectible, $714.15. M219.
    17. Received cash in full payment of Kingston Corporation's account, previously written off as uncollectible, $247.60. M223 and R461.
    22. Received cash in full payment of Peterson, Inc.'s account, previously written off as uncollectible, $523.30. M225 and R476.

3. Journalize the following transactions for December. Use page 12 of a general journal and page 12 of a cash receipts journal. Prove the cash receipts journal. Post the transactions to the customer accounts and general ledger accounts.

Transactions:

Dec.   3. Wrote off Fiber-Tech's past-due account as uncollectible, $829.35. M226.
    9. Received cash in full payment of Burrell Company's account, previously written off as uncollectible, $714.15. M229 and R514.
    28. Received cash in full payment of Gentry Corporation's account, previously written off as uncollectible, $482.50. M235 and R547.

4. Journalize the December 31 adjusting entry for estimated uncollectible accounts expense for the year. Use page 13 of the general journal. Uncollectible accounts expense is estimated as 1.0% of total sales on account. Total sales on account for the year were $1,051,080.00. Post the transaction to the general ledger accounts.

✔ Mastery Problem 20-4

Adjusting entry: debit Uncollectible Accounts Expense and credit Allowance for Uncollectible Accounts, 10,510.80

Ending balances: Accounts Receivable, 62,313.40; Allowance for Uncollectible Accounts, 11,752.95

APPLIED SKILLS

WORD PROCESSING

If you wish to integrate word processing into your accounting course, you may direct students to answer the Terms Reviews, Audit Your Understanding questions, and Cases for Critical Thinking using their word processing software.

20-5 CHALLENGE PROBLEM
Recording entries for uncollectible accounts

Information from the accounting records of Rosedale Company concerning uncollectible accounts during the past five years follows (presented in thousands of dollars).

	20X1	20X2	20X3	20X4	20X5
Sales on account	$575	$700	$850	$1,050	$1,200
Ending Accounts Receivable	50	60	80	90	100
Uncollectible Accounts Expense	8	8	15	15	15
Ending Allowance for Uncollectible Accounts	5	1	4	3	1
Accounts written off	10	13	14	18	19
Accounts collected after being written off	1	1	2	2	2

The controller of the company has asked you to evaluate the prior annual adjustments to Allowance for Uncollectible Accounts. If the company expects to have sales of $1,400,000.00 next year, what amount would you suggest be expensed to Uncollectible Accounts Expense? Support your answer.

Applied Communication

For many years the accounting staff at St. Charles Furniture have written off uncollectible accounts receivable by debiting Uncollectible Accounts Expense and crediting Accounts Receivable. Despite relatively constant sales and collections on account, the annual amount of Uncollectible Accounts Expense has fluctuated between $5,000.00 and $90,000.00 during the past six years. Management admits that the amount of accounts written off depends largely on the time the managers have devoted to evaluating accounts receivable for possible collection problems.

Instructions: Prepare a memorandum to Duane Smith, president of St. Charles Furniture, explaining the correct way to account for uncollectible accounts receivable. The memorandum should pursuade him to implement a change from the current accounting procedure.

APPLIED SKILLS

WRITING ACROSS THE CURRICULUM

Writing Paragraphs and Short Essays. The Cases for Critical Thinking are short, practical applications of the accounting principles developed in the chapter. Some cases are planned to present problems related to the chapter but not specifically discussed and answered in the chapter. These cases present an opportunity for critical thinking and decision making. These cases also require more than a short, objective-type response. Therefore, they provide ideal practice in writing paragraphs and short essays.

Cases for Critical Thinking

Case 1 Crain Corporation has always assumed that an account receivable is good until the account is proven to be uncollectible. When an account proves to be uncollectible, the credit manager notifies the accounting clerk to write off the account. The accounting clerk then debits Uncollectible Accounts Expense and credits Accounts Receivable. Recently the company's new accountant, Dawn Mitchner, suggested that the method be changed for recording uncollectible accounts expense. Ms. Mitchner recommended that the company estimate uncollectible accounts expense based on a percentage of total sales on account. Ms. Mitchner stated that the change would provide more accurate information on the income statement and balance sheet. Do you agree with Ms. Mitchner that her recommended method would provide more accurate information? Explain.

Case 2 Tupelo Industries credits Accounts Receivable for the amount of estimated uncollectible accounts expense at the end of each fiscal period. Bluff Company credits Allowance for Uncollectible Accounts for the amount of estimated uncollectible accounts expense at the end of each fiscal period. Which company is using the better method? Why?

Case 3 Some businesses have a policy of accepting only cash sales. Depending on economic conditions or the time of year, many potential customers may not be able to pay with currency, check, or debit card. Businesses with cash-only policies will lose those potential sales. As has been discussed in previous chapters, other businesses encourage more sales by selling on account to customers with approved credit. The key decision is defining what is *approved credit*. Employees responsible for meeting the sales goals of a business would have one set of standards for approving credit. Employees responsible for maintaining merchandise inventory and filling orders would have another set of standards for approving credit. What role, if any, do you believe that accounting employees should play in setting a company's standards for approving credit? What contributions can accounting employees make to discussions about credit standards?

CASE 1 The percentage of total sales on account method recommended by Ms. Mitchner should provide more accurate financial statements. Risk of loss occurs when a business makes a sale on account. This potential loss is present even though several months may pass before the actual uncollectible account is determined. Recording uncollectible accounts expense in the same fiscal period the revenue is earned is an application of the *Matching Expenses with Revenue* concept. Accurate financial reporting requires that expenses be included in the accounting period in which the expenses contribute to earning revenue.

CASE 2 Bluff Company is using the better method. As long as the amount being recorded is only an estimate, it should not be charged to the accounts receivable account. Only when it is known for sure that a customer cannot or will not pay the amount owed should the amount be credited to Accounts Receivable. Also, the total of Tupelo Industries' accounts receivable ledger will not balance with the controlling account.

CASE 3 The definition of approved credit should be carefully considered, and input from employees in various departments of the company should be considered. Those who are responsible for sales will want to maximize sales; and while their incentives might lead to a very loose credit approval standard, increasing sales is the reason for selling on credit in the first place. Sales people may also have insights into the ability of customers to pay their accounts. Employees who maintain merchandise inventory and filling orders might desire a tighter credit policy to minimize their workload; on the other hand, they might also encourage a looser policy to increase their job security. Accounting employees may be more objective, and some may have credit experience with other companies or knowledge about the credit industry. A company may also have a credit manager who makes the ultimate decision on which customers are granted credit. There is always a risk that even the best customers may default on a payment, but it is a calculated risk weighed against the benefits of selling on credit to increase sales.

PORTFOLIO ASSESSMENT

Proper and accurate accounting for uncollectible accounts is critical to a business, and credit departments can employ a large number of people in very large companies. Because there are many career possibilities in accounts receivable, students should emphasize their learning of this topic by selecting an example of a comprehensive sample of their work in this chapter, either the mastery problem or a problem from a test, to include in their portfolio. A copy of the Portfolio Assessment form (blackline master in the Teacher's Resource Guide) should be completed by the student, and the Description section should include any comments regarding how the student mastered these concepts and procedures. Alternatively, students might include in their portfolios printed reports from an Automated Accounting problem.

❑ Explain that the adjustment for uncollectible accounts expense is recorded in the general journal at the end of the fiscal period.

❑ Explain that uncollectible accounts receivable are written off when efforts to collect amounts due have been exhausted.

❑ Explain that the journal entry to write off an account receivable is recorded in the general journal.

❑ Explain that when a previously written-off account receivable is collected, two journal entries are needed: (1) an entry to reopen the account receivable, which is recorded in the general journal, and (2) an entry to record the cash received on account, which is recorded in the cash receipts journal.

DEMONSTRATE

Journalizing adjustment for uncollectible accounts expense

❑ Demonstrate how to record a adjustment for uncollectible accounts expense in the General Journal screen.

❑ Demonstrate using Adj.Ent. as the Reference for this adjusting entry.

❑ Demonstrate the debit to Uncollectible Account Expense.

❑ Demonstrate the credit to Allowance for Uncollectible Accounts.

❑ Explain that after a transaction is entered, the Post button must be pressed to allow an additional transaction to be entered.

Journalizing writing off an uncollectible account receivable

❑ Demonstrate writing off an account receivable.

❑ Demonstrate entering the information in each of the fields.

❑ Demonstrate that after the credit amount is entered for the Accounts Receivable account, the drop-down list of customers will be available for selecting the specific account receivable being written off.

AUTOMATED ACCOUNTING

AUTOMATED ENTRIES FOR UNCOLLECTIBLE ACCOUNTS AND WRITE-OFFS

Many businesses allow sales on account. Before granting credit, businesses investigate the creditworthiness of the customer. These investigations minimize the amount of losses from uncollectible accounts. Businesses maintain a separate customer file. The total owed by all customers maintained in a customer file is summarized in a single general ledger asset account called Accounts Receivable. If the business fails to collect from a customer, the business loses part of the asset Accounts Receivable. This loss is a regular expense of doing business.

Recording Estimated Uncollectible Accounts

In order to properly match revenues with expenses at the end of the fiscal period, each business that sells on account must estimate the amount of current Accounts Receivable that will not be collected during the next period. A business may use a percentage of sales on account to make the estimate. The estimated amount is recorded in a contra asset account, Allowance for Uncollectible Accounts. An adjusting entry is made for the estimated amount.

To record the adjusting entry:
1. Click the Journal toolbar button.
2. Click the General Journal tab.

3. Enter the transaction date and press Tab.
4. Enter Adj. Ent. in the Refer. text box and press Tab.
5. Enter the account numbers for Uncollectible Account Expense and Allowance for Uncollectible Accounts, and the estimated amount of the loss. Press the Tab key as needed.
6. Click the Post button.

Writing Off an Uncollectible Account Receivable

When a specific account is determined to be uncollectible, the balance of the account must be removed. The debit is made to Allowance for Uncollectible Accounts. The total of Accounts Receivable and the customer's account in the accounts receivable ledger are reduced by a credit.
1. Click the Journal toolbar button.
2. Click the General Journal tab.
3. Enter the transaction date and press Tab.
4. Enter the source document number in the Refer. text box and press Tab. A memorandum is generally prepared as the source document.
5. Enter the account number for Allowance for Uncollectible Accounts, and the debit amount.
6. Enter the account number

for Accounts Receivable and the credit amount.
7. Tab to the Customer column and select the customer from the drop-down list.
8. Click the Post button.

Collecting a Previously Written-Off Account Receivable

When a previously written-off account is collected, the customer account is first reinstated. Once the account is reinstated, the cash receipt is recorded in the cash receipts journal.

To reinstate the account:
1. Click the Journal toolbar button.
2. Click the General Journal tab.
3. Enter the transaction date and press Tab.
4. Enter the source document number in the Refer. text box and press Tab. A memorandum is generally prepared as the source document.
5. Enter the account number for Accounts Receivable and the debit amount.
6. Tab to the Customer column and select the customer from the drop-down list.
7. Tab to the next line and enter the account number for Allowance for Uncollectible Accounts and the credit amount.
8. Click the Post button.

AUTOMATED ACCOUNTING

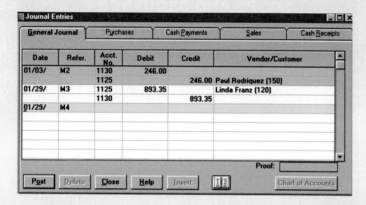

To record the cash receipt:

1. Click the Journal toolbar button.
2. Click the Cash Receipts tab.
3. Enter the transaction date and press Tab.
4. Enter the source document number in the Refer. text box and press Tab to move to the A.R. Credit text box.
5. Enter the Accounts Receivable credit amount. The debit to Cash will be automatically calculated. Press Tab to move to the Customer text box.
6. Choose the customer name from the Customer drop-down list.
7. Click the Post button.

AUTOMATING APPLICATION PROBLEM 20-3: Recording entries related to uncollectible accounts expense
Instructions:
1. Load *Automated Accounting* 7.0 or higher software.

2. Select database F20-1 from the appropriate directory/folder.
3. Select File from the menu bar and choose the Save As menu command. Key the path to the drive and directory that contains your data files. Save the database with a file name of XXX201 (where XXX are your initials).
4. Access Problem Instructions through the Help menu. Read the Problem Instructions screen.
5. Key the data listed on pages 538–539.
6. Exit the *Automated Accounting* software.

AUTOMATING MASTERY PROBLEM 20-4: Recording entries for uncollectible accounts
Instructions:
1. Load *Automated Accounting* 7.0 or higher software.

2. Select database F20-2 from the appropriate directory/folder.
3. Select File from the menu bar and choose the Save As menu command. Key the path to the drive and directory that contains your data files. Save the database with a file name of XXX202 (where XXX are your initials).
4. Access Problem Instructions through the Help menu. Read the Problem Instructions screen.
5. Key the data listed on page 539.
6. Exit the *Automated Accounting* software.

CHAPTER 20   Accounting for Uncollectible Accounts Receivable   **545**

Collecting a previously written-off account receivable—reopening the account

❑ Demonstrate reopening an account receivable in the General Journal screen.
❑ Demonstrate entering the account number for Accounts Receivable and the debit amount. Point out that after the debit amount is entered, the drop-down list of customers will be available for selecting the specific account receivable being written off.
❑ Demonstrate entering the account number for Allowance for Uncollectible Accounts and the credit amount.

Collecting a previously written-off account receivable—recording the cash receipt

❑ Demonstrate journalizing the cash receipt in the Cash Receipts screen.
❑ Demonstrate entering the date and reference.
❑ Demonstrate entering the amount in the A.R. Credit field. Emphasize that the debit to Cash will be automatically calculated.
❑ Demonstrate choosing the customer name from the Customer Drop-down list.

PRACTICE

❑ Assign Automating Application Problem 20-3: Recording entries related to uncollectible accounts expense.
❑ Assign Automating Mastery Problem 20-4: Recording entries for uncollectible accounts.

ASSESSMENT

❑ Use the Electronic Auditor to assess student understanding.

PORTFOLIO ASSESSMENT

Students should be encouraged to print at least one report from one of the *Automated Accounting* problems to include in their portfolio to demonstrate mastery of automated accounting systems. A copy of the Portfolio Assessment form (blackline master in the Teacher's Resource Guide) should be completed by the student, and the Description section should include any comments regarding how the student mastered these concepts and procedures.

CHAPTER 21

	SCOPE AND SEQUENCE		ENHANCING	
	NEW	**REVIEW/ EXTENSION**	**SPECIAL FEATURES**	
INTRODUCE THE CHAPTER			Accounting in Your Career: Secrets of the Competition Thinking about Careers	
Categories of assets				
LESSSON 21-1 BUYING PLANT ASSETS AND PAYING PROPERTY TAX			Math Work Sheet, Chapter 21, Part A	
Recording buying plant assets	✓			
Calculating and paying property tax	✓			
LESSSON 21-2 CALCULATING DEPRECIATION EXPENSE			Math Work Sheet, Chapter 21, Part B	
Depreciation	✓		Math Work Sheet, Chapter 21, Part C	
Calculating straight-line depreciation	✓		Math Work Sheet, Chapter 21, Part D	
Calculating depreciation for part of a year	✓		Cultural Diversity: Valuing Diversity in the Workplace	
Calculating accumulated depreciation	✓			
LESSSON 21-3 JOURNALIZING DEPRECIATION EXPENSE				
Preparing plant asset records	✓			
Recording annual depreciation expense	✓			
LESSSON 21-4 DISPOSING OF PLANT ASSETS			Math Work Sheet, Chapter 21, Part E	
Sale of a plant asset for book value	✓			
Recording partial year's depreciation expense	✓			
Sale of a plant asset for more than book value	✓			
Sale of a plant asset for less than book value	✓			
LESSSON 21-5 DECLINING-BALANCE METHOD OF DEPRECIATION			Math Work Sheet, Chapter 21, Part F	
Calculating depreciation using the double declining-balance method	✓		Legal Issues in Accounting: Dissolving a Corporation	
Calculating the last year's depreciation expense	✓			
Comparing straight-line and double declining-balance depreciation	✓			
PUTTING IT ALL TOGETHER			Explore Accounting Internet Activity Applied Communication Cases for Critical Thinking 1 and 2	

ACCOUNTING FOR PLANT ASSETS AND DEPRECIATION

INSTRUCTION		PRACTICE AND ASSESSMENT		
TECHNOLOGY AND MEDIA	TEACHING STRATEGIES	GUIDED PRACTICE	INDEPENDENT PRACTICE	RETEACHING AND ENRICHMENT
Internet Activity	Software Focus			
Transparency L	Building Study Skills	Terms Review Audit Your Understanding Work Together	On Your Own Application Problem 21-1 Ongoing Assessment, p. 549	Reteach, p. 549 Enrich, p. 550
Automated Accounting Spreadsheet Accounting	Applied Skills: Mathematics	Terms Review Audit Your Understanding Work Together	On Your Own Application Problem 21-2 Ongoing Assessment, p. 553	Reteach, p. 553 Enrich, p. 554
CNN Accounting Video Transparencies 21-1 and M	Print Learner	Term Review Audit Your Understanding Work Together	On Your Own Application Problem 21-3 Application Problem 21-4 Ongoing Assessment, p. 557	Reteach, p. 557 Enrich, p. 558
Transparencies M and O	Visual Learner Kinesthetic Learner	Terms Review Audit Your Understanding Work Together	On Your Own Application Problem 21-5 Ongoing Assessment, p. 562	Reteach, p. 562 Enrich, p. 563
	Expanding Beyond the Classroom	Term Review Audit Your Understanding Work Together	On Your Own Application Problem 21-6 Ongoing Assessment, p. 566	Reteach, p. 566 Enrich, p. 567

Transparency 21-2
Automated Accounting
Spreadsheet Accounting
Accounting Connection
	Auditory Learner
	Limited English Proficiency
	    (LEP) Students
	Applied Skills: Writing Across
	    the Curriculum
			Mastery Problem 21-7
			Study Guide 21
			Chapter 21 Test
			ExamViewPro or Westest,
			    Chapter 21
			Portfolio Assessment
				Enrich, p. 568
				Challenge Problem 21-8
				Reteach, p. 568
				Recycling Problem 21-1
				Accounting Connection

PREVIEW ACCOUNTING TERMS
- ❏ Read each term out loud to verify pronunciation for students.
- ❏ Point out terms or parts of terms that should already be familiar to most students, such as assets, property, and salvage.

PREVIEW CHAPTER OBJECTIVES
- ❏ Point out that students have already learned how to journalize and post using a cash payments journal, cash receipts journal, and general journal.
- ❏ Point out that this chapter will introduce two ways to categorize assets.
- ❏ Note that this chapter presents the accounting procedures for expensing the cost of long-lived assets.

INTRODUCTION
- ❏ Have students read the two paragraphs under the heading "Categories of Assets." Asking a student to read the paragraphs out loud to the class is a good technique for improving the student's public speaking skills.
- ❏ Ask students to identify assets that would be classified as current assets.
- ❏ Ask students to identify items in their school that would be classified as plant assets.

TERMS PREVIEW

current assets
plant assets
real property
personal property
assessed value
depreciation
  expense
estimated salvage
  value
straight-line
  method of
  depreciation
accumulated
  depreciation
book value of a
  plant asset
plant asset record
gain on plant
  assets
loss on plant
  assets
declining-balance
  method of
  depreciation

546

21 Accounting for Plant Assets and Depreciation

AFTER STUDYING CHAPTER 21, YOU WILL BE ABLE TO:

1. Define accounting terms related to plant assets, depreciation, and property tax expense.

2. Identify accounting concepts and practices related to accounting for plant assets, depreciation, and property tax expense.

3. Record the buying of a plant asset and the paying of property tax.

4. Calculate depreciation expense and book value using the straight-line method of depreciation.

5. Prepare plant asset records and journalize annual depreciation expense.

6. Record entries related to disposing of plant assets.

7. Calculate depreciation expense using the double declining-balance method of depreciation.

CATEGORIES OF ASSETS

Most businesses use two broad categories of assets in their operations. Cash and other assets expected to be exchanged for cash or consumed within a year are called **current assets.** Assets that will be used for a number of years in the operation of a business are called **plant assets.** Some of the more significant current assets used by Winning Edge are cash, accounts receivable, merchandise inventory, supplies, and prepaid insurance. Some of Winning Edge's plant assets are computers, cash registers, sales display cases, and furniture. Winning Edge's complete list of current and plant assets is in the chart of accounts on page 459.

Businesses may have three major types of plant assets—equipment, buildings, and land. Winning Edge owns equipment that it uses to operate the business. However, the company rents the building and the land where the business is located. Therefore, Winning Edge has accounts for equipment, which is the only type of plant asset it owns. To provide more detailed financial information, Winning Edge records its equipment in two different equipment accounts—**Office Equipment** and **Store Equipment.** (CONCEPT: Adequate Disclosure)

SOFTWARE FOCUS

Software may be used for independent practice or enrichment as the instructor deems appropriate. For this chapter, the following software may be used: Automated Accounting 7.0 or higher for Application Problem 21-2 and Mastery Problem 21-7; Spreadsheet Accounting Template for Application Problem 21-2 and Mastery Problem 21-7; and Accounting Connection, Chapter 21.

Instructors may wish to cover the Automated Accounting feature on page 573, even if the Automated Accounting software is not being used in the classroom, so students get a sense of how the chapter's accounting procedures would be implemented in an automated environment.

ACCOUNTING IN YOUR CAREER

SECRETS OF THE COMPETITION

Keith Birchhill is a senior accountant at GenSys Inc., a medical and scientific research company. Keith prepares the company's financial statements and federal tax returns, and supervises a team of accounting clerks. He is also well known in the company as an able researcher on the Internet. So it is not unusual that Marta Boswell, Chief Executive Officer, has asked to see him regarding a new research project.

Marta is interested in knowing whether any competing research firms have the electron microscopes and other expensive laboratory equipment that would be needed to pursue a new line of research on cancer treatment. She says that only the newest models of most lab equipment have the capacity needed for this research. At the end of her presentation, she emphasizes that only publicly available information should be used.

"Don't worry, Marta," Keith replies after some thought. "I think I can get the information right off the published financial statements. So you won't have to be concerned with ethical issues."

"That's amazing, Keith," Marta says. "Financial statements are included in annual reports that are public information. But I've read all those financial statements, and I don't remember seeing anything like what I'm asking you for."

"You just have to know where to look, Marta. That's what you pay me for."

Critical Thinking:

1. The balance sheet of GenSys's major competitor, MedTech, Inc., shows: Laboratory Equipment, $5,500,000; Accumulated Depreciation—Laboratory Equipment, $4,000,000. GenSys's balance sheet reports: Laboratory Equipment, $7,500,000, and Accumulated Depreciation—Laboratory Equipment, $2,500,000. What percentage of lab equipment is undepreciated to date for the two companies? Notes to the financial statements report that the straight-line depreciation method is used for both companies.

2. What can Keith Birchhill conclude about the newness of the two companies' lab equipment?

ACCOUNTING IN YOUR CAREER

❏ This feature illustrates how financial statements provide a significant amount of information to individuals who understand the accounting principles used to prepare the statements.

❏ Ask students to read the feature or have one or more students read the feature out loud.

❏ Give students 5–10 minutes to jot down some ideas for answering the Critical Thinking questions, then discuss the answers in class.

❏ As an alternative, you can use brainstorming techniques to generate possible solutions to the questions. With this approach, you may also wish to record the suggestions and save them for additional discussion after the chapter is completed.

THINKING ABOUT CAREERS

❏ Use this feature to encourage additional thinking about accounting careers.

❏ Ask students what kind of education and experience Keith Burchhill would need to be a senior accountant. *(Keith should have at least a bachelor's degree in accounting. However, Keith appears to be the type of individual who will advance as the company grows. Keith would want to have a master's degree in accounting and an accounting certification [CPA or CMA] to support his advancement to higher positions of responsibility.)*

❏ Ask students what kinds of personal qualities are desirable in a senior accountant. *(Keith needs to be able to work on several projects at one time. He also needs to be able to deal with unstructured problems—problems for which there is no established method for obtaining the solution.)*

SUGGESTED ANSWERS

1. MedTech, Inc.: 27.3% ($1,500,000/$5,500,000); GenSys, Inc., 66.7% ($5,000,000/$7,500,000).
2. MedTech, Inc., has older equipment because most of it has already had depreciation allocated. GenSys's equipment can be assumed to be newer because a much smaller percentage has been depreciated. Therefore, MedTech, Inc., does not have the equipment necessary to pursue this research.

OBJECTIVES

❏ Define accounting terms related to plant assets and property tax expense.
❏ Identify accounting concepts and practices related to accounting for plant assets and property tax expense.
❏ Record the buying of a plant asset and the paying of property tax.

MOTIVATE

Plant assets are the largest asset category for many businesses. Ask students to identify the types of plant assets required to operate a specific business in their community.

Preview

❏ Preview accounting terms and definitions introduced in this lesson: current assets, plant assets, real property, personal property, and assessed value.
❏ Direct students to read the headings at the top of each page in this lesson and to examine the illustrations given.

EXPLAIN

❏ Remind students that they have already learned to record the purchase of items, such as supplies, in a cash payments journal.
❏ Explain why the normal balance of Store Equipment is a debit.
❏ Explain that the cost of a plant asset would include all costs to obtain the item, including taxes, shipping costs, and installation.

DEMONSTRATE

Analyze Store Equipment

❏ Draw a T account on the board for Store Equipment. Label the increase/decrease, debit/credit, and normal balance sides.

Record and post the transaction

❏ Use Transparency L to illustrate recording the transaction in the cash payments journal or direct students to the illustration.
❏ Direct students to journalize and post the transactions, following the four steps shown.
❏ Remind students that the account title is written in the Account Title column for the amount in the General Debit column.
❏ Direct students to the illustration to walk through posting this entry.

548

RECORDING THE BUYING OF A PLANT ASSET

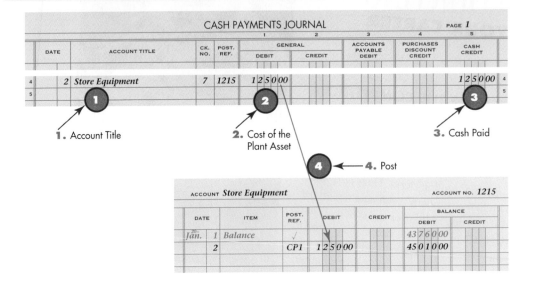

1. Account Title
2. Cost of the Plant Asset
3. Cash Paid
4. Post

Procedures for recording the buying of a plant asset are similar to procedures for recording the buying of current assets such as supplies. The amount paid for a plant asset is debited to a plant asset account with a title such as Store Equipment. *(CONCEPT: Historical Cost)*

January 2, 20X1. Paid cash for a display case, $1,250.00. Check No. 7.

The entry in the General Debit column of the cash payments journal is posted individually to the account named in the Account Title column.

S T E P S Journalizing and posting the buying of a plant asset

1. Write the plant asset account, *Store Equipment*, in the Account Title column of the cash payments journal.
2. Enter the cost of the plant asset, *$1,250.00*, in the General Debit column.
3. Enter the same amount, *$1,250.00*, in the Cash Credit column.
4. Post the entry in the General Debit column to the general ledger.

548 CHAPTER 21 Accounting for Plant Assets and Depreciation

MATERIALS

❏ Transparencies:
 L, Blank Cash Payments Journal (5-Column)
❏ Working Papers
 Teacher's Edition of the Working Papers for Lesson 21-1
❏ Work Sheets:
 Math Work Sheet, Chapter 21, Part A

CALCULATING AND PAYING PROPERTY TAX

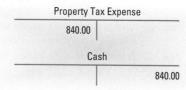

		CASH PAYMENTS JOURNAL										PAGE 3	
						1	2	3	4	5
DATE	ACCOUNT TITLE	CK. NO.	POST. REF.	GENERAL DEBIT	GENERAL CREDIT	ACCOUNTS PAYABLE DEBIT	PURCHASES DISCOUNT CREDIT	CASH CREDIT
1	Feb 1	Property Tax Expense	187		8 4 0 00					8 4 0 00
2									

For tax purposes, state and federal governments define two kinds of property—real and personal. Land and anything attached to the land is called **real property.** Real property is sometimes referred to as real estate. All property not classified as real property is called **personal property.** For tax purposes, these definitions apply whether the property is owned by a business or an individual.

The value of an asset determined by tax authorities for the purpose of calculating taxes is called the **assessed value.** Assessed value is usually based on the judgment of persons referred to as assessors. Assessors are elected by citizens or are specially trained employees of a governmental unit.

Most governmental units with taxing power have a tax based on the value of real property. The real property tax is used on buildings and land. Some governmental units also tax personal property such as cars, boats, trailers, and airplanes.

A governmental taxing unit determines a tax rate to use in calculating taxes. The tax rate is multiplied by an asset's *assessed value,* not the value recorded on a business's records.

Harrison Manufacturing's plant assets have been assessed for a total of $70,000.00. The city tax rate is 1.2%.

Assessed Value	×	Tax Rate	=	Annual Property Tax
$70,000.00	×	1.2%	=	$840.00

Paying Property Tax on Plant Assets

February 1. Harrison Manufacturing paid cash for property tax, $840.00. Check No. 187.

Payment of property taxes is necessary if a firm is to continue in business. Therefore, Harrison Manufacturing classifies property tax as an operating expense.

Property Tax Expense	
840.00	

Cash	
	840.00

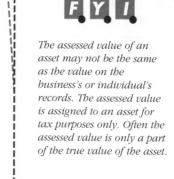

F.Y.I.

The assessed value of an asset may not be the same as the value on the business's or individual's records. The assessed value is assigned to an asset for tax purposes only. Often the assessed value is only a part of the true value of the asset.

Terms Review
Call on students to define the terms in the Terms Review. Ask the class if the definitions are correct and whether the complete definitions have been given or if anything needs to be added. Suggested definitions for all terms are given in the Glossary.

Audit Your Understanding
Call on students to answer the Audit Your Understanding questions. Ask the class if the answer is correct and/or complete. Answers are given in Appendix D of the textbook.

Work Together
Have students write the solutions to the Work Together problems as you guide the class through the examples.
❑ Direct students to record each transaction in the journal as you elicit class participation in analyzing and recording each transaction.
❑ Call on students to describe how to post amounts in the general columns of a cash payments journal.

INDEPENDENT PRACTICE

On Your Own
❑ Assign the On Your Own problems to be worked independently.
❑ Use the Ongoing Assessment techniques to diagnose student understanding.

Application Problem
❑ Assign Application Problem 21-1: Journalizing buying plant assets and paying property tax.

TERMS REVIEW

current assets

plant assets

real property

personal property

assessed value

AUDIT YOUR UNDERSTANDING

1. What are the two broad categories of assets used by most businesses in their operations?

2. What accounts are affected, and how, when cash is paid for office equipment?

3. What items are included in real property?

4. Who determines the assessed value of plant assets?

WORK TOGETHER

Journalizing buying plant assets and paying property tax

The cash payments journal and selected general ledger accounts for Bargain Center are given in the *Working Papers.* Your instructor will guide you through the following examples.

5. Journalize the following transactions completed during the current year. Use page 1 of a cash payments journal. The abbreviation for a check is C.
   Transactions:
   Jan. 2. Paid cash for a computer printer, $900.00. C130.
        3. Paid cash for a cash register, $800.00. C132.
   Feb. 26. Paid property taxes on real property with an assessed value of $120,000.00. The tax rate in the city where the property is located is 1.5% of assessed value. C167.
   Apr. 2. Paid cash for a telephone system in the store, $1,500.00. C193.

6. Post the general columns of the cash payments journal.

ON YOUR OWN

Journalizing buying plant assets and paying property tax

The cash payments journal and selected general ledger accounts for Nelson Paint Store are given in the *Working Papers.* Work these problems independently.

7. Journalize the following transactions completed during the current year. Use page 1 of a cash payments journal. The abbreviation for a check is C.
   Transactions:
   Jan. 3. Paid cash for a paint mixer, $500.00. C142.
        5. Paid cash for an office chair, $400.00. C145.
   Feb. 26. Paid property taxes on real property with an assessed value of $80,000.00. The tax rate in the city where the property is located is 3.0% of assessed value. C182.
   July 2. Paid cash for a filing cabinet, $260.00. C216.

8. Post the general columns of the cash payments journal.

ENRICH

❑ Invite a local government official to speak to the class regarding property taxes. Work with the students prior to the presentation to prepare a list of questions. Students should be encouraged to talk with a relative or friend who owns property for assistance in writing the questions.

CLOSE

❑ Ask students to briefly summarize the procedures for journalizing transactions to buy plant assets and pay property taxes.

DEPRECIATING PLANT ASSETS

A business buys plant assets to use in earning revenue. Winning Edge bought a new lighted display case to display sport watches. Winning Edge knows that the display case will be useful only for a limited period of time. After several years, most display cases become worn from use and no longer attractively display the products. Winning Edge replaces worn display cases with newer models. Thus, each display case has a limited useful life to the business.

In order to match revenue with the expenses used to earn the revenue, the cost of a plant asset should be expensed over the plant asset's useful life. A portion of a plant asset's cost is transferred to an expense account in each fiscal period that a plant asset is used to earn revenue. (CONCEPT: Matching Expenses with Revenue) The portion of a plant asset's cost that is transferred to an expense account in each fiscal period during a plant asset's useful life is called **depreciation expense.**

Three factors are considered in calculating the annual amount of depreciation expense for a plant asset.

1. *Original Cost.* The original cost of a plant asset includes all costs paid to make the asset usable to a business. These costs include the price of the asset, delivery costs, and any necessary installation costs.

2. *Estimated Salvage Value.* Generally, a business removes a plant asset from use and disposes of it when the asset is no longer usable. The amount that will be received for an asset at the time of its disposal is not known when the asset is bought. Thus, the amount that may be received at disposal must be estimated. The amount an owner expects to receive when a plant asset is removed from use is called **estimated salvage value.** Estimated salvage value may also be referred to as residual value or scrap value.

3. *Estimated Useful Life.* The total amount of depreciation expense is distributed over the estimated useful life of a plant asset. When a plant asset is bought, the exact length of useful life is impossible to predict. Therefore, the number of years of useful life must be estimated. Two factors affect the useful life of a plant asset: (1) physical depreciation and (2) functional depreciation. Physical depreciation is caused by wear from use and deterioration from aging and weathering. Functional depreciation occurs when a plant asset becomes inadequate or obsolete. An asset is inadequate when it can no longer satisfactorily perform the needed service. An asset is obsolete when a newer asset can operate more efficiently or produce better service.

Because of its permanent nature, land is generally not subject to depreciation. Buildings, after years of use, eventually become unusable. A building may be torn down and a new building constructed on the same land. Since land can be used indefinitely, it is considered permanent and is not depreciated.

The estimated useful life should be based on prior experience with similar assets and on available guidelines. Trade associations frequently publish guidelines for specialized plant assets. The Internal Revenue Service publishes depreciation guidelines for plant assets.

> *Depreciation expense differs from many other business expenses in one significant way. For most business expenses, cash is paid out in the same fiscal period in which the expense is recorded. Cash is paid out in the fiscal period during which a plant asset is purchased, but the related depreciation expense is recorded over several years.*

OBJECTIVES

❏ Define accounting terms related to depreciation.
❏ Identify accounting concepts and practices related to depreciation.
❏ Calculate depreciation expense and book value using the straight-line method of depreciation.

MOTIVATE

Most plant assets wear out or become technologically obsolete over a period of time. This loss of value is an expense to the business that should be recorded in the financial statements.

Preview

❏ Preview the accounting terms and definitions introduced in this lesson: depreciation expense, estimated salvage value, straight-line method of depreciation, accumulated depreciation, and book value of a plant asset.
❏ Direct students to read the headings at the top of each page in this lesson and to examine the illustrations given.

EXPLAIN

❏ Explain that depreciation is an estimate that attempts to match the expense of using plant assets with the revenue earned using those plant assets.
❏ Ask students to identify the three factors used to calculate depreciation.
❏ Ask students to identify which of the three factors are estimates.
❏ Ask students to identify the two factors that affect the useful life of a plant asset.
❏ Explain why land is not depreciated.
❏ Ask students to read the F.Y.I. to reinforce how depreciation expense is different from most other expenses.

MATERIALS

❏ Work Sheets:
  Math Work Sheet, Chapter 21, Part B
  Math Work Sheet, Chapter 21, Part C
  Math Work Sheet, Chapter 21, Part D
❏ Working Papers:

Teacher's Edition of the Working Papers for Lesson 21-2
❏ Software:
  Automated Accounting 7.0 or higher and Accounting Textbook Template
  Spreadsheet Accounting Template

STRAIGHT-LINE DEPRECIATION

Original Cost	–	Estimated Salvage Value	=	Estimated Total Depreciation Expense
$1,250.00	–	$250.00	=	**1** $1,000.00

Estimated Total Depreciation Expense	÷	Years of Estimated Useful Life	=	Annual Depreciation Expense
$1,000.00	÷	5	=	**2** $200.00

Charging an *equal* amount of depreciation expense for a plant asset in each year of useful life is called the **straight-line method of depreciation.**

On January 2, 20X1, Winning Edge bought a lighted display case for $1,250.00 with an estimated salvage value of $250.00 and an estimated useful life of 5 years.

Using the straight-line method of depreciation, the annual depreciation expense is the same for each full year in which the asset is used.

S T E P S

Calculating annual depreciation expense

1. Subtract the asset's estimated salvage value from the asset's original cost. This difference is the estimated total depreciation expense for the asset's entire useful life.

2. Divide the estimated total depreciation expense by the years of estimated useful life. The result is the annual depreciation expense.

CALCULATING DEPRECIATION EXPENSE FOR PART OF A YEAR

Annual Depreciation Expense	÷	Months in a Year	=	Monthly Depreciation Expense
$900.00	÷	12	=	**1** $75.00

Monthly Depreciation Expense	×	Number of Months Asset Is Used	=	Partial Year's Depreciation Expense
$75.00	×	5	=	**2** $375.00

A month is the smallest unit of time used to calculate depreciation. A plant asset may be placed in service at a date other than the first day of a fiscal period. In such cases, depreciation expense is calculated to the nearest first of a month.

Winning Edge bought a computer on August 2, 20X1. The annual straight-line depreciation expense is $900.00. The depreciation expense for the part of the year Winning Edge used the computer is $375.00.

S T E P S

Calculating partial year's depreciation expense

1. Divide the annual depreciation expense by 12, the number of months in a year. The result is the monthly depreciation expense.

2. Multiply the monthly depreciation expense by the number of months the plant asset is used in a year. The result is the partial year's depreciation expense.

552 CHAPTER 21 Accounting for Plant Assets and Depreciation

APPLIED SKILLS

MATHEMATICS

Use the math work sheet in the Masters and Solutions to Enrichment/Application section of the Teacher's Resource Guide to integrate applied mathematics. In this work sheet, students will apply math concepts to calculate amounts for plant assets and depreciation, using a variety of methods. Students will calculate rates, percentages, and accumulated amounts.

Calculating Accumulated Depreciation

The total amount of depreciation expense that has been recorded since the purchase of a plant asset is called **accumulated depreciation.**

First, the depreciation expense that has accumulated over all prior years is determined. Second, the depreciation expense for the current year is calculated. Third, the prior accumulated depreciation and the current depreciation expense are added.

20X2 Accumulated Depreciation	+	20X3 Depreciation Expense	=	20X3 Accumulated Depreciation
$400.00	+	$200.00	=	$600.00

Calculating Book Value

The original cost of a plant asset minus accumulated depreciation is called the **book value of a plant asset.** For the first year, the beginning book value is the original cost. Thereafter, the book value is calculated by subtracting the accumulated depreciation from the original cost of the asset. The ending book value is the beginning book value for the next year.

Original Cost	–	Accumulated Depreciation	=	Ending Book Value
$1,250.00	–	$600.00	=	$650.00

The book value can also be calculated by subtracting the year's depreciation from that year's beginning book value. Either method of calculating a book value is acceptable because both methods calculate the same amount.

Beginning Book Value	–	Annual Depreciation	=	Ending Book Value
$850.00	–	$200.00	=	$650.00

CULTURAL DIVERSITY

VALUING DIVERSITY IN THE WORKPLACE

Employees in the U.S. have diverse cultural backgrounds. This diversity reflects the cultural differences in society.

All employees bring their cultural backgrounds and values with them to the workplace. In order to work effectively with people of other cultures, we need to understand each other.

Cultural differences do not exist only between people from different countries. They may arise with anyone in the workplace perceived to be different from the norm. Consider the differences in employees who are younger or older than average, who are physically handicapped, or who speak English as a second language.

Enlightened companies will encourage "valuing diversity" in the workplace. This means valuing the cultural backgrounds of each individual. It means respecting each person for what he or she can contribute to the goals of the organization.

Terms Review
Call on students to define the terms in the Terms Review. Ask the class if the definitions are correct and whether the complete definitions have been given or if anything needs to be added. The suggested definition is given in the Glossary.

Audit Your Understanding
Call on students to answer the Audit Your Understanding questions. Ask the class if the answer is correct and/or complete. Answers are given in Appendix D of the textbook.

Work Together
Have students write the solution to the Work Together problem as you guide the class through the example.

❏ Ask students to identify the number of months the asset should be depreciated in the first year.

❏ Call on a student to describe the calculation of the depreciation expense for the first year.

❏ Call on students to describe the calculation of the accumulated depreciation and book value for the first year.

❏ Direct students to complete the depreciation tables.

❏ Remind students to save their work to complete Work Together in Lesson 3.

INDEPENDENT PRACTICE

On Your Own
❏ Assign the On Your Own problem to be worked independently.

❏ Remind students to save their work to complete On Your Own in Lesson 3.

❏ Use the Ongoing Assessment techniques to diagnose student understanding.

Application Problem
❏ Assign Application Problem 21-2: Calculating depreciation.

TERMS REVIEW

depreciation expense

estimated salvage value

straight-line method of depreciation

accumulated depreciation

book value of a plant asset

AUDIT YOUR UNDERSTANDING

1. Which accounting concept is being applied when depreciation expense is recorded for plant assets?

2. What three factors are used to calculate a plant asset's annual depreciation expense?

3. Why is annual depreciation not recorded for land?

WORK TOGETHER

Calculating depreciation

Depreciation tables for Gabriel, Inc., are given in the *Working Papers*. Your instructor will guide you through the following example.

4. The following assets were bought during 20X1. Complete a depreciation table for each asset using the straight-line depreciation method. If the asset was not bought at the beginning of 20X1, calculate the depreciation expense for the part of 20X1 in which the company owned the asset. Save your work to complete Work Together on page 558.

Transactions:

Jan. 4. Bought a television costing $700.00 for use in a sales display; estimated salvage value, $100.00; estimated useful life, 3 years.

May 27. Bought an office desk, $920.00; estimated salvage value, $200.00; estimated useful life, 6 years.

ON YOUR OWN

Calculating depreciation

Depreciation tables for Yeatman Co. are given in the *Working Papers*. Work this problem independently.

5. The following assets were bought during 20X1. Complete a depreciation table for each asset using the straight-line depreciation method. If the asset was not bought at the beginning of 20X1, calculate the depreciation expense for the part of 20X1 in which the company owned the asset. Save your work to complete On Your Own on page 558.

Transactions:

Jan. 3. Bought a security camera costing $850.00; estimated salvage value, $250.00; estimated useful life, 5 years.

June 29. Bought a copy machine, $3,500.00; estimated salvage value, $500.00; estimated useful life, 4 years.

ENRICH

❏ Assign the Automated Accounting feature on page 573 to automate Application Problem 21-2.

❏ Assign the Spreadsheet Accounting Template for Application Problem 21-2.

CLOSE

❏ Ask students to briefly summarize the procedures for calculating depreciation expense, using the straight-line method.

21-3 Journalizing Depreciation Expense

PREPARING PLANT ASSET RECORDS

PLANT ASSET RECORD No. **123**

General Ledger Account No. **1215**

Description **Display Case**

General Ledger Account **Store Equipment**

Date Bought **January 2, 20X1**   Serial Number **B672981**   Original Cost **$1,250.00**

Estimated Useful Life **5 years**   Estimated Salvage Value **$250.00**   Depreciation Method **Straight-line**

Disposed of: Discarded _____   Sold _____   Traded _____

Date _____   Disposal Amount _____

YEAR	ANNUAL DEPRECIATION EXPENSE	ACCUMULATED DEPRECIATION	ENDING BOOK VALUE
20X1	$200.00	$ 200.00	$1,050.00
20X2	200.00	400.00	850.00
20X3	200.00	600.00	650.00
20X4	200.00	800.00	450.00
20X5	200.00	1,000.00	250.00

Continue record on back of card

A separate record is kept for each plant asset. An accounting form on which a business records information about each plant asset is called a **plant asset record.**

Plant asset records may vary in arrangement for different businesses, but most records contain similar information. Winning Edge's plant asset record has three sections. Section 1 is prepared when a plant asset is bought. Section 2 provides space for recording the disposition of the plant asset. When the asset is disposed of, this information will be filled in. Section 3 provides space for recording annual depreciation expense and the changing book value of the asset each year it is used.

At the end of each fiscal period, Winning Edge brings each plant asset record up to date by recording three amounts: (1) annual depreciation expense, (2) accumulated depreciation, and (3) ending book value.

The amount recorded in the Annual Depreciation Expense column is the amount calculated for each year. These amounts may be different if the asset is bought or sold at a time other than near the fiscal year end.

Accumulated depreciation for the first year is the annual depreciation expense for the first year. In later years, accumulated depreciation is the depreciation expense that has accumulated over all prior years added to that year's annual depreciation expense.

The ending book value is the original cost less that year's accumulated depreciation.

S T E P S Preparing a plant asset record

1. Write the information in Section 1 when the plant asset is purchased.
2. Do *not* write in Section 2 until the asset is disposed of.
3. Each year the asset is owned, record the year's annual depreciation expense in Section 3. Calculate and record accumulated depreciation and ending book value.

CHAPTER 21   Accounting for Plant Assets and Depreciation   **555**

- ❑ Point out that depreciation is recorded on the work sheet and journalized in the general journal.
- ❑ Explain that Accumulated Depreciation is a contra asset account having a normal credit balance.
- ❑ Point out that recording annual depreciation has no effect on the plant asset account.

DEMONSTRATE

Analyze the accumulated depreciation account

- ❑ Draw a T account on the board for Store Equipment. Label its increase/decrease, debit/credit, and normal balance sides.
- ❑ Draw a T account on the board for Accumulated Depreciation—Store Equipment. Explain that this account is a contra account to Store Equipment.
- ❑ Ask students to identify the increase/decrease, debit/credit, and normal balance sides as you label the account.

Analyze the transaction

- ❑ Draw three T accounts on the board and enter the balance amounts shown in the illustration.
- ❑ Read the transaction statement.
- ❑ Ask students to analyze the transaction by answering: what accounts are affected, are they increased or decreased, and are they debited or credited? Complete the T accounts as the information is provided.

Record the transaction

- ❑ Use Transparency M to illustrate recording the transaction in the general journal or direct students to the illustration.
- ❑ Direct students to record the transaction, following the three steps shown.
- ❑ Remind students that no source document notation is necessary in the general journal for adjusting entries recorded on a work sheet.

JOURNALIZING ANNUAL DEPRECIATION EXPENSE

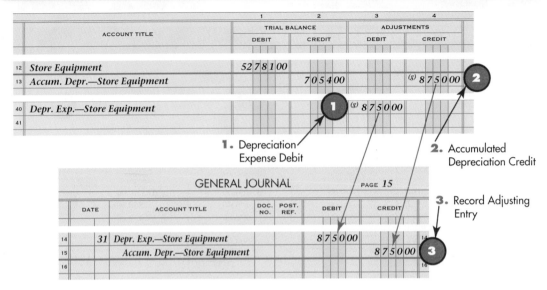

1. Depreciation Expense Debit

2. Accumulated Depreciation Credit

3. Record Adjusting Entry

At the end of the fiscal year, Winning Edge calculates the depreciation expense for each plant asset. The depreciation expense for each asset is recorded on its plant asset record. Next, the total depreciation expense is calculated for all plant assets recorded in the same plant asset account.

Winning Edge determined that total depreciation expense for store equipment is $8,750.00. An adjustment is planned in the Adjustments columns of the work sheet. Using this information, an adjusting entry is then recorded in a general journal.

It is important to retain original cost information for plant assets. Rather than credit the plant asset account, depreciation is recorded to the contra asset account Accumulated Depreciation.

Accumulated Depreciation

Debit	Credit

At any time, the book value of plant assets can be calculated by subtracting Accumulated Depreciation from the plant asset account.

Store Equipment

| Dec. 31 Bal. | 52,781.00 | |

Depreciation Expense—Store Equipment

| Dec. 31 Adj. | 8,750.00 | |

Accumulated Depreciation—Store Equipment

	Jan. 1 Bal.	7,054.00
	Dec. 31 Adj.	8,750.00
	Dec. 31 Bal.	15,804.00

Analyzing and journalizing annual depreciation expense

1. Write the total annual depreciation expense, *$8,750.00,* in the Adjustments Debit column on the Depreciation Expense—Store Equipment line of the work sheet. Label the adjustment *(g),* with a small letter in parentheses.
2. Write the same amount, *$8,750.00,* in the Adjustments Credit column on the Accumulated Depreciation—Store Equipment line of the work sheet. Label the adjustment using the same letter, *(g).*
3. Use the debit and credit accounts on the work sheet to record an adjusting entry in a general journal.

556 CHAPTER 21 Accounting for Plant Assets and Depreciation

TEACHING STRATEGIES DIFFERENT LEARNING STYLES

Print Learner. When learning formulas, the print learner would prefer to be able to study the formula as given in the textbook or as printed on a separate handout. The print material should show the formula as well as an example of performing the calculations.

POSTING AN ADJUSTING ENTRY FOR DEPRECIATION EXPENSE

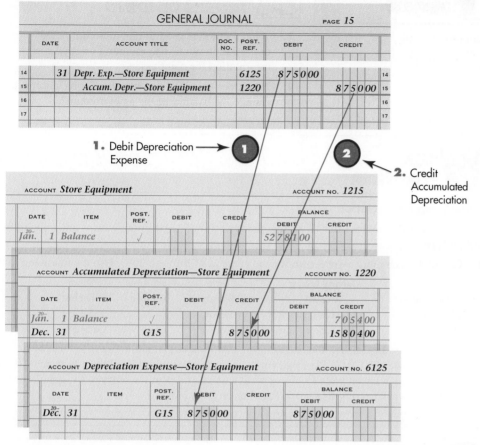

1. Debit Depreciation Expense

2. Credit Accumulated Depreciation

EXPLAIN

- ❏ Point out that students have already learned how to post transactions from a general journal to the general ledger.
- ❏ Remind students that the depreciation expense adjustment does not impact the plant asset account.
- ❏ Point out that the balances in the plant asset and related accumulated depreciation accounts can be used to calculate the book value of plant assets.
- ❏ Ask students to read the Remember to reinforce that depreciation expense transactions are recorded for each category of plant assets (except land).

DEMONSTRATE

- ❏ Direct students to the illustration and describe the steps to post the adjusting entry, following the two steps shown.
- ❏ Ask students to identify the individual steps for posting from a general journal to a general ledger.

ONGOING ASSESSMENT

- ❏ Assessment is an ongoing process. Circulate through the classroom or lab, observing which students have problems with the assignments.
- ❏ Troubleshooting: Diagnose what kinds of problems students have with this lesson. Students may have trouble (1) understanding the purpose of the accumulated depreciation account and (2) understanding what the account balance represents.
- ❏ Assess student understanding by checking solutions to Independent Practice assignments.

The adjustment for depreciation expense planned on the work sheet is recorded as an adjusting entry in the general journal. The adjusting entry is then posted to the general ledger.

After posting, Store Equipment has a debit balance showing the original cost of all store equipment. The contra account Accumulated Depreciation—Store Equipment has a credit balance showing the accumulated depreciation recorded to date.

The debit balance of Depreciation Expense—Store Equipment is the portion of the cost of plant assets allocated to expense during the fiscal period.

S T E P S Posting an adjusting entry for depreciation expense

1. Post the debit, *$8,750.00,* to the Depreciation Expense—Store Equipment account.

2. Post the credit, *$8,750.00,* to the Accumulated Depreciation—Store Equipment account.

REMEMBER

An adjusting entry is made to record the depreciation expense for each category of plant assets. Winning Edge also records an adjusting entry to Depreciation Expense—Office Equipment and Accumulated Depreciation—Office Equipment.

RETEACH

- ❏ Ask students to identify the four places where depreciation expense is recorded *(plant asset record, work sheet, general journal, and general ledger account).*
- ❏ Ask students to identify the adjusting entry to record depreciation expense.

- ❏ Encourage students to evaluate the balance in an accumulated depreciation account with the related plant asset account (thus, the book value).

Term Review

Call on students to define the term in the Term Review. Ask the class if the definition is correct and whether the complete definition has been given or if anything needs to be added. Suggested definitions for all terms are given in the Glossary.

Audit Your Understanding

Call on students to answer the Audit Your Understanding questions. Ask the class if the answer is correct and/or complete. Answers are given in Appendix D of the textbook.

Work Together

Have students write the solutions to the Work Together problems as you guide the class through the examples.

❑ Remind students to use the problem started in Lesson 2.

❑ Ask students to complete the plant asset record for each asset.

❑ Direct students to record the adjusting entry on the work sheet.

❑ Direct students to record the adjusting entry in the general journal.

❑ Direct students to post the adjusting entry to the general ledger.

❑ Remind students to save their work to complete Work Together in Lesson 4.

On Your Own

❑ Assign the On Your Own problems to be worked independently.

❑ Remind students to use the problem started in Lesson 2.

❑ Remind students to save their work to complete On Your Own in Lesson 4.

❑ Use the Ongoing Assessment techniques to diagnose student understanding.

Application Problem

❑ Assign Application Problem 21-3: Preparing plant asset records.

❑ Assign Application Problem 21-4: Journalizing annual depreciation expense.

558

TERM REVIEW

plant asset record

AUDIT YOUR UNDERSTANDING

1. What method is used to record accumulated depreciation while also retaining original cost information for plant assets?

2. How does an adjusting entry for depreciation expense change the balance of the asset account?

WORK TOGETHER

Journalizing depreciation

Use the depreciation tables from Work Together on page 554. Additional forms are given in the *Working Papers*. Your instructor will guide you through the following examples.

3. Complete each plant asset record for the years 20X1 through 20X3. Use the following table:

Description	General Ledger Account	Date Bought	Plant Asset Number	Serial Number
Television	1215-Store Equipment	Jan. 4	134	15SG152
Office Desk	1205-Office Equipment	May 27	135	GE572N

4. On December 31, Gabriel, Inc., determined that total depreciation expense for office equipment was $3,120.00. Plan the work sheet adjustment and label the adjustment (*f*). Record the adjusting entry on page 18 of a general journal and post the entry to the general ledger. Save your work to complete Work Together on page 563.

ON YOUR OWN

Journalizing depreciation

Use the depreciation tables from On Your Own on page 554. Additional forms are given in the *Working Papers*. Work these problems independently.

5. Complete each plant asset record from the years 20X1 through 20X3. Use the following table:

Description	General Ledger Account	Date Bought	Plant Asset Number	Serial Number
Security Camera	1215-Store Equipment	Jan. 3	253	G1234MN2
Copy Machine	1205-Office Equipment	June 29	254	1776CM123

6. On December 31, Yeatman Co. determined that total depreciation expense for store equipment was $8,770.00. Plan the work sheet adjustment and label the adjustment (*g*). Record the adjusting entry on page 13 of a general journal and post the entry to the general ledger. Save your work to complete On Your Own on page 563.

ENRICH

❑ Direct students to obtain the annual report of a publicly-traded company. Instruct the students to locate the amount of depreciation expense as reported on either the income statement or statement of cash flows. What percent of total operating expenses resulted from depreciation expense?

❑ Show the CNN Accounting Video.

CLOSE

❑ Ask students to summarize the sections of a plant asset record.

❑ Ask students to explain how to journalize and post the adjusting entry to record depreciation expense.

SALE OF A PLANT ASSET FOR BOOK VALUE

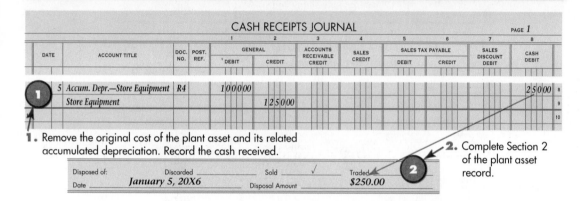

CASH RECEIPTS JOURNAL — PAGE 1

DATE	ACCOUNT TITLE	DOC. NO.	POST. REF.	GENERAL DEBIT	GENERAL CREDIT	ACCOUNTS RECEIVABLE CREDIT	SALES CREDIT	SALES TAX PAYABLE DEBIT	SALES TAX PAYABLE CREDIT	SALES DISCOUNT DEBIT	CASH DEBIT
5	Accum. Depr.—Store Equipment	R4		1 000 00							2 50 00
	Store Equipment				1 2 50 00						

1. Remove the original cost of the plant asset and its related accumulated depreciation. Record the cash received.

2. Complete Section 2 of the plant asset record.

Disposed of: Discarded _____ Sold _✓_ Traded _____
Date _January 5, 20X6_ Disposal Amount _$250.00_

A plant asset may no longer be useful to a business for a number of reasons. When a plant asset is no longer useful to a business, the asset may be disposed of. The old plant asset may be sold, traded for a new asset, or discarded.

When a plant asset is disposed of, a journal entry is recorded that achieves the following:
1. Removes the original cost of the plant asset and its related accumulated depreciation.
2. Recognizes any cash or other asset received for the old plant asset.
3. Recognizes any gain or loss on the disposal.

After five years of use, Winning Edge sold a display case.

> *January 5, 20X6. Received cash from sale of display case, $250.00: original cost, $1,250.00; total accumulated depreciation through December 31, 20X5, $1,000.00. Receipt No. 4.*

The amount of gain or loss, if any, is calculated by subtracting the book value from the cash received.

The display case was sold for its book value. Therefore, no gain or loss exists.

Cash received		$250.00
Less: Book value of asset sold:		
Cost	$1,250.00	
Accum. Depr.	1,000.00	250.00
Gain (loss) on sale of plant asset		$ 0.00

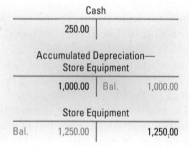

Cash

250.00	

Accumulated Depreciation— Store Equipment

1,000.00	Bal.	1,000.00

Store Equipment

Bal.	1,250.00		1,250.00

Recording sale of a plant asset for book value

1. Record an entry in the cash receipts journal to remove the original cost, *$1,250.00*, from Store Equipment and *$1,000.00* from Accumulated Depreciation—Store Equipment. Record the cash received from the sale, *$250.00*, as a debit to Cash.
2. Check the type of disposal, *Sold*, and write the date, *January 5, 20X6*, and disposal amount, *$250.00*, in Section 2 of the plant asset record.

EXPLAIN

□ Remind students that they have already learned how to calculate a partial year's depreciation expense when a plant asset is purchased during the fiscal year.

□ Point out that plant assets can be sold any time during the year.

□ Ask students to describe why depreciation expense should be recorded for a partial year if the asset is being sold or disposed of. *(Use of the asset during a portion of the year is an expense that should be matched with the revenue the asset helped to generate.)*

□ Point out that two journal entries are typically required to discard a plant asset: one entry updates depreciation expense and the other entry records the disposition.

DEMONSTRATE

Calculate depreciation expense

□ Ask students to use a calculator to calculate the partial year's depreciation, as shown in the math box.

Record the transaction

□ Draw two T accounts on the board and enter the balance amounts.

□ Read the transaction statement.

□ Ask students to analyze the transaction by answering: what accounts are affected, are they increased or decreased, and are they debited or credited? Complete the T accounts as the information is provided.

□ Use Transparency M to illustrate recording the transaction in the general journal or direct students to the illustration.

□ Direct students to record the journal entry, following the first two steps shown.

□ Discuss that the plant asset record would also be updated as shown.

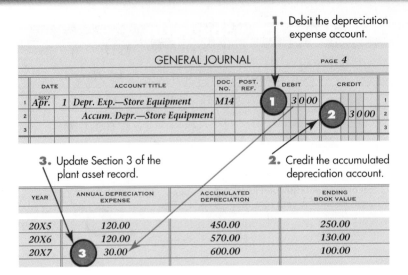

1. Debit the depreciation expense account.

3. Update Section 3 of the plant asset record.

2. Credit the accumulated depreciation account.

A plant asset may be sold at any time during the asset's useful life. When a plant asset is sold, its depreciation from the beginning of the current fiscal year to the date of disposal is recorded.

On April 1, 20X7, Winning Edge intends to sell a cash register that was bought on August 1, 20X2. Annual depreciation expense for the cash register is $120.00. Depreciation recorded through December 31, 20X6, is $570.00.

The method to calculate a partial year's depreciation is the same as calculating depreciation when an asset is purchased during the fiscal year. The monthly depreciation expense is multiplied by the number of months the asset is used during the current fiscal year.

	Annual Depreciation Expense	÷	Months in a Year	=	Monthly Depreciation Expense
	$120.00	÷	12	=	$10.00

	Monthly Depreciation Expense	×	Number of Months Asset Is Used	=	Partial Year's Depreciation Expense
	$10.00	×	3	=	$30.00

April 1, 20X7. Recorded a partial year's depreciation on cash register to be sold, $30.00. Memorandum No. 14.

Depreciation Expense—Store Equipment

Add. Depr. 30.00	

Accumulated Depreciation— Store Equipment

	Bal. 570.00
	Add. Depr. 30.00
	(New Bal. 600.00)

The depreciation is also recorded on the plant asset record for the cash register.

ⓢⓣⒺⓟⓢ Recording a partial year's depreciation

1. Record a debit, *$30.00*, to Depreciation Expense—Store Equipment in the general journal.

2. Record a credit, *$30.00*, to Accumulated Depreciation—Store Equipment in the general journal.

3. Record the depreciation expense in Section 3 of the plant asset record for the cash register. Calculate and record accumulated depreciation and ending book value.

TEACHING STRATEGIES   DIFFERENT LEARNING STYLES

Visual Learner. Formulas, such as those used to calculate depreciation expense, should be illustrated on the chalkboard to assist visual learners. The instructor should also complete the calculations for a few depreciable assets to show the process to visual learners.

SALE OF A PLANT ASSET FOR MORE THAN BOOK VALUE

CASH RECEIPTS JOURNAL
PAGE 10

				GENERAL		ACCOUNTS RECEIVABLE CREDIT	SALES CREDIT	SALES TAX PAYABLE		SALES DISCOUNT DEBIT	CASH DEBIT	
DATE	ACCOUNT TITLE	DOC. NO.	POST. REF.	DEBIT	CREDIT			DEBIT	CREDIT			
20X7 Apr. 1	Accum. Depr.—Store Equipment	R39		600 00							125 00	1
	Store Equipment				700 00							2
	Gain on Plant Assets				25 00							3

1. Record an entry to remove asset, record gain, and record cash.

2. Complete Section 2 of the plant asset record.

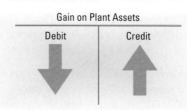

Disposed of: Discarded ___ Sold ✓ Traded ___
Date __April 1, 20X7__ Disposal Amount __$125.00__

YEAR	ANNUAL DEPRECIATION EXPENSE	ACCUMULATED DEPRECIATION	ENDING BOOK VALUE

Revenue that results when a plant asset is sold for more than book value is called **gain on plant assets.** Winning Edge is selling a cash register for $125.00. After the partial year's depreciation is recorded, a journal entry is made to record the sale of the cash register.

> *April 1, 20X7. Received cash from sale of a cash register, $125.00: original cost, $700.00; accumulated depreciation through April 1, 20X7, $600.00. Receipt No. 39.*

The gain or loss on the sale of a plant asset is the book value subtracted from cash received.

Cash received		$125.00
Less: Book value of asset sold:		
Cost	$700.00	
Accum. Depr.	600.00	100.00
Gain (loss) on sale of plant asset		$ 25.00

The gain realized on the disposal of a plant asset is credited to a revenue account titled Gain on Plant Assets.

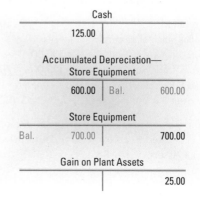

Gain on Plant Assets

Debit	Credit
▼	▲

A gain from the sale of plant assets is not an operating revenue. Therefore, Gain on Plant Assets is listed in a classification titled Other Revenue in the chart of accounts.

Cash
125.00	

Accumulated Depreciation— Store Equipment
600.00	Bal. 600.00

Store Equipment
Bal. 700.00	700.00

Gain on Plant Assets
	25.00

CHAPTER 21 Accounting for Plant Assets and Depreciation **561**

EXPLAIN

☐ Point out that plant assets can be sold as productive assets or for scrap.

☐ Emphasize that the gain on plant assets account is a revenue account that appears in the Other Revenue section in the chart of accounts. It is not an operating revenue account because the company is not in the business of selling its assets.

☐ Review the calculation of the gain or loss on the sale of the plant asset.

☐ Ask students to identify the difference between this entry and the entry shown earlier in this lesson. *(This entry requires three lines, rather than two, because the asset was sold for a gain.)*

DEMONSTRATE

Analyze the gain on plant assets account

☐ Draw a T account on the board for Gain on Plant Assets.

☐ Ask students to identify the increase/decrease, debit/credit, and normal balance side as you label the account. Explain that because the account is a revenue account, it has the same normal balance side as the sales account.

Analyze the transaction

☐ Draw four T accounts on the board and enter the balance amounts.

☐ Read the transaction statement.

☐ Ask students to analyze the transaction by answering: what accounts are affected, are they increased or decreased, and are they debited or credited? Complete the T accounts as the information is provided.

Record the transaction

☐ Use Transparency O to illustrate recording the transaction in the cash receipts journal or direct students to the illustration.

☐ Direct students to record the transaction in the cash receipts journal and the plant asset record, following the two steps shown.

DATE	ACCOUNT TITLE	DOC. NO.	POST. REF.	GENERAL DEBIT	GENERAL CREDIT	ACCOUNTS RECEIVABLE CREDIT	SALES CREDIT	SALES TAX PAYABLE DEBIT	SALES TAX PAYABLE CREDIT	SALES DISCOUNT DEBIT	CASH DEBIT	
20X7 Sept. 1	Accum. Depr.—Office Equipment	R281		1 3 0 0 00							5 0 0 00	1
	Loss on Plant Assets			2 0 0 00								2
	Office Equipment				2 0 0 0 00							3

1. Record an entry to dispose of the asset, record a loss on plant assets, and record cash.

Disposed of:	Discarded _____	Sold _____ ✓	Traded _____
Date _____ September 1, 20X7		Disposal Amount _____	$500.00

2. Complete Section 2 of the plant asset record.

The loss that results when a plant asset is sold for less than book value is called **loss on plant assets.** Winning Edge sold a computer after three years of use. After the partial year's depreciation is recorded, a journal entry is made to record the sale of the computer.

> **September 1, 20X7. Received cash from sale of a computer, $500.00: original cost, $2,000.00; total accumulated depreciation through September 1, 20X7, $1,300.00. Receipt No. 281.**

The gain or loss on the sale of a plant asset is the book value subtracted from cash received.

Cash received		$ 500.00
Less: Book value of asset sold:		
Cost	$2,000.00	
Accum. Depr.	1,300.00	700.00
Gain (loss) on sale of plant asset		$ (200.00)

The loss realized on the disposal of a plant asset is debited to an expense account titled Loss on Plant Assets.

Loss on Plant Assets

Debit	Credit
↑	↓

A loss from the sale of plant assets is not an operating expense. Therefore, Loss on Plant Assets is listed in a classification titled Other Expenses in the chart of accounts.

Cash

500.00	

Accumulated Depreciation— Office Equipment

	1,300.00	Bal.	1,300.00

Loss on Plant Assets

200.00	

Office Equipment

Bal.	2,000.00	2,000.00

(S) Recording sale of a plant asset for less than book value

T
1. Record an entry in the cash receipts journal to remove the original cost, $2,000.00, from Office Equipment and $1,300.00 from Accumulated Depreciation—Office Equipment. Record the loss on sale, $200.00, as a debit to Loss on Plant Assets. Record the cash received from the sale, $500.00, as a debit to Cash.
E
P 2. Check the type of disposal, *Sold,* and write the date, *Sept. 1, 20X7,* and disposal amount, $500.00, in Section 2 of the plant asset record for the computer.
S

TERMS REVIEW

gain on plant assets

loss on plant assets

AUDIT YOUR UNDERSTANDING

1. What is recorded on plant asset records for plant assets that have been disposed of?

2. When an asset is disposed of after the beginning of the fiscal year, what entry may need to be recorded before an entry is made for the discarding of a plant asset?

3. What is the formula to compute the gain or loss on the sale of a plant asset?

4. In what account classification is Loss on Plant Assets listed?

WORK TOGETHER

Recording the disposal of plant assets

Use the plant asset records from Work Together on page 558. Your instructor will guide you through the following examples.

5. For each of the following transactions completed in 20X4, journalize an entry for additional depreciation, if needed. Use page 3 of a general journal given in the *Working Papers*. Source documents are abbreviated as follows: check, C; memorandum, M; receipt, R.

Transactions:

Jan. 3. Received cash for sale of a television, plant asset No.134, $100.00. R3.

June 30. Received cash for sale of an office desk, plant asset No.135, $400.00. M25 and R45.

6. Use page 3 of a cash receipts journal to record the disposal of each plant asset.

7. Make appropriate notations in the plant asset records.

ON YOUR OWN

Recording the disposal of plant assets

Use the plant asset records from On Your Own on page 558. Work these problems independently.

8. For each of the following transactions completed in 20X4, journalize an entry for additional depreciation, if needed. Use page 4 of a general journal given in the *Working Papers*. Source documents are abbreviated as follows: check, C; memorandum, M; receipt, R.

Transactions:

Jan. 2. Received cash for sale of a copy machine, plant asset No. 254, $1,800.00. R8.

Apr. 29. Received cash for sale of a security camera, plant asset No. 253, $450.00. M4 and R45.

9. Use page 1 of a cash receipts journal to record the disposal of each plant asset.

10. Make appropriate notations in the plant asset records.

ENRICH

❑ Ask students to discuss when a business should sell a plant asset. *(An asset should be sold when it is no longer productive or the asset could be sold and the cash received used to purchase more productive assets. The gain or loss on the sale should not typically impact the sales decision.)*

CLOSE

❑ Ask students to list the information required to record the sale of a plant asset.

❑ Ask students to explain how to calculate the gain or loss on the sale of a plant asset.

OBJECTIVES

❏ Define the accounting terms related to plant assets and depreciation.
❏ Identify accounting concepts and practices related to plant assets and depreciation.
❏ Calculate depreciation expense using the double declining-balance method of depreciation.

MOTIVATE

Several methods can be used to calculate depreciation expense. Unlike the straight-line method of depreciation, the declining-balance method results in a higher amount of depreciation expense in the first years of an asset's useful life. These depreciation methods are known as accelerated depreciation methods.

Preview
❏ Preview the accounting term "declining-balance method of depreciation" and its definition, introduced in this lesson.
❏ Direct students to read the headings at the top of each page in this lesson and to examine the illustrations given.

EXPLAIN

❏ Ask students how the double declining-balance rate is calculated.
❏ Ask students to identify what amount is constant *(the depreciation rate)*.
❏ Describe the method used to calculate annual depreciation expense.
❏ Point out that the salvage value is not used in the depreciation calculation for the years shown.

DEMONSTRATE

❏ Draw five columns on the board and label the columns as shown in the illustration.
❏ Ask a student to calculate the double declining-balance rate.
❏ Ask a student to calculate and record the amounts for year 1.
❏ Ask students to take turns completing the table for years 2–4.
❏ Retain the schedule on the board for use in the demonstration for the following page.

564

CALCULATING DEPRECIATION USING THE DOUBLE DECLINING-BALANCE METHOD

Plant Asset: Truck Depreciation Method: Declining-Balance		Original Cost: $22,000.00 Estimated Salvage Value: $2,200.00 Estimated Useful Life: 5 years		
Year	Beginning Book Value	Declining-Balance Rate	Annual Depreciation	Ending Book Value
1	$22,000.00	40%	$8,800.00	$13,200.00
2	13,200.00	40%	5,280.00	7,920.00

4. Transfer the book value to the following year.

2. Determine the annual depreciation expense.

3. Determine the ending book value.

The straight-line method of depreciation charges an equal amount of depreciation expense each year. However, not all assets depreciate the same amount each year. Many plant assets depreciate more in the early years of useful life than in later years. For example, a truck's value will decrease more in the first year of service than in later years. Therefore, charging more depreciation expense in the early years of a plant asset may be more accurate than charging the same amount each year. (*CONCEPT: Matching Expenses with Revenue*)

Multiplying the book value by a constant depreciation rate at the end of each fiscal period is called the **declining-balance method of depreciation.**

The declining-balance depreciation rate is a multiple of the straight-line rate. Many businesses use a declining-balance rate that is two times the straight-line rate. This method of depreciation is referred to as the double declining-balance method.

Calculating depreciation using the double declining-balance method

1. Calculate the double-declining balance rate. An example of a plant asset with a five-year life is shown.

Estimated Depreciation Expense	÷	Years of Estimated Useful Life	=	Straight-Line Rate of Depreciation
100%	÷	5	=	20%

Straight-Line Rate of Depreciation	×	2	=	Double Declining- Balance Rate
20%	×	2	=	40%

2. Multiply the double-declining balance rate by the beginning book value to determine the annual depreciation expense for a given year ($22,000.00 × 40% = $8,800.00).

3. Subtract the annual depreciation expense from the beginning book value to determine the ending book value ($22,000.00 − $8,800.00 = $13,200.00).

4. Transfer the ending book value to the beginning book value for the following year. Repeat this process for all remaining years except for the last year of useful life. Calculating the depreciation expense in the last year of an asset's life is covered on the next page.

MATERIALS

❏ Work Sheets:
Math Work Sheet, Chapter 21, Part F
❏ Transparencies:
21-2, Chapter Summary
❏ Working Papers:
Teacher's Edition of the Working Papers for Lesson 21-5

❏ Software:
Accounting Connection, Chapter 21
Automated Accounting 7.0 or higher and Accounting Textbook Template
Spreadsheet Accounting Template

CALCULATING THE LAST YEAR'S DEPRECIATION EXPENSE

Plant Asset: Truck Depreciation Method: Declining-Balance	Original Cost: $22,000.00 Estimated Salvage Value: $2,200.00 Estimated Useful Life: 5 years			
Year	Beginning Book Value	Declining-Balance Rate	Annual Depreciation	Ending Book Value
1	$22,000.00	40%	$8,800.00	$13,200.00
2	13,200.00	40%	5,280.00	7,920.00
3	7,920.00	40%	3,168.00	4,752.00
4	4,752.00	40%	1,900.80	2,851.20
5	① 2,851.20 ←		② 651.20	③ 2,200.00
Total Depreciation			$19,800.00	

1. Transfer the book value. **2.** Determine the last year's depreciation. **3.** Verify the ending book value.

Although the depreciation rate is the same each year, the annual depreciation expense declines from one year to the next.

A plant asset is never depreciated below its estimated salvage value. Therefore, in the last year, only enough depreciation expense is recorded to reduce the book value of the plant asset to its salvage value.

Sometimes in the last year of a plant asset's useful life, the formula for the double declining-balance method of depreciation results in an ending book value greater than the estimated salvage value. In other words, the depreciation formula does not create enough accumulated depreciation to reduce the book value down to what is a relatively small estimated salvage value.

When this situation exists, most companies that use the declining-balance method of depreciation switch to the straight-line method sometime during the life of the plant asset. To determine when to switch to the straight-line method of depreciation, each year a company compares the annual depreciation expense calculated using the straight-line method to the annual depreciation expense calculated using the declining-balance method. If the annual depreciation expense using the straight-line method is greater than the annual depreciation expense using the declining-balance method, the company should use the straight-line method.

S **Calculating the last year's depreciation expense**
T
E **1.** Transfer the ending book value from Year 4 to the beginning book value of Year 5.
P **2.** Subtract the salvage value of the plant asset from the beginning book value to determine the depreciation
S expense for the last year of useful life ($2,851.20 − $2,200.00 = $651.20).
3. Verify that the ending book value is equal to the salvage value.

REMEMBER

Unlike the straight-line method, the declining-balance method does not use the estimated salvage value to calculate depreciation. The estimated salvage value is used only to limit the last year's depreciation expense.

EXPLAIN

❏ Point out that both depreciation methods are generally accepted.

❏ Point out that the adjusting entry for depreciation is the same, regardless of the depreciation method used.

❏ Remind students that each depreciation method results in the same amount of depreciation over the useful life of the asset.

DEMONSTRATE

Ask a student to draw on the board a graph of the annual depreciation amounts for the five years. Ask students to describe why the double declining-balance method is referred to as an accelerated depreciation method.

LEGAL ISSUES IN ACCOUNTING

The Legal Issues in Accounting feature describes aspects of law that affect business organizations. Take time to discuss the legal ramifications of dissolving a corporation.

ONGOING ASSESSMENT

❏ Assessment is an ongoing process. Circulate through the classroom or lab, observing which students have problems with the assignments.

❏ Troubleshooting: Diagnose what kinds of problems students have with this lesson. Students may have difficulty (1) understanding how to calculate annual double declining-balance depreciation expense, especially after having learned the calculations required for the straight-line method, or (2) remembering that accumulated depreciation cannot reduce book value below salvage value.

❏ Assess student understanding by checking solutions to Independent Practice assignments.

Plant Asset: Computer
Depreciation Method: Comparison of Two Methods

Original Cost: $2,000.00
Estimated Salvage Value: $200.00
Estimated Useful Life: 5 years

Year	Straight-Line Method			Double Declining-Balance Method		
	Beginning Book Value	Annual Depreciation	Ending Book Value	Beginning Book Value	Annual Depreciation	Ending Book Value
1	$2,000.00	$360.00	$1,640.00	$2,000.00	$800.00	$1,200.00
2	1,640.00	360.00	1,280.00	1,200.00	480.00	720.00
3	1,280.00	360.00	920.00	720.00	288.00	432.00
4	920.00	360.00	560.00	432.00	172.80	259.20
5	560.00	360.00	200.00	259.20	59.20	200.00
Total Depreciation	—	$1,800.00	—	—	$1,800.00	—

Regardless of the depreciation method used, the total depreciation expense over the useful life of a plant asset is the same. The accounts used in the journal entries to record depreciation expense and the sale of plant assets are also the same.

Each depreciation method is acceptable according to generally accepted accounting principles. The straight-line method is easy to calculate. The same amount of depreciation expense is recorded for each year of estimated useful life.

The double declining-balance method is slightly more complicated. This method records a greater depreciation expense in the early years than the straight-line method. The declining-balance method is referred to as an accelerated depreciation method. The method accelerates the recording of depreciation in the early years of the asset's useful life.

LEGAL ISSUES IN ACCOUNTING

DISSOLVING A CORPORATION

Because the corporation is the most complex form of business, dissolution involves many legal procedures. Thus, the board of directors should seek the legal advice of an attorney.

In some states, the Secretary of State may take action to dissolve a corporation if one or more of the three following conditions exists: (1) The corporation is 60 days late in paying franchise taxes. (2) The corporation does not file its annual report within 60 days of the due date. (3) The corporation does not have a registered agent or office for 60 days or more.

Judicial proceedings may be brought against a corporation if the corporation acts beyond the powers it has been granted or engages in illegal activity. These proceedings may force the corporation to give up its charter.

Once a corporation is dissolved, the liquidation process can begin. Noncash assets usually are sold, and the available cash is used to pay creditors. The procedure for selling noncash assets is similar to that for proprietorships and partnerships. However, because a corporation's earnings are taxable, the gains and losses on the sale of noncash assets are subject to taxation. Therefore, additional tax reports for the corporation must be filed.

566

RETEACH

❏ Assign Math Worksheet, Chapter 21, Part F.

❏ List the information required to depreciate a plant asset, using the double declining-balance method of depreciation.

❏ Ask students to estimate the original cost, salvage value, and useful life for several assets.

❏ Direct students to depreciate the assets, using both the straight-line and double declining-balance method of depreciation.

 **TERM REVIEW**

declining-balance method
of depreciation

 **AUDIT YOUR UNDERSTANDING**

1. When calculating depreciation expense using the declining-balance method, what number stays constant each fiscal period?

2. What term is used for the declining-balance method using twice the straight-line rate?

3. What change occurs in the annual depreciation expense calculated using the declining-balance method?

4. An asset is never depreciated below what amount?

 **WORK TOGETHER**

Calculating depreciation using the double declining-balance depreciation method

Depreciation tables for Clearwater Clothiers are given in the *Working Papers.* Your instructor will guide you through the following example.

5. Complete a depreciation table for each of the following plant assets purchased during the current year. Use the double declining-balance depreciation method.

Date	Description	Original Cost	Estimated Salvage Value	Estimated Useful Life
Jan. 3	Computer	$2,300.00	$200.00	4 years
Jan. 4	Cash Register	$1,200.00	$100.00	5 years
Jan. 5	Clothing Rack	$ 500.00	$ 50.00	5 years

 **ON YOUR OWN**

Calculating depreciation using the double declining-balance depreciation method

Depreciation tables for Hilltop Bikes are given in the *Working Papers.* Work this problem independently.

6. Complete a depreciation table for each of the following plant assets purchased during the current year. Use the double declining-balance depreciation method. Round amounts to the nearest cent.

Date	Description	Original Cost	Estimated Salvage Value	Estimated Useful Life
Jan. 2	Bike Rack	$1,000.00	$100.00	4 years
Jan. 4	Sales Counter	$3,200.00	$250.00	5 years
Jan. 6	Filing Cabinet	$ 400.00	$ 50.00	8 years

GUIDED PRACTICE

Term Review
Call on students to define the term in the Term Review. Ask the class if the definition is correct and whether the complete definition has been given or if anything needs to be added. Suggested definitions for all terms are given in the Glossary.

Audit Your Understanding
Call on students to answer the Audit Your Understanding questions. Ask the class if the answer is correct and/or complete. Answers are given in Appendix D of the textbook.

Work Together
Have students write the solution to the Work Together problem as you guide the class through the example.
- Call on students to explain the calculation of the double declining-balance rate.
- Call on a student to explain the calculation of the amounts for year 1.
- Instruct students to complete the depreciation table as you elicit class participation in calculating each amount.
- Call on a student to explain the calculation of the depreciation amount for the last year.

INDEPENDENT PRACTICE

On Your Own
- Assign the On Your Own problem to be worked independently.
- Use the Ongoing Assessment techniques to diagnose student understanding.

Application Problem
- Assign Application Problem 21-6: Calculating depreciation using the double declining-balance depreciation method.

ENRICH

- Assign the Legal Issues in Accounting feature on page 566.
- Ask students to determine which depreciation method would be most appropriate for depreciating personal computers. Remind students that depreciation expenses the cost of a plant asset over its productive life. Is a computer more productive in the first years of its useful life?

CLOSE

- Ask students to briefly summarize the method for calculating double declining-balance depreciation.
- Ask students to compare the impact of the depreciation methods on the amount of depreciation expense recorded at the beginning and end of a plant asset's useful life.

PUTTING IT ALL TOGETHER

❑ Review the Chapter Summary.

❑ Use Transparency 21-2 to review the transactions presented in this chapter.

❑ Ask students to prepare a list of the new concepts introduced in this chapter.

INDEPENDENT PRACTICE

❑ Assign **Mastery Problem 21-7** to students who need the reinforcement of a problem that combines all concepts and transactions from the chapter in one problem; this will be most students.

❑ Assign **Challenge Problem 21-8** to accelerated students who do not require the reinforcement of the mastery problem.

❑ Assign **Study Guide 21**.

ONGOING ASSESSMENT

Review solutions to the assigned problems in class, diagnosing troublespots.

RETEACH

❑ Call on students to describe how they avoid the troublespots diagnosed.

❑ Use reteaching suggestions from lesson plans as required.

❑ Assign Recycling Problem 21-1 if needed.

❑ Assign Accounting Connection, Chapter 21.

ENRICH

❑ Assign the Explore Accounting feature. Ask students to share the data they have gathered in a report to the class.

❑ Assign the Internet Activity.

❑ Assign the Applied Communication activity.

❑ Assign Cases 1 and 2 of Cases for Critical Thinking.

❑ Assign the Automated Accounting feature on page 573 to automate Mastery Problem 21-7.

❑ Assign the Spreadsheet Accounting Template for Mastery Problem 21-7.

CHAPTER 21 SUMMARY

After completing this chapter, you can

1. Define accounting terms related to plant assets, depreciation, and property tax expense.
2. Identify accounting concepts and practices related to accounting for plant assets, depreciation, and property tax expense.
3. Record the buying of a plant asset and the paying of property tax.
4. Calculate depreciation expense and book value using the straight-line method of depreciation.
5. Prepare plant asset records and journalize annual depreciation expense.
6. Record entries related to disposing of plant assets.
7. Calculate depreciation expense using the double declining-balance method of depreciation.

EXPLORE ACCOUNTING

ACCOUNTING FOR LEASES

Leasing has become a popular alternative to purchasing a new car. The customer, called the lessee, has use of the car during the lease period. At the end of the lease term the car dealer, called the lessor, may give the lessee the option to purchase the car.

The accounting for a lease and the buying of an asset on account are very different. Normally, a leased asset is not recorded on the balance sheet as a plant asset, and the future lease payments are not recorded as a liability. Lease payments are charged to Rent Expense when paid. In contrast, an asset bought on account is recorded on the balance sheet

as a plant asset and the total payments are recorded as a liability. Each month, Depreciation Expense is charged and the interest expense is recorded on the monthly note payment. In addition, the liability account is debited; the cash and accumulated depreciation accounts are credited. Thus, the decision to lease or buy plant assets can have a dramatic impact on the financial statements of a company.

Accountants often apply the concept of substance over form when accounting for economic transactions. Substance refers to the underlying nature of the transaction. Form considers only the appearance of the transaction. FASB

(Financial Accounting Standards Board) Statement No. 13, *Accounting for Leases,* provides accountants with guidelines for evaluating lease agreements. If one of four criteria is met, the lease is recorded as if the asset were purchased, referred to as a capital lease.

Research: Investigate the terms of leases offered by a local car dealership and an apartment complex. Identify factors, such as lease term and maintenance, that differ between the two leases. Disregarding the rules of FASB Statement No. 13, would you consider the substance of either lease to be a purchase of the asset?

568 CHAPTER 21 Accounting for Plant Assets and Depreciation

EXPLORE ACCOUNTING

If needed, give students direction on contacting local businesses to obtain the required information.

Although car leases can be purchases in substance, the rental of an apartment would rarely be considered a purchase. The lease on an apartment is typically a short period compared to the building's useful life.

This feature illustrates how determining the appropriate debits and credits of a transaction is only a part of recording process. Accountants must understand accounting authoritative

pronouncements, such as those issued by the FASB, that provide guidance on determining the appropriate amounts to be used in recording transactions.

This feature also presents the important concept of substance versus form. Accountants must look past the form of a transaction to identify the substance of the economic event. Having this information enables accountants to prepare financial statements to correctly present the financial activities of the business.

21-1

APPLICATION PROBLEM
Journalizing buying plant assets and paying property tax

The cash payments journal and selected general ledger accounts for Bates Grocery Stores are given in the *Working Papers*.

Instructions:

1. Journalize the following transactions completed during the current year. The abbreviation for a check is C.

Transactions:

Jan. 3. Paid cash for computer printer, $300.00. C126.
       6. Paid cash for a freezer, $1,200.00. C130.
Feb. 27. Paid property taxes on real property with an assessed value of $180,000.00. The tax rate in the city where the property is located is 1.75% of assessed value. C214.
Apr. 5. Paid cash for a lobster tank, $850.00. C310.

2. Post the general columns of the cash payments journal.

21-2

APPLICATION PROBLEM
Calculating depreciation

Planter Stores depreciates plant assets using the straight-line depreciation method. If the asset was not bought at the beginning of 20X1, calculate the depreciation expense for the part of 20X1 that the company owned the asset.

Instructions:

Prepare a depreciation table for each of the following plant assets bought by Planter Stores during 20X1. Depreciation tables are given in the *Working Papers*. Save your work to complete Application Problem 21-3.

Transactions:

Jan. 4. Bought a cooler costing $1,400.00; estimated salvage value, $350.00; estimated useful life, 7 years; plant asset No. 311; serial number, 47367BX34.
Mar. 30. Bought an office chair, $500.00; estimated salvage value, $50.00; estimated useful life, 5 years; plant asset No. 312; serial number, 1727X6B3.
Aug. 2. Bought a sale sign, $350.00; estimated salvage value, $50.00; estimated useful life, 5 years; plant asset No. 313; serial number, BC762761.

21-3

APPLICATION PROBLEM
Preparing plant asset records

Instructions:

Using the depreciation tables prepared in Application Problem 21-2, prepare a plant asset record for each plant asset. Plant asset records are given in the *Working Papers*. Record the depreciation and book values for 20X1-20X4. Save the plant asset records for use in Application Problem 21-5.

CHAPTER 21   Accounting for Plant Assets and Depreciation   **569**

FORMAL EVALUATION

Chapter 21 Test
ExamViewPro or Westest for Chapter 21
Assessment by Portfolio

❑ Review answers to all tests administered as a class activity. If time is limited, review only the items that were frequently incorrectly answered.

❑ Ask students if there are any questions about the chapter before proceeding to the next chapter.

CHECK FIGURES

✔ **Application Problem 21-1**
General Debit amounts: 300.00, 1,200.00, 3,150.00, 850.00

✔ **Application Problem 21-2**
Year 1 depreciation, 150.00, 67.50, 25.00
Year 2 depreciation, 150.00, 90.00, 60.00

✔ **Application Problem 21-3**
Year 1 book values, 1,250.00, 432.50, 325.00

See Teacher's Edition of the Working Papers for Chapter 21 for complete solutions.

TEACHING STRATEGIES   DIFFERENT LEARNING STYLES

Auditory Learner. The auditory learner can reinforce the learning of formulas by verbally explaining the formula and/or calculations to other students in a small group. In a group of three, for example, each student should get the opportunity to "teach" the formula to the other two students. Through this process, each student in the group will teach the formula once and learn the formula two times.

✔ Application Problem 21-4
Credit Accumulated Depreciation—Office Equipment, 7,840.00

✔ Application Problem 21-5
Jan. 6 gain on sale, 100.00; Mar. 29 sold for book value; July 8 loss on sale, 425.00

✔ Application Problem 21-6
Year 1 depreciation, 360.00, 22,500.00, 600.00

Year 2 depreciation, 216.00, 11,250.00, 450.00

✔ Mastery Problem 21-7
Year 1 depreciation, 1,000.00, 150.00

Year 2 depreciation, 600.00, 180.00

Jan. 3 gain on sale, 376.00

June 28 loss on sale, 170.00

21-4 APPLICATION PROBLEM
Journalizing annual depreciation expense

Instructions:

On December 31, Baumann, Inc., determined that total depreciation expense for office equipment was $7,840.00. Plan the work sheet adjustment and label the adjustment *(f)*. Record the adjusting entry on page 13 of a general journal and post the transaction to the general ledger. Forms are given in the *Working Papers*.

21-5 APPLICATION PROBLEM
Recording the disposal of plant assets

During 20X5, Planter Stores had the following transactions involving the sale of plant assets. Use the plant asset records completed in Application Problem 21-3. Journals are given in the *Working Papers*.

Transactions:

Jan.   6. Received cash for sale of an office chair, plant asset No. 312, $250.00. R4.

Mar. 29. Received cash for sale of a sale sign, plant asset No. 313, $130.00. M3 and R53.

July   8. Received cash for sale of a cooler, plant asset No. 311, $300.00. M34 and R125.

Instructions:

1. For each plant asset disposed of in 20X5, journalize an entry for additional depreciation, if needed. Use page 3 of a general journal. Source documents are abbreviated as follows: check, C; memorandum, M; receipt, R.
2. Use page 3 of a cash receipts journal to record the disposal of each plant asset.
3. Make appropriate notations in the plant asset records.

21-6 APPLICATION PROBLEM
Calculating depreciation using the double declining-balance depreciation method

Instructions:

Depreciation tables are given in the *Working Papers*. Complete a depreciation table for each of the following plant assets purchased during the current year. Use the double declining-balance depreciation method. Round amounts to the nearest cent.

Date	Description	Original Cost	Estimated Salvage Value	Estimated Useful Life
Jan. 3	Computer Desk	$ 900.00	$ 100.00	5 years
Jan. 5	Truck	$45,000.00	$5,000.00	4 years
Jan. 8	Sound System	$ 2,400.00	$ 250.00	8 years

21-7 MASTERY PROBLEM
Recording transactions for plant assets

Ocean View Apartments records plant assets in two accounts: Room Furnishings, Account No. 1205, and Equipment, Account No. 1215. Room furnishings are depreciated using the double declining-balance method. Equipment is depreciated using the straight-line method. Forms are given in the *Working Papers*.

TEACHING STRATEGIES   DIFFERENT LEARNING ABILITIES

Limited English Proficiency (LEP) Students. Allow for longer pauses when you ask questions. Non-native speakers need more time to formulate their answers.

Instructions:

1. Record the following transactions completed during 20X1 on page 1 of a cash payments journal.

Transactions:

Jan. 4. Bought an entertainment center for room 214: cost, $2,500.00; estimated salvage value, $300.00; estimated useful life, 5 years; plant asset No. 413; serial number, 16143G52. C125.

Feb. 27. Paid property taxes on plant assets assessed at $500,000.00. The tax rate is 1.2%. C167.

Mar. 2. Bought a vacuum cleaner: cost, $1,000.00; estimated salvage value, $100.00; estimated useful life, 5 years; plant asset No. 414; serial number, BD324RT23. C175.

2. Complete Section 1 of a plant asset record for each new plant asset.

3. Prepare a depreciation table for each new plant asset.

4. Complete Section 3 of the plant asset record for 20X1-20X4.

5. Record the following transactions completed during 20X5. Use page 2 of a cash receipts journal and page 2 of a general journal.

Transactions:

Jan. 3. Received cash for sale of an entertainment center, plant asset No. 413, $700.00. R3.

June 28. Received cash for sale of a vacuum cleaner, plant asset No. 414, $50.00. M29 and R67.

Dec. 31. Recorded the adjusting entry for depreciation expense—room furnishings. Total 20X5 depreciation expense of room furnishings was $42,534.00.

6. Complete the plant asset records for each plant asset sold during 20X5.

CHALLENGE PROBLEM
Calculating a partial year's depreciation using the double declining-balance method

Blette and Associates uses the double declining-balance depreciation method for its office equipment. Because many purchases are made during the year, Blette must calculate a partial year's depreciation in the first year. Blette uses the same method to calculate a partial year's depreciation as was described for Winning Edge in this chapter. The annual depreciation expense is divided by 12 to calculate a monthly depreciation. The monthly depreciation is then multiplied by the number of months the plant asset was owned during the year. For subsequent years, the annual depreciation is calculated using the normal method—book value multiplied by the depreciation rate.

Instructions:

Depreciation tables are given in the *Working Papers*. Prepare depreciation tables for the following assets purchased in 20X1. Round to the nearest cent.

Transactions:

Mar. 29. Bought an office desk system, $2,600.00; estimated salvage value, $250.00; estimated useful life, 8 years.

June 1. Purchased an MICR scanner, $3,800.00; estimated salvage value, $300.00; estimated useful life, 5 years.

✔ **Challenge Problem 21-8**
Year 1 depreciation, 487.53, 886.69
Year 2 depreciation, 528.12, 1,165.32

APPLIED SKILLS

WRITING ACROSS THE CURRICULUM

Writing Paragraphs and Short Essays. The Cases for Critical Thinking are short, practical applications of the accounting principles developed in the chapter. Some cases are planned to present problems related to the chapter but not specifically discussed and answered in the chapter. These cases present an opportunity for critical thinking and decision making. These cases also require more than a short, objective-type response. Therefore, they provide ideal practice in writing paragraphs and short essays.

THE MOST EFFICIENT QUANTITY OF INVENTORY

To determine the most efficient quantity of inventory, a business makes frequent analysis of purchases, sales, and inventory records. Many businesses fail because too much or too little merchandise inventory is kept on hand. A business that stocks merchandise that does not satisfy the demand of its customers is also likely to fail.

A merchandise inventory that is larger than needed may decrease the net income of a business for several reasons.

1. Excess inventory requires that a business spend money for expensive store and warehouse space.

2. Excess inventory uses capital that could be invested in other assets to earn a profit for the business.

3. Excess inventory requires that a business spend money for expenses, such as taxes and insurance premiums, that increase with the cost of the merchandise inventory.

4. Excess inventory may become obsolete and unsalable.

Merchandise inventory that is smaller than needed may also decrease the net income of a business for several reasons.

1. Sales may be lost to competitors if items wanted by customers are not on hand.

2. Sales may be lost to competitors if there is an insufficient variety of merchandise to satisfy customers.

3. When a business frequently orders small quantities of an item, the price paid is often more per unit than when merchandise is ordered in large quantities.

METHODS USED TO DETERMINE THE QUANTITY OF MERCHANDISE INVENTORY

The quantity of items in inventory at the end of a fiscal period must be determined in order to calculate the cost of merchandise sold.

Two principal methods are used to determine the quantity of each item of merchandise on hand.

1. A merchandise inventory determined by counting, weighing, or measuring items of merchandise on hand is called a **periodic inventory.** A periodic inventory is also referred to as a physical inventory.

2. A merchandise inventory determined by keeping a continuous record of increases, decreases, and balance on hand is called a **perpetual inventory.** A perpetual inventory is also referred to as a book inventory.

Because controlling the quantity of merchandise inventory is so important to a business's success, many methods of keeping inventory records are used. Today, most companies use computers to keep track of the inventory on hand.

Keeping track of merchandise inventory also involves knowing the ideal quantity for each kind of merchandise in inventory. To ensure having the appropriate quantity, companies frequently establish an ideal minimum quantity and an ideal reorder quantity. When the minimum quantity is reached, new merchandise is ordered.

Minimum quantity levels must be established with consideration for how long it may take to receive new inventory. Otherwise, merchandise may not be available when a customer wants to buy it. Those who order new merchandise must also be aware of the ideal quantities to order to get the best prices and trade discounts.

576 CHAPTER 22 Accounting for Inventory

1. Stock Number and Description

3. Unit Price and Total Cost

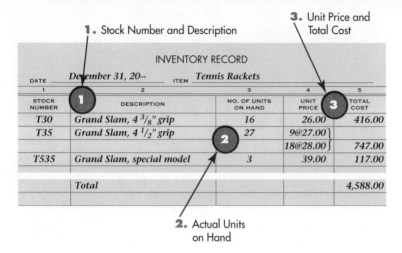

INVENTORY RECORD

DATE _December 31, 20--_   ITEM _Tennis Rackets_

1	2	3	4	5
STOCK NUMBER	DESCRIPTION	NO. OF UNITS ON HAND	UNIT PRICE	TOTAL COST
T30	Grand Slam, 4 3/8" grip	16	26.00	416.00
T35	Grand Slam, 4 1/2" grip	27	9@27.00 ⎱	
			18@28.00 ⎰	747.00
T535	Grand Slam, special model	3	39.00	117.00
	Total			4,588.00

2. Actual Units on Hand

Counting, weighing, or measuring merchandise on hand for a periodic inventory is commonly referred to as "taking an inventory." Employees count each item of inventory and record the quantities on special forms. To assure an accurate and complete count, a business will typically be closed during the periodic inventory.

Businesses frequently establish their fiscal period to end when inventory is at a minimum because it takes less time to count a smaller inventory. For example, a department store may take an inventory at the end of December. The amount of merchandise on hand is smaller because of holiday sales. Few purchases of additional merchandise are made in December after the holiday sales. All of these activities make the merchandise inventory smaller at the end of December.

A form used during a periodic inventory to record information about each item of merchandise on hand is called an **inventory record.** The inventory record has space to record the stock number, description, number of units on hand, unit price, and total cost of each item. Columns 1-3 are completed when the business is taking an inventory. Columns 4-5 are completed after the taking of inventory. The methods used to determine the unit prices are discussed later in this chapter.

F.Y.I. _Taking an inventory is an involved and expensive task. An efficient inventory count requires extensive management planning and employee training. Some businesses hire independent companies that specialize in taking inventories to assist in planning for and counting the inventory._

Preparing an inventory record

S T E P S

1. Write the stock number and description before the periodic inventory begins.

2. Write the actual count in the No. of Units on Hand column.

3. Write the unit price and calculate the total cost after the physical inventory is completed. These columns are usually completed by the accounting department.

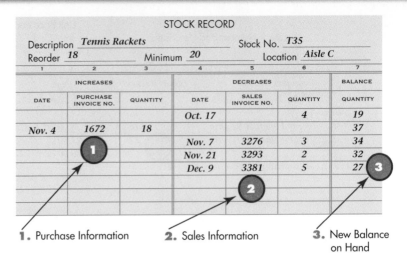

STOCK RECORD

Description **Tennis Rackets**   Stock No. **T35**
Reorder **18**   Minimum **20**   Location **Aisle C**

	INCREASES			DECREASES		BALANCE
1	2	3	4	5	6	7
DATE	PURCHASE INVOICE NO.	QUANTITY	DATE	SALES INVOICE NO.	QUANTITY	QUANTITY
			Oct. 17		4	19
Nov. 4	1672	18				37
			Nov. 7	3276	3	34
			Nov. 21	3293	2	32
			Dec. 9	3381	5	27

1. Purchase Information   **2.** Sales Information   **3.** New Balance on Hand

Some businesses keep inventory records that show continuously the quantity on hand for each kind of merchandise. A form used to show the kind of merchandise, quantity received, quantity sold, and balance on hand is called a **stock record.** A separate stock record is prepared for each kind of merchandise on hand. A file of stock records for all merchandise on hand is called a **stock ledger.**

A perpetual inventory system provides day-to-day information about the quantity of merchandise on hand. The minimum balance allowed before a reorder must be placed is also shown on each stock record. The minimum balance is the quantity that will typically last until the ordered merchandise can be received from the vendors. When the quantity falls below the minimum, additional merchandise is ordered in the quantity shown on the reorder line of the stock record. A stock record shows the quantity but usually not the cost of the merchandise.

Purchase information is recorded in the Increases columns when additional merchandise is received. Sales information is recorded in the Decreases columns when merchandise is sold. The new balance on hand is recorded after each purchase and sale.

When a perpetual inventory is kept, errors may be made in recording or calculating amounts. Also, some stock records may be incorrect because merchandise is taken from stock and not recorded on stock records. A business should take a periodic inventory at least once a fiscal period. The perpetual records are corrected to reflect the actual quantity on hand as determined by the periodic inventory.

PERPETUAL INVENTORY USING A COMPUTER

Many merchandising businesses use a computer to keep perpetual inventory records. The computer is connected to special cash registers known as point-of-sale terminals. The terminals read the Universal Product Codes (UPC) marked on products.

The stock ledger is stored in the computer. When a UPC is read at the terminal, the product description and the sales price are retrieved from the stock ledger and displayed on the terminal. The computer reduces the units on hand to reflect the item sold. The computer may also periodically check the quantities in the stock ledger and print a list of items that need to be reordered.

578 CHAPTER 22 Accounting for Inventory

TERMS REVIEW

periodic inventory

perpetual inventory

inventory record

stock record

stock ledger

AUDIT YOUR UNDERSTANDING

1. Why do successful businesses need an effective inventory system?

2. Identify four reasons why a merchandise inventory that is larger than needed may decrease the net income of a business.

3. When are periodic inventories normally taken?

4. How do inventory levels affect the period a business selects for its fiscal year? Why?

5. How is the accuracy of a perpetual inventory checked?

WORK TOGETHER

Preparing a stock record

A stock record for Riverville Electronics is given in the *Working Papers*. Your instructor will guide you through the following example.

6. Enter the following transactions on the stock record of Model No. XW142 cable adapter. Source documents are abbreviated as follows: purchase invoice, P; sales invoice, S.

   Transactions:
   Oct. 22. Received 9 XW142 cable adapters. P321
   Nov. 12. Sold 6 XW142 cable adapters. S1816.
       23. Sold 3 XW142 cable adapters. S1839.
   Dec. 14. Sold 2 XW142 cable adapters. S1898.

ON YOUR OWN

Preparing a stock record

A stock record for Fernandez Jewelry is given in the *Working Papers*. Work this problem independently.

7. Enter the following transactions on the stock record of Model No. C310 crystal biscuit barrel. Source documents are abbreviated as follows: purchase invoice, P; sales invoice, S.

   Transactions:
   Dec. 9. Received 20 C310 crystal biscuit barrels. P2076.
       10. Sold 4 C310 crystal biscuit barrels. S6206.
       13. Sold 1 C310 crystal biscuit barrels. S6271.
       16. Sold 3 C310 crystal biscuit barrels. S6351.

GUIDED PRACTICE

Terms Review
Call on students to define the terms in the Terms Review. Ask the class if the definitions are correct and whether the complete definitions have been given or if anything needs to be added. Suggested definitions for all terms are given in the Glossary.

Audit Your Understanding
Call on students to answer the Audit Your Understanding questions. Ask the class if the answer is correct and/or complete. Answers are given in Appendix D of the textbook.

Work Together
Have students write the solution to the Work Together problem as you guide the class through the example.

❏ Direct students to record each transaction in the stock record as you elicit class participation.

❏ Call on students to describe how to calculate the quantity balance.

INDEPENDENT PRACTICE

On Your Own
❏ Assign the On Your Own problem to be worked independently.

❏ Use the Ongoing Assessment techniques to diagnose student understanding.

Application Problem
❏ Assign Application Problem 22-1: Preparing a stock record.

ENRICH

❏ Assign the Automated Accounting feature on pages 592–593 to automate Application Problem 22-1.

❏ Direct students to take a physical inventory of items at their school or home. The students could prepare a stock record for each item. After several days, instruct students to perform another physical inventory.

CLOSE

❏ Ask students to briefly summarize the records used to determine the quantity of merchandise inventory.

FIRST-IN, FIRST-OUT INVENTORY COSTING METHOD

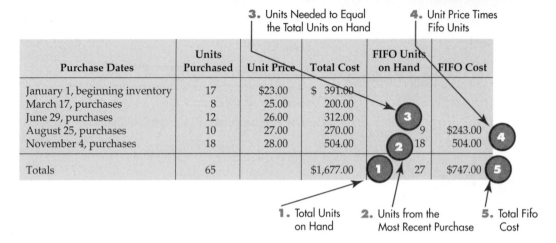

3. Units Needed to Equal the Total Units on Hand

4. Unit Price Times Fifo Units

Purchase Dates	Units Purchased	Unit Price	Total Cost	FIFO Units on Hand	FIFO Cost
January 1, beginning inventory	17	$23.00	$ 391.00		
March 17, purchases	8	25.00	200.00		
June 29, purchases	12	26.00	312.00		
August 25, purchases	10	27.00	270.00	9	$243.00
November 4, purchases	18	28.00	504.00	18	504.00
Totals	65		$1,677.00	27	$747.00

1. Total Units on Hand **2.** Units from the Most Recent Purchase **5.** Total Fifo Cost

Costs are not recorded on inventory records at the time a periodic inventory is taken. After the quantities of merchandise on hand are counted, purchase invoices are used to find merchandise unit prices. The total costs are then calculated using the quantities and unit prices recorded on the inventory records. Most businesses use one of three inventory costing methods: (1) first-in, first-out, (2) last-in, first-out, or (3) weighted-average.

Winning Edge uses the most recent invoices for purchases to determine the unit price of an item in inventory. The earliest invoices for purchases, therefore, are used to determine the cost of merchandise sold. Using the price of merchandise purchased first to calculate the cost of merchandise sold first is called the **first-in, first-out inventory costing method.** The first-in, first-out method is frequently abbreviated as *fifo.*

On December 31, a periodic inventory of Model No. T35 tennis racket showed 27 rackets on hand. Using the fifo method, the most recent purchase, November 4, is used to cost 18 of the 27 rackets in ending inventory. The remaining 9 rackets in ending inventory are costed using the next most recent purchase, August 25.

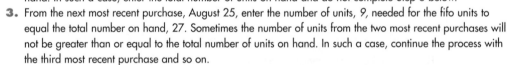

S T E P S **Costing inventory using the fifo method**

1. Enter the total number of units on hand, *27.*
2. From the most recent purchase, November 4, enter the number of units purchased, *18.* In some cases, the number of units of the most recent purchase will be greater than or equal to the total number of units on hand. In such a case, enter the total number of units on hand and do not complete Step 3 below.
3. From the next most recent purchase, August 25, enter the number of units, *9,* needed for the fifo units to equal the total number on hand, *27.* Sometimes the number of units from the two most recent purchases will not be greater than or equal to the total number of units on hand. In such a case, continue the process with the third most recent purchase and so on.
4. Multiply the unit price of each appropriate purchase times the fifo units on hand to determine the fifo cost.
5. Add the individual fifo costs to determine the fifo cost of the total number of units in ending inventory.

MATERIALS

LAST-IN, FIRST-OUT INVENTORY COSTING METHOD

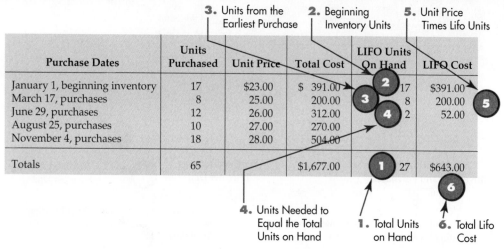

Labels on illustration:
- **3.** Units from the Earliest Purchase
- **2.** Beginning Inventory Units
- **5.** Unit Price Times Lifo Units

Purchase Dates	Units Purchased	Unit Price	Total Cost	LIFO Units On Hand	LIFO Cost
January 1, beginning inventory	17	$23.00	$ 391.00	17	$391.00
March 17, purchases	8	25.00	200.00	8	200.00
June 29, purchases	12	26.00	312.00	2	52.00
August 25, purchases	10	27.00	270.00		
November 4, purchases	18	28.00	504.00		
Totals	65		$1,677.00	27	$643.00

- **4.** Units Needed to Equal the Total Units on Hand
- **1.** Total Units on Hand
- **6.** Total Lifo Cost

Using the price of merchandise purchased last to calculate the cost of merchandise sold first is called the **last-in, first-out inventory costing method.** The last-in, first-out method is frequently abbreviated as *lifo.* This method is based on the idea that the most recent costs of merchandise should be charged against current revenue. *(CONCEPT: Matching Expenses with Revenue)*

Using the lifo method, each item on the inventory records is recorded at the earliest prices paid for the merchandise.

The earliest prices for the 27 tennis rackets would consist of the 17 units in the January 1 beginning inventory. The next earliest purchase, March 17, of 8 units is then used to cost 8 units in ending inventory. The remaining 2 units in ending inventory are costed using the next earliest purchase, June 29. On the inventory record, the 27 tennis rackets would show a total cost of $643.00.

Costing inventory using the lifo method

1. Enter the total number of units on hand, *27.*
2. Enter the number of units in beginning inventory, *17.* In some cases, the number of units of beginning inventory will be greater than or equal to the total number of units on hand. In such a case, enter the total number of units on hand and do not complete Steps 3 and 4 below.
3. From the earliest purchase, March 17, enter the number of units purchased, *8.*
4. From the next earliest purchase, June 29, enter the number of units, *2,* needed for the lifo units to equal the total number of units on hand, *27.*
5. Multiply the unit price of the beginning inventory times the lifo units on hand to determine the lifo cost for beginning inventory. Repeat this process for each appropriate purchase.
6. Add the lifo cost for the beginning inventory and each appropriate purchase to determine the lifo cost of the total number of units in ending inventory.

REMEMBER

In the lifo method, the latest purchases are assumed to be sold first (first-out). Therefore, ending inventory consists of the units purchased the earliest, and the earliest purchase invoice costs are used to value the ending inventory.

EXPLAIN

❏ Emphasize that lifo uses the most recent purchases to determine the cost of merchandise sold.
❏ Ask students to identify which costs are used to determine the cost of merchandise inventory using the lifo method *(the unit costs of the beginning inventory and earliest purchases).*
❏ Ask students to read the Remember to reinforce which costs are used for the lifo method.

DEMONSTRATE

❏ Direct students to draw six columns on a sheet of paper and copy the information in the first four columns of the illustration.
❏ Emphasize that the information in these first four columns represents the cost of merchandise available for sale; this information is the same for both fifo and lifo calculations.
❏ Direct students to follow the six steps shown for costing merchandise inventory using the lifo method.
❏ To reinforce the lifo method, instruct students to cost merchandise inventory assuming ending inventory consists of 30 rackets *($721.00).*

| Purchases | | | Total |
Date	Units	Unit Price	Cost
January 1, beginning inventory	17	$23.00	$ 391.00
March 17, purchases	8	25.00	200.00
June 29, purchases	12	26.00	312.00
August 25, purchases	10	27.00	270.00
November 4, purchases	18	28.00	504.00
Totals	65		$1,677.00

1. Total Cost of Inventory Available

Total of Beginning Inventory and Purchases $1,677.00 ÷ Total Units 65 = Weighted-Average Price per Unit $25.80

2. Weighted-Average Price per Unit

Units in Ending Inventory 27 × Weighted-Average Price per Unit $25.80 = Cost of Ending Inventory $696.60

3. Cost of Ending Inventory

Using the average cost of beginning inventory plus merchandise purchased during a fiscal period to calculate the cost of merchandise sold is called the **weighted-average inventory costing method.** The average unit price of the total inventory available is calculated. This average unit price is used to calculate both ending inventory and cost of merchandise sold. The average cost of merchandise is then charged against current revenue. *(CONCEPT: Matching Expenses with Revenue)*

Using the weighted-average method, the inventory is costed at the average price per unit of the beginning inventory plus the cost of all purchases during the fiscal year. On the inventory record, the 27 tennis rackets would show a total cost of $696.60.

S T E P S

Costing inventory using the weighted-average method

1. Calculate the total cost of beginning inventory and each purchase, $1,677.00, by multiplying the units by each unit price.

2. Calculate the weighted-average price per unit, $25.80, by dividing the total cost, $1,677.00, by the number of units available, 65.

3. Calculate the cost of ending inventory, $696.60, by multiplying the weighted-average price per unit, $25.80, by the units in ending inventory, 27.

F.Y.I

A business usually determines the order in which products are sold based on the type of inventory. A grocery store, for example, must sell its earliest purchases first. A hardware store, however, could sell its most recent purchases first. The inventory costing method used to calculate the cost of merchandise sold should not, however, be determined by the order in which items are sold. A business should choose the inventory costing method that provides its managers with the best accounting information.

582 CHAPTER 22 Accounting for Inventory

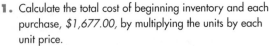

CALCULATING THE COST OF MERCHANDISE SOLD

The cost of ending inventory determined using any of the three inventory costing methods can be used to calculate the cost of merchandise sold. The cost of ending inventory is subtracted from the total cost of units available for sale. Although the formula is the same, under each inventory costing method the amount determined will be different. Winning Edge uses the fifo method. Therefore, the fifo cost of $747.00 is subtracted from the total cost of merchandise available for sale, $1,677.00, to calculate the cost of merchandise sold of $930.00.

Cost of Merchandise Available for Sale	−	Fifo Cost of Ending Inventory	=	Cost of Merchandise Sold
$1,677.00	−	$747.00	=	$930.00

COMPARISON OF INVENTORY METHODS

	Fifo	Lifo	Weighted Average
Cost of Merchandise Sold:			
Merchandise Inventory, Jan. 1	$ 391.00	$ 391.00	$ 391.00
Net Purchases	1,286.00	1,286.00	1,286.00
Merchandise Available for Sale	$1,677.00	$1,677.00	$1,677.00
Less Ending Inventory, Dec. 31	747.00	643.00	696.60
Cost of Merchandise Sold	$ 930.00	$1,034.00	$ 980.40
In a period of rising prices:			
Relative Cost of Ending Inventory	highest	lowest	intermediate
Relative Cost of Merchandise Sold	lowest	highest	intermediate

In a period of rising prices, the fifo method gives the highest possible ending inventory cost and the lowest cost of merchandise sold. The lifo method gives the lowest possible ending inventory cost and the highest cost of merchandise sold. The weighted-average method gives ending inventory cost and cost of merchandise sold between fifo and lifo. As the cost of merchandise sold increases, gross profit and net income decrease. Thus, net income is highest under the fifo method, lowest under the lifo method, and intermediate under the weighted-average method.

In a period of declining prices, the results for the fifo and lifo methods are reversed.

All three inventory costing methods are acceptable accounting practices. A business should select one method and use that same method continuously for each fiscal period. If a business changed inventory costing methods, part of the difference in gross profit and net income would be caused by the change in methods. To provide financial statements that can be analyzed and compared with statements of other fiscal periods, the same inventory costing method should be used each fiscal period. (*CONCEPT: Consistent Reporting*)

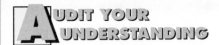

GUIDED PRACTICE

Terms Review

Call on students to define the terms in the Terms Review. Ask the class if the definitions are correct and whether the complete definitions have been given or if anything needs to be added. The suggested definition is given in the Glossary.

Audit Your Understanding

Call on students to answer the Audit Your Understanding questions. Ask the class if the answer is correct and/or complete. Answers are given in Appendix D of the textbook.

Work Together

Have students write the solution to the Work Together problem as you guide the class through the example. For the fifo and lifo methods:

❑ Call on a student to identify the first purchase to be used to cost the merchandise inventory.

❑ Call on another student to explain how to determine the number of units to be included from this purchase.

❑ Repeat this process until all the units have been identified.

❑ Ask a student to write the weighted-average method calculation on the board.

INDEPENDENT PRACTICE

On Your Own

❑ Assign the On Your Own problem to be worked independently.

❑ Use the Ongoing Assessment techniques to diagnose student understanding.

Application Problem

❑ Assign Application Problem 22-2: Determining the cost of inventory using the fifo, lifo, and weighted-average inventory costing methods.

TERMS REVIEW

first-in, first-out inventory costing method

last-in, first-out inventory costing method

weighted-average inventory costing method

AUDIT YOUR UNDERSTANDING

1. When the fifo method is used, how is the cost of each kind of ending merchandise inventory determined?

2. On what idea is the lifo method based?

3. In a period of rising prices, which inventory costing method gives the highest cost of merchandise sold?

4. Why should a business select one inventory costing method and use that same method continuously for each fiscal period?

WORK TOGETHER

Determining the cost of inventory using the fifo, lifo, and weighted-average inventory costing methods

Inventory costing information for Riverville Electronics is given in the *Working Papers.* Your instructor will guide you through the following example.

5. Calculate the cost of ending inventory using the fifo, lifo, and weighted-average methods. There are 16 units in ending inventory.

ON YOUR OWN

Determining the cost of inventory using the fifo, lifo, and weighted-average inventory costing methods

Inventory costing information for Fernandez Jewelry is given in the *Working Papers.* Work this problem independently.

6. Calculate the cost of ending inventory using the fifo, lifo, and weighted-average methods. There are 25 units in ending inventory.

584 CHAPTER 22 Accounting for Inventory

ENRICH

❑ Assign the Automated Accounting feature on pages 592–593 to automate Application Problem 22-2.

❑ Assign the Spreadsheet Accounting Template for Application Problem 22-2.

❑ Show the CNN Accounting Video.

CLOSE

❑ Ask students to briefly summarize the procedures for calculating the cost of inventory, using the fifo, lifo, and weighted-average inventory costing methods.

22-3 Estimating Inventory

GROSS PROFIT METHOD OF ESTIMATING INVENTORY

STEP 1

Beginning inventory, January 1		$ 238,750.00
Plus net purchases for January 1 to January 31		+ 125,450.00
Equals cost of merchandise available for sale		$ 364,200.00

STEP 2

Net sales for January 1 to January 31		$ 206,250.00
Times previous year's gross profit percentage		× 48.00%
Equals estimated gross profit on operations		$ 99,000.00

STEP 3

Net sales for January 1 to January 31		$ 206,250.00
Less estimated gross profit on operations		− 99,000.00
Equals estimated cost of merchandise sold		$ 107,250.00

STEP 4

Cost of merchandise available for sale		$ 364,200.00
Less estimated cost of merchandise sold		− 107,250.00
Equals estimated ending merchandise inventory		$ 256,950.00

Winning Edge
Income Statement
For Month Ended January 31, 20--

		% of Net Sales
Operating Revenue:		
Net Sales	$206,250.00	100.0
Cost of Merchandise Sold:		
Beginning Inventory, January 1	$238,750.00	
Net Purchases	125,450.00	
Merchandise Available for Sale	$364,200.00	
Less Est. Ending Inv., January 31	256,950.00	
Cost of Merchandise Sold	107,250.00	52.0
Gross Profit on Operations	$ 99,000.00	48.0
Operating Expenses	79,200.00	38.4
Net Income	$ 19,800.00	9.6

Estimating inventory by using the previous year's percentage of gross profit on operations is called the **gross profit method of estimating inventory.** The gross profit method is often used to estimate the cost of the ending inventory reported on monthly financial statements. The gross profit method is a less expensive method of calculating inventory costs than taking a periodic inventory or maintaining a perpetual inventory system.

Four values are needed to perform the four-step process. Actual net sales and net purchases amounts are obtained from the general ledger. The beginning inventory amount is obtained from the prior period's financial statements. The gross profit percentage is estimated by management based on the previous year's actual percentage, adjusted for any significant changes in economic conditions.

When the gross profit method of estimating inventory is used for months other than the first month of the fiscal period, the process is the same as that just illustrated. Net sales and purchases amounts are obtained from the general ledger. For the sales account, the previous month's ending balance is subtracted from the current month's ending balance to calculate the amount of sales for just the current month. The same process is used for the purchases account. The beginning inventory for the month is the same as the ending inventory from the previous month. Note that both the beginning and ending inventory amounts will be based on estimated amounts.

TECHNOLOGY FOR BUSINESS

ELECTRONIC SPREADSHEETS HELP ANSWER "WHAT IF?" QUESTIONS

F inancial statements are important tools for providing information to businesses. Illustrated here is an electronic spreadsheet that will be analyzed by the owner of a rug-cleaning business. For example, the owner may ask several "what if?" questions to determine what action might improve net income and the net income component percentage. What if the amount spent on advertising is increased to $300.00? The owner estimates that this would increase sales to $5,000.00. Rugcare will then need additional supplies to clean more rugs. Therefore, the owner estimates that supplies expense will increase to $2,900.00.

Electronic spreadsheets eliminate the need to manually erase data and recalculate totals each time a change is made. When data is keyed on the spreadsheet, formulas use the new data to recalculate other values. Formulas may consist of values, mathematical operations, and cell addresses. The electronic spreadsheet uses the standard mathematical operations of addition (+), subtraction (−), multiplication (*), and division (/). The formula to calculate the net income component percentage, +E19/E7, divides the value currently displayed at E19 by the value currently displayed in E7.

Spending $300.00 on advertising would improve net income and the net income component percentage. In the future, the owner can retrieve the spreadsheet, key new data, and instantly analyze the revised net income and net income component percentage.

```
F7     (P1) +E7/E7
       A      B           C        D        E        F       G
1                            Rugcare
2                        Income Statement
3                    Projection of Net Income
4                                                    % of
5                                                    Sales
6      Revenue:                                      -------
7        Sales                                5,000.00  100.0%
8      Expenses:
9        Advertising Expense        300.00
10       Insurance Expense          100.00
11       Miscellaneous Expense      105.00
12       Rent Expense               250.00
13       Repair Expense             110.00
14       Supplies Expense         2,900.00
15       Utilities Expense          115.00
16                               ----------
17       Total Expenses                      3,880.00   77.6%
18                                          ----------
19     Net Income                            1,120.00   22.4%
20                                          ==========
```

586

TERM REVIEW

gross profit method of estimating inventory

AUDIT YOUR UNDERSTANDING

1. When neither a perpetual system is maintained nor a periodic inventory is taken, how can an ending merchandise inventory be determined that is accurate enough for a monthly income statement?

2. What amounts are needed to estimate ending merchandise inventory?

3. What amount is used for beginning inventory for a month that is not the first month of a fiscal period?

WORK TOGETHER

Estimating ending inventory using the gross profit method

A form for making inventory calculations and a form for completing an income statement are given in the *Working Papers*. Your instructor will guide you through the following examples.

4. Use the following information obtained from the records and management of Evans Company to estimate the cost of the ending inventory on June 30.

Estimated beginning inventory, June 1	$154,800.00
Actual net purchases for June	$ 47,900.00
Actual net sales for June	$245,000.00
Estimated gross profit percentage	45.0%
Actual operating expenses for June	$ 76,930.00

5. Prepare an income statement for the month ended June 30 of the current year.

ON YOUR OWN

Estimating ending inventory using the gross profit method

A form for making inventory calculations and a form for completing an income statement are given in the *Working Papers*. Work independently to complete these problems.

6. Use the following information obtained from the records and management of Tabora Stores to estimate the cost of the ending inventory on April 30.

Estimated beginning inventory, April 1	$48,900.00
Actual net purchases for April	$24,100.00
Actual net sales for April	$65,000.00
Estimated gross profit percentage	60.0%
Actual operating expenses for April	$21,125.00

7. Prepare an income statement for the month ended April 30 of the current year.

GUIDED PRACTICE

Term Review
Call on students to define the term in the Term Review. Ask the class if the definition is correct and whether the complete definition has been given or if anything needs to be added. Suggested definitions for all terms are given in the Glossary.

Audit Your Understanding
Call on students to answer the Audit Your Understanding questions. Ask the class if the answer is correct and/or complete. Answers are given in Appendix D of the textbook.

Work Together
Have students write the solutions to the Work Together problems as you guide the class through the examples.
- ❏ Ask four students to each write one of the four calculations on the board.
- ❏ Direct students to prepare the income statement.

INDEPENDENT PRACTICE

On Your Own
- ❏ Assign the On Your Own problems to be worked independently.
- ❏ Use the Ongoing Assessment techniques to diagnose student understanding.

Application Problem
- ❏ Assign Application Problem 22-3: Estimating ending inventory using the gross profit method.

ENRICH

- ❏ Assign the Technology for Business feature on page 586. Students can practice writing formulas for the income statement on paper rather than actually booting spreadsheet software if time is a factor.
- ❏ Assign Spreadsheet Accounting Template for Application Problem 22-3.

CLOSE

- ❏ Ask students to summarize the purpose of the gross profit method of estimating inventory.
- ❏ Ask students to explain the four steps for estimating merchandise inventory using the gross profit method of estimating inventory.

PUTTING IT ALL TOGETHER

- ❑ Review the Chapter Summary.
- ❑ Ask students to prepare a list of the new concepts introduced in this chapter.
- ❑ Use Transparency 22-2 to review the chapter.
- ❑ Discuss that the methods presented in this chapter are used to determine the actual historical cost or an estimate of merchandise inventory.

INDEPENDENT PRACTICE

- ❑ Assign **Mastery Problem 22-4** to students who need the reinforcement of a problem that combines all concepts from the chapter in one problem; this will be most students.
- ❑ Assign **Challenge Problem 22-5** to accelerated students who do not require the reinforcement of the mastery problem.
- ❑ Assign **Study Guide 22**.

ONGOING ASSESSMENT

Review solutions to the assigned problems in class, diagnosing troublespots.

RETEACH

- ❑ Call on students to describe how they avoid the troublespots diagnosed.
- ❑ Use reteaching suggestions from lesson plans as required.
- ❑ Assign Recycling Problem 22-1 if needed.
- ❑ Assign Accounting Connection, Chapter 22.

ENRICH

- ❑ Assign the Explore Accounting feature. Ask students to share the information they have gathered in a report to the class.
- ❑ Assign the Internet Activity.
- ❑ Assign the Applied Communication activity.
- ❑ Assign Cases 1 and 2 of Cases for Critical Thinking.
- ❑ Assign the Automated Accounting feature on pages 592–593 to automate Mastery Problem 22-4.

CHAPTER 22 SUMMARY

After completing this chapter, you can

1. Define accounting terms related to inventory.
2. Identify accounting concepts and practices related to inventory.
3. Prepare a stock record.
4. Determine the cost of merchandise inventory using the fifo, lifo, and weighted-average inventory costing methods.
5. Estimate the cost of merchandise inventory using the gross profit method of estimating inventory.

EXPLORE ACCOUNTING

COSTING A CD CAN MAKE YOUR HEAD SPIN

Determining the cost of an item of inventory, often referred to as *costing* an item, is a relatively easy task for a merchandising business. However, costing can be a complex task for the company that manufactures the item.

Consider the challenge of a music company costing a music CD. Stardust Music has signed a new group, SeaMist, to its first contract. Included in the cost of the CD is all the labor required to produce the CD. Stardust Music will pay SeaMist $1.50 for every CD sold. Studio artists, however, were paid a fixed fee totalling $30,000.

If Stardust Music sells 100,000 CDs, its labor cost will be $180,000 or $1.80 per CD—$150,000 to SeaMist and $30,000 to the studio artists. If the CD is an unexpected smash hit, selling 300,000 CDs, Stardust's labor cost will be $480,000 or $1.60 per CD—$450,000 to SeaMist and $30,000 for the studio artists.

The artist cost, $1.50 per CD, is referred to as a variable cost. The *total* artist cost *varies*, depending on the number of units sold. The studio artist cost of $30,000 is referred to as a fixed cost because the *total* studio artist cost is *fixed* (constant), regardless of the number of units sold.

When preparing the first monthly financial statement after the release of SeaMist's CD, Stardust's accountants must assign a labor cost to SeaMist's CD. What amount should be used? $1.80? $1.60? Another amount?

Accountants must make good sales estimates and constantly reevaluate these estimates to compute the most accurate cost information possible. Accountants must constantly communicate with the sales staff to update sales projections.

Required: Calculate the total and unit labor costs for SeaMist's second CD using the following assumptions: (1) SeaMist receives $1.75 per CD. (2) Studio artists cost $60,000. (3) A famous guest artist used on one track receives $30,000 plus $0.10 for every CD sold. Prepare estimates for 400,000; 500,000; and 600,000 unit sales.

EXPLORE ACCOUNTING

This feature presents new concepts of inventory in a setting very familiar to students—compact discs (CDs). For a manufacturing company, every cost of the product can be classified as a fixed or variable cost. Changes in the number of items produced have a different impact on fixed and variable costs. Accountants must be able to analyze these costs to prepare financial statements and operating budgets.

The feature illustrates how accountants need to communicate with management in other areas of the business in order to obtain the information necessary to prepare financial transactions.

The cost of the guest artist has both fixed and variable cost components. This type of cost is known as a mixed cost. *(Calculations are shown in the continuation on the next page.)*

22-1 APPLICATION PROBLEM
Preparing a stock record

A stock record for Harrison Sound is given in the *Working Papers*.

Instructions:

Enter the following transactions on the stock record of Model No. BE211, speaker wire. Source documents are abbreviated as follows: purchase invoice, P; sales invoice, S.

Transactions:

Nov.　8. Received 88 BE211 speaker wire. P2960.

　　13. Sold 20 BE211 speaker wire. S3527.

　　30. Sold 30 BE211 speaker wire. S3698.

Dec.　5. Sold 15 BE211 speaker wire. S3729.

22-2 APPLICATION PROBLEM
Determining the cost of inventory using the fifo, lifo, and weighted-average inventory costing methods

Forms for costing inventory for Harrison Sound are given in the *Working Papers*. There are 182 units in ending inventory.

Purchase Date	Quantity	Unit Price
January 1, beginning inventory	90	$1.00
March 29, purchases	78	1.10
May 6, purchases	80	1.25
August 28, purchases	84	1.30
November 8, purchases	88	1.40

Instructions:

Calculate the cost of ending inventory using the fifo, lifo, and weighted-average methods.

22-3 APPLICATION PROBLEM
Estimating ending inventory using the gross profit method

Use the following information obtained from the records and management of Cutshaw Company. A form for making inventory calculations and a form for completing an income statement are given in the *Working Papers*.

Instructions:

1. Estimate the cost of the ending inventory on August 31.

Estimated beginning inventory, August 1	$158,900.00
Actual net purchases for August	$ 64,800.00
Actual net sales for August	$254,800.00
Estimated gross profit percentage	30.0%
Actual operating expenses for August	$ 70,070.00

2. Prepare an income statement for the month ended August 31 of the current year.

EXPLORE ACCOUNTING (continued)

400,000 units:
($1.75 × 400,000) + $60,000 + 30,000 + ($0.10 × 400,000) = $830,000 total labor cost divided by 400,000 units = $2.08 unit labor cost.

500,000 units: ($1.75 × 500,000) + $60,000 + 30,000 + ($0.10 × 500,000) = $1,015,000 total labor cost divided by

unit labor cost.

600,000 units: ($1.75 × 600,000) + $60,000 + 30,000 + ($0.10 × 600,000) = $1,200,000 total labor cost divided by 600,000 units = $2.00 unit labor cost.

500,000 units = $2.03

✔ **Mastery Problem 22-4**
Fifo, 930.50
Lifo, 879.80
Weighted-average, 902.70

✔ **Challenge Problem 22-5**
45%
Inv. destroyed, 101,090.00
Net income, 18,300.00

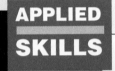

APPLIED SKILLS

LANGUAGE ARTS
Exploring Spelling Checker Software. Students may rely too heavily on the spelling checker feature of their word processing software. A word may be spelled correctly, but it may not be the word that should be used. Spend some time giving examples of incorrect words that the spelling checker cannot identify as misspelled ("if" instead of "is"; "its" instead of "it's"; "the" instead of "them"; etc.). Ask students to supply other pairs of words.

22-4 MASTERY PROBLEM
Determining the cost of inventory using the fifo, lifo, and weighted-average inventory costing methods

Chou Enterprises made the following purchases of a part during the fiscal year. There are 34 units in ending inventory. Forms are given in the *Working Papers*.

Purchase Date	Quantity	Unit Price
January 1, beginning inventory	6	$25.30
January 8, purchases	25	26.00
April 2, purchases	25	26.00
September 13, purchases	25	27.00
December 20, purchases	25	27.50

Instructions:
1. Calculate the cost of ending inventory using the fifo, lifo, and weighted-average methods.
2. Which of the inventory costing methods resulted in the highest cost of merchandise sold?

22-5 CHALLENGE PROBLEM
Determining the cost of merchandise inventory destroyed in a fire

A fire completely destroyed the warehouse of Wright Plumbing Company on the night of October 10 of the current year. The accounting records of the company and $3,500.00 of merchandise inventory remained safe in the company's showroom. The company does not maintain a perpetual inventory system. The insurance company therefore has requested an estimate of the merchandise inventory destroyed in the fire. Forms are given in the *Working Papers*.

The following income statement is for the previous fiscal year.

Wright Plumbing Company Income Statement For Year Ended July 31, 20--		
Operating Revenue:		
Net Sales..............................		$958,700.00
Cost of Merchandise Sold:		
Estimated Beginning Inventory, August 1.......	$119,060.00	
Net Purchases............................	534,607.60	
Merchandise Available for Sale	$653,667.60	
Less Estimated Ending Inventory, July 31	128,300.00	
Cost of Merchandise Sold...................		525,367.60
Gross Profit on Operations..................		$433,332.40
Operating Expenses.......................		325,180.00
Net Income.............................		$108,152.40

The following additional financial information is obtained from the current year's accounting records.

Net purchases, August 1 to October 10	$ 57,800.00
Net sales, August 1 to October 10	148,200.00
Operating expenses, August 1 to October 10	48,390.00

Instructions:
1. Calculate the prior year's gross profit on operations as a percentage of net sales. Round the percentage calculation to the nearest whole percent.

APPLIED SKILLS

WRITING ACROSS THE CURRICULUM
Writing Paragraphs and Short Essays. The Cases for Critical Thinking are short, practical applications of the accounting principles developed in the chapter. Some cases are planned to present problems related to the chapter but not specifically discussed and answered in the chapter. These cases present an opportunity for critical thinking and decision making. These cases also require more than a short, objective-type response. Therefore, they provide ideal practice in writing paragraphs and short essays.

2. Use the percentage calculated in Instruction 1 and the current year's financial information to calculate an estimate of the total merchandise inventory as of October 10.

3. To calculate the cost of the inventory destroyed in the fire, subtract the cost of the merchandise inventory that was not destroyed from the estimate of the total merchandise inventory as of October 10.

4. Prepare an income statement for the period August 1 to October 10.

The insurance company maintains that it is liable for paying only the book value of the inventory destroyed by fire. Wright Plumbing Company maintains that the insurance company should pay the replacement cost of the destroyed inventory.

Instructions:

5. What is meant by the book value and the replacement value of the inventory?

6. Wright Plumbing Company uses the fifo inventory costing method. How does that affect the difference between the book value and the replacement value of the destroyed inventory?

7. What should determine which value the insurance company uses?

INTERNET ACTIVITY

Point your browser to

http://accounting.swpco.com

Choose **First-Year Course**, choose **Activities**, and complete the activity for Chapter 22.

Applied Communication

Arrange with your instructor to call the manager of a local merchandising company. Ask the manager questions concerning how the company maintains a count and cost of its merchandise inventory. Suggested questions include:

1. Does the company maintain a perpetual inventory system?
2. How often does the company take an inventory?
3. Who counts the inventory during a periodic inventory?
4. What method is used to cost the ending inventory?
5. If a perpetual inventory is used, how closely do the year-end quantities match the periodic counts?

Cases for Critical Thinking

Case 1 Ballston Company uses the fifo method of costing its merchandise inventory. The manager is considering a change to the lifo method. Costs have increased steadily over the past three years. What effect will the change have on the following items? (1) The amount of net income on the income statement. (2) The amount of income taxes to be paid. (3) The quantity of each item of merchandise that must be kept in stock. Why?

Case 2 The Pet Center stocks many kinds of merchandise. The store has always taken a periodic inventory at the end of a fiscal year. The store has not kept a perpetual inventory because of the cost. However, the manager wants a reasonably accurate cost of merchandise inventory at the end of each month. The manager needs the amount to prepare monthly income statements and to help in making decisions about the business. What would you recommend?

INTERNET ACTIVITY

Because Internet sites can change frequently, the requirements of the Internet Activity are posted on a South-Western site where they can be updated as needed. Direct students to follow the directions given on their student page.

APPLIED COMMUNICATION

This activity requires students to talk with a local business manager. Two difficult parts of a conversation with an unknown individual are the introduction and the closing. Some students may need assistance formulating a plan for these parts of the conversation. Conducting a mock interview in class may be helpful.

CASES FOR CRITICAL THINKING

CASE 1 (1) The net income on the income statement will be less because the lifo method gives the lowest possible ending inventory cost during a period of rising prices. Therefore, the cost of merchandise sold will be higher, using the lifo method. Thus, net income will also be less. (2) The amount of income taxes to be paid will be less because of the lower net income. (3) There will be no effect upon the quantity of each item that should be kept in stock because inventory costing methods do not affect the amount of merchandise needed.

CASE 2 The manager could use the gross profit method of estimating inventory. The estimate will be accurate enough to prepare monthly income statements and to manage the inventory. Therefore, it is not necessary to take a periodic inventory monthly or to maintain a perpetual inventory.

PORTFOLIO ASSESSMENT

Proper and accurate accounting for merchandise inventory is critical to a business. Large businesses may have millions of dollars worth of merchandise inventory on hand, and accurate records may make the difference in a business's success. Students should emphasize their learning of this topic by selecting an example of a comprehensive sample of their work in this chapter, either the mastery problem or a problem from a test, to include in their portfolio. A copy of the Portfolio Assessment form (blackline master in the Teacher's Resource Guide) should be completed by the student, and the Description section should include any comments regarding how the student mastered these concepts and procedures. Alternatively, students might include in their portfolios printed reports from an Automated Accounting or Spreadsheet Accounting problem.

AUTOMATED INVENTORY SYSTEMS

EXPLAIN

- ❑ Preview the terms used or introduced in this feature: inventory stock maintenance and inventory stock record.
- ❑ Explain that a computerized inventory system allows businesses better access to accurate information about the inventory.
- ❑ Explain that inventory data may be updated as often as necessary—daily, weekly, monthly.
- ❑ Explain that an inventory system must have a record for each kind of merchandise in the inventory.
- ❑ Explain that information about inventory is maintained in the stock records and this information can be changed, added, or deleted.
- ❑ Explain that all inventory transactions are recorded in the Other Activities Inventory window, including sales, purchases, and returns and allowances.

DEMONSTRATE

Inventory stock maintenance

- ❑ Demonstrate clicking the Accounts toolbar button and then clicking the Inventory tab.
- ❑ Demonstrate entering the data in the inventory fields.
- ❑ Demonstrate clicking the Add Item button to record the data entered.
- ❑ Demonstrate changing data for an inventory stock item by clicking in the cell that needs to be changed, correcting the data, and clicking the Change Item button to record the change.
- ❑ Demonstrate deleting an inventory item by clicking on the item and clicking the Delete button. Point out that an inventory item may be deleted only after current transaction data has been deleted or purged.

A merchandising business is a business that purchases and resells goods. Merchandise inventory may consist of thousands of different items. The total cost of the inventory consists of many different costs, including:

- The cost of purchasing the inventory.
- The cost of storing the inventory.
- The cost of record keeping.
- Taxes and insurance on the inventory.
- The cost of losses due to theft and damage.

A computerized inventory system allows business better access to accurate information about the inventory. Managers need information about which items are selling, the number of items currently in inventory, and when to reorder an item.

Inventory Stock Maintenance

An inventory stock record is created for each item in inventory. The inventory stock record retains information such as stock number, description, unit of measure, reorder point, retail price, quantity sold, quantity ordered, quantity received, and purchase price. This data may be updated as often (daily, weekly, monthly) as necessary. All normal transactions related to inventory are entered into the system. Periodic inventory reports are generated.

To add or change inventory stock data:

1. Click the Accounts toolbar button.
2. Click the Inventory tab.
3. To add a new inventory stock item:
   a. Enter the stock number.
   b. Enter a short description for the item.
   c. Enter the unit of measure. Common units of measure are EA for Each, CS for Case, and BX for Box.
   d. Enter the reorder point. Merchandising businesses can sell only the goods they have in stock. The reorder point is set so that the item will not be out of stock.
   e. Enter the retail price, or the price the business charges its customers. (The cost of the item will be entered when each order is received.)
4. Click the Add Item button.
5. To change data for a current inventory stock item:
   a. Select the stock item by clicking the text cell containing the data you wish to change.
   b. Enter the correct data.
   c. Click the Change Item button, or click the Delete button to remove the item from the database. (Inventory items may be deleted only after current transaction data has been deleted or purged.)

Inventory Transactions

All inventory transactions are recorded in the Other Activities Inventory window. These transactions include sales, purchases ordered, purchases received, and sales and purchases returns.

To enter inventory transactions:

1. Click the Other toolbar button.
2. Click the Inventory tab.
3. Enter the date of the inventory transaction.
4. Select the inventory item from the Inventory drop-down list.
5. Enter the transaction data in the appropriate text boxes.
6. Click OK.

To correct or delete an inventory transaction:

1. Select the transaction by clicking the text box containing the data you wish to correct.
2. Enter the correct data and click OK, or click the Delete button to remove the transaction.

Automated Accounting 8.0 has a more complete inventory system:

1. When inventory items are ordered, a purchase order is recorded in the Purch. Order tab of the Other Activities window.
2. When an order is received, a purchase invoice is issued and recorded in the Purch. Invoice tab of the Other Activities window.
3. When merchandise is sold, the sales invoice is entered in

AUTOMATED ACCOUNTING

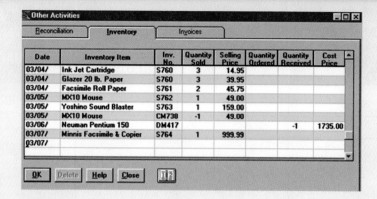

the Sales Invoice tab of the Other Activities window.

Inventory Reports

Several inventory reports are available. Managers use these reports in planning and controlling inventory. To display inventory reports:

1. Click the Reports toolbar button, or choose the Reports Selection menu item from the Reports menu.
2. When the Report Selection dialog appears, choose the Inventory Reports option button from the Select a Report Group list.
3. Choose the inventory report you would like to display from the Choose a Report to Display list.
4. Click the OK button.

AUTOMATING APPLICATION PROBLEM 22-1: Preparing a stock record
Instructions:
1. Load *Automated Accounting*

7.0 or higher software.
2. Select database F22-1 from the appropriate directory/folder.
3. Select File from the menu bar and choose the Save As menu command. Key the path to the drive and directory that contains your data files. Save the database with a file name of XXX221 (where XXX are your initials).
4. Access Problem Instructions through the Help menu. Read the Problem Instructions screen.
5. Key the data listed on page 589.
6. Exit the *Automated Accounting* software.

AUTOMATING MASTERY PROBLEM 22-4: Determining the cost of inventory using the fifo, lifo, and weighted-average inventory costing methods
Instructions:
1. Load *Automated Accounting*

7.0 or higher software.
2. Select database F22-2 from the appropriate directory/folder.
3. Select File from the menu bar and choose the Save As menu command. Key the path to the drive and directory that contains your data files. Save the database with a file name of XXX222 (where XXX are your initials).
4. Access Problem Instructions through the Help menu. Read the Problem Instructions screen.
5. Key the data listed on page 590.
6. Exit the *Automated Accounting* software.

CHAPTER 22 Accounting for Inventory **593**

DEMONSTRATE

Recording inventory transactions
❑ Demonstrate Clicking the Other toolbar button and then clicking the Inventory tab.
❑ Demonstrate selecting the inventory item from the inventory drop-down list.
❑ Demonstrate entering transaction data in the appropriate fields.
❑ Demonstrate clicking OK to record the transaction.
❑ *Automated Accounting 8.0* integrates the inventory, purchases, and sales systems to keep a perpetual inventory. Demonstrate how purchase orders, purchase invoices, and sales invoices are entered in the Other Activities window to update inventory stock records.

Generating inventory reports
❑ Demonstrate clicking the Reports toolbar button and choosing the Inventory Reports option button from the Select a Report Group list.
❑ Demonstrate choosing an inventory report from the Choose a Report to Display list.
❑ Demonstrate clicking OK to display the report.
❑ Repeat the demonstration for each different inventory report.
❑ Mention to students that *Automated Accounting* calculates the weighted-average method differently than the manual process described in the chapter. The automated report may not match their manual solution.

PRACTICE

❑ Assign Automating Application Problem 22-1: Preparing a stock record.
❑ Assign Automating Mastery Problem 22-4: Determining the cost of inventory using the fifo, lifo, and weighted-average inventory costing methods.

PORTFOLIO ASSESSMENT

Students should be encouraged to print at least one report from one of the *Automated Accounting* problems to include in their portfolio to demonstrate mastery of automated accounting systems. A copy of the Portfolio Assessment form (blackline master in the Teacher's Resource Guide) should be completed by the student, and the Description section should include any comments regarding how the student mastered these concepts and procedures.

ASSESSMENT

❑ Use the Electronic Auditor to assess student understanding.

CHAPTER 23

	SCOPE AND SEQUENCE		ENHANCING	
	NEW	**REVIEW/ EXTENSION**	**SPECIAL FEATURES**	
INTRODUCE THE CHAPTER			Accounting in Your Career: How to Choose a Loan Thinking about Careers	
When lending and borrowing are necessary	✓			
LESSSON 23-1 PROMISSORY NOTES			Math Work Sheet, Chapter 22, Part A Math Work Sheet, Chapter 22, Part B Math Work Sheet, Chapter 22, Part C Math Work Sheet, Chapter 22, Part D	
Uses of promissory notes	✓			
Calculating interest on promissory notes	✓			
Calculating maturity value and maturity date of promissory notes	✓			
LESSSON 23-2 NOTES PAYABLE			Accounting at Work: Arthur R. Velasquez	
Journalizing signing a note payable	✓			
Journalizing paying principal and interest on a note payable	✓			
Journalizing signing a note payable for an extension of time on account	✓			
Journalizing paying a note payable issued for an extension of time on account	✓			
LESSSON 23-3 NOTES RECEIVABLE				
Journalizing accepting a note receivable from a customer	✓			
Journalzing collecting principal and interest on a note receivable	✓			
Journalizing a dishonored note receivable	✓			
PUTTING IT ALL TOGETHER			Explore Accounting Internet Activity Applied Communication Cases for Critical Thinking 1 and 2	

ACCOUNTING FOR NOTES AND INTEREST

INSTRUCTION		PRACTICE AND ASSESSMENT		
TECHNOLOGY AND MEDIA	TEACHING STRATEGIES	GUIDED PRACTICE	INDEPENDENT PRACTICE	RETEACHING AND ENRICHMENT
Internet Activity	Software Focus			
Transparencies 23-1 Automated Accounting Spreadsheet Accounting	Applied Skills: Mathematics	Terms Review Audit Your Understanding Work Together	On Your Own Application Problem 23-1 Ongoing Assessment, p. 598	Reteach, p. 598 Enrich, p. 599
South-Western Accounting Video: Accounting Field Trip—Notes Payable Transparencies L, M, and O	Building Study Skills Expanding Beyond the Classroom	Terms Review Audit Your Understanding Work Together	On Your Own Application Problem 23-2 Ongoing Assessment, p. 603	Reteach, p. 603 Enrich, p. 604
CNN Accounting Video Transparencies M and O	Limited English Proficiency (LEP) Students	Terms Review Audit Your Understanding Work Together	On Your Own Application Problem 23-3 Ongoing Assessment, p. 607	Reteach, p. 607 Enrich, p. 608
Transparency 23-2 Automated Accounting Accounting Connection	Applied Skills: Language Arts Applied Skills: Writing Across the Curriculum		Application Problem 23-4 Mastery Problem 23-5 Study Guide 23 Chapter 23 Test ExamViewPro or Westest, Chapter 23 Portfolio Assessment	Enrich, p. 609 Challenge Problem 23-6 Reteach, p. 609 Recycling Problem 23-1 Accounting Connection

TERMS PREVIEW

number of a note
date of a note
payee of a note
time of a note
principal of a note
interest rate of a note
maturity date of a note
maker of a note
promissory note
creditor
notes payable
interest
maturity value
current liabilities
interest expense
notes receivable
interest income
dishonored note

594

23

Accounting for Notes and Interest

AFTER STUDYING CHAPTER 23, YOU WILL BE ABLE TO:

1. Define accounting terms related to notes and interest.

2. Identify accounting concepts and practices related to notes and interest.

3. Calculate interest and maturity dates for notes.

4. Analyze and record transactions for notes payable.

5. Analyze and record transactions for notes receivable.

WHEN LENDING AND BORROWING ARE NECESSARY

Cash is the primary medium of exchange for business transactions. *(CONCEPT: Unit of Measurement)* Cash is used to purchase merchandise and to pay salaries and other expenses. In turn, businesses receive cash when they sell their products or services and collect payment. The cash received for products or services can be used to purchase more merchandise and continue to pay salaries and other expenses. Thus, the business cycle continues.

Sometimes a business receives more cash from sales than is needed to pay for purchases and expenses. When this occurs, a business may deposit the extra cash in a bank or other financial institution for a short period. At other times, the receipt of cash from sales does not occur at the same time and in amounts sufficient to pay for needed purchases and expenses. When this occurs, a business needs to borrow additional cash or make arrangements with its vendors to delay payment for a period of time. Generally, when a bank or other business lends money to another business, the loan agreement is made in writing.

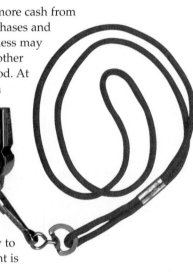

ACCOUNTING IN YOUR CAREER

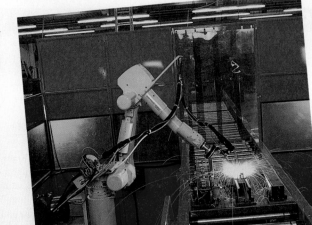

HOW TO CHOOSE A LOAN

Alisa Chavez is an experienced mechanical engineer and inventor who has financed the startup of a new company, Roboco, Inc. After two years of operations, the company is profitable, but most of the profits are reinvested in research. The research group has perfected a new kind of robotic arm that will allow manufacturers to produce their products faster and cheaper. It is expected that the sales of this new arm will dramatically increase revenues and profits for Roboco, Inc. However, new equipment costing $250,000 will be needed to produce these new arms.

Robert Greeley, accounting manager, has sought loans from the company's bankers to purchase this new equipment. One bank is offering a 10-year, 12% loan and another an 8-year, 11.5% loan. Both banks are also willing to finance the acquisition of the equipment with a 1-year, 9% loan. All the loans would require monthly payments of principal plus interest.

Robert explains to Alisa that it will take four months to acquire the equipment and get it set up to begin production. The first arms would be available for sale in about six months. Alisa does not like to carry much debt and has never borrowed on a long-term basis before. Therefore, she favors the 1-year loan. Robert says, "I recommend that we discuss this some more before making a decision. The 1-year loan might not be the best decision for the company right now."

Critical Thinking:
1. Why would banks require higher interest rates on longer-term loans?
2. The interest rate on the 1-year loan is clearly the lowest. Why would Robert suggest that the long-term loans might be better?

SUGGESTED ANSWERS

1. *The longer the terms of a loan, the more risk there is that conditions could change and a company would be unable to pay back the rest of the loan. The higher interest rate reflects this greater risk. Banks also want to allow for the possibility that inflation will decrease the amount of profit they make from loaning money.*

2. *Robert Greeley knows that the new equipment will not generate any new revenue for at least six months. Therefore, half of the new loan would have to be paid back before the equipment bought with the loan proceeds begins to generate any revenue. Therefore, Robert is not enthusiastic about a fast repayment of the loan.*

USES OF PROMISSORY NOTES

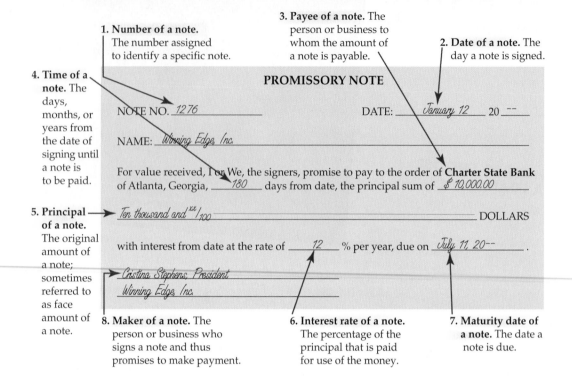

1. **Number of a note.** The number assigned to identify a specific note.

2. **Date of a note.** The day a note is signed.

3. **Payee of a note.** The person or business to whom the amount of a note is payable.

4. **Time of a note.** The days, months, or years from the date of signing until a note is to be paid.

5. **Principal of a note.** The original amount of a note; sometimes referred to as face amount of a note.

6. **Interest rate of a note.** The percentage of the principal that is paid for use of the money.

7. **Maturity date of a note.** The date a note is due.

8. **Maker of a note.** The person or business who signs a note and thus promises to make payment.

A written and signed promise to pay a sum of money at a specified time is called a **promissory note.** A person or organization to whom a liability is owed is called a **creditor.** Promissory notes signed by a business and given to a creditor are called **notes payable.** A note payable is frequently referred to as a note.

Promissory notes are used when money is borrowed for a period of time from a bank or other lending agency. Sometimes a business requests a note from a customer who wants credit beyond the usual time given for sales on account. Notes have an advantage over oral promises and accounts receivable or payable. Notes can be useful in a court of law as written evidence of a debt.

596 CHAPTER 23 Accounting for Notes and Interest

INTEREST ON PROMISSORY NOTES

An amount paid for the use of money for a period of time is called **interest.** Banks and other lending institutions charge interest on money loaned to their customers. The interest rate is stated as a percentage of the principal. *Interest at 10% means that 10 cents will be paid for the use of each dollar borrowed for a full year.*

When businesses borrow money from banks, other lending institutions, or other businesses, promissory notes should be prepared to provide written evidence of the transaction.

Sometimes partial payments on a note are made each month. This arrangement is particularly true when an individual buys a car and signs a note for the amount owed. The monthly payment includes part of the principal and part of the interest to be paid.

To calculate interest for one year, the principal is multiplied by the interest rate. The interest on a $1,000.00, 12% note for one year is $120.00.

Principal	×	Interest Rate	×	Time in Years	=	Interest for One Year	
$1,000.00	×	12%	×	1	=	$120.00	

The time of a note issued for less than one year is typically stated as a number of days, such as 30 days, 60 days, or 90 days. The time used in calculating interest is usually stated as a fraction of 360 days. The interest on a $1,000.00, 12% note for 60 days is $20.00.

Principal	×	Interest Rate	×	Time as Fraction of Year	=	Interest for Fraction of Year	
$1,000.00	×	12%	×	$\frac{60}{360}$	=	$20.00	

The amount that is due on the maturity date of a note is called the **maturity value.** A 60-day note with a principal of $1,000.00 and interest rate of 12% will have a maturity value of $1,020.00.

Principal	+	Interest	=	Maturity Value	
$1,000.00	+	$20.00	=	$1,020.00	

CHAPTER 23   Accounting for Notes and Interest   **597**

MATURITY DATE OF PROMISSORY NOTES

EXPLAIN

- Point out that the date of the note is not counted as one of the days.
- Point out the maturity date is often written on a note.
- Point out that the method of determining the maturity date is the same, regardless of whether the business is the payee or maker of the note.
- Ask students to read the F.Y.I. to learn more about how interest rates can be entered in a calculator or electronic spreadsheet program.
- Ask students to read the F.Y.I. about the number of days in a year used for interest calculations.

DEMONSTRATE

- Demonstrate the calculation of the maturity date shown in the textbook on the blackboard. As you read a step, ask students to write the amounts on a sheet of paper.
- Ask a student to summarize each step as it is completed.
- Ask students to prepare original date and times for three notes.
- Direct students to determine the maturity date for each note.

ONGOING ASSESSMENT

- Assessment is an ongoing process. Circulate through the classroom or lab, observing which students have problems with the assignments.
- Troubleshooting: Diagnose what kinds of problems students have with this lesson. Students may have trouble (1) understanding that interest rates are stated as annual interest rates, (2) calculating interest, (3) calculating maturity dates, or (4) calculating maturity value.
- Assess student understanding by checking solutions to Independent Practice assignments.

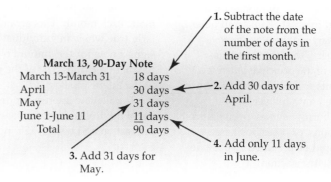

March 13, 90-Day Note

March 13–March 31	18 days
April	30 days
May	31 days
June 1–June 11	11 days
Total	90 days

1. Subtract the date of the note from the number of days in the first month.
2. Add 30 days for April.
3. Add 31 days for May.
4. Add only 11 days in June.

The time between the date a note is signed and the date a note is due is typically expressed in days. The maturity date is calculated by counting the exact number of days. The date the note is written is not counted, but the maturity date is counted. For example, a 90-day note dated March 13 is due on June 11.

Calculating the maturity date of a note

1. Calculate the number of days remaining in March, *18,* by subtracting the date of the note, *13,* from the number of days in March, *31.*
2. Calculate the number of days remaining in the term of the note, *72,* by subtracting the number of days in the previous month, *18,* from the term of the note, *90.* Because 72 is greater than the number of days in April, *30,* add all of the days in April.
3. Calculate the number of days remaining in the term of the note, *42,* by subtracting the number of days in the previous months, *48 (18 + 30),* from the term of the note, *90.* Because 42 is greater than the number of days in May, *31,* add all of the days in May.
4. Calculate the number of days remaining in the term of the note, *11,* by subtracting the number of days in the previous months, *79 (18 + 30 + 31),* from the term of the note, *90.* Because 11 is less than the number of days in June, *30,* add only *11* days in June.

> **F.Y.I.**
>
> *Agencies of the federal government generally use a 365-day year when calculating interest. Consumer interest is also generally calculated on a 365-day year. However, many banks use a 360-day year when calculating interest. Therefore, the interest calculations in this textbook use a 360-day year.*

> **F.Y.I.**
>
> *An interest rate can be entered on a calculator or electronic spreadsheet either by using the Percent key (%) or the decimal equivalent of the interest rate. For example, 12% could be keyed as 0.12.*

598 CHAPTER 23 Accounting for Notes and Interest

RETEACH

- Ask students to describe how to calculate interest for a year and a fraction of a year.
- Call on students to describe how to calculate the maturity date of a note.
- Call on students to describe how to calculate the maturity value of a note.
- Assign Math Work Sheet, Chapter 23, Parts A, B, C, and D.

 **TERMS REVIEW**

number of a note

date of a note

payee of a note

time of a note

principal of a note

interest rate of a note

maturity date of a note

maker of a note

promissory note

creditor

notes payable

interest

maturity value

 **AUDIT YOUR UNDERSTANDING**

1. What conditions would cause a business to have extra cash to deposit in a bank, yet at another time of year need to borrow extra cash from a bank?

2. What is the advantage of a promissory note over an account receivable?

3. What does interest at 10% mean?

4. How is interest calculated for a fraction of a year?

GUIDED PRACTICE

Terms Review
Call on students to define the terms in the Terms Review. Ask the class if the definitions are correct and whether the complete definitions have been given or if anything needs to be added. The suggested definitions are given in the Glossary.

Audit Your Understanding
Call on students to answer the Audit Your Understanding questions. Ask the class if the answer is correct and/or complete. Answers are given in Appendix D of the textbook.

Work Together
Have students write the solution to the Work Together problem as you guide the class through the example.
❏ Call on two students to write their interest calculations on the board.
❏ Call on another two students to write their maturity date calculations on the board.
❏ Call on another two students to write their maturity value calculations on the board.
❏ Remind students to save their work to complete Work Together in Lesson 2.

 **WORK TOGETHER**

Calculating interest, maturity dates, and maturity values for promissory notes

Write the answers to the following problem in the *Working Papers*. Your instructor will guide you through the following example.

5. For each of the following promissory notes, calculate (a) the interest on the note, (b) the maturity date of the note, and (c) the maturity value of the note. Save your work to complete Work Together on page 604.

Date	Principal	Interest Rate	Time
March 3	$6,000.00	12%	90 days
March 18	$2,000.00	18%	60 days

 **ON YOUR OWN**

Calculating interest, maturity dates, and maturity values for promissory notes

Write the answers to the following problem in the *Working Papers*. Work this problem independently.

6. For each of the following promissory notes, calculate (a) the interest on the note, (b) the maturity date of the note, and (c) the maturity value of the note. Save your work to complete On Your Own on page 604.

Date	Principal	Interest Rate	Time
June 6	$10,000.00	10%	60 days
June 23	$ 4,200.00	18%	90 days

INDEPENDENT PRACTICE

On Your Own
❏ Assign the On Your Own problem to be worked independently.
❏ Remind students to save their work to complete On Your Own in Lesson 2.
❏ Use the Ongoing Assessment techniques to diagnose student understanding.

Application Problem
❏ Assign Application Problem 23-1: Calculating interest, maturity dates, and maturity values for promissory notes.

ENRICH

❏ Assign the Automated Accounting feature on pages 614–615 to automate Application Problem 23-1.
❏ Assign the Spreadsheet Accounting Template for Application Problem 23-1.
❏ Direct students to obtain current certificate of deposit rates. For an assumed amount of money, ask students to calculate the maturity date and value.

CLOSE

❏ Ask students to briefly summarize the procedures for determining the interest, maturity value, and maturity date of a note.

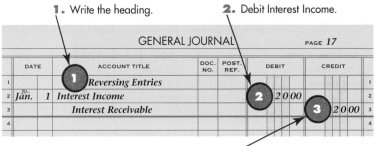

1. Write the heading.

2. Debit Interest Income.

3. Credit Interest Receivable.

EXPLAIN

❏ Explain that after the closing entry, Interest Income has a zero balance because part of the interest revenue that is not yet due has been recorded in the account and then removed by the closing entry.

❏ Explain that when the cash for the note receivable is received in the next fiscal period, the cash will include the interest that was closed from this account at the end of the fiscal period.

❏ Explain that if the full amount of interest is recorded in the next fiscal period, the part that was recorded in the previous fiscal period will have been recorded twice.

❏ Explain that reversing entries are recorded to avoid erroneously recording interest twice.

❏ Explain that the effect of the reversing entry creates a debit balance in Interest Income, a balance opposite to the normal balance of an other revenue account.

❏ Explain that reversing entries are the exact opposite of the adjusting entries for the same accounts.

DEMONSTRATE

Analyze the transaction

❏ Draw two T accounts on the blackboard and enter the pre-adjustment balance in Interest Income.

❏ Describe the adjusting and closing entries while recording these entries in the T accounts.

❏ Describe the reversing entry.

❏ Ask students to analyze the reversing entry by answering: what accounts are affected, are they increased or decreased, and are they debited or credited? Complete the T accounts as the information is provided.

Record the transaction

❏ Use Transparency M or direct students to the illustration to demonstrate recording the reversing entry in the general journal.

On December 31, Interest Income is closed as part of the regular closing entry for income statement accounts with credit balances. Interest Income is debited for $88.00 to reduce the account balance to zero.

Adjusting entries for accrued revenues have an effect on transactions to be recorded in the following fiscal period. On the maturity date of the outstanding 90-day note receivable, Winning Edge will receive interest of $30.00.

However, an adjusting entry was made to record the amount of interest earned last year, $20.00. Thus, $20.00 of the $30.00 total interest income has already been recorded as revenue. The remaining $10.00 of the $30.00 total interest will be earned during the current fiscal period.

It is inconvenient to determine how much, if any, of cash received from notes receivable relates to interest accrued during the prior fiscal period. To avoid this inconvenience, an entry is made at the beginning of the new fiscal period

to reverse the adjusting entry. An entry made at the beginning of one fiscal period to reverse an adjusting entry made in the previous fiscal period is called a **reversing entry.**

Interest Income

Dec. 31 Closing	88.00	Dec. 31 Bal.	68.00
Jan. 1 Rev.	20.00	Dec. 31 Adj.	20.00
(New Bal.	*20.00)*		

Interest Receivable

| Dec. 31 Adj. | 20.00 | Jan. 1 Rev. | 20.00 |
| *(New Bal. zero)* | | | |

The reversing entry is the opposite of the adjusting entry. The entry creates a debit balance of $20.00 in Interest Income. A debit balance is the opposite of the normal balance of Interest Income. When the full amount of interest is received, the $30.00 will be credited to Interest Income, resulting in a $10.00 credit balance ($30.00 credit − $20.00 debit), the amount of interest earned in the new year.

The reversing entry reduced the balance in Interest Receivable to zero. When the interest is received, no entry will be made to Interest Receivable. Instead, the total amount of interest received will be credited to Interest Income.

S T E P S

Reversing an adjusting entry for accrued interest income

1. Write the heading *Reversing Entries* in the middle of the general journal's Account Title column. This heading explains all the reversing entries that follow. Therefore, indicating a source document is unnecessary.

2. Record a debit, *$20.00,* to Interest Income.

3. Record a credit, *$20.00,* to Interest Receivable.

TEACHING STRATEGIES   BUILDING STUDY SKILLS

Two new accounts, Interest Receivable and Interest Payable, are introduced in this chapter. Direct students to create a Quick Reference Guide (QRG) on a small card or sheet of paper to use as an aid in analyzing transactions. T accounts should be used to show normal balance sides.

COLLECTING A NOTE RECEIVABLE ISSUED IN A PREVIOUS FISCAL PERIOD

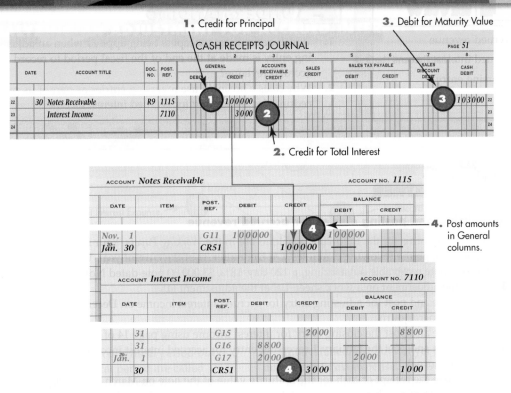

1. Credit for Principal

3. Debit for Maturity Value

2. Credit for Total Interest

4. Post amounts in General columns.

On January 30, Winning Edge received the maturity value of the only note receivable on hand on December 31, the end of the previous fiscal year.

January 30. Received cash for the maturity value of a 90-day, 12% note: principal, $1,000.00, plus interest, $30.00; total, $1,030.00. Receipt No. 9.

Cash

Jan. 30 Rec'd	1,030.00

Notes Receivable

Nov. 1	1,000.00	Jan. 30 Rec'd	1,000.00

Interest Income

Dec. 31 Closing	88.00	Dec. 31 Bal.	68.00
Jan. 1 Rev.	20.00	Dec. 31 Adj.	20.00
		Jan. 30 Rec'd	30.00
		(New Bal.	*10.00)*

The total interest, $30.00, was earned during two fiscal periods—$20.00 during the previous fiscal period and $10.00 during the current fiscal period. The reversing entry created a $20.00 debit balance in Interest Income. After the $30.00 credit is posted, Interest Income has a credit balance of $10.00, the amount of interest earned during the current fiscal period.

S T E P S

Collecting a note receivable issued in a previous fiscal period

1. Record a credit to Notes Receivable in the General Credit column of a cash receipts journal for the principal of the note, *$1,000.00*.

2. Record a credit to Interest Income in the General Credit column for the total interest, *$30.00*.

3. Record a debit in the Cash Debit column for the maturity value of the note, *$1,030.00*.

4. Post the amounts in the General columns of the cash receipts journal.

RETEACH

❑ Ask students to discuss the purpose of a reversing entry.
❑ Assign Math Work Sheet, Chapter 24, Parts A and B.
❑ Ask students to identify how to record the adjusting and reversing entries for accrued interest revenue.
❑ Ask students how to record the cash receipt for a note receivable.

EXPLAIN

❑ Explain that students learned to record the collecting of a note receivable in the previous chapter.
❑ Explain that the entry to record the collection of a note receivable is the same, regardless of when the note was issued.
❑ Ask students to explain how much of the interest income received in cash was earned in the current period *($10.00)*.
❑ Point out that the entry has no impact on Interest Receivable.

DEMONSTRATE

Analyze the transaction

❑ Direct students to use a calculator to calculate the interest income.
❑ Read the transaction statement.
❑ Ask students to analyze the entry by answering: what accounts are affected, are they increased or decreased, and are they debited or credited? Complete the T accounts as the information is provided.
❑ Point out that because Interest Income had a debit balance of $20.00, the credit entry of $30.00 interest on the note has the effect of recording only the $10.00 interest earned in the current period in the account.

Record the transaction

❑ Use Transparency 0 or direct students to the illustration to demonstrate recording the transaction in the cash receipts journal.
❑ Direct students to the illustration to demonstrate posting the transaction.

ONGOING ASSESSMENT

❑ Assessment is an ongoing process. Circulate through the classroom or lab, observing which students have problems with the assignments.
❑ Troubleshooting: Diagnose what kinds of problems students have with this lesson. Students may have difficulty (1) understanding the purpose of a reversing entry and its impact on transactions recorded in the future, (2) calculating the accrued interest income, (3) calculating the maturity value, (4) journalizing a reversing entry, or (5) journalizing the subsequent collection of a note receivable.
❑ Assess student understanding by checking solutions to Independent Practice assignments.

GUIDED PRACTICE

Terms Review

Call on students to define the terms in the Terms Review. Ask the class if the definitions are correct and whether the complete definitions have been given or if anything needs to be added. The suggested definitions are given in the Glossary.

Audit Your Understanding

Call on students to answer the Audit Your Understanding questions. Ask the class if the answer is correct and/or complete. Answers are given in Appendix D of the textbook.

Work Together

Have students write the solutions to the Work Together problems as you guide the class through the examples.

❑ Ask students to explain their calculation of total interest expense.

❑ Direct students to record the adjusting, closing, and reversing entries in the general journal as you elicit class participation in analyzing and recording the transactions.

❑ Direct students to record the transaction for the cash payment in the cash payments journal as you elicit class participation in analyzing and recording the transaction.

INDEPENDENT PRACTICE

On Your Own

❑ Assign the On Your Own problems to be worked independently.

❑ Use the Ongoing Assessment techniques to diagnose student understanding.

Application Problem

❑ Assign Application Problem 24-2: Journalizing and posting entries for accrued expenses.

❑ Assign Application Problem 24-3: Journalizing and posting entries for accrued expenses.

accrued expenses

accrued interest expense

1. Why should accrued expenses be recorded by an adjusting entry before financial statements are prepared at the end of a fiscal period?

2. What accounts are affected, and how, by the reversing entry for accrued interest expense?

Journalizing and posting entries for accrued expenses

The accounting forms for the following problems are in the *Working Papers*. Your instructor will guide you through the following examples. On December 31 of the current year, Powers Corporation has one note payable outstanding, a 90-day, 18%, $2,000.00 note dated December 1.

3. Plan the adjustment on a work sheet. Label the adjustment *(h)*.

4. Journalize and post the adjusting entry for accrued interest expense on December 31. Use page 14 of a general journal.

5. Journalize and post the closing entry for interest expense using page 14 of a general journal.

6. Journalize and post the January 1 reversing entry for accrued interest expense on page 15 of a general journal.

7. Journalize the payment of cash for the maturity value of the note on March 1, Check No. 543. Use page 25 of a cash payments journal. Post the amounts in the General columns.

Journalizing and posting entries for accrued expenses

The accounting forms for the following problems are in the *Working Papers*. Work these problems independently. On December 31 of the current year, Bartlett Industries has one note payable outstanding, a 180-day, 12%, $10,000.00 note dated September 2.

8. Plan the adjustment on a work sheet. Label the adjustment *(h)*.

9. Journalize and post the adjusting entry for accrued interest expense on December 31. Use page 14 of a general journal.

10. Journalize and post the closing entry for interest expense using page 14 of a general journal.

11. Journalize and post the January 1 reversing entry for accrued interest expense on page 15 of a general journal.

12. Journalize the payment of cash for the maturity value of the note on March 1, Check No. 845. Use page 29 of a cash payments journal. Post the amounts in the General columns.

ENRICH

❑ Assign the Accounting at Work feature on page 627.

❑ Assign the Automated Accounting feature on pages 634–635 to automate Application Problem 24-2.

❑ Show the South-Western Accounting Video: Accounting Field Trip—Accrued Revenue and Expenses.

CLOSE

❑ Ask students to briefly summarize the recording of adjusting, closing, and reversing entries for accrued interest expense.

After completing this chapter, you can

1. Define accounting terms related to accrued revenue and accrued expenses.

2. Identify accounting concepts and practices related to accrued revenue and accrued expenses.

3. Record adjusting, closing, and reversing entries for accrued revenue.

4. Record adjusting, closing, and reversing entries for accrued expenses.

EXPLORE ACCOUNTING

ANNUAL REPORTS— FINANCIAL INFORMATION AND MORE

Corporations publish annual reports to communicate the results of operations to interested parties, such as stockholders, creditors, and government agencies. The typical annual report is a colorful, soft-cover brochure printed on $8\frac{1}{2}$-by-11-inch glossy paper and measuring 40 to 60 pages in length. The reports are grouped in two sections:

1. *Management's Analysis and Discussion.* This section provides management with an opportunity to promote the corporation. Through the use of pictures, graphs, and narrative, management can highlight the achievements of the past fiscal year and present its plans. Some corporations report on how the volunteer work of their employees is having a positive impact in their communities. Discussions of environmental and recycling programs could demonstrate

how the corporation is socially responsible.

The ultimate objective of any corporation is to increase the market price of its stock, thereby raising stockholders' investment. By "putting its best foot forward" in this section, management can increase the demand for the corporation's products and stock, thus increasing the stock's price.

2. *Financial Statements.* The financial statements section contains several items in addition to basic financial statements. Most of the additional items are required by GAAP or the Securities and Exchange Commission. As a result, these items are similar among corporations.

(a) *Notes to the Financial Statements.* The notes contain additional, detailed information about items presented on the financial statements. For example, the note related to long-term debt would include the

projected loan repayments for the next five years.

(b) *Auditor's Report.* The report of the independent auditor states that a public accounting firm has tested the financial statements for accuracy and fair presentation. The report gives the reader confidence to use the financial statements to make business decisions.

(c) *Financial Analysis.* Summary financial information, such as total assets, net income, and common financial ratios, are presented for several years.

Required: Obtain an annual report and prepare a detailed outline of its contents. Summarize the major topics in management's analysis and discussion. Did management do a good job of "putting its best foot forward"? Would you recommend that a friend purchase the corporation's stock? Support your answers.

EXPLORE ACCOUNTING

This feature presents the two major sections of published annual reports. Assist students in obtaining the annual report for a publicly-traded company. Many companies now publish their annual reports on the Internet. Students should be encouraged to share the findings of their research with their classmates.

PUTTING IT ALL TOGETHER

❏ Review the Chapter Summary.
❏ Ask students to prepare a list of the new concepts introduced in this chapter.
❏ Use Transparency 24-1 to summarize the chapter.
❏ Ask students to identify why adjusting entries are recorded for accrued revenue and expenses *(to match expenses with revenue, thereby improving the accuracy of financial statements).*

INDEPENDENT PRACTICE

❏ Assign **Mastery Problem 24-4** to students who need the reinforcement of a problem that combines all concepts and transactions from the chapter in one problem; this will be most students.
❏ Assign **Challenge Problem 24-5** to accelerated students who do not require the reinforcement of the mastery problem.
❏ Assign **Study Guide 24**.

ONGOING ASSESSMENT

Review solutions to the assigned problems in class, diagnosing troublespots.

RETEACH

❏ Call on students to describe how they avoid the troublespots diagnosed.
❏ Use reteaching suggestions from lesson plans as required.
❏ Assign Recycling Problem 24-1 if needed.
❏ Assign Accounting Connection, Chapter 24.

ENRICH

❏ Assign the Explore Accounting feature. Ask students to share the information they have gathered in a report to the class.
❏ Assign the Internet Activity.
❏ Assign the Applied Communication activity.
❏ Assign Cases 1 and 2 of Cases for Critical Thinking.
❏ Assign the Automated Accounting feature on pages 634–635 to automate Mastery Problem 24-4.

629

❑ Explain that when a transaction affects more than one accounting period, an adjusting entry may be needed to match revenues and expenses.

❑ Explain that the accounting cycle is completed by recording adjusting entries, generating financial statements, and generating and posting closing entries. A post-closing trial balance is prepared, and then reversing entries, if needed, are journalized and posted at the beginning of the next fiscal period.

❑ Explain that a preliminary trial balance is prepared to aid in analyzing needed adjusting entries.

❑ Explain that adjusting entries are needed for accrued revenue to recognize revenue that has been earned in the current fiscal period but not yet received.

❑ Explain that adjusting entries are needed for accrued expenses to recognize expenses that have been incurred in the current fiscal period but not yet paid.

DEMONSTRATE

Recording adjusting entries

❑ Demonstrate how to record adjusting entries in the General Journal screen.

❑ Demonstrate clicking the Journal toolbar button and then clicking the General Journal tab.

❑ Demonstrate entering the relevant information in the fields for the first line of the first adjusting entry. Point out that Adj.Ent. is used in the Refer. field.

❑ Demonstrate clicking the Post button after each complete adjusting entry.

AUTOMATED ACCOUNTING

AUTOMATED ADJUSTING AND CLOSING ENTRIES FOR ACCRUED REVENUES AND EXPENSES

During the fiscal period, numerous transactions are analyzed, journalized, and posted. When a transaction affects more than one accounting period, an adjusting entry may be needed to match revenues and expenses. To complete the accounting cycle, adjusting entries are entered into the computer and verified for accuracy. The financial statements are generated, and then closing entries are generated and posted by the software.

Adjusting Entries

After all the usual transactions of the business are entered as journal entries, a preliminary trial balance is generated. This trial balance and period-end adjustment data are used as the basis for the adjusting entries. Adjusting entries are made for assets that have been consumed during the period and become expenses. In addition, adjusting entries are needed for accrued revenue and accrued expenses. Adjusting entries for accrued revenue recognize revenue that has been earned in the current fiscal period, but not yet received. Adjusting entries for accrued expenses recognize expenses incurred in the current fiscal period, but not actually paid until the next period.

To record adjusting entries:
1. Click the Journal toolbar button.
2. Click the General Journal tab.
3. Enter the transaction date and press Tab. All adjusting entries are made on the last day of the fiscal period.
4. Enter Adj. Ent. in the Refer. text box and press Tab.
5. Enter the account numbers and amounts for the adjusting entries. Press the Tab key to move among the text boxes.
6. Click the Post button.

Closing Entries for Accrued Revenues and Expenses

Closing entries are made to close all temporary accounts at the end of the accounting period. *Automated Accounting 7.0* automatically prepares and posts closing entries.

To generate closing entries:
1. Choose Generate Closing Journal Entries from the Options menu.

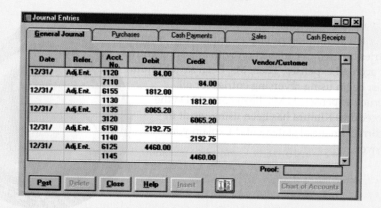

AUTOMATED ACCOUNTING

2. Click Yes to generate the closing entries.

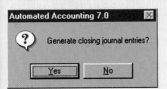

Automated Accounting 7.0

❓ Generate closing journal entries?

[Yes] [No]

3. The general journal will appear, containing the journal entries.
4. Click the Post button.
5. To display a post-closing trial balance report:
   a. Click on the Reports toolbar button, or choose the Reports Selection menu item from the Reports menu.
   b. Select the Ledger Reports option button from the Report Selection dialog box.
   c. Choose Trial Balance report.

AUTOMATING APPLICATION PROBLEM 24-2: Journalizing and posting entries for accrued expenses

Instructions:

1. Load *Automated Accounting 7.0* or higher software.
2. Select database F24-1 from the appropriate directory/folder.
3. Select File from the menu bar and choose the Save As menu command. Key the path to the drive and directory that contains your data files. Save the database with a file name of XXX241 (where XXX are your initials).
4. Access Problem Instructions through the Help menu. Read the Problem Instructions screen.
5. Refer to page 630 for data used in this template.
6. Exit the *Automated Accounting* software.

AUTOMATING MASTERY PROBLEM 24-4: Journalizing and posting entries for accrued interest revenue and expense

Instructions:

1. Load *Automated Accounting 7.0* or higher software.
2. Select database F24-2 from the appropriate directory/folder.
3. Select File from the menu bar and choose the Save As menu command. Key the path to the drive and directory that contains your data files. Save the database with a file name of XXX242 (where XXX are your initials).
4. Access Problem Instructions through the Help menu. Read the Problem Instructions screen.
5. Refer to page 631 for data used in this template.
6. Exit the *Automated Accounting* software.

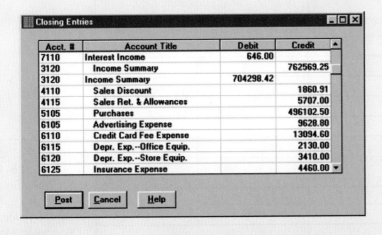

Closing Entries

Acct. #	Account Title	Debit	Credit
7110	Interest Income	646.00	
3120	Income Summary		762569.25
3120	Income Summary	704298.42	
4110	Sales Discount		1860.91
4115	Sales Ret. & Allowances		5707.00
5105	Purchases		496102.50
6105	Advertising Expense		9628.80
6110	Credit Card Fee Expense		13094.60
6115	Depr. Exp.--Office Equip.		2130.00
6120	Depr. Exp.--Store Equip.		3410.00
6125	Insurance Expense		4460.00

[Post] [Cancel] [Help]

DEMONSTRATE

Generating closing entries and post-closing trial balance

❑ Demonstrate choosing Generate Closing Journal Entries from the Options menu.
❑ Demonstrate choosing Yes from the dialog box to generate the closing entries.
❑ Direct students to verify that the closing entries are correct; then demonstrate clicking the Post button to post the closing entries.
❑ Demonstrate clicking the Reports toolbar button or choosing the Reports Selection menu item from the Reports menu.
❑ Demonstrate selecting the Ledger Reports option button from the Report Selection dialog box.
❑ Demonstrate choosing Trial Balance report to display the post-closing trial balance.

Recording reversing entries

❑ Demonstrate clicking the Journal toolbar button and then clicking the General Journal tab.
❑ Demonstrate entering the relevant information in the fields for the first line of the first reversing entry. Point out that Rev.Ent. is used in the Refer. field.
❑ Demonstrate clicking the Post button after each complete reversing entry.

PRACTICE

❑ Assign Automating Application Problem 24-2: Journalizing and posting entries for accrued expenses.
❑ Assign Automating Mastery Problem 24-4: Journalizing and posting entries for accrued interest revenue and expense.

ASSESSMENT

❑ Use the Electronic Auditor to assess student understanding.

PORTFOLIO ASSESSMENT

Students should be encouraged to print at least one report from one of the *Automated Accounting* problems to include in their portfolio to demonstrate mastery of automated accounting systems. A copy of the Portfolio Assessment form (blackline master in the Teacher's Resource Guide) should be completed by the student, and the Description section should include any comments regarding how the student mastered these concepts and procedures.

	SCOPE AND SEQUENCE		ENHANCING	
	NEW	REVIEW/EXTENSION	SPECIAL FEATURES	
INTRODUCE THE CHAPTER			Accounting in Your Career: Taxes on Businesses Thinking about Careers	
Accounting for a corporation		✓		
LESSSON 25-1 DISTRIBUTING CORPORATE DIVIDENDS TO STOCKHOLDERS				
Stockholders' equity accounts used by a corporation	✓			
Declaring a dividend	✓			
Paying a dividend	✓			
LESSSON 25-2 PREPARING A WORK SHEET FOR A CORPORATION			Small Business Spotlight	
Adjustment for interest income		✓		
Adjustment for uncollectible accounts expense		✓		
Adjustment for merchandise inventory		✓		
Adjustment for supplies		✓		
Adjustment for prepaid insurance		✓		
Adjustment for depreciation expense		✓		
Adjustment for interest expense		✓		
LESSSON 25-3 CALCULATING FEDERAL INCOME TAX AND COMPLETING A WORK SHEET			Math Work Sheet, Chapter 25, Part A Math Work Sheet, Chapter 25, Part B Technology for Business: Spending More Than Time on the Web	
Adjusting for federal income tax expense	✓			
Calculating federal income tax expense	✓			
Completing a work sheet		✓		
PUTTING IT ALL TOGETHER			Explore Accounting Internet Activity Applied Communication Cases for Critical Thinking 1, 2, and 3	

PREPARING A WORK SHEET

INSTRUCTION		PRACTICE AND ASSESSMENT		
TECHNOLOGY AND MEDIA	TEACHING STRATEGIES	GUIDED PRACTICE	INDEPENDENT PRACTICE	RETEACHING AND ENRICHMENT
Internet Activity	Software Focus			
South-Western Accounting Video: Computerized Accounting— Adjusting Entries for a Merchandising Business Transparencies L and M	Building Study Skills	Term Review Audit Your Understanding Work Together	On Your Own Application Problem 25-1 Application Problem 25-2 Ongoing Assessment, p. 640	Reteach, p. 640 Enrich, p. 641
CNN Accounting Video	Expanding Beyond the Classroom Limited English Proficiency (LEP) Students	Audit Your Understanding Work Together	On Your Own Application Problem 25-3 Ongoing Assessment, p. 646	Reteach, p. 646 Enrich, p. 647
	Applied Skills: Mathematics Applied Skills: Language Arts Limited English Proficiency (LEP) Students	Audit Your Understanding Work Together	On Your Own Application Problem 25-4 Ongoing Assessment, p. 653	Reteach, p. 653 Enrich, p. 654
Transparency 25-1 Automated Accounting Accounting Connection	Cooperative Learning Applied Skills: Writing Across the Curriculum		Mastery Problem 25-5 Study Guide 25 Chapter 25 Test ExamViewPro or Westest, Chapter 25 Portfolio Assessment	Enrich, p. 655 Challenge Problem 25-6 Reteach, p. 655 Recycling Problem 25-1 Accounting Connection

PREVIEW **ACCOUNTING TERMS**

❑ Read each term out loud to verify pronunciation for students.

❑ Point out terms or parts of terms that should already be familiar to most students, such as corporation, stockholder, and dividend.

PREVIEW **CHAPTER OBJECTIVES**

❑ Point out that students have already learned to record adjusting entries on a work sheet and complete the work sheet.

❑ Point out that students have already learned to record transactions in the cash payments and general journals.

❑ Note that this chapter presents procedures to record federal income taxes and payments to owners of a corporation.

INTRODUCTION

❑ Ask students to discuss what they think might be the differences between preparing a work sheet for a partnership and preparing a work sheet for a corporation. Students should realize that the equity accounts are different, but may not be aware that corporations pay dividends or that they pay federal income tax on their earnings.

❑ Point out that corporations are the only form of business organization that pays federal income taxes.

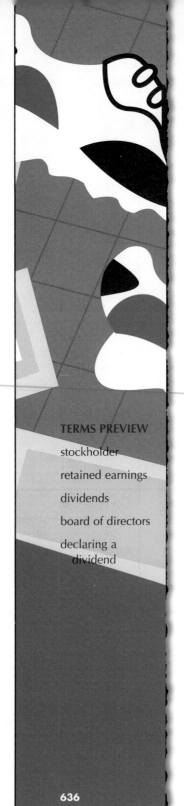

25

Distributing Dividends and Preparing a Work Sheet

AFTER STUDYING CHAPTER 25, YOU WILL BE ABLE TO:

1. Define accounting terms related to distributing dividends and preparing a work sheet for a merchandising business organized as a corporation.

2. Identify accounting concepts and practices related to distributing dividends and preparing a work sheet for a merchandising business organized as a corporation.

3. Journalize the declaration and payment of a dividend for a merchandising business organized as a corporation.

4. Plan end-of-fiscal-period adjustments for a merchandising business organized as a corporation.

5. Calculate federal income tax, plan an adjustment for federal income tax expense, and complete a work sheet.

TERMS PREVIEW

stockholder

retained earnings

dividends

board of directors

declaring a dividend

636

ACCOUNTING FOR A CORPORATION

Many accounting procedures used for a corporation are similar to the procedures used for a proprietorship or a partnership. Consequently, preparing a work sheet for a corporation is similar to preparing a work sheet for a proprietorship or a partnership.

There are, however, three principal differences between accounting for a proprietorship or partnership and accounting for a corporation: (1) Different accounts are used to record owners' equity. (2) Different procedures are used to distribute income to owners. (3) Corporations calculate and pay federal income tax. Corporations must pay federal income tax on their net income. Proprietorship and partnership net income is treated as part of each owner's personal income for income tax purposes. Thus, federal income tax is not calculated for a proprietorship or partnership business.

SOFTWARE FOCUS

Software may be used for independent practice or enrichment as the instructor deems appropriate. For this chapter, the following software may be used: Automated Accounting 7.0 or higher and Accounting Connection, Chapter 25. In this chapter, the Automated Accounting software's Loan Planner feature is covered. Therefore, the software is not applied to a specific end-of-chapter problem. Instead, students learn how to forecast the number and amount of loan payments for money borrowed.

Instructors may wish to cover the Automated Accounting feature on pages 660–661, even if the Automated Accounting software is not being used in the classroom, so students get a sense of how the chapter's accounting procedures would be implemented in an automated environment.

ACCOUNTING IN YOUR CAREER

TAXES ON BUSINESSES

Jody Meehan has just lost her job in a corporate downsizing. Her company was generous, however, and Jody has a substantial amount of cash to invest in a new business. She is looking at a small local factory that she can buy and refit to produce car care chemicals, such as waxes and upholstery cleaners. She is uncertain about whether to organize her business as a proprietorship or a corporation. She knows some of the advantages and disadvantages of both forms of businesses, and she has decided to incorporate if the tax effect is equitable. She has hired Midori Tanaka, a tax accountant, to advise her on corporate income taxes.

At their first meeting, Jody explains what kind of business she is planning to start and the budget for the first year of operations. She also details what income she expects to make from the first year of operations. She forecasts net income of $100,000 during each of the first few years and wants to draw a salary of $35,000 each year.

Midori explains that both forms of business would be taxed on net income, the amount of revenue after expenses are deducted. But the salary is treated differently by the two forms of business. In a proprietorship, the business would not consider the $35,000 as a salary, and therefore the owner would pay tax on the entire net income of $100,000. In a corporation, the $35,000 salary would be deducted from the company's revenue as an expense. Jody would still have to pay personal income tax on the $35,000 salary, however.

Jody says, "Midori, I can't really understand the effect unless I do some calculations to compare the differences. Can you give me some tax rates to use?"

Critical Thinking:

1. In this scenario, what is the tax for the proprietorship using a personal income tax rate of 25% for this level of earnings?
2. How much tax does the corporation pay if corporate income tax rates are 15% on the first $50,000 plus 25% of the next $25,000? How much personal income tax will Jody pay on her salary using a 25% personal income tax rate?
3. Which form of business organization has the lower tax consequence in this scenario?

SUGGESTED ANSWERS

1. $100,000 × 25% = $25,000 tax.
2. Corporation: $100,000 − 35,000 = $65,000 net income.
   15% × $50,000 = $7,500. $15,000 × 25% = $3,750.
   Jody's personal income tax: $35,000 salary × 25% = $8,750. Total tax = $7,500 + 3,750 + 8,750 = $20,000.

3. The corporate organization actually has the lower tax consequences at this level of income. However, when a corporation earns over $100,000 net income, the tax rate increases to 39% and the advantage may shift to a proprietorship.

STOCKHOLDERS' EQUITY ACCOUNTS USED BY A CORPORATION

(3000) STOCKHOLDERS' EQUITY
3105 Capital Stock
3110 Retained Earnings
3115 Dividends
3120 Income Summary

A corporation's ownership is divided into units. Each unit of ownership in a corporation is known as a share of stock. An owner of one or more shares of a corporation is called a **stockholder.** Each stockholder is an owner of a corporation.

A separate general ledger owner's equity account is maintained for each owner of a proprietorship or a partnership. However, a corporation may have many stockholders. Therefore, a separate owner's equity account is not maintained for each owner of a corporation. Instead, a single owners' equity account, titled Capital Stock, is used for the investment of all owners.

Owners' equity accounts for a corporation normally are listed under a major chart of accounts division titled Stockholders' Equity.

A second stockholders' equity account is used to record a corporation's earnings. Net income increases a corporation's total stockholders' equity. Some income may be retained by a corporation for business expansion. An amount earned by a corporation and not yet distributed to stockholders is called **retained earnings.**

Retained Earnings is the title of the account used to record a corporation's earnings.

A third stockholders' equity account is used to record the distribution of a corporation's earnings to stockholders. Some income may be given to stockholders as a return on their investments. Earnings distributed to stockholders are called **dividends.** A corporation's dividend account is a temporary account similar to a proprietorship's or partnership's drawing account. Each time a dividend is declared, an account titled Dividends is debited. At the end of each fiscal period, the balance in the dividends account is closed to Retained Earnings.

REMEMBER

Dividends is a temporary account that is closed to Retained Earnings at the end of the fiscal period.

638 CHAPTER 25 Distributing Dividends and Preparing a Work Sheet

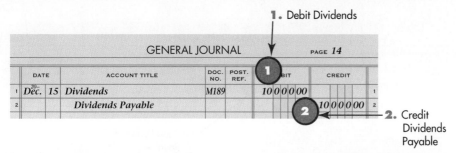

1. Debit Dividends

GENERAL JOURNAL   PAGE 14

	DATE		ACCOUNT TITLE	DOC. NO.	POST. REF.	DEBIT	CREDIT	
1	20-- Dec.	15	Dividends	M189		10 0 0 0 00		1
2			Dividends Payable				10 0 0 0 00	2

2. Credit Dividends Payable

A group of persons elected by the stockholders to manage a corporation is called a **board of directors.** Dividends can be distributed to stockholders only by formal action of a corporation's board of directors. (CONCEPT: Business Entity)

Action by a board of directors to distribute corporate earnings to stockholders is called **declaring a dividend.** Dividends normally are declared on one date and paid on a later date. A corporation's board of directors is not required to declare a dividend. In fact, declared dividends cannot exceed the balance of the retained earnings account. However, when a board of directors does declare a dividend, the corporation is then obligated to pay the dividend. The dividend is a liability that must be recorded in the corporation's accounts.

Winning Edge's board of directors declares a dividend every three months so that stockholders can share the corporation's earnings throughout the year. Winning Edge declares dividends each March 15, June 15, September 15, and December 15. The dividends are then paid on the 15th of the month following the declaration.

December 15. Winning Edge's board of directors declared a quarterly dividend of $1.00 per share; capital stock issued is 10,000 shares; total dividend, $10,000.00. Date of payment is January 15. Memorandum No. 189.

Dividends	
3/15 Decl.	10,000.00
6/15 Decl.	10,000.00
9/15 Decl.	10,000.00
12/15 Decl.	**10,000.00**

Dividends Payable			
4/15 Paid	10,000.00	3/15 Decl.	10,000.00
7/15 Paid	10,000.00	6/15 Decl.	10,000.00
10/15 Paid	10,000.00	9/15 Decl.	10,000.00
		12/15 Decl.	10,000.00

The stockholders' equity account, Dividends, has a normal debit balance and is increased by a $10,000.00 debit. Dividends Payable is credited for $10,000.00 to show the increase in this liability account.

Number of Shares Outstanding		Quarterly Dividend per Share		Total Quarterly Dividend
	×		=	
10,000	×	$1.00	=	$10,000.00

❏ Remind students that Dividends Payable is a current liability.

❏ Point out that students have previously learned to pay other current liabilities.

❏ Explain that the check written transfers cash into a special account used solely for dividend checks.

❏ Ask students to read the F.Y.I. to learn more about how dividends are paid to stockholders.

DEMONSTRATE

Analyze the transaction

❏ Draw two T accounts on the board.

❏ Describe each previous transaction as it is recorded in the T accounts.

❏ Read the transaction statement.

❏ Ask students to analyze the transaction by answering: what accounts are affected, are they increased or decreased, and are they debited or credited? Complete the T accounts as the information is provided.

Record the transaction

❏ Use Transparency L or direct students to the figure to demonstrate recording the transaction in the cash payments journal.

❏ Record each item in the cash payments journal, following the two steps shown.

ONGOING ASSESSMENT

❏ Assessment is an ongoing process. Circulate through the classroom or lab, observing which students have problems with the assignments.

❏ Troubleshooting: Diagnose what kinds of problems students have with this lesson. Students may have trouble (1) understanding that dividends are not an expense of the corporation, (2) understanding how dividends are paid to the stockholders, or (3) debiting and crediting the correct accounts for dividends transactions.

❏ Assess student understanding by checking solutions to Independent Practice assignments.

PAYING A DIVIDEND

2. Credit Cash

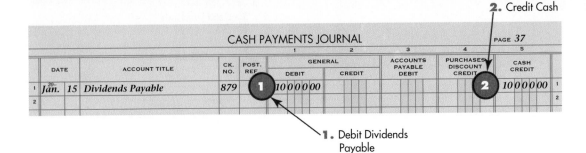

	DATE	ACCOUNT TITLE	CK. NO.	POST. REF.	GENERAL DEBIT	GENERAL CREDIT	ACCOUNTS PAYABLE DEBIT	PURCHASES DISCOUNT CREDIT	CASH CREDIT	
1	Jan. 15	Dividends Payable	879		10 0 0 0 00				10 0 0 0 00	1
2										2

CASH PAYMENTS JOURNAL — PAGE 37

1. Debit Dividends Payable

Winning Edge issues one check for the amount of the total dividend to be paid. This check is deposited in a special dividend checking account. A separate check for each stockholder is drawn on this special account. The special account avoids a large number of cash payments journal entries and also reserves cash specifically for paying dividends.

A check is often made payable to an agent, such as a bank. The agent then handles the details of sending dividend checks to individual stockholders.

January 15. Paid cash for quarterly dividend declared December 15, $10,000.00. Check No. 879.

Dividends Payable			
4/15 Paid	10,000.00	3/15 Decl.	10,000.00
7/15 Paid	10,000.00	6/15 Decl.	10,000.00
10/15 Paid	10,000.00	9/15 Decl.	10,000.00
1/15 Paid	10,000.00	12/15 Decl.	10,000.00

Cash			
1/15 Paid	10,000.00		

S T E P S

Journalizing the payment of dividends

1. Record a debit for the total amount of dividends, $10,000.00, to Dividends Payable in the General Debit column of a cash payments journal.

2. Record a credit, $10,000.00, in the Cash Credit column.

When this entry is posted, the dividends payable account has a zero balance.

F Y I *Dividends are declared on one date and paid on a later date. Only stockholders owning the stock on the date of record specified by the board of directors receive the dividend. Stockholders owning the stock on the date of record receive the entire dividend, regardless of how long they have owned the stock.*

RETEACH

❏ Call on students to identify the equity accounts of a corporation.

❏ Ask students to describe how to calculate the amount of dividends declared.

❏ Call on students to describe how dividends are declared and paid.

❏ Ask students to make up transactions for declaring and paying dividends. Call students to the blackboard to analyze the transactions in T accounts.

TERMS REVIEW

stockholder

retained earnings

dividends

board of directors

declaring a dividend

AUDIT YOUR UNDERSTANDING

1. How does accounting for a corporation differ from accounting for a proprietorship or partnership?
2. How many accounts are kept for the investment of all owners of a corporation?
3. What account does a corporation use to record earnings not yet distributed to stockholders?
4. What action is required before a corporation can distribute income to its stockholders?

WORK TOGETHER

Journalizing dividends

Journals are given in the *Working Papers*. Your instructor will guide you through the following examples.

PTC Corporation completed the following transactions during December of the current year and January of the next year.

Transactions:

Dec. 15. The board of directors declared a dividend of $10.00 per share; capital stock issued is 2,500 shares. M212.

Jan. 15. Paid cash for dividend declared December 15. C543.

5. Use page 12 of a general journal. Journalize the dividend declared on December 15.
6. Use page 15 of a cash payments journal. Journalize payment of the dividend on January 15.

ON YOUR OWN

Journalizing dividends

Journals are given in the *Working Papers*. Work these problems independently.

Lucita Manufacturing Corporation completed the following transactions during December of the current year and January of the next year.

Transactions:

Dec. 15. The board of directors declared a dividend of $3.50 per share; capital stock issued is 40,000 shares. M126.

Jan. 15. Paid cash for dividend declared December 15. C432.

7. Use page 24 of a general journal. Journalize the dividend declared on December 15.
8. Use page 18 of a cash payments journal. Journalize payment of the dividend.

GUIDED PRACTICE

Terms Review
Call on students to define the terms in the Terms Review. Ask the class if the definitions are correct and whether the complete definitions have been given or if anything needs to be added. The suggested definitions are given in the Glossary.

Audit Your Understanding
Call on students to answer the Audit Your Understanding questions. Ask the class if the answer is correct and/or complete. Answers are given in Appendix D of the textbook.

Work Together
Have students write the solutions to the Work Together problems as you guide the class through the examples.

❏ Call on students to write their dividend calculation on the board.

❏ Direct students to record each transaction in the journals as you elicit class participation in analyzing and recording each transaction.

INDEPENDENT PRACTICE

On Your Own
❏ Assign the On Your Own problems to be worked independently.

❏ Use the Ongoing Assessment techniques to diagnose student understanding.

Application Problem
❏ Assign Application Problem 25-1: Journalizing dividends.

❏ Assign Application Problem 25-2: Journalizing dividends.

ENRICH

❏ Students can research the dividend policies of corporations in their local areas or state.

❏ Show the South-Western Accounting Video: Computerized Accounting—Adjusting Entries for a Merchandising Business.

CLOSE

❏ Ask students to briefly summarize the procedures for determining the amount of dividends and journalizing the declaration and payment of dividends.

USE OF A WORK SHEET

Work sheets for proprietorships, partnerships, and corporations are similar. Businesses use work sheets to plan adjustments and provide information needed to prepare financial statements. Winning Edge may prepare a work sheet at any time financial statements are needed. However, Winning Edge always prepares a work sheet and financial statements at the end of a fiscal year. (CONCEPT: Accounting Period Cycle)

Entering a Trial Balance on a Work Sheet

To prepare a work sheet, a trial balance is first entered in the Trial Balance columns. All general ledger accounts are listed in the same order as they appear in the general ledger. Trial Balance columns are totaled to prove equality of debits and credits.

On December 31, Winning Edge enters its trial balance on a work sheet. A corporation's accounts are similar to those of a proprietorship or partnership except for the capital stock, retained earnings, dividends, and federal income tax accounts.

Planning Adjustments on a Work Sheet

Some general ledger accounts need to be brought up to date before financial statements are prepared. Accounts are brought up to date by planning and entering adjustments on a work sheet. Most adjustments on a corporation's work sheet are similar to those for proprietorships and partnerships.

The adjustments for merchandise inventory, supplies, and prepaid insurance are described in earlier chapters. Winning Edge makes nine adjustments: (1) Interest Income, (2) Uncollectible Accounts Expense, (3) Merchandise Inventory, (4) Supplies, (5) Prepaid Insurance, (6) Depreciation Expense—Office Equipment, (7) Depreciation Expense—Store Equipment, (8) Interest Expense, and (9) Federal Income Tax Expense.

Adjustments for depreciation expense, uncollectible accounts expense, interest income, and interest expense could also be made by proprietorships and partnerships. However, the adjustment for federal income tax is unique to corporations. This adjustment is not made for proprietorships and partnerships because taxes are paid by the owners, not the business. Adjustments generally are made in the order that accounts are listed on a work sheet.

SMALL BUSINESS SPOTLIGHT

Three to four million new small businesses form every year. Individuals are more willing to risk investing their time and money in small business ventures in a strong economy. However, about 60% of new small businesses will be out of business in five years.

642 CHAPTER 25 Distributing Dividends and Preparing a Work Sheet

MATERIALS

❑ Working Papers:
Teacher's Edition of the Working Papers for Lesson 25-2

❑ Videos:
CNN Accounting Video

INTEREST INCOME ADJUSTMENT

1. Debit Interest Receivable

	ACCOUNT TITLE	TRIAL BALANCE		ADJUSTMENTS	
		DEBIT	CREDIT	DEBIT	CREDIT
4	Interest Receivable			(a) 20 00	
51	Interest Income		68 00		(a) 20 00

2. Credit Interest Income

Interest income earned during the current fiscal period but not yet received needs to be recorded. Two accounts are used for the adjustment for accrued interest income: Interest Receivable and Interest Income. An analysis of Winning Edge's adjustment for accrued interest income is described in Chapter 24.

S T E P S

Planning a work sheet adjustment for interest income

1. Enter the accrued interest income amount, $20.00, in the Adjustments Debit column on the Interest Receivable line of the work sheet. Label the adjustment (a).

2. Enter the same amount, $20.00, in the Adjustments Credit column on the Interest Income line. Label the adjustment (a).

UNCOLLECTIBLE ACCOUNTS EXPENSE ADJUSTMENT

1. Credit Allowance for Uncollectible Accounts

	ACCOUNT TITLE	TRIAL BALANCE		ADJUSTMENTS	
		DEBIT	CREDIT	DEBIT	CREDIT
6	Allowance for Uncollectible Accounts		32 00		(b) 9 828 00
48	Uncollectible Accounts Expense			(b) 9 828 00	

2. Debit Uncollectible Accounts Expense

The estimated amount of uncollectible accounts expense for a fiscal period needs to be brought up to date. Two accounts are used for the adjustment for uncollectible accounts expense: Uncollectible Accounts Expense and Allowance for Uncollectible Accounts. An analysis of Winning Edge's uncollectible accounts expense adjustment is described in Chapter 20.

S T E P S

Planning a work sheet adjustment for uncollectible accounts expense

1. Enter the estimated uncollectible amount, $9,828.00, in the Adjustments Credit column on the Allowance for Uncollectible Accounts line of the work sheet. Label the adjustment (b).

2. Enter the same amount, $9,828.00, in the Adjustments Debit column on the Uncollectible Accounts Expense line. Label the adjustment (b).

CHAPTER 25 Distributing Dividends and Preparing a Work Sheet **643**

EXPLAIN

❑ Ask students to describe the purpose of the adjustment for interest income.
❑ Ask students to identify the classification of each account affected by the adjustment.

DEMONSTRATE

❑ Draw two T accounts on the board.
❑ Describe the work sheet adjustment.
❑ Ask students to analyze the transaction by answering: what accounts are affected, are they increased or decreased, and are they debited or credited? Complete the T accounts as the information is provided.
❑ Direct students to the illustration to review the recording of a work sheet adjustment using the two steps shown.

EXPLAIN

❑ Ask students to describe the purpose of the adjustment for uncollectible accounts expense.
❑ Ask students to identify the classification of each account affected by the adjustment.

DEMONSTRATE

❑ Draw two T accounts on the board.
❑ Describe the work sheet adjustment.
❑ Ask students to analyze the transaction by answering: what accounts are affected, are they increased or decreased, and are they debited or credited? Complete the T accounts as the information is provided.
❑ Direct students to the illustration to review the recording of a work sheet adjustment using the two steps shown.

TEACHING STRATEGIES EXPANDING BEYOND THE CLASSROOM

Invite a tax accountant as a guest speaker to discuss tax planning issues related to corporations, partnerships, and proprietorships. The tax accountant should also explain the tax implications for corporations.

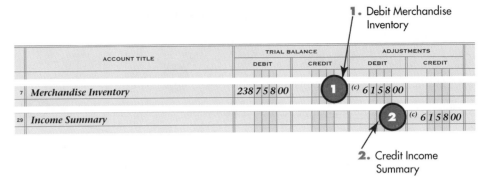

1. Debit Merchandise Inventory

ACCOUNT TITLE	TRIAL BALANCE		ADJUSTMENTS	
	DEBIT	CREDIT	DEBIT	CREDIT
7 Merchandise Inventory	238 758 00		(c) 6 158 00	
29 Income Summary				(c) 6 158 00

2. Credit Income Summary

The merchandise inventory account balance in a trial balance is the beginning inventory for a fiscal period. The amount of the ending inventory is determined by counting the merchandise on hand at the end of the fiscal period. An adjusting entry is made to bring merchandise inventory up to date so that the end-of-fiscal-period balance will be shown in the merchandise inventory account. The procedure used to adjust Winning Edge's merchandise inventory account is the same as that described for a merchandising business organized as a partnership in Chapter 15.

Winning Edge's beginning merchandise inventory, $238,758.00, is shown on line 7 in the Trial Balance Debit column on the work sheet.

Winning Edge's ending merchandise inventory on December 31 is counted and determined to be $244,916.00. To bring Winning Edge's merchandise inventory account up to date, the balance of Merchandise Inventory needs to be increased by $6,158.00. Merchandise Inventory is debited for the amount of the increase, $6,158.00. Income Summary is credited for the same amount.

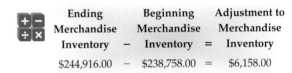

Ending Merchandise Inventory	−	Beginning Merchandise Inventory	=	Adjustment to Merchandise Inventory
$244,916.00	−	$238,758.00	=	$6,158.00

Planning a work sheet adjustment for merchandise inventory

S **T** **E** **P** **S**

1. Enter the increase in merchandise inventory, *$6,158.00,* in the Adjustments Debit column on the Merchandise Inventory line of the work sheet. Label the adjustment *(c).*

2. Enter the same amount, *$6,158.00,* in the Adjustments Credit column on the Income Summary line of the work sheet. Label the adjustment *(c).*

REMEMBER

If the ending merchandise inventory is less than the beginning merchandise inventory, the difference (decrease) is debited to Income Summary and credited to Merchandise Inventory.

SUPPLIES ADJUSTMENT

1. Credit Supplies

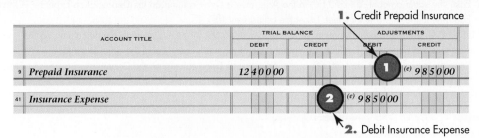

	ACCOUNT TITLE	TRIAL BALANCE		ADJUSTMENTS	
		DEBIT	CREDIT	DEBIT	CREDIT
8	Supplies	9 1 5 8 00		①	(d) 7 4 7 2 00
47	Supplies Expense			② (d) 7 4 7 2 00	

2. Debit Supplies Expense

The balance of Supplies in the trial balance, $9,158.00, is the cost of supplies on hand at the beginning of the year plus the supplies purchased during the year. The supplies on hand on December 31 are counted and determined to be $1,686.00. To bring the account up to date, the balance of Supplies needs to be decreased by $7,472.00 ($9,158.00 − $1,686.00), the cost of supplies used during the year. Supplies Expense is debited and Supplies is credited for the amount of the decrease.

S T E P S **Planning a work sheet adjustment for supplies**

1. Enter the amount of supplies used, *$7,472.00,* in the Adjustments Credit column on the Supplies line of the work sheet. Label the adjustment *(d).*

2. Enter the same amount, *$7,472.00,* in the Adjustments Debit column on the Supplies Expense line of the work sheet. Label the adjustment *(d).*

PREPAID INSURANCE ADJUSTMENT

1. Credit Prepaid Insurance

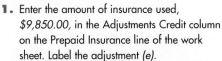

	ACCOUNT TITLE	TRIAL BALANCE		ADJUSTMENTS	
		DEBIT	CREDIT	DEBIT	CREDIT
9	Prepaid Insurance	12 4 0 0 00		①	(e) 9 8 5 0 00
41	Insurance Expense			② (e) 9 8 5 0 00	

2. Debit Insurance Expense

Insurance premiums are debited to a prepaid insurance account when paid. During the year, Winning Edge paid $12,400.00 of insurance premiums.

Winning Edge determined that the value of prepaid insurance on December 31 is $2,550.00. Therefore, the value of insurance used during the year is $9,850.00 ($12,400.00 − $2,550.00). Prepaid Insurance is credited and Insurance Expense is debited at the end of the fiscal period for the value of insurance used.

S T E P S **Planning a work sheet adjustment for prepaid insurance**

1. Enter the amount of insurance used, *$9,850.00,* in the Adjustments Credit column on the Prepaid Insurance line of the work sheet. Label the adjustment *(e).*

2. Enter the same amount, *$9,850.00,* in the Adjustments Debit column on the Insurance Expense line of the work sheet. Label the adjustment *(e).*

EXPLAIN

- ❏ Ask students to describe the purpose of the adjustments for depreciation expense.
- ❏ Ask students to describe the purpose of the adjustment for interest expense.
- ❏ Ask students to identify the classification of each account affected by the adjustments.

DEMONSTRATE

- ❏ Draw T accounts on the board and record the beginning balances.
- ❏ Describe the work sheet adjustments.
- ❏ Ask students to analyze the transactions by answering: what accounts are affected, are they increased or decreased, and are they debited or credited? Complete the T accounts as the information is provided.
- ❏ Direct students to review the recording of work sheet adjustments using the steps shown.

ONGOING ASSESSMENT

- ❏ Assessment is an ongoing process. Circulate through the classroom or lab, observing which students have problems with the assignments.
- ❏ Troubleshooting: Diagnose what kinds of problems students have with this lesson. This lesson is a review of work sheet adjustments first presented in previous chapters. Students may have a problem remembering (1) the accounts used in the adjustments and (2) the methods used to calculate the adjustment amounts.
- ❏ Assess student understanding by checking solutions to Independent Practice assignments.

DEPRECIATION EXPENSE ADJUSTMENTS

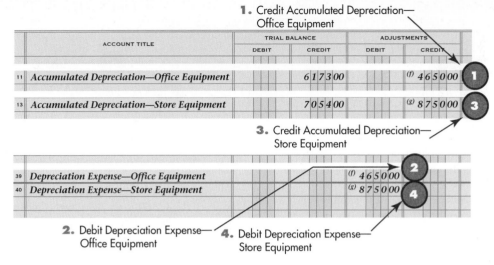

An analysis of Winning Edge's depreciation expense adjustments is described in Chapter 21. Winning Edge has two plant asset accounts: Office Equipment and Store Equipment. A separate adjustment is planned to record the depreciation for each type of equipment.

S T E P S

Planning a work sheet adjustment for depreciation expense

1. Enter the office equipment depreciation amount, *$4,650.00,* in the Adjustments Credit column on the Accumulated Depreciation—Office Equipment line of the work sheet. Label the adjustment *(f).*
2. Enter the same amount, *$4,650.00,* in the Adjustments Debit column on the Depreciation Expense—Office Equipment line of the work sheet. Label the adjustment *(f).*
3. Enter the store equipment depreciation amount, *$8,750.00,* in the Adjustments Credit column on the Accumulated Depreciation—Store Equipment line of the work sheet. Label the adjustment *(g).*
4. Enter the same amount, *$8,750.00,* in the Adjustments Debit column on the Depreciation Expense—Store Equipment line of the work sheet. Label the adjustment *(g).*

INTEREST EXPENSE ADJUSTMENT

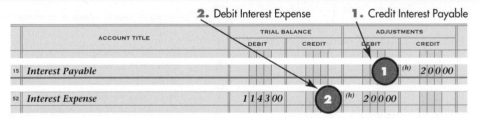

Interest expense incurred during the current fiscal period but not yet paid needs to be recorded. Two accounts are used for the adjustment for accrued interest expense: Interest Payable and Interest Expense. An analysis of Winning Edge's adjustment for accrued interest expense is described in Chapter 24.

646 CHAPTER 25 Distributing Dividends and Preparing a Work Sheet

RETEACH

- ❏ Call on students to summarize the purpose of each adjustment.
- ❏ Call on students to identify whether the balance of an account is used in calculating the adjustment amount.

AUDIT YOUR UNDERSTANDING

1. What circumstances would require an adjustment that debits Merchandise Inventory?
2. What circumstances would require an adjustment that credits Merchandise Inventory?

WORK TOGETHER

Preparing a work sheet for a corporation

Webster Corporation's work sheet is given in the *Working Papers*. Your instructor will guide you through the following example.

3. For the current year ended December 31, record the adjustments on the work sheet using the following information. Do not total the Adjustments columns. Save your work to complete Work Together on page 654.

Accrued interest income . . . . $	277.20
Uncollectible accounts expense estimated as 1.5% of sales on account.	
Sales on account for year, $499,000.00.	
Merchandise inventory	90,066.26
Supplies inventory	327.88
Value of prepaid insurance	3,023.60
Annual depreciation expense—office equipment	2,690.00
Annual depreciation expense—store equipment	1,607.60
Accrued interest expense	545.16

ON YOUR OWN

Preparing a work sheet for a corporation

Osborn Corporation's work sheet is given in the *Working Papers*. Work this problem independently.

4. For the current year ended December 31, record the adjustments on the work sheet using the following information. Do not total the Adjustments columns. Save your work to complete On Your Own on page 654.

Accrued interest income . . . . $	543.20
Uncollectible accounts expense estimated as 1.5% of sales on account.	
Sales on account for year, $869,000.00.	
Merchandise inventory	106,597.06
Supplies inventory	896.53
Value of prepaid insurance	5,370.00
Annual depreciation expense—office equipment	5,480.00
Annual depreciation expense—store equipment	6,876.00
Accrued interest expense	523.25

650

EXPLAIN

- ❏ Explain that the federal income tax payable is the federal income tax less any estimated tax payments made in previous quarters.
- ❏ Point out that the income tax expense adjustment is recorded on a work sheet, using the same method as all other adjustments.

DEMONSTRATE

Analyze the federal income tax expense account

- ❏ Ask students to identify the classification of the federal income tax expense account.
- ❏ Draw a T account on the board for Federal Income Tax Expense. Label the account as you ask students to identify the increase/decrease, debit/credit, and normal balance sides.

Analyze the federal income tax payable account

- ❏ Ask students to identify the classification of the federal income tax payable account.
- ❏ Draw a T account on the board for Federal Income Tax Payable. Label the account as you ask students to identify the increase/decrease, debit/credit, and normal balance sides.

Analyze the adjustment

- ❏ Ask students to use a calculator to compute the federal income tax adjustment.
- ❏ Draw two T accounts on the board and enter the balance amounts.

Record the adjustment

- ❏ Describe the work sheet adjustment.
- ❏ Direct students to record the adjustment, following the three steps shown.

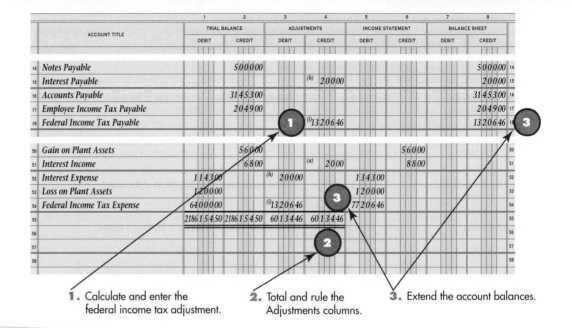

1. Calculate and enter the federal income tax adjustment.

2. Total and rule the Adjustments columns.

3. Extend the account balances.

S T E P S

Planning a work sheet adjustment for federal income tax expense

1. Calculate the amount of the federal income tax expense adjustment. The adjustment is the difference between the federal income tax for the year and the taxes paid during the year.

Federal Income Tax..............................	$77,206.46
Less Total of Quarterly Installments....................	−64,000.00
Equals Federal Income Tax Adjustment.................	$13,206.46

Enter the federal income tax expense adjustment, *$13,206.46,* in the Adjustments Credit column on the Federal Income Tax Payable line of the work sheet. Enter the same amount in the Adjustments Debit column of the Federal Income Tax Expense line of the work sheet. Label both parts of the adjustment *(i).*

2. Total and rule the Adjustments columns.

3. Extend the federal income tax expense account balance, *$77,206.46,* to the Income Statement Debit column. Extend the amount for Federal Income Tax Payable, *$13,206.46,* to the Balance Sheet Credit column.

Federal Income Tax Expense

4/15	16,000.00
6/15	16,000.00
9/15	16,000.00
12/15	16,000.00
(12/15 Bal.	64,000.00)
12/31 Adj. (i)	13,206.46
(New Bal.	77,206.46)

Federal Income Tax Payable

12/31 Adj. (i)	13,206.46

		1	2	3	4	5	6	7	8	
	ACCOUNT TITLE	TRIAL BALANCE		ADJUSTMENTS		INCOME STATEMENT		BALANCE SHEET		
		DEBIT	CREDIT	DEBIT	CREDIT	DEBIT	CREDIT	DEBIT	CREDIT	
14	Notes Payable		5 0 0 0 00						5 0 0 0 00	14
15	Interest Payable				(h) 2 0 0 00				2 0 0 00	15
16	Accounts Payable		31 4 5 3 00						31 4 5 3 00	16
17	Employee Income Tax Payable		2 0 4 9 00						2 0 4 9 00	17
18	Federal Income Tax Payable				(i) 13 2 0 6 46				13 2 0 6 46	18
50	Gain on Plant Assets		5 6 0 00				5 6 0 00			50
51	Interest Income		6 8 00	(a) 2 0 00			8 8 00			51
52	Interest Expense	1 1 4 3 00		(h) 2 0 0 00		1 3 4 3 00				52
53	Loss on Plant Assets	1 2 0 0 00				1 2 0 0 00				53
54	Federal Income Tax Expense	64 0 0 0 00		(i) 13 2 0 6 46		77 2 0 6 46				54
55		2186 1 5 4 50	2186 1 5 4 50	60 1 3 4 46	60 1 3 4 46	1776 7 4 3 96	1940 4 5 1 50	452 2 2 3 00	288 5 1 5 46	55
56	Net Income after Federal Income Tax					163 7 0 7 54			163 7 0 7 54	56
57						1940 4 5 1 50	1940 4 5 1 50	452 2 2 3 00	452 2 2 3 00	57
58										58

After the adjustment for federal income tax expense has been recorded, the work sheet is ready to be completed. Income Statement column totals are used to calculate net income after federal income tax. Winning Edge's completed work sheet is shown on the following two pages.

Completing a work sheet

1. Total the Income Statement and Balance Sheet columns.

2. Write the words *Net Income after Federal Income Tax* on line 56 of the work sheet. Calculate and enter the net income after federal income tax, *$163,707.54*, in the Income Statement Debit column on this new line of the work sheet.

Total of Income Statement Credit column	$1,940,451.50
Less Total of Income Statement Debit column	−1,776,743.96
Equals Net Income after Federal Income Tax	$ 163,707.54

3. Extend the net income after federal income tax amount, *$163,707.54*, to the Balance Sheet Credit column.

4. Total the four Income Statement and Balance Sheet columns. Determine that the totals of each pair of columns are in balance.

5. Rule double lines across the Income Statement and Balance Sheet columns to show that the totals have been verified as correct.

❏ Point out that the process of completing a work sheet is the same for a corporation, partnership, or proprietorship.

❏ Ask students to identify the steps involved in completing a work sheet.

❏ Direct students to the illustration to demonstrate completing the work sheet, following the five steps shown.

❏ Ask students to identify how a net loss would be recorded on the work sheet.

APPLIED SKILLS

LANGUAGE ARTS

Paraphrasing, Writing Complete Sentences, and Identifying Active and Passive Verbs. For additional practice in language arts skills, direct students to answer the Terms Review and Audit Your Understanding questions at the end of each lesson. Students should write the answers in their own words and in complete sentences. To further practice language arts skills, ask students to underline all active verbs and circle all passive verbs in the answers.

GUIDED PRACTICE

❏ Explain
page ill
sheet f
year en
ments
recorde

❏ Ask stu
that we
to desc
each ac

Audit Your Understanding

Call on students to answer the Audit Your Understanding questions. Ask the class if the answer is correct and/or complete. Answers are given in Appendix D of the textbook.

Work Together

Have students write the solutions to the Work Together problems as you guide the class through the examples.

❏ Remind students to use the work sheet from Lesson 2.

❏ Ask several students to write their calculation of federal income tax expense on the board.

❏ Direct students to record the federal income tax adjustment on the work sheet.

❏ Direct students to complete the work sheet.

❏ Direct s
review
require

❏ Ask stu
extende
Balance
that are

❏ Ask stu
were us
Stateme

INDEPENDENT PRACTICE

On Your Own

❏ Assign the On Your Own problems to be worked independently.

❏ Remind students to use the work sheet from Lesson 2.

❏ Use the Ongoing Assessment techniques to diagnose student understanding.

Application Problem

❏ Assign Application Problem 25-4: Completing a work sheet for a corporation.

EXPLAIN

❏ Remind students that in this chapter the adjustment for federal income tax is labeled (i).

AUDIT YOUR UNDERSTANDING

1. What must a corporation do if actual federal income tax owed is greater than estimated tax paid?

2. Why is federal income tax expense not calculated until all other adjustments have been planned on a work sheet?

WORK TOGETHER

Completing a work sheet for a corporation

Use the work sheet from Work Together on page 647. Your instructor will guide you through the following examples.

3. Extend all amounts except Federal Income Tax Expense to the appropriate Income Statement or Balance Sheet columns. Do not total the columns.

4. On the form provided in the *Working Papers*, total the work sheet's Income Statement columns. Calculate the difference between the debit and credit totals. This difference becomes the net income before federal income tax expense.

5. Using the tax table shown in this chapter, calculate federal income tax expense and record the income tax adjustment on the work sheet. Complete the work sheet.

ON YOUR OWN

Completing a work sheet for a corporation

Use the work sheet from On Your Own on page 647. Work these problems independently.

6. Extend all amounts except Federal Income Tax Expense to the appropriate Income Statement or Balance Sheet columns. Do not total the columns.

7. On the form provided in the *Working Papers*, total the work sheet's Income Statement columns. Calculate the difference between the debit and credit totals. This difference becomes the net income before federal income tax expense.

8. Using the tax table shown in this chapter, calculate federal income tax expense and record the income tax adjustment on the work sheet. Complete the work sheet.

654 CHAPTER 25 Distributing Dividends and Preparing a Work Sheet

ENRICH

❏ As the size of a work sheet increases, the chance of making an error also increases. Discuss how a company could use an electronic spreadsheet to prepare its work sheet. Discuss what formulas might be used.

❏ Research federal income tax rates for corporations.

❏ Assign the Technology for Business feature on page 648.

CLOSE

❏ Ask students to briefly summarize the procedures for calculating federal income tax expense and completing a work sheet for a corporation.

CHAPTER 25 SUMMARY

After completing this chapter, you can

1. Define accounting terms related to distributing dividends and preparing a work sheet for a merchandising business organized as a corporation.
2. Identify accounting concepts and practices related to distributing dividends and preparing a work sheet for a merchandising business organized as a corporation.
3. Journalize the declaration and payment of a dividend for a merchandising business organized as a corporation.
4. Plan end-of-fiscal-period adjustments for a merchandising business organized as a corporation.
5. Calculate federal income tax, plan an adjustment for federal income tax expense, and complete a work sheet.

EXPLORE ACCOUNTING

AUDITS PROVIDE STOCKHOLDERS WITH POSITIVE ASSURANCE

Stockholders want assurance that the financial statements of their corporation accurately present its financial condition and results of operations. To provide this assurance, corporations hire independent public accountants to audit the financial statements. These accountants, referred to as auditors, provide a written opinion that informs stockholders whether the financial statements can be relied upon for making informed business decisions.

Auditors examine documents, journals, ledgers, and other accounting records to collect evidence that supports five declarations, or assertions, about each amount in the financial statements. Each assertion addresses a unique quality about the amount in the financial statements. These assertions are summarized as follows.

1. *Existence or Occurrence.* All assets and liabilities actually exist and all income statement transactions actually occurred during the period.
2. *Completeness.* All assets and liabilities that exist have been reported and all revenue and expense events have been recorded.
3. *Rights and Obligations.* All assets and liabilities are those of the corporation

and not of its owners or another corporation.
4. *Valuation or Allocation.* Transactions are reported using amounts that correctly reflect the value of the item or event.
5. *Presentation and Disclosure.* Accounts are properly classified, described, and disclosed in conformity with generally accepted accounting principles.

Required: Create a table that shows how the five financial statement assertions relate to any one particular amount reported on the financial statements.

Chapter 25 Test

ExamViewPro or Westest for Chapter 25

Assessment by Portfolio

❑ Review answers to all tests administered as a class activity. If time is limited, review only the items that were
frequently incorrectly answered.

❑ Ask students if there are any questions
about the chapter before proceeding to
the next chapter.

CHECK FIGURES

✔ **Application Problem 25-1**
Dec. 15: debit Dividends and credit
Dividends Payable, 1,500.00

✔ **Application Problem 25-2**
Jan. 15: debit Dividends Payable and
credit Cash, 65,000.00

✔ **Application Problem 25-3**
Debit Merchandise Inventory and credit
Income Summary, 2,326.50

*See Teacher's Edition of the Working
Papers for Chapter 25 for complete
solutions.*

25-1 APPLICATION PROBLEM
Journalizing dividends

Journals are given in the *Working Papers*. Lewis Corporation completed the following transactions during
December of the current year and January of the next year.

Transactions:

Dec. 15. The board of directors declared a dividend of $0.06 per share; capital stock issued is 25,000
shares. M321.

Jan. 15. Paid cash for dividend declared December 15. C659.

Instructions:

1. Use page 18 of a general journal. Journalize the dividend declared on December 15.
2. Use page 24 of a cash payments journal. Journalize payment of the dividend on January 15.

25-2 APPLICATION PROBLEM
Journalizing dividends

Journals are given in the *Working Papers*. Lynchburg Corporation's board of directors met on December
15 and raised the company's quarterly dividend to $6.50 per share. The company currently has 10,000
shares of stock outstanding. The dividends will be paid in one month.

Instructions:

1. Use page 12 of a general journal. Journalize the dividend declared using M177 as the source
document.
2. Use page 18 of a cash payments journal to journalize the dividend payment using Check No. 865.

25-3 APPLICATION PROBLEM
Preparing a work sheet for a corporation

Instructions:

Donovan Lumber Corporation's work sheet is given in the *Working Papers*. For the current year ended
December 31, record the adjustments on the work sheet using the following information. Do not total the
Adjustments columns. Save your work to complete Application Problem 25-4.

Adjustment Information, December 31

Accrued interest income	$ 312.00
Uncollectible accounts expense estimated as 1.0% of sales on account. Sales on account for year, $687,000.00.	
Merchandise inventory	82,184.50
Supplies inventory	1,840.50
Value of prepaid insurance	4,200.00
Annual depreciation expense—office equipment	3,028.00
Annual depreciation expense—store equipment	3,489.00
Accrued interest expense	250.00

TEACHING STRATEGIES
COOPERATIVE LEARNING

Use the Explore Accounting Feature. Direct students to identify and read the auditor's report included in the annual
report of a publicly-traded company. Divide the class into groups and direct each group to identify examples for one of
the five financial statement assertions. Direct groups to make an oral presentation of their work.

✔ **Application Problem 25-4**
Federal Income Tax Expense, 13,768.35

25-4 APPLICATION PROBLEM
Completing a work sheet for a corporation

Use the work sheet from Application Problem 25-3 to complete this problem.

Tax Table

15% of net income before taxes, zero to $50,000.00
Plus 25% of net income before taxes, $50,000.00 to $75,000.00
Plus 34% of net income before taxes, $75,000.00 to $100,000.00
Plus 39% of net income before taxes, $100,000.00 to $335,000.00
Plus 34% of net income before taxes over $335,000.00

Instructions:

1. Extend all amounts except Federal Income Tax Expense to the appropriate Income Statement or Balance Sheet columns. Do not total the columns.
2. On the form provided in the *Working Papers,* total the work sheet's Income Statement columns. Calculate the difference between the debit and credit totals. This difference becomes the net income before federal income tax expense.
3. Using the tax table above, calculate federal income tax expense and record the income tax adjustment on the work sheet. Complete the work sheet.

25-5 MASTERY PROBLEM
Journalizing dividends and preparing a work sheet for a corporation

✔ **Mastery Problem 25-5**
Federal Income Tax Expense, 90,630.22

EXPLAIN

Remind students that in this chapter the adjustment for federal income tax is labeled (*i*).

Accounting forms are given in the *Working Papers*. Pennington Corporation completed the following transactions during December of the current year and January of the next year.

Transactions:

Dec. 15. The board of directors declared a dividend of $0.25 per share; capital stock issued is 40,000 shares. M327.

Jan. 15. Paid cash for dividend declared December 15. C983.

Instructions:

1. Use page 12 of a general journal. Journalize the dividend declared on December 15.
2. Use page 18 of a cash payments journal. Journalize payment of the dividend on January 15.
3. Prepare Pennington Corporation's work sheet for the current year ended December 31. Record the adjustments on the work sheet using the following information. Do not total the Adjustments columns.

Adjustment Information, December 31

Accrued interest income	$ 684.00
Uncollectible accounts expense estimated as 1.0% of sales on account. Sales on account for year, $956,000.00.	
Merchandise inventory	218,687.20
Supplies inventory	332.40
Value of prepaid insurance	4,200.00
Annual depreciation expense—office equipment	5,847.00
Annual depreciation expense—store equipment	4,520.00
Accrued interest expense	300.00

INTERNET ACTIVITY

Because Internet sites can change frequently, the requirements of the Internet Activity are posted on a South-Western site where they can be updated as needed. Direct students to follow the directions given on their student page.

APPLIED COMMUNICATION

Student answers to this activity will differ. When preparing written instructions of accounting procedures, individuals often make incorrect assumptions about the reader's knowledge. As a result, instructions are often too brief or combine too many steps in a single instruction.

An entertaining activity can be used to illustrate the need for detailed instructions. Obtain two identical sets of children's blocks. Instruct several students to create a structure with one set of blocks. Do not allow students in a second group to see the structure. Direct the first group to verbalize instructions that enable the second group to replicate the structure. To simulate written instructions, the first group cannot watch the second group create their structure and the second group cannot ask any questions. How well did the second group replicate the structure?

4. Extend all amounts except Federal Income Tax Expense to the appropriate Income Statement or Balance Sheet columns. Do not total the columns.

5. On the form provided in the *Working Papers*, total the work sheet's Income Statement columns. Calculate the difference between the debit and credit totals. This difference becomes the net income before federal income tax expense.

6. Using the tax table in Application Problem 25-4, calculate federal income tax expense and record the income tax adjustment on the work sheet. Complete the work sheet.

CHALLENGE PROBLEM

25-6 Completing a work sheet for a corporation

Matthew Williams, the accountant for Petal Corporation, has recorded all adjustments on the work sheet except for the income tax expense adjustment. Mr. Williams has written below the work sheet the column totals (excluding the $40,000.00 estimated tax payments in the income statement columns) before the income tax adjustment.

Instructions:

1. On the form provided in the *Working Papers*, record the totals of the work sheet's Income Statement columns. Calculate the difference between the debit and credit totals. This difference becomes the net income before federal income tax expense.

2. Using the tax table in Application Problem 25-4, calculate federal income tax expense and record the income tax adjustment on the work sheet. Complete the work sheet.

3. Proposals have been made to replace the corporate federal income tax with a national sales or consumption tax. How would such a change in taxes affect the way that businesses account for federal tax expense?

INTERNET ACTIVITY

Point your browser to

http://accounting.swpco.com

Choose **First-Year Course**, choose **Activities**, and complete the activity for Chapter 25.

Applied Communication

Corporations maintain written documentation about their accounting procedures. The Securities and Exchange Commission requires regulated companies to maintain written documentation of their accounting systems. The documentation is also useful for auditors and employees to learn how the accounting system operates.

Instructions: Prepare the written procedures for completing a work sheet, assuming a company has a net loss. In this circumstance, the company would receive a refund for income taxes paid during the year. In addition, the company would be able to receive a refund of taxes paid in prior years, calculated using the tax rates applied to the net loss. For example, if a company with net income of $50,000.00 would pay income taxes of $7,500.00, a company with a net loss of $50,000.00 would receive a tax refund of $7,500.00.

APPLIED SKILLS

WRITING ACROSS THE CURRICULUM

Writing Paragraphs and Short Essays. The Cases for Critical Thinking are short, practical applications of the accounting principles developed in the chapter. Some cases are planned to present problems related to the chapter but not specifically discussed and answered in the chapter. These cases present an opportunity for critical thinking and decision making. These cases also require more than a short, objective-type response. Therefore, they provide ideal practice in writing paragraphs and short essays.

Cases for Critical Thinking

Case 1 Harris Company's net income has been fluctuating between a small net income and a small net loss during the first four years of the corporation's existence, resulting in a retained earnings balance of $45,000.00. The company is hoping to earn $500,000.00 during its fifth year. Janet Crosland, newly appointed president of Harris Company, believes the corporation needs to take some positive action to regain the confidence of the stockholders. She suggests the corporation declare a $600,000.00 dividend December 15, to be paid February 1. Ms. Crosland also suggests that if the net income is not as high as expected, the board of directors can cancel the declared dividend before it is paid. Do you agree with Ms. Crosland's proposal? Explain.

Case 2 At the beginning of the current year, Liang Company changed its organization from a partnership to a corporation. The president suggested that since the same six individuals owned the corporation as had owned the partnership, the same procedures should be used for paying income tax on the earnings of the business. The net income of the corporation would be treated as part of each corporation owner's personal income for income tax purposes. "If this procedure is followed," said the president, "the corporation will not need to pay any income tax." Do you agree with the president's suggestion? Explain.

Case 3 The board of directors of Christina's Gift Shops, Inc., has not declared a dividend in any of the last five years. The net income from each year has been added to the corporation's retained earnings. Excess cash has been invested in opening new stores and upgrading store equipment in older stores. At the corporation's annual meeting last week, some stockholders supported the actions of the board of directors. Several other stockholders, however, disagreed strongly with the board's policy of not declaring dividends. These stockholders said that they invested in the corporation in the expectation of earning steady income from dividends. If you were the chairperson of the board of directors, how would you respond to the disagreement among the stockholders?

CASES FOR CRITICAL THINKING

CASE 1 Ms. Crosland's proposal is not acceptable for two major reasons: (1) A corporation cannot declare a dividend that exceeds the balance in retained earnings. (2) When dividends are declared, the corporation is obligated to pay the dividends and a liability is recorded in the accounts. Thus, once declared, a dividend cannot later be canceled.

CASE 2 The president's suggestion is not acceptable. Partnership income is correctly treated as part of the owner's personal income for income tax purposes. However, corporations are required to calculate and pay income tax on their net income.

CASE 3 The board chairperson should calmly apologize to the stockholders who are disappointed in the lack of dividends. The chairperson should further explain that there are two primary reasons for buying stock: (1) to increase the value of the individual's stock holdings through an increase in value of the company, a long-term investment strategy, and (2) to obtain current income from declared dividends. The chairperson should suggest that it is not always possible to achieve both goals and that the corporation has decided on the long-term growth strategy. The chair should suggest that stockholders who are more interested in dividends should pursue other investments; the chairperson might also point out that when these stockholders go to sell their stock to purchase other stock, they should find that the stock is worth considerably more than what they paid for it, due to the long-term growth strategy.

PORTFOLIO ASSESSMENT

Dividends are unique to corporations and important to stockholders of a corporation. In addition, the federal income tax paid by corporations is also unique to the corporate form of business organization. Students should emphasize their learning of this topic by selecting an example of a comprehensive sample of their work in this chapter, either the mastery problem or a problem from a test, to include in their portfolio. A copy of the Portfolio Assessment form (blackline master in the Teacher's Resource Guide) should be completed by the student, and the Description section should include any comments regarding how the student mastered these concepts and procedures. Alternatively, students might include in their portfolios printed reports from an Automated Accounting problem.

	SCOPE AND SEQUENCE		ENHANCING	
	NEW	**REVIEW/ EXTENSION**	**SPECIAL FEATURES**	
INTRODUCE THE CHAPTER			Accounting in Your Career: Trying on a New Accounting System Thinking about Careers	
Financial statements for corporations		✓		
LESSSON 26-1 PREPARING AN INCOME STATEMENT			Math Work Sheet, Chapter 26, Part A Professional Business Ethics: Is This Really a Business Expense?	
Preparing an income statement for a corporation		✓		
Analyzing an income statement for a corporation		✓		
LESSSON 26-2 PREPARING A STATEMENT OF STOCKHOLDERS' EQUITY			Math Work Sheet, Chapter 26, Part B	
Preparing the capital stock section of the statement of stockholders'equity	✓			
Preparing the retained earnings section of the statement of stockholders' equity	✓			
LESSSON 26-3 PREPARING A BALANCE SHEET			Math Work Sheet, Chapter 26, Part C	
Preparing a balance sheet for a corporation		✓		
Preparing the assets section of a balance sheet		✓		
Preparing the liabilities section of a balance sheet		✓		
Preparing the stockholders' equity section of a balance sheet		✓		
Analyzing a balance sheet	✓			
Calculating working capital	✓			
Calculating the current ratio	✓			
LESSSON 26-4 ADJUSTING, CLOSING, AND REVERSING ENTRIES FOR A CORPORATION				
Recording adjusting entries for a corporation		✓		
Recording closing entries for a corporation		✓		
Closing entry for credit balance accounts		✓		
Closing entry for debit balance accounts		✓		
Closing entry to record net income		✓		
Closing entry for dividends	✓			
Reversing entries		✓		
Accounting cycle for a merchandising business organized as a corporation		✓		
PUTTING IT ALL TOGETHER			Explore Accounting Internet Activity Applied Communication Cases for Critical Thinking 1 and 2	

OF-FISCAL-PERIOD ENTRIES FOR A CORPORATION

INSTRUCTION		PRACTICE AND ASSESSMENT		
TECHNOLOGY AND MEDIA	TEACHING STRATEGIES	GUIDED PRACTICE	INDEPENDENT PRACTICE	RETEACHING AND ENRICHMENT
Internet Activity	Software Focus			
Automated Accounting South-Western Accounting Video: Global Perspective— Financial Statements	Applied Skills: Mathematics	Terms Review Audit Your Understanding Work Together	On Your Own Application Problem 26-1 Ongoing Assessment, p. 666	Reteach, p. 666 Enrich, p. 667
South-Western Accounting Video: Cultural Diversity— What Is Papyrus?		Terms Review Audit Your Understanding Work Together	On Your Own Application Problem 26-2 Ongoing Assessment, p. 669	Reteach, p. 669 Enrich, p. 670
CNN Accounting Video	Cooperative Learning Kinesthetic Learner Cooperative Learning	Terms Review Audit Your Understanding Work Together	On Your Own Application Problem 26-3 Ongoing Assessment, p. 675	Reteach, p. 675 Enrich, p. 676
	Auditory Learner Print Learner Cooperating Learning Tactile Learner	Audit Your Understanding Work Together	On Your Own Application Problem 26-4 Ongoing Assessment, p. 682	Reteach, p. 682 Enrich, p. 683
Transparency 26-1 Automated Accounting Spreadsheet Accounting Accounting Connection	Limited English Proficiency (LEP) Students Software Focus Simulation Milestone Applied Skills: Writing Across the Curriculum		Mastery Problem 26-5 Study Guide 26 Chapter 26 Test ExamViewPro or Westest, Chapter 26 Portfolio Assessment	Enrich, p. 684 Challenge Problem 26-6 Reteach, p. 684 Recycling Problem 26-1 Accounting Connection

INTRODUCE THE CHAPTER

PREVIEW ACCOUNTING TERMS
- ❑ Read each term out loud to verify pronunciation for students.
- ❑ Point out terms or parts of terms that should already be familiar to most students, such as net, stockholder, and equity.

PREVIEW CHAPTER OBJECTIVES
- ❑ Point out that students have already learned to prepare financial statements.
- ❑ Point out that this chapter will present the preparation of the income statement, statement of stockholders' equity, and balance sheet for a corporation.
- ❑ Note that this chapter will introduce ratios used to evaluate financial statements.
- ❑ Note that this chapter presents the adjusting, closing, and reversing entries for a corporation.

INTRODUCTION
- ❑ Ask students to identify how often corporations may prepare financial statements.
- ❑ Point out that the income statement and the balance sheet of a corporation are very similar to the statements for a partnership or proprietorship.
- ❑ Note that a new statement is introduced in this chapter to report the changes in the stockholders' equity in the corporation.

TERMS PREVIEW

net sales

net purchases

statement of stockholders' equity

par value

long-term liabilities

working capital

ratio

current ratio

662

INTERNET ACTIVITY

Point your browser to

http://accounting.swpco.com

Choose **First-Year Course**, choose **Activities**, and complete the activity for Chapter 26.

26

Financial Statements and End-of-Fiscal-Period Entries for a Corporation

AFTER STUDYING CHAPTER 26, YOU WILL BE ABLE TO:

1. Define accounting terms related to financial statements for a merchandising business organized as a corporation.

2. Identify accounting concepts and practices related to financial statements and end-of-fiscal-period entries for a merchandising business organized as a corporation.

3. Prepare and analyze an income statement for a merchandising business organized as a corporation.

4. Prepare a statement of stockholders' equity for a merchandising business organized as a corporation.

5. Prepare and analyze a balance sheet for a merchandising business organized as a corporation.

6. Record adjusting, closing, and reversing entries for a merchandising business organized as a corporation.

FINANCIAL STATEMENTS FOR CORPORATIONS

Corporations prepare financial statements that provide financial information similar to that reported by proprietorships and partnerships. To furnish the corporation's managers and stockholders with information on how well the corporation is progressing, financial statements are prepared annually and sometimes monthly or quarterly. *(CONCEPT: Accounting Period Cycle)*

Financial statements are used to report a business's financial progress and condition as well as changes in the owners' equity. To report this information, Winning Edge prepares three financial statements: (1) income statement, (2) statement of stockholders' equity, and (3) balance sheet.

A corporation prepares an income statement and a balance sheet similar to those used by proprietorships and partnerships. However, a corporation reports changes in owners' equity differently. First, owners' equity for all owners is reported as a single amount rather than for each owner. Second, owners' equity is reported in two categories: (1) capital contributed by the owners and (2) capital earned by the corporation.

SOFTWARE FOCUS

Software may be used for independent practice or enrichment as the instructor deems appropriate. For this chapter, the following software may be used: Automated Accounting 7.0 or higher for Application Problem 26-1 and Mastery Problem 26-5; Spreadsheet Accounting Template for Mastery Problem 26-5; and Accounting Connection, Chapter 26.

Instructors may wish to cover the Automated Accounting feature on pages 688–689, even if the Automated Accounting software is not being used in the classroom, so students get a sense of how the chapter's accounting procedures would be implemented in an automated environment.

ACCOUNTING IN YOUR CAREER

TRYING ON A NEW ACCOUNTING SYSTEM

Eva Perez is anxious to get to the office today to do the end-of-fiscal-period work for the year just ended. She has been the accounting manager for GenTelsys, Inc., for five years and has done the year-end accounting work before. But this time it's different.

For the past three months, Eva and her assistant, Ed Duncan, have been using a new computerized accounting system. They have continued to keep all accounting records manually as well as enter all data into the new accounting system. For three months they have compared results from these two systems to be sure the computerized system was producing accurate results. So far everything has matched. But today they will close the year and get the final test before abandoning the manual system.

Eva rushes to a meeting while Ed keys the adjusting entries. The adjusted trial balance prints just as Eva returns from the meeting. A quick check confirms that it matches the manually-prepared trial balance. In a short while the financial statements are printed and they too match. Ed then selects the option for posting the closing entries and prints the post-closing trial balance. A quick comparison reveals that the computerized report shows a balance for Charitable Contributions Expense, a new account added in December, and for Loss on Plant Assets—accounts that should have been closed.

"Ed, that's not too bad," says Eva. "I think we can load the backup and fix this quickly. Everything should match then, and we can stop keeping both systems going at the same time. Then maybe things will get back to normal around here."

Critical Thinking:

1. What would explain why two accounts were not closed in the computerized closing entries?
2. Eva Perez referred to a backup. Once the system is permanently in place, would you recommend that the company continue to keep a backup of the accounting system?
3. Would your opinion about a backup be the same if the backup equipment and supplies were expensive and if considerable labor time was involved in each backup?

ACCOUNTING IN YOUR CAREER

- ❏ This feature demonstrates how accounting professionals should test new computer systems before discontinuing the traditional manual system. This process is referred to as "running parallel systems."
- ❏ Ask students to read the feature or have one or more students read the feature out loud.
- ❏ Give students 5–10 minutes to jot down some ideas for answering the Critical Thinking questions, then discuss the answers in class.
- ❏ As an alternative, you can use brainstorming techniques to generate possible solutions to the questions. With this approach, you may also wish to record the suggestions and save them for additional discussion after the chapter is completed.

THINKING ABOUT CAREERS

- ❏ Use this feature to encourage additional thinking about accounting careers.
- ❏ Ask students what kind of education and experience Eva Perez would need in order to be an accounting manager. *(Eva would need to have an accounting degree and expertise in computer processing and controls.)*
- ❏ Ask students what kinds of personal qualities are desirable for an accounting manager. *(Eva needs good computer and communication skills. She also needs to have a willingness to accept responsibility. The process of converting from a manual to a computer accounting system can be a significant task, one which some employees may be unwilling to make. Thus, Eva must accept the responsibility not only to develop the new system but also to assure that employees are properly trained and motivated to support the new computer system.)*

SUGGESTED ANSWERS

1. *Apparently these two accounts were not specified as part of the closing entries when they were added to the chart of accounts. IIt should be simple, however, to change the setup for these two accounts to be included in the closing entries.*
2. *The company should continue the backup process. The possibility of system or human error is too great to risk not having a backup. Furthermore, a fire or other disaster could also result in data loss.*
3. *The cost of the backup should be compared with the cost of losing the accounting data altogether. Most companies would not find the risk acceptable. Relatively low cost backups can be made with commercially-available hardware and software, such as tape backups and zip drives. The labor time should be contrasted with the labor time involved if a system had to be recreated from scratch.*

OBJECTIVES

- Define accounting terms related to financial statements for a merchandising business organized as a corporation.
- Identify accounting concepts and practices related to financial statements for a merchandising business organized as a corporation.
- Prepare and analyze an income statement for a merchandising business organized as a corporation.

MOTIVATE

Ask students why the income statement of a corporation is important to the stockholders. Students should understand that the stockholders of large corporations are not employed by the company nor do they have any other method to monitor the corporation's activities. These stockholders are referred to as absentee owners because they are absent from the day-to-day activities of the corporation. These stockholders rely heavily on the income statement to inform them of the corporation's ability to make a profit.

Preview

- Preview accounting terms and definitions introduced in this lesson: net sales and net purchases.
- Direct students to read the headings at the top of each page in this lesson and to examine the figures given.

INCOME STATEMENT

Winning Edge, Inc.
Income Statement
For Year Ended December 31, 20--

				% of Net Sales
Operating Revenue:				
Sales			$1,917,955.50	1. Net Sales
Less: Sales Discount	$ 7,584.00			
Sales Ret. and Allow.	21,486.00	29,070.00		
Net Sales			$1,888,885.50	100.0
Cost of Merchandise Sold:				
Merchandise Inv., Jan. 1, 20--			$ 238,758.00	
Purchases		$1,045,832.00		
Less: Purchases Discount	$10,548.00			
Purch. Ret. and Allow.	5,142.00	15,690.00		
Net Purchases			1,030,142.00	
Total Cost of Mdse. Avail. for Sale			$1,268,900.00	
Less Mdse. Inventory, Dec. 31, 20--			244,916.00	
Cost of Merchandise Sold			1,023,984.00	54.2
Gross Profit on Operations			$ 864,901.50	45.8
Operating Expenses:				
Advertising Expense		$ 28,472.00		
Cash Short and Over		7.00		
Credit Card Fee Expense		18,489.00		
Depreciation Exp.—Office Equip.		4,650.00		
Depreciation Exp.—Store Equip.		8,750.00		
Insurance Expense		9,850.00		
Miscellaneous Expense		28,398.17		
Payroll Taxes Expense		29,310.05		
Rent Expense		60,000.00		
Repair Expense		4,872.00		
Salary Expense		393,844.28		
Supplies Expense		7,472.00		
Uncollectible Accounts Expense		9,828.00		
Utilities Expense		18,150.00		
Total Operating Expenses			622,092.50	32.9
Income from Operations			$ 242,809.00	12.9
Other Revenue:				
Gain on Plant Assets	$ 560.00			
Interest Income	88.00			
Total Other Revenue		$ 648.00		
Other Expenses:				
Interest Expense	$ 1,343.00			
Loss on Plant Assets	1,200.00			
Total Other Expenses		2,543.00		
Net Deduction			1,895.00	0.1
Net Income before Fed. Inc. Tax			$ 240,914.00	12.8
Less Federal Income Tax Exp.			77,206.46	
Net Income after Fed. Inc. Tax			$ 163,707.54	

1. Net Sales

2. Net Purchases

3. Income from Operations

4. Net Income before and after Federal Income Tax

MATERIALS

- Work Sheets:
  Math Work Sheet, Chapter 26, Part A
- Working Papers:
  Teacher's Edition of the Working Papers for Lesson 26-1

- Software:
  Automated Accounting 7.0 or higher and Accounting Textbook Template
- Videos:
  South-Western Accounting Video

USES OF AN INCOME STATEMENT

An income statement reports the financial progress of a business during a fiscal period. (CONCEPT: Accounting Period Cycle) Revenue, cost of merchandise sold, gross profit on operations, operating expenses, and net income or net loss are reported on an income statement. (CONCEPT: Adequate Disclosure) To help make decisions about current and future operations, Winning Edge also analyzes relationships between revenue and expense items. Based on this analysis, Winning Edge reports component percentages for all major income statement items.

Winning Edge's income statement differs from Omni Import's income statement shown in Cycle 2. Winning Edge has more accounts to report on the income statement. Because Winning Edge is a corporation, it must also report its federal income tax expense. As shown in the steps, there are four elements in the income statement of Winning Edge that do not appear in the income statement of Omni Import.

The work sheet Winning Edge used to prepare the financial statements in this chapter is shown in Chapter 25 on pages 652–653.

STEPS New elements in the income statement for Winning Edge

1. Subtract Sales Discount, *$7,584.00,* and Sales Returns and Allowances, *$21,486.00,* from Sales, *$1,917,955.50.* Total sales less sales discount and sales returns and allowances is called **net sales.**

2. Subtract Purchases Discount, *$10,548.00,* and Purchases Returns and Allowances, *$5,142.00,* from Purchases, *$1,045,832.00.* Total purchases less purchases discount and purchases returns and allowances is called **net purchases.**

3. Income from operations, *$242,809.00,* is reported separately from net income. Income from operations is the income earned only from normal business activities. Winning Edge's normal business activities are selling sports equipment. Other revenue and expenses, such as interest income, interest expense, and gains or losses on plant assets, are not normal business activities. Other revenue and expenses are not included in calculating income from operations.

4. Net income before federal income tax, *$240,914.00,* and net income after federal income tax, *$163,707.54,* are reported separately. Reporting net income before and after federal income tax is unique to corporation income statements.

PROFESSIONAL BUSINESS ETHICS

Is This Really a Business Expense?

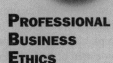

ameron Duermit owns a computer consulting business. Each year he must report the amount of revenue and expenses involved in operating the firm. He must pay federal income tax on the amount by which revenues exceed expenses.

Instructions

Use the three-step checklist to help determine whether or not each of these actions demonstrates ethical behavior.

Situation 1. Mr. Duermit often makes personal long-distance phone calls from his office. He charges these calls to the business account.

Situation 2. Mr. Duermit hired his teenage son to work after school as an office assistant. Tyler comes in to the office every afternoon and earns $6.00 per hour. During this time he does homework and telephones friends. Mr. Duermit knows the business does not really need an assistant, but this is a good way for Tyler to earn spending money.

665

EXPLAIN

❏ Point out that the number of component percentages for this income statement is more than was calculated in Cycle 2. This income statement reports activities, such as the sale of plant assets, that were not included in previous income statements.

❏ Ask students to read the F.Y.I. to learn why component percentages are not calculated for federal income tax expense and net income after federal income tax.

❏ Explain that after component percentages are calculated, each percentage is evaluated against the company's standards to determine whether action is required to improve performance.

DEMONSTRATE

❏ Explain that cost and expense items are stated in terms of "not more than . . ." Using the Total Operating Expenses standard of not more than 35.0%, write some percentages on the blackboard (such as 33.2%, 29.8%, 53.0%, and 37.4%). Ask students whether the higher or the lower percentages are more acceptable for Total Operating Expenses. Ask students which of the percentages written on the board are "not more than 35.0%."

❏ Explain that revenue, profit, and income items are stated in terms of "not less than . . ." Using the Income from Operations standard of not less than 7.0%, write some percentages on the blackboard (such as 3.2%, 9.8%, 7.5%, and 6.7%). Ask students whether the higher or the lower percentages are more acceptable for Income from Operations. Ask students which of the percentages written on the board are "not less than 7.0%."

ONGOING ASSESSMENT

❏ Assessment is an ongoing process. Circulate through the classroom or lab, observing which students have problems with the assignments.

❏ Troubleshooting: Students may have trouble with (1) being overwhelmed by the amount of information on the income statement, (2) the format of the income statement, (3) calculating component percentages, or (4) analyzing component percentages.

❏ Assess student understanding by checking solutions to Independent Practice assignments.

Income Statement Items	Acceptable Component Percentages	Actual Component Percentages
Net sales	100.0%	100.0%
Cost of merchandise sold	not more than 58.0%	54.2%
Gross profit on operations	not less than 42.0%	45.8%
Total operating expenses	not more than 35.0%	32.9%
Income from operations	not less than 7.0%	12.9%
Net deduction	not more than 0.1%	0.1%
Net income before federal income tax	not less than 6.9%	12.8%

For a business to determine whether it is progressing satisfactorily, results of operations are compared with industry standards and/or previous fiscal periods. By analyzing revenues, costs, and expenses, management can gain information that it can use to improve future operations.

The percentage relationship between one financial statement item and the total that includes that item is known as a component percentage. Winning Edge prepares component percentages for six major items on its income statement, as shown in the illustration. Winning Edge uses net sales as the base for calculating component percentages.

The amount of each item on the income statement is divided by the amount of net sales. Thus, each component percentage shows the percentage that item is of net sales. For example, the cost of merchandise sold component percentage indicates that Winning Edge spent 54.2 cents out of each $1.00 of sales for the merchandise sold.

Cost of Merchandise Sold	÷	Net Sales	=	Cost of Merchandise Sold Component Percentage
$1,023,984.00	÷	$1,888,885.50	=	54.2%

Acceptable Component Percentages

Based on comparisons with industry standards as well as previous accounting periods, Winning Edge has determined acceptable component percentages for each major item of cost and expense on its income statement.

If the component percentage of any cost or expense item for a fiscal period exceeds the acceptable percentage, that cost or expense is reviewed further to determine the reason. After determining the reason why a cost or expense exceeded the acceptable percentage, ways are sought to bring the expense within acceptable limits.

> **F.Y.I.** *Component percentages are not calculated for federal income tax expense and net income after federal income tax. Corporations do not have much control over the amount of federal income taxes to be paid. Thus, the net income before federal income tax is the best measure the corporation has to assess its profitability.*

RETEACH

❏ Call on students to identify the primary parts of the income statement. Work with students to divide the income statement into smaller parts that are easier to comprehend.

❏ Review each amount column on the income statement and explain which amounts are recorded in which column.

❏ Assign Math Work Sheet, Chapter 26, Part A.

❏ Review each component percentage and its performance standard and ask students to explain which are acceptable and which are not.

 **TERMS REVIEW**

net sales

net purchases

 **AUDIT YOUR UNDERSTANDING**

1. In what two ways does a corporation report changes in owners' equity differently from a proprietorship or partnership?
2. Why are other revenue and other expenses reported separately on the income statement from sales, cost of merchandise sold, and operating expenses?
3. What information is shown by component percentages on an income statement?

 **WORK TOGETHER**

Preparing an income statement for a corporation

The completed work sheet for Webster Corporation and a blank income statement form are given in the *Working Papers*. Your instructor will guide you through the following examples.

4. Prepare an income statement for the current year. Calculate and record the following component percentages: (a) cost of merchandise sold; (b) gross profit on operations; (c) total operating expenses; (d) income from operations; (e) net addition or deduction resulting from other revenue and expenses; and (f) net income before federal income tax. Round percentage calculations to the nearest 0.1%.
5. The acceptable component percentages are given in the *Working Papers*. Analyze the income statement by determining if component percentages are within acceptable levels. If any component percentage is not within an acceptable level, suggest steps that the company should take. Save your work to complete Work Together on page 670.

 **ON YOUR OWN**

Preparing an income statement for a corporation

The completed work sheet you completed for Osborn Corporation and a blank income statement form are given in the *Working Papers*. Work these problems independently.

6. Prepare an income statement for the current year. Calculate and record the following component percentages: (a) cost of merchandise sold; (b) gross profit on operations; (c) total operating expenses; (d) income from operations; (e) net addition or deduction resulting from other revenue and expenses; and (f) net income before federal income tax. Round percentage calculations to the nearest 0.1%.
7. The acceptable component percentages are given in the *Working Papers*. Analyze the income statement by determining if component percentages are within acceptable levels. If any component percentage is not within an acceptable level, suggest steps that the company should take. Save your work to complete On Your Own on page 670.

GUIDED PRACTICE

Terms Review
Call on students to define the terms in the Terms Review. Ask the class if the definitions are correct and whether the complete definitions have been given or if anything needs to be added. The suggested definitions are given in the Glossary.

Audit Your Understanding
Call on students to answer the Audit Your Understanding questions. Ask the class if the answer is correct and/or complete. Answers are given in Appendix D of the textbook.

Work Together
Have students write the solutions to the Work Together problems as you guide the class through the examples.
❏ Direct students to prepare the income statement.
❏ Ask students to write their calculations of the component percentages on the board.
❏ Direct students to evaluate the income statement, using the component percentages.
❏ Lead a class discussion to identify possible steps to correct problems identified using the component percentages.
❏ Remind students to save their work to complete Work Together in Lesson 2.

INDEPENDENT PRACTICE

On Your Own
❏ Assign the On Your Own problems to be worked independently.
❏ Remind students to save their work to complete On Your Own in Lesson 2.
❏ Use the Ongoing Assessment techniques to diagnose student understanding.

Application Problem
❏ Assign Application Problem 26-1: Preparing an income statement for a corporation.

ENRICH

❏ Assign the Automated Accounting feature on pages 688–689 to automate Application Problem 26-1.
❏ Show the South-Western Accounting Video: Global Perspective—Financial Statements.

CLOSE

❏ Ask students to briefly summarize the new parts of the income statement presented in this lesson.

CAPITAL STOCK SECTION OF THE STATEMENT OF STOCKHOLDERS' EQUITY

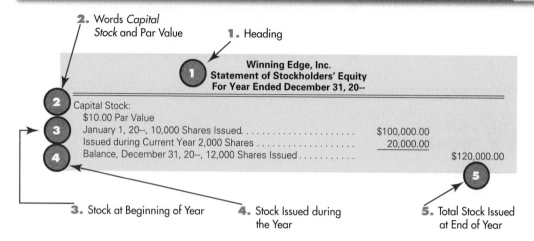

2. Words *Capital Stock* and Par Value   **1.** Heading

Winning Edge, Inc.
Statement of Stockholders' Equity
For Year Ended December 31, 20--

Capital Stock:
$10.00 Par Value
January 1, 20--, 10,000 Shares Issued $100,000.00
Issued during Current Year 2,000 Shares 20,000.00
Balance, December 31, 20--, 12,000 Shares Issued $120,000.00

3. Stock at Beginning of Year   **4.** Stock Issued during the Year   **5.** Total Stock Issued at End of Year

A financial statement that shows changes in a corporation's ownership for a fiscal period is called a **statement of stockholders' equity.** A statement of stockholders' equity is similar to the owners' equity statement for a partnership.

A statement of stockholders' equity contains two major sections: (1) capital stock and (2) retained earnings.

The amount of capital stock issued as of the beginning of the year is the beginning balance of the capital stock account. Any additional stock transactions recorded in the general ledger during the fiscal year would be added up to calculate the amount of stock issued during the fiscal year. Thus, the amounts in the capital stock section of the income statement are obtained from the general ledger account, Capital Stock.

Each share of stock issued by a corporation has a monetary value. A value assigned to a share of stock and printed on the stock certificate is called **par value.**

S T E P S **Preparing the capital stock section of a statement of stockholders' equity**

1. Write the heading: company name, *Winning Edge, Inc.*; statement name, *Statement of Stockholders' Equity*; and fiscal period, *For Year Ended December 31, 20—*, in the statement heading.

2. Write the the words *Capital Stock* and the par value of the stock, *$10.00 Par Value.*

3. Write the number of shares, *10,000*, and dollar amount, *$100,000.00*, of stock issued as of the beginning of the year.

4. Write the number of shares, *2,000*, and dollar amount, *$20,000.00*, of stock issued during the year.

5. Calculate the total dollar amount of stock issued as of the end of the fiscal year, *$120,000.00*, by adding the dollar amount of beginning stock, *$100,000.00*, and the dollar amount of shares issued during the year, *$20,000.00*.

RETAINED EARNINGS SECTION OF THE STATEMENT OF STOCKHOLDERS' EQUITY

EXPLAIN

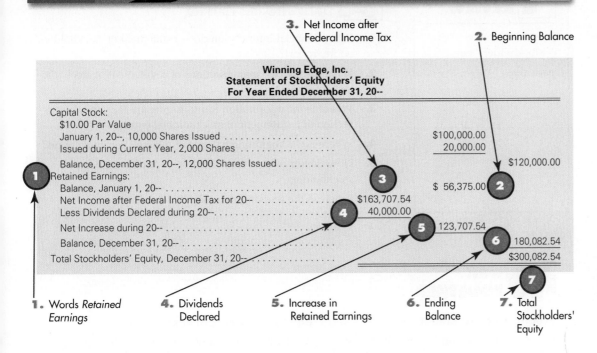

3. Net Income after Federal Income Tax

2. Beginning Balance

Winning Edge, Inc.
Statement of Stockholders' Equity
For Year Ended December 31, 20--

Capital Stock:
$10.00 Par Value
January 1, 20--, 10,000 Shares Issued $100,000.00
Issued during Current Year, 2,000 Shares 20,000.00
Balance, December 31, 20--, 12,000 Shares Issued $120,000.00

① Retained Earnings:
Balance, January 1, 20-- . . . . $ 56,375.00 ②
Net Income after Federal Income Tax for 20-- . . . . $163,707.54 ③
Less Dividends Declared during 20--. . . . . ④ 40,000.00
Net Increase during 20-- . . . . ⑤ 123,707.54
Balance, December 31, 20-- . . . . ⑥ 180,082.54
Total Stockholders' Equity, December 31, 20-- . . . . $300,082.54 ⑦

1. Words *Retained Earnings*   4. Dividends Declared   5. Increase in Retained Earnings   6. Ending Balance   7. Total Stockholders' Equity

Net income increases a corporation's total capital. Some income may be retained by a corporation for business expansion. Some income may be distributed as dividends to provide stockholders with a return on their investments. During the year, Winning Edge's board of directors declared $40,000.00 in dividends.

Amounts used to prepare the statement of stockholders' equity are obtained from the income statement and balance sheet columns of the work sheet shown in Chapter 25.

STEPS

Preparing the retained earnings section of a statement of stockholders' equity

1. Write the words *Retained Earnings*.
2. Write the beginning balance of retained earnings, *$56,375.00*, from the Balance Sheet Credit column.
3. Write the net income after federal income tax, *$163,707.54*, from the Income Statement Debit column.
4. Write the amount of dividends, *$40,000.00*, from the Balance Sheet Debit column.
5. Subtract dividends, *$40,000.00*, from net income after federal income tax, *$163,707.54*, to calculate the increase in retained earnings, *$123,707.54*.
6. Add the beginning balance of retained earnings, *$56,375.00*, and the increase in retained earnings, *$123,707.54*, to calculate the ending balance of retained earnings, *$180,082.54*.
7. Add the ending amounts of capital stock, *$120,000.00*, and retained earnings, *$180,082.54*, to calculate the total amount of stockholders' equity, *$300,082.54*.

RETEACH

❏ Call on students to identify the major sections of the statement of stockholders' equity.
❏ Call on students to summarize the information presented in each section of the statement.
❏ Assign Math Work Sheet, Chapter 26, Part B.
❏ Call on students to describe where to obtain the information presented in the statement.

EXPLAIN

❏ Ask students to again identify the two major sections of the statement of stockholders' equity.
❏ Direct students to identify the source of each amount in the Retained Earnings section of the statement.
❏ Remind students that retained earnings is not equivalent to cash.
❏ Note that a single individual can own all the stock of a corporation. In this case, the statement title would include the word "Stockholder's."

DEMONSTRATE

❏ Ask students to continue writing the statement of stockholders' equity started when completing the Capital Stock section of the statement.
❏ Direct students to complete the statement while you read each of the seven steps shown.
❏ When you demonstrate Step 3, point out that this step is comparable to adding the net income amount to the owner's capital account for a partnership or a proprietorship.
❏ When you demonstrate Steps 4 and 5, point out that these steps are comparable to deducting drawing amounts from the net income amount for a partnership or a proprietorship.

ONGOING ASSESSMENT

❏ Assessment is an ongoing process. Circulate through the classroom or lab, observing which students have problems with the assignments.
❏ Troubleshooting: Diagnose what kinds of problems students have with this lesson. The statement of stockholders' equity is a new statement for students. Thus, students may have trouble (1) remembering how to prepare the statement, (2) calculating the retained earnings section, or (3) understanding how the statement interacts with the income statement and balance sheet.
❏ Assess student understanding by checking solutions to Independent Practice assignments.

Terms Review

Call on students to define the terms in the Terms Review. Ask the class if the definitions are correct and whether the complete definitions have been given or if anything needs to be added. The suggested definitions are given in the Glossary.

Audit Your Understanding

Call on students to answer the Audit Your Understanding questions. Ask the class if the answer is correct and/or complete. Answers are given in Appendix D of the textbook.

Work Together

Have students write the solution to the Work Together problem as you guide the class through the example.

❏ Remind students to use the problem started in Lesson 1.
❏ Direct students to prepare the statement heading.
❏ Direct students to prepare the Capital Stock section.
❏ Direct students to prepare the Retained Earnings section.
❏ Remind students to save their work to complete Work Together in Lesson 3.

On Your Own

❏ Assign the On Your Own problem to be worked independently.
❏ Remind students to use the problem started in Lesson 1.
❏ Remind students to save their work to complete On Your Own in Lesson 3.
❏ Use the Ongoing Assessment techniques to diagnose student understanding.

Application Problem

❏ Assign Application Problem 26-2: Preparing a statement of stockholders' equity for a corporation.

TERMS REVIEW

statement of
   stockholders' equity
par value

AUDIT YOUR UNDERSTANDING

1. What financial information does a statement of stockholders' equity report?

2. What are the two major sections of a statement of stockholders' equity?

3. Where is the information found to prepare the capital stock section of a statement of stockholders' equity?

4. Where is the beginning balance of retained earnings found?

5. How does a corporation distribute a portion of income to stockholders?

6. Where is the amount of dividends found?

WORK TOGETHER

Preparing a statement of stockholders' equity for a corporation

Use the work sheet and income statement for Webster Corporation from Work Together on page 667. A form for the statement of stockholders' equity is given in the *Working Papers.* Your instructor will guide you through the following example.

7. Prepare a statement of stockholders' equity for the current year. As of January 1, Webster Corporation had issued 9,000 shares of capital stock with a par value of $10.00 per share. During the fiscal year, the corporation issued 1,000 additional shares of capital stock. Save your work to complete Work Together on page 676.

ON YOUR OWN

Preparing a statement of stockholders' equity for a corporation

Use the work sheet and income statement for Osborn Corporation from On Your Own on page 667. A form for the statement of stockholders' equity is given in the *Working Papers.* Work this problem independently.

8. Prepare a statement of stockholders' equity for the current year. As of January 1, Osborn Corporation had issued 75,000 shares of capital stock with a par value of $1.00 per share. During the fiscal year, the corporation issued 5,000 additional shares of stock. Save your work to complete On Your Own on page 676.

670 CHAPTER 26 Financial Statements and End-of-Fiscal-Period Entries for a Corporation

ENRICH

❏ Publicly-held corporations report a three-year income statement and statement of stockholders' equity and a two-year balance sheet. Compare the style of the statement of stockholders' equity in an annual report to the statement shown in this text.
❏ Show the South-Western Accounting Video: Cultural Diversity—What Is Papyrus?

CLOSE

❏ Ask students to briefly summarize the procedures for preparing a statement of stockholders' equity.

ASSETS SECTION OF A BALANCE SHEET

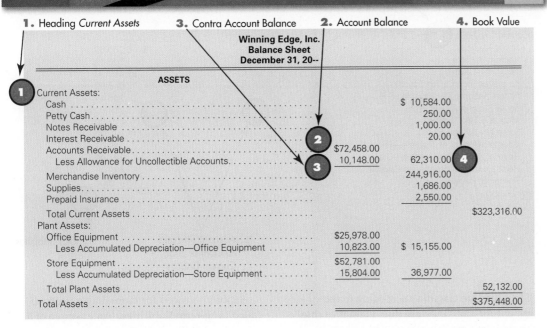

1. Heading *Current Assets*   **3.** Contra Account Balance   **2.** Account Balance   **4.** Book Value

Winning Edge, Inc.
Balance Sheet
December 31, 20--

ASSETS

1 Current Assets:			
Cash		$ 10,584.00	
Petty Cash		250.00	
Notes Receivable		1,000.00	
Interest Receivable		20.00	
Accounts Receivable	$72,458.00		
Less Allowance for Uncollectible Accounts	10,148.00	62,310.00 **4**	
Merchandise Inventory		244,916.00	
Supplies		1,686.00	
Prepaid Insurance		2,550.00	
Total Current Assets			$323,316.00
Plant Assets:			
Office Equipment	$25,978.00		
Less Accumulated Depreciation—Office Equipment	10,823.00	$ 15,155.00	
Store Equipment	$52,781.00		
Less Accumulated Depreciation—Store Equipment	15,804.00	36,977.00	
Total Plant Assets			52,132.00
Total Assets			$375,448.00

A corporation's balance sheet reports assets, liabilities, and stockholders' equity on a specific date. (*CONCEPT: Accounting Period Cycle*) A balance sheet is prepared from information found in the Balance Sheet columns of the work sheet and the statement of stockholders' equity.

Procedures for preparing Winning Edge's balance sheet are similar to those used by Omni Import in Cycle 2. However, Winning Edge must report the results of its accounting for accounts receivable and plant assets.

Winning Edge classifies its assets as current

assets and plant assets. A business owning both current and plant assets usually lists them under separate headings on a balance sheet.

Some of Winning Edge's asset accounts have related contra accounts that reduce the related account on the balance sheet. The difference between an asset's account balance and its related contra account balance is known as book value. An asset's book value is reported on a balance sheet by listing three amounts: (1) the balance of the asset account, (2) the balance of the asset's contra account, and (3) book value.

S T E P S **Calculating the book value of accounts receivable**

1. Write the heading *Current Assets*.
2. Write the total amount of accounts receivable, *$72,458.00*, in the first amount column.
3. Write the words *Less Allowance for Uncollectible Accounts* on the next line, indented about one centimeter, and the amount, *$10,148.00*, below the amount of accounts receivable, *$72,458.00*.
4. Subtract the allowance for uncollectible accounts, $10,148.00, from the total amount of accounts receivable, $72,458.00, to calculate the book value of accounts receivable, *$62,310.00*. Write the amount in the second amount column on the same line. Use the same procedure to report book values of the plant asset accounts.

MATERIALS

❏ Work Sheets:
Math Work Sheet, Chapter 26, Part C
❏ Working Papers:
Teacher's Edition of the Working Papers for Lesson 26-3
❏ Videos:
CNN Accounting Video

OBJECTIVES

❏ Identify accounting concepts and practices related to financial statements for a merchandising business organized as a corporation.
❏ Prepare and analyze a balance sheet for a merchandising business organized as a corporation.

MOTIVATE

Both the income statement and the statement of stockholders' equity report the financial activity of a business over a period of time. In contrast, the balance sheet reports the financial condition of the business as of a single date.

Preview

❏ Preview accounting terms and definitions introduced in this lesson: long-term liabilities, working capital, ratio, and current ratio.
❏ Note that some accounting procedures learned in this part of the textbook, such as the allowance for uncollectible accounts and accumulated depreciation, increase the amount of information reported on a balance sheet.
❏ Direct students to read the headings at the top of each page in this lesson and to examine the figures given.

EXPLAIN

❏ Note that this page presents only the Assets section of a balance sheet.
❏ Ask students to identify the two classifications of assets.

DEMONSTRATE

❏ Ask students to write the balance sheet on a piece of paper while you read each of the four steps shown.
❏ Demonstrate which columns are used for which amounts: section totals in the far-right columns, next-most-significant amounts and calculations in the next-to-the-far-right columns, etc.
❏ Point out that only the features of the balance sheet introduced in this part of the textbook are highlighted by the steps shown.
❏ Point out that students will complete the balance sheet using the steps on the following pages.

❑ Note that this page presents only the Liabilities section of a balance sheet.

❑ Call on students to identify the accounts that have been introduced in this part of the textbook (notes payable, interest payable, dividends payable).

❑ Explain the difference between current and long-term liabilities. Ask students if they can think of any examples of long-term liabilities.

❑ Ask students to read the F.Y.I. to learn more about how long-term liabilities would be reported.

DEMONSTRATE

❑ Ask students to continue preparing the balance sheet started when completing the Assets section.

❑ Direct students to complete the Liabilities section of the balance sheet while you read each of the three steps shown.

❑ Point out that students will complete the balance sheet using the steps on the following page.

LIABILITIES SECTION OF A BALANCE SHEET

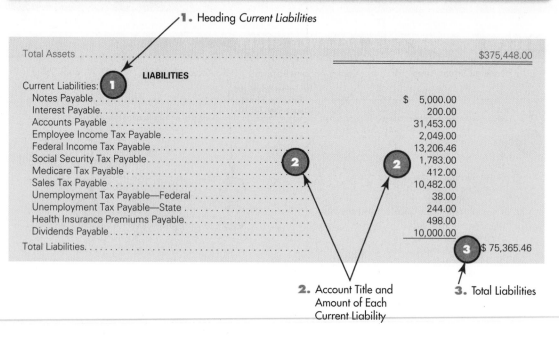

1. Heading *Current Liabilities*

Total Assets	$375,448.00

LIABILITIES

Current Liabilities: **1**

Notes Payable	$ 5,000.00
Interest Payable.	200.00
Accounts Payable	31,453.00
Employee Income Tax Payable	2,049.00
Federal Income Tax Payable	13,206.46
Social Security Tax Payable	1,783.00
Medicare Tax Payable	412.00
Sales Tax Payable	10,482.00
Unemployment Tax Payable—Federal	38.00
Unemployment Tax Payable—State	244.00
Health Insurance Premiums Payable.	498.00
Dividends Payable	10,000.00
Total Liabilities. **3**	$ 75,365.46

2. Account Title and Amount of Each Current Liability

3. Total Liabilities

Liabilities are classified according to the length of time until they are due. Liabilities due within a short time, usually within a year, are known as current liabilities. All of Winning Edge's liabilities are current liabilities because they come due within a year.

Liabilities owed for more than a year are called **long-term liabilities.** An example of a long-term liability is Mortgage Payable. On December 31 of the current year, Winning Edge does not have any long-term liabilities.

Preparing the liabilities section of a balance sheet

S T E P S

1. Write the heading *Current Liabilities*.

2. Write the account title and amount of each current liability account.

3. Calculate and write the amount of total liabilities, *$75,365.46*.

F.Y.I. *A company having both current liabilities and long-term liabilities would include headings and totals for each category. The process is similar to preparing the asset section of a balance sheet.*

672 CHAPTER 26 Financial Statements and End-of-Fiscal-Period Entries for a Corporation

TEACHING STRATEGIES — COOPERATIVE LEARNING

Explain What Component Percentages Measure. Assign students to groups of three. Each group is to plan, prepare, and deliver a presentation to nonaccountants. The presentation should explain what component percentages are and how they are used to analyze financial statements. Time frame: Class time 15–30 minutes over a few class periods; additional time outside class will be required to prepare the presentation.

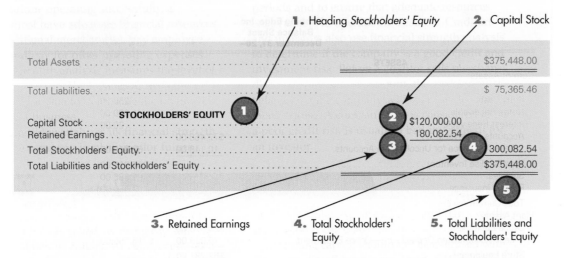

1. Heading *Stockholders' Equity*
2. Capital Stock

Total Assets	$375,448.00
Total Liabilities	$ 75,365.46
STOCKHOLDERS' EQUITY	
Capital Stock	$120,000.00
Retained Earnings	180,082.54
Total Stockholders' Equity	300,082.54
Total Liabilities and Stockholders' Equity	$375,448.00

3. Retained Earnings
4. Total Stockholders' Equity
5. Total Liabilities and Stockholders' Equity

A major difference between corporation balance sheets and proprietorship or partnership balance sheets is the owners' equity section. The owners' equity section of Winning Edge's balance sheet is labeled Stockholders' Equity. Some corporations use the same label, Owners' Equity, as proprietorships and partnerships. Either label is acceptable.

The stockholders' equity section contains the total amounts of capital stock and retained earnings. These amounts are calculated and reported on the statement of stockholders' equity.

Winning Edge's completed balance sheet is shown on the following page.

S T E P S

Preparing the stockholders' equity section of a balance sheet

1. Write the heading *Stockholders' Equity*.
2. Write the amount of capital stock, *$120,000.00,* calculated on the statement of stockholders' equity.
3. Write the amount of retained earnings, *$180,082.54,* calculated on the statement of stockholders' equity.
4. Add the amount of capital stock, $120,000.00, and retained earnings, $180,082.54, to calculate the total of stockholders' equity, *$300,082.54.*
5. Add the amount of total liabilities, $75,365.46, and total stockholders' equity, $300,082.54, to calculate the total of liabilities and stockholders' equity, *$375,448.00.* Verify accuracy by comparing the total amount of assets and the total amount of liabilities and stockholders' equity. These two amounts must be the same.

REMEMBER

Total assets must equal the total of liabilities and stockholders' equity. If these totals are not equal, identify the errors before preparing closing and reversing entries.

❏ Ask students to identify the four closing entries for a corporation.
❏ Ask students to identify the closing entry that is unique to a corporation.

EXPLAIN

❏ Ask students to identify the two types of accounts with credit balances that are closed.
❏ Explain that the credit entry to Income Summary does not have any meaning other than being the sum of credit accounts.

DEMONSTRATE

❏ Direct students to the illustration as you demonstrate recording the closing entry, following the two steps shown.
❏ Refer students to the work sheet illustration in Chapter 25 to emphasize that the closing entries come directly from the Income Statement Credit column of the work sheet.

CLOSING ENTRIES FOR A CORPORATION

Closing entries for a corporation are made from information in a work sheet. Closing entries for revenue and expense accounts are similar to those for proprietorships or partnerships. A corporation's closing entries to close net income and temporary equity accounts are similar to those for a partnership or proprietorship. However, these closing entries affect different accounts. A corporation records four closing entries:

1. Closing entry for income statement accounts with credit balances (revenue and contra cost accounts).
2. Closing entry for income statement accounts with debit balances (cost, contra revenue, and expense accounts).
3. Closing entry to record net income or net loss in the retained earnings account and close the income summary account.
4. Closing entry for the dividends account.

CLOSING ENTRY FOR ACCOUNTS WITH CREDIT BALANCES

1. Enter the balance of accounts in the Income Statement credit column as a debit.

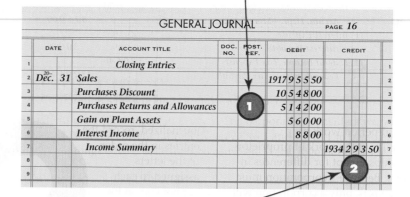

2. Enter the total of debit entries as a credit to Income Summary.

Income statement credit balance accounts are the revenue (Sales, Gain on Plant Assets, and Interest Income) and the contra cost accounts (Purchases Discount and Purchases Returns and Allowances). Information needed for closing income statement credit balance accounts is obtained from the work sheet. Closing entries are recorded on a new page of the general journal.

S T E P S

Journalizing a closing entry for accounts with credit balances

1. Except for Income Summary, enter the balance of every account in the Income Statement credit column of the work sheet as a debit entry in a general journal.
2. Enter the total of the debit entries, *$1,934,293.50,* as a credit to Income Summary.

TEACHING STRATEGIES   DIFFERENT LEARNING STYLES

Auditory Learner. The auditory learner can reinforce the learning of formulas by verbally explaining the formula and/or calculations to other students in a small group. In a group of three, for example, each student should get the opportunity to "teach" the formula to the other two students. Through this process, each student in the group will "teach" the formula once and "learn" the formula two times.

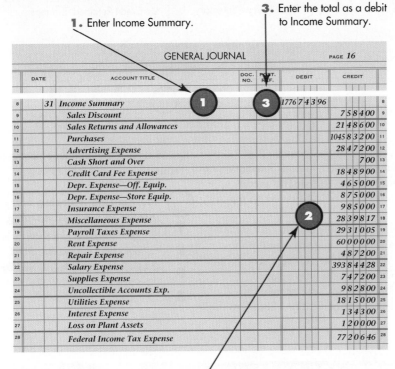

1. Enter Income Summary.

3. Enter the total as a debit to Income Summary.

GENERAL JOURNAL   PAGE 16

	DATE	ACCOUNT TITLE	DOC. NO.	POST. REF.	DEBIT	CREDIT	
8	31	*Income Summary*			1776 743 96		8
9		*Sales Discount*				7 584 00	9
10		*Sales Returns and Allowances*				21 486 00	10
11		*Purchases*				1045 832 00	11
12		*Advertising Expense*				28 472 00	12
13		*Cash Short and Over*				7 00	13
14		*Credit Card Fee Expense*				18 489 00	14
15		*Depr. Expense—Off. Equip.*				4 650 00	15
16		*Depr. Expense—Store Equip.*				8 750 00	16
17		*Insurance Expense*				9 850 00	17
18		*Miscellaneous Expense*				28 398 17	18
19		*Payroll Taxes Expense*				29 310 05	19
20		*Rent Expense*				60 000 00	20
21		*Repair Expense*				4 872 00	21
22		*Salary Expense*				393 844 28	22
23		*Supplies Expense*				7 472 00	23
24		*Uncollectible Accounts Exp.*				9 828 00	24
25		*Utilities Expense*				18 150 00	25
26		*Interest Expense*				1 343 00	26
27		*Loss on Plant Assets*				1 200 00	27
28		*Federal Income Tax Expense*				77 206 46	28

2. Enter the balance of every account in the Income Statement debit column as a credit.

Income statement debit balance accounts are the contra revenue accounts (Sales Discount and Sales Returns and Allowances) and the cost (Purchases) and expense accounts. Information needed for closing income statement debit balance accounts is obtained from the work sheet's Income Statement Debit column.

If Cash Short and Over has a credit balance, the account balance amount is closed to Income Summary with the credit balance accounts.

Journalizing a closing entry for accounts with debit balances

STEPS

1. Enter the account title Income Summary.

2. Enter the balance of every account in the Income Statement debit column of the work sheet as a credit entry in a general journal.

3. Enter the total of the credit entries, $1,776,743.96, as a debit on the line with the account title, Income Summary.

CHAPTER 26   Financial Statements and End-of-Fiscal-Period Entries for a Corporation   **679**

EXPLAIN

❑ Ask students to identify the three types of accounts with debit balances that are closed (*contra revenue, cost, and expense accounts*).

❑ Explain that the debit entry to Income Summary does not have any meaning other than being the sum of debit accounts.

❑ Point out that the cash short and over account, if it had a credit balance, would have been included in the closing entry shown on the previous page.

❑ Ask students which account in this closing entry is unique to a corporation (*Federal Income Tax Expense*).

DEMONSTRATE

❑ Direct students to the illustration as you demonstrate recording the closing entry, following the three steps shown.

❑ Refer students to the work sheet illustration in Chapter 25 to emphasize that the closing entries come directly from the Income Statement Debit column of the work sheet.

TEACHING STRATEGIES   DIFFERENT LEARNING STYLES

Print Learner. When learning formulas, the print learner would prefer to be able to study the formula as given in the textbook or as printed on a separate handout. The print material should show the formula as well as an example of performing the calculations.

- Ask students to identify the three trans-actions that have created the balance in Income Summary *(the merchandise inventory adjusting entry; the closing entry for income statement accounts with credit balances; and the closing entry for income statement accounts with debit balances).*
- Explain that the balance of Income Summary is the same as the net income amount on the work sheet and income statement.
- Ask students to explain why Dividends is closed to Retained Earnings.
- Ask students to identify the similar closing entry for a partnership.

Closing entry to record net income

- Draw a T account on the blackboard for Income Summary. Record the adjusting entry for merchandise inventory ($6,158.00 credit), the closing entry for the credit balance accounts ($1,934,293.50 credit), and the closing entry for the debit balance accounts ($1,776,743.96 debit). Ask students to calculate the balance of this account, which should be the same as the net income amount, $163,707.54 credit.
- Draw a T account for Retained Earnings and record the January 1 balance, $56,375.00 credit.
- Record the entry to close net income in the T accounts.
- Direct students to the illustration as you demonstrate recording the closing entry for net income in the general journal, following the two steps shown.

Closing entry for dividends

- Continue with the T account for Retained Earnings.
- Draw a T account for Dividends and record the December 31 balance of $40,000.00 debit.
- Record the entry to close Dividends in the T accounts.
- Direct students to the illustration as you demonstrate recording the closing entry for Dividends in the general journal, following the two steps shown.

CLOSING ENTRY TO RECORD NET INCOME

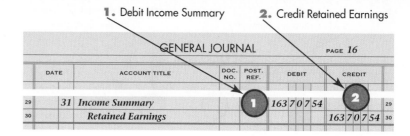

After closing entries for the income statement accounts are posted, Income Summary has a credit balance of $163,707.54. This credit balance equals the net income calculated on the work sheet.

A corporation's net income should be recorded in the retained earnings account at the end of the fiscal year. After the closing entry is posted, Income Summary has a zero balance.

If a corporation has a net loss, Income Summary has a debit balance. Retained Earnings would then be debited and Income Summary credited for the net loss amount.

S T E P S

Journalizing a closing entry for net income to retained earnings

1. Record a debit to Income Summary for the amount of net income, $163,707.54.
2. Record a credit to Retained Earnings for the same amount, $163,707.54.

CLOSING ENTRY FOR DIVIDENDS

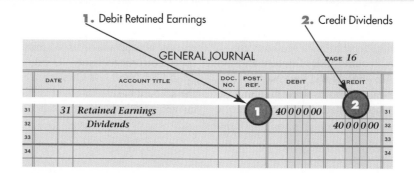

Because dividends decrease the earnings retained by a corporation, the dividends account is closed to Retained Earnings. After the closing entry for the dividends account is posted, Dividends has a zero balance. The amount of the dividends, $40,000.00, has reduced the balance of Retained Earnings.

S T E P S

Journalizing a closing entry for dividends

1. Record a debit to Retained Earnings for the amount of dividends, $40,000.00.
2. Record a credit to Dividends for the same amount, $40,000.00.

680 CHAPTER 26 Financial Statements and End-of-Fiscal-Period Entries for a Corporation

---

TEACHING STRATEGIES

COOPERATIVE LEARNING

Develop a Better Way to Classify Assets. Assign students to groups of three. Give students a deck of cards with one asset listed on each card. Ask each group to physically group these asset cards to develop a better system of classifying assets. Each group should explain their system to one other group. Time frame: 30 minutes.

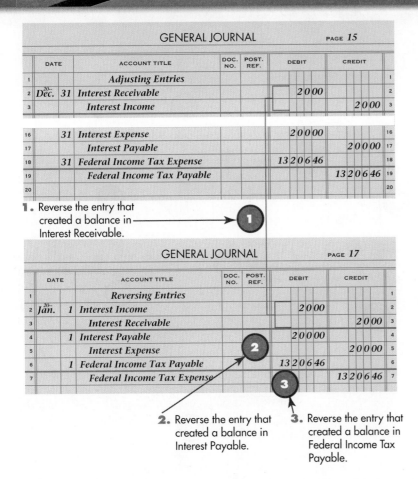

1. Reverse the entry that created a balance in Interest Receivable.

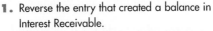

2. Reverse the entry that created a balance in Interest Payable.

3. Reverse the entry that created a balance in Federal Income Tax Payable.

If an adjusting entry creates a balance in an asset or liability account, the adjusting entry should be reversed. A review of Winning Edge's adjusting entries shows that three adjusting entries created a balance in an asset or liability account.

1. The adjusting entry for accrued interest income created a balance in the interest receivable account.

2. The adjusting entry for accrued interest expense created a balance in the interest payable account.

3. The adjusting entry for federal income tax expense created a balance in the federal income tax payable account.

S T E P S **Journalizing reversing entries**

1. Reverse the entry that created a balance in Interest Receivable.

2. Reverse the entry that created a balance in Interest Payable.

3. Reverse the entry that created a balance in Federal Income Tax Payable.

R E M E M B E R

A post-closing trial balance is prepared to prove the equality ot debits and credits in the general ledger after adjusting and closing entries have been posted.

❑ Remind students that they have now completed the accounting cycle for three different businesses.

❑ Call on students to take turns reading the nine steps shown.

❑ After a student reads a step, ask the student to provide additional information about the step.

ONGOING ASSESSMENT

❑ Assessment is an ongoing process. Circulate through the classroom or lab, observing which students have problems with the assignments.

❑ Troubleshooting: Diagnose what kinds of problems students have with this lesson. This lesson is a review of information taught in previous cycles as well as selected chapters in this part. Thus, students should not have many problems with this lesson. Students may have trouble with (1) recording the closing entries for Net Income and Dividends or (2) recording the reversing entries.

❑ Assess student understanding by checking solutions to Independent Practice assignments.

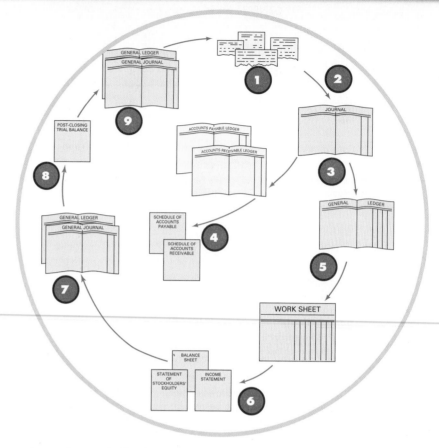

The accounting cycles are similar for merchandising businesses organized as either partnerships or corporations. Variations occur in preparing financial statements. Variations also occur when reversing entries are recorded.

Accounting cycle for a merchandising business organized as a corporation

STEPS

1. Source documents are checked for accuracy, and transactions are analyzed into debit and credit parts.
2. Transactions, from information on source documents, are recorded in journals.
3. Journal entries are posted to the accounts payable, accounts receivable, and general ledgers.
4. Schedules of accounts payable and accounts receivable are prepared from the subsidiary ledgers.
5. A work sheet, including a trial balance and an adjustment for federal income tax expense, is prepared from the general ledger.
6. Financial statements are prepared from the work sheet.
7. Adjusting and closing entries are journalized from the work sheet and posted to the general ledger.
8. A post-closing trial balance of the general ledger is prepared.
9. Reversing entries are journalized and posted to the general ledger.

RETEACH

❑ Call on students to summarize how to record adjusting, closing, and reversing entries.

❑ Call on students to explain the steps in an accounting cycle.

AUDIT YOUR UNDERSTANDING

1. What adjusting entry is recorded only for a corporation?
2. What closing entry is recorded only for a corporation?
3. To what account is Dividends closed at the fiscal year end?

WORK TOGETHER

Journalizing adjusting, closing, and reversing entries for a corporation

Use the work sheet and financial statements from Work Together on page 676. General journal pages are given in the *Working Papers*. Your instructor will guide you through the following examples.

4. For the current year, journalize the adjusting entries using page 15 of a general journal.
5. For the current year, journalize the closing entries using page 16 of a general journal.
6. For the following year, journalize the reversing entries using page 17 of a general journal.

ON YOUR OWN

Journalizing adjusting, closing, and reversing entries for a corporation

Use the work sheet and financial statements from On Your Own on page 676. General journal pages are given in the *Working Papers*. Work these problems independently.

7. For the current year, journalize the adjusting entries using page 18 of a general journal.
8. For the current year, journalize the closing entries using page 19 of a general journal.
9. For the following year, journalize the reversing entries using page 20 of a general journal.

GUIDED PRACTICE

Audit Your Understanding
Call on students to answer the Audit Your Understanding questions. Ask the class if the answer is correct and/or complete. Answers are given in Appendix D of the textbook.

Work Together
Have students write the solutions to the Work Together problems as you guide the class through the examples.
- ❑ Remind students to use the problem started in Lesson 1 and continued in Lessons 2 and 3.
- ❑ Direct students to prepare the adjusting entries.
- ❑ Direct students to prepare the closing entries.
- ❑ Direct students to prepare the reversing entries.

INDEPENDENT PRACTICE

On Your Own
- ❑ Assign the On Your Own problems to be worked independently.
- ❑ Remind students to use the problem started in Lesson 1 and continued in Lessons 2 and 3.
- ❑ Use the Ongoing Assessment techniques to diagnose student understanding.

Application Problem
- ❑ Assign Application Problem 26-4: Journalizing adjusting, closing, and reversing entries for a corporation.

ENRICH

- ❑ More companies select a December 31 fiscal year end than any other year end. Ask students to identify the fiscal year end of companies in available annual reports. Ask students to suggest reasons why companies selected their particular fiscal year end.

CLOSE

- ❑ Ask students to summarize the procedures for recording adjusting, closing, and reversing entries.

CHAPTER 26 SUMMARY

After completing this chapter, you can

1. Define accounting terms related to financial statements for a merchandising business organized as a corporation.
2. Identify accounting concepts and practices related to financial statements and end-of-fiscal-period entries for a merchandising business organized as a corporation.
3. Prepare and analyze an income statement for a merchandising business organized as a corporation.
4. Prepare a statement of stockholders' equity for a merchandising business organized as a corporation.
5. Prepare and analyze a balance sheet for a merchandising business organized as a corporation.
6. Record adjusting, closing, and reversing entries for a merchandising business organized as a corporation.

EXPLORE ACCOUNTING

STATEMENT OF CASH FLOWS

The income statement and balance sheet are prepared using the accrual basis of accounting. These accrual-basis financial statements do not, however, provide detailed information about the sources and uses of cash in a business. A financial statement that reports the cash flows of a business for a fiscal period is called a *statement of cash flows*.

A statement of cash flows is comprised of three primary sections. The first section, Cash Flows from Operating Activities, reports the amount of cash generated from the sale of goods and services. This section can be compared to an income statement, except that revenue, merchandise purchases, and expenses are

reported on a cash basis. For example, a sale on account that remains unpaid at the fiscal year end does not result in an increase in cash. In addition, only expenses that are paid during the fiscal year result in a decrease in cash. For example, depreciation is an accrual-basis expense that requires no cash payment. Therefore, depreciation expense is not a use of cash as reported in this statement.

The section Cash Flows from Investing Activities reports the cash used to purchase plant assets and other long-term assets. The section Cash Flows from Financing Activities reports the cash generated by issuing long-term debt and capital stock. This section also reports the cash used to repay long-term debt and pay dividends.

The net change in cash, reported at the end of the statement, is an important measure of the financial strength of the company. A company must have an adequate supply of cash to finance its daily operations and long-term expansions.

Required: (1) Obtain the Statement of Cash Flows for a corporation. Identify the major sections of the statement. Did the corporation have an increase in cash from operations? What did the corporation do with this increase in cash? (2) Explain how a corporation could have net income yet have a decrease in cash. Does this situation indicate a positive or negative sign of financial strength?

684   CHAPTER 26   Financial Statements and End-of-Fiscal-Period Entries for a Corporation

26-1 APPLICATION PROBLEM
Preparing an income statement for a corporation

Use the work sheet provided in the *Working Papers* to complete this problem.

Instructions:

1. Prepare an income statement for Donovan Lumber Corporation for the fiscal year ending December 31 of the current year.
2. Calculate and record the following component percentages: (a) cost of merchandise sold; (b) gross profit on operations; (c) total operating expenses; (d) income from operations; (e) net addition or deduction resulting from other revenue and expenses; and (f) net income before federal income tax. Round percentage calculations to the nearest 0.1%.
3. Analyze the corporation's income statement by determining if component percentages are within acceptable levels. If any component percentage is not within an acceptable level, suggest steps that the company should take. The corporation considers the following component percentages acceptable. Save your work to complete Application Problem 26-2.

Cost of merchandise sold	Not more than 70.0%
Gross profit on operations	Not less than 30.0%
Total operating expenses	Not more than 25.0%
Income from operations	Not less than 5.0%
Net deduction from other revenue and expenses	Not more than 0.1%
Net income before federal income tax	Not less than 4.9%

26-2 APPLICATION PROBLEM
Preparing a statement of stockholders' equity for a corporation

Use the work sheet and income statement from Application Problem 26-1 to complete this problem.

Instructions:

Prepare a statement of stockholders' equity for Donovan Lumber Corporation for the fiscal year ended on December 31 of the current year. Use the following additional information. Save your work to complete Application Problem 26-3.

January 1 balance of capital stock account	$40,000.00
(8,000 shares issued for $5.00 per share)	
Shares issued during the year	2,000 shares

26-3 APPLICATION PROBLEM
Preparing and analyzing a balance sheet for a corporation

Use the work sheet and financial statements from Application Problem 26-2 to complete this problem.

Instructions:

1. Prepare a balance sheet for Donovan Lumber Corporation as of December 31 of the current year.
2. Calculate the corporation's (a) working capital and (b) current ratio. Determine if these items are within acceptable levels. The corporation considers the following levels acceptable. Save your work to complete Application Problem 26-4.

Working capital	Not less than $100,000.00
Current ratio	Between 3.0 to 1 and 3.5 to 1

TEACHING STRATEGIES   DIFFERENT LEARNING ABILITIES

Limited English Proficiency (LEP) Students. In some cultures, "Yes" is the response to every question. It may mean "I heard your question" rather than "I understand."

✔ **Application Problem 26-4**
Adjusting entry: debit Federal Income Tax Expense and credit Federal Income Tax Payable, 1,278.49

✔ **Mastery Problem 26-5**
Net Income before Federal Income Tax, 18.6%

Net increase in Retained Earnings, 144,886.67

Current ratio, 4.60 to 1

SOFTWARE
FOCUS

Reinforcement Activity 3 and/or Putting Green Golf Supply: A Business Simulation may be automated using Automated Accounting 7.0 or higher.

SIMULATION

To give students an opportunity to apply accounting concepts from the third accounting cycle, assign students Putting Green Golf Supply: A Business Simulation to demonstrate their understanding of the complete accounting cycle.

MILESTONE

Chapters 18 through 26 of the textbook complete an accounting cycle for a merchandising business organized as a corporation. Mastery of these chapters is the foundation for studying a second year of accounting. Courses that follow this one will expand upon this foundation with concepts of increasing complexity.

26-4

APPLICATION PROBLEM
Journalizing adjusting, closing, and reversing entries for a corporation

Use the work sheet and financial statements from Application Problem 26-3 to complete this problem.

Instructions:

1. For the current year, journalize the adjusting entries using page 15 of a general journal.
2. For the current year, journalize the closing entries using page 16 of a general journal.
3. For the following year, journalize the reversing entries using page 17 of a general journal.

26-5

MASTERY PROBLEM
Preparing financial statements and end-of-fiscal-period entries for a corporation

Use the work sheet provided in the *Working Papers* for Pennington Corporation to prepare the financial statements and end-of-fiscal-period entries for the corporation for the current year.

Instructions:

1. Prepare an income statement. Calculate and record the following component percentages: (a) cost of merchandise sold; (b) gross profit on operations; (c) total operating expenses; (d) income from operations; (e) net addition or deduction resulting from other revenue and expenses; and (f) net income before federal income tax. Round percentage calculations to the nearest 0.1%.
2. Analyze the corporation's income statement by determining if component percentages are within acceptable levels. If any component percentage is not within an acceptable level, suggest steps that the company should take. The corporation considers the following component percentages acceptable.

Cost of merchandise sold	Not more than 65.0%
Gross profit on operations	Not less than 35.0%
Total operating expenses	Not more than 16.0%
Income from operations	Not less than 19.0%
Net deduction from other revenue and expenses	Not more than 0.5%
Net income before federal income tax	Not less than 18.5%

3. Prepare a statement of stockholders' equity. Use the following additional information.

January 1 balance of capital stock account	$100,000.00
(100,000 shares issued for $1.00 per share)	
Shares issued during the year	None

4. Prepare a balance sheet.
5. Calculate the corporation's (a) working capital and (b) current ratio. Determine if these items are within acceptable levels. The corporation considers the following levels acceptable.

Working capital	Not less than $150,000.00
Current ratio	Between 3.0 to 1 and 4.0 to 1

6. Journalize the adjusting entries using page 15 of a general journal.
7. Journalize the closing entries using page 16 of a general journal.
8. Journalize the reversing entries using page 17 of a general journal.

WRITING ACROSS THE CURRICULUM

Writing Paragraphs and Short Essays. The Cases for Critical Thinking are short, practical applications of the accounting principles developed in the chapter. Some cases are planned to present problems related to the chapter but not specifically discussed and answered in the chapter. These cases present an opportunity for critical thinking and decision making. These cases also require more than a short, objective-type response. Therefore, they provide ideal practice in writing paragraphs and short essays.

Instructions:

1. Obtain the financial statements of two corporations from two different industries. Calculate the amount of working capital and the current ratio of each corporation. Discuss the usefulness of each measure of financial strength between the companies in each industry and among the different industries.

2. The current ratio is often considered to be acceptable within a specified range. Investigate why a current ratio being too high might be undesirable.

INTERNET ACTIVITY

Point your browser to
http://accounting.swpco.com
Choose **First-Year Course**, choose **Activities**, and complete the activity for Chapter 26.

Applied Communication

Congratulations on completing your study of accounting in this textbook. You have learned a wide variety of facts and concepts about accounting and the business world. Regardless of your future educational and career goals, this knowledge will provide you with a sound foundation to become a productive member of society.

Instructions: Prepare an essay to discuss how your knowledge of accounting will be useful to you in the future. How will accounting help you to complete your education, obtain a job, start a business, make personal investment decisions, and be successful in other facets of your life?

Cases for Critical Thinking

Case 1 The president of Wilson Company asked the accounting department to provide as much information as possible to help management improve the company's net income. Peter Lance, a new accountant, suggests that an income statement showing all the revenue and expense amounts should provide all the information management needs to analyze the company's results of operations. Do you agree with the accountant's suggestion? If not, what additional information do you recommend? Explain your answer.

Case 2 LMP Company recently organized as a corporation with five stockholders. Tammy Kellogg, a CPA, is developing the accounting system. She suggested that although there are five stockholders, only one equity account be used. The account would be titled Corporation Capital. The president of Riverside questions the accountant's recommendation. Is this recommendation acceptable? If not, how should capital be recorded and reported? Explain your answer.

✔ **Challenge Problem 26-6**
Solutions will vary.

INTERNET ACTIVITY

Because Internet sites can change frequently, the requirements of the Internet Activity are posted on a South-Western site where they can be updated as needed. Direct students to follow the directions given on their student page.

APPLIED COMMUNICATION

Students' answers to this activity will differ, depending on the student's future employment and educational goals. Students seeking employment or additional education in accounting might focus on accounting procedures. Students seeking employment or additional education in non-business fields might be more general in their responses, focusing on the purpose of accounting information.

CASES FOR CRITICAL THINKING

CASE 1 Do not agree with the accountant. The income statement does report each of the revenue and expense amounts and net income for the current accounting period. However, if component percentages are added for each amount, better relative comparisons can be made of each expense as a percentage of net sales. These percentages can be compared with the company's previous accounting periods as well as industry standard percentages. This additional information will help management identify expense items that are higher than they should be, compared with industry standards. This information will also help identify undesirable trends earlier by comparing component percentages for each expense item with percentages for previous periods.

CASE 2 The CPA is correct. Since a corporation has the legal rights of one individual, separate capital accounts are not kept for each owner (stockholders). However, corporations normally are required to keep separate accounts for stock issued (capital contributed by the stockholders) and for earnings kept in the business. This permits any interested person reading the balance sheet to determine how much equity was contributed by the stockholders and how much was earned. Riverside Company should have at least two equity accounts: Capital Stock and Retained Earnings.

PORTFOLIO ASSESSMENT

Students should emphasize their learning of these topics by selecting an example of a comprehensive sample of their work in this chapter, either the mastery problem or a problem from a test, to include in their portfolio. A copy of the Portfolio Assessment form (blackline master in the Teacher's Resource Guide) should be completed by the student, and the Description lesson should include any comments regarding how the student mastered these concepts and proce-

dures. Alternatively, students might include in their portfolios printed reports from an Automated Accounting or Spreadsheet Accounting problem.

If you assign Reinforcement Activity 3, Parts A and B, or Putting Green Golf Supply: A Business Simulation advise students that their work on this activity may also be included in their portfolio.

Recording adjusting entries

❑ Explain that in an automated accounting system, adjusting entries are planned using a trial balance. A work sheet is not prepared.

❑ Demonstrate how adjusting entries are entered and posted using the General Journal tab within the Journal Entries window.

❑ Explain that Adj.Ent. is used as the reference for adjusting entries since there is no source document.

Generating financial statements

❑ Demonstrate that a financial statement can be generated in one of three ways:
(1) click the Reports toolbar button,
(2) click the Reports menu and choose the Reports Selection menu item, or
(3) use Ctrl+R.

❑ Demonstrate selecting the Financial Statements option button from the Select a Report Group list.

❑ Demonstrate choosing the income statement from the Choose a Report to Display list and clicking OK.

❑ Demonstrate that other financial statements can be displayed by choosing other option buttons in the Choose a Report to Display list.

❑ Explain that displayed financial statements should be checked for accuracy before printing.

❑ Explain that if errors are found on financial statements, corrections to journal entries should be made before financial statements are printed.

AUTOMATED ACCOUNTING

END-OF-FISCAL-PERIOD WORK FOR A CORPORATION

During the fiscal period, numerous transactions are analyzed, journalized, and posted. When a transaction affects more than one accounting period, an adjusting entry may be needed to match revenues and expenses with the appropriate accounting period. To complete the accounting cycle, adjusting entries are recorded in the computer and verified for accuracy. The financial statements are generated, and then closing entries are generated and posted by the software.

Adjusting Entries

Adjusting entries are planned and recorded in the computerized accounting system. The general journal is used to record the adjusting entries. All adjusting entries are recorded on the last day of the accounting period. The entries are referenced by Adj. Ent. in the Refer. text box. Adjusting entries:

• Transfer to expenses the amounts of assets consumed (for example, office supplies and prepaid insurance).
• Update the merchandise inventory account.
• Recognize accrued revenues and accrued expenses.

Financial Statements for a Corporation

The reports that summarize information from the ledgers are known as financial statements. The most common financial statements for a business organized as a corporation are the balance sheet and the income statement.

To display financial statements:

1. Click the Reports toolbar button, or choose the Reports Selection menu item from the Reports menu.
2. When the Report Selection dialog appears, choose the Financial Statements option button from the Select a Report Group list.
3. Choose the financial statement report you would like to display from the Choose a Report to Display list.
4. Click the OK button.

The up-to-date account balances stored by the software are used to calculate and display the current financial statements.

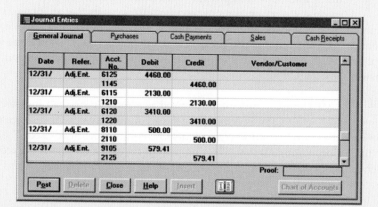

AUTOMATED ACCOUNTING

Closing Entries for a Corporation

In an automated accounting system, closing entries are generated and posted by the software. The software automatically closes net income to the retained earnings account after closing the revenue and expense accounts. The dividend account is closed as well.

1. Choose Generate Closing Journal Entries from the Options menu.
2. Click Yes to generate the closing entries.
3. The general journal will appear, containing the journal entries.
4. Click the Post button.

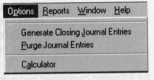

| Options | Reports | Window | Help |

Generate Closing Journal Entries
Purge Journal Entries
Calculator

AUTOMATING APPLICATION PROBLEM 26-1: Preparing an income statement for a corporation

Instructions:

1. Load *Automated Accounting* 7.0 or higher software.
2. Select database F26-1 from the appropriate directory/folder.
3. Select File from the menu bar and choose the Save As menu command. Key the path to the drive and directory that contains your data files. Save the database with a file name of XXX261 (where XXX are your initials).
4. Access Problem Instructions through the Help menu. Read the Problem Instructions screen.
5. Refer to page 685 for data used in this template.
6. Exit the *Automated Accounting* software.

AUTOMATING MASTERY PROBLEM 26-5: Preparing financial statements and end-of-fiscal-period entries for a corporation

Instructions:

1. Load *Automated Accounting* 7.0 or higher software.
2. Select database F26-2 from the appropriate directory/folder.
3. Select File from the menu bar and choose the Save As menu command. Key the path to the drive and directory that contains your data files. Save the database with a file name of XXX262 (where XXX are your initials).
4. Access Problem Instructions through the Help menu. Read the Problem Instructions screen.
5. Refer to page 686 for data used in this template.
6. Exit the *Automated Accounting* software.

Closing Entries

Acct. #	Account Title	Debit	Credit
4105	Sales	970998.47	
5110	Purchases Discount	4917.24	
5115	Purchases Ret. and Allow.	2444.52	
7105	Gain on Plant Assets	99.00	
7110	Interest Income	805.00	
3120	Income Summary		979264.23
3120	Income Summary	913218.66	
4110	Sales Discount		1802.52
4115	Sales Ret. and Allowances		7512.48
5105	Purchases		663734.50
6105	Advertising Expense		14353.20

| Post | Cancel | Help |

PORTFOLIO ASSESSMENT

Students should be encouraged to print at least one report from one of the *Automated Accounting* problems to include in their portfolio to demonstrate mastery of automated accounting systems. A copy of the Portfolio Assessment form (blackline master in the Teacher's Resource Guide) should be completed by the student, and the Description section should include any comments regarding how the student mastered these concepts and procedures.

KINDS OF COMPUTER KEYBOARDS

The computer has a keypad on the right side of the keyboard called the *numeric keypad*. Even though several styles of keyboards for the IBM® and compatible computers are found, there are two basic layouts for the numeric keypad. The standard layout and enhanced layout are shown in the illustration. On the standard keyboard the directional arrow keys are found on the number keys. To use the numbers, press the key called *Num Lock*. (This key is found above the "7" key.) When the *Num Lock* is turned on, numbers are entered when the keys on the keypad are pressed. When the Num Lock is off, the arrow, Home, Page Up, Page Down, End, Insert, and Delete keys can be used.

The enhanced keyboards have the arrow keys and the other directional keys mentioned above to the left of the numeric keypad. When using the keypad on an enhanced keyboard, Num Lock can remain on.

The asterisk (*) performs a different function on the computer than the calculator. The asterisk on the calculator is used for the total while the computer uses it for multiplication.

Another difference is the division key. The computer key is the forward slash key (/). The calculator key uses the division key (÷).

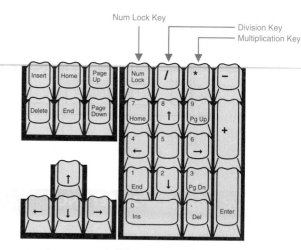

Standard
Keyboard Layout

Enhanced
Keyboard Layout

TEN-KEY TOUCH SYSTEM

Striking the numbers 0 to 9 on a calculator or numeric keypad without looking at the keyboard is called the *touch system*. Using the touch system develops both speed and accuracy.

The 4, 5, and 6 keys are called the *home row*. If the right hand is used for the keyboard, the index finger is placed on the 4 key, the middle finger on the 5 key, and the ring finger on the 6 key. If the left hand is used, the ring finger is placed on the 4 key, the middle finger on the 5 key, and the index finger on the 6 key.

Place the fingers on the home row keys. Curve the fingers and keep the wrist straight. These keys may feel slightly concaved or the 5 key may have a raised dot. The differences in the home row allow the operator to recognize the home row by touch rather than by sight.

Maintain the position of the fingers on the home row. The finger used to strike the 4 key will also strike the 7 key and the 1 key. Stretch the finger up to reach the 7; then stretch the finger down to reach the 1 key. Visualize the position of these keys.

Again, place the fingers on the home row. Stretch the finger that strikes the 5 key up to reach the 8 key, then down to reach the 2 key. Likewise, stretch the finger that strikes the 6 key up to strike the 9 and down to strike the 3 key. This same finger will stretch down again to hit the decimal point.

If the right hand is used, the thumb will be used to strike the 0 and 00 keys and the little finger to strike the addition key. If the left hand is used, the little finger will be used to strike the 0 and 00 keys and the thumb to strike the addition key.

HAND-HELD CALCULATORS

Hand-held calculators are slightly different from desktop calculators, not only in their size and features but also in their operation. Refer to the operator's manual for specific instructions for the calculator being used.

On a hand-held calculator, the numeric keys are usually very close together. In addition, the keys do not respond to touch as easily as on a desktop calculator. Therefore, the touch system is usually not used on a hand-held calculator.

PERFORMING MATHEMATICAL OPERATIONS ON DESKTOP CALCULATORS

Mathematical operations can be performed on a calculator both quickly and efficiently. The basic operations of addition, subtraction, multiplication, and division are used frequently on a calculator.

Addition

Each number to be added is called an *addend*. The answer to an addition problem is called the *sum.*

Addition is performed by entering an addend and striking the addition key (+). All numbers are entered on a calculator in the exact order they are given. To enter the number 4,455.65, strike the 4, 4, 5, 5, decimal, 6, and 5 keys in that order, and then strike the addition key. Commas are not entered. Continue in this manner until all addends have been entered. To obtain the sum, strike the total key on the calculator.

Subtraction

The top number or first number of a subtraction problem is called the *minuend*. The number to be subtracted from the minuend is called the *subtrahend*. The answer to a subtraction problem is called the *difference*.

Subtraction is performed by first entering the minuend and striking the addition key (+). The subtrahend is then entered, followed by the minus key (−), followed by the total key.

Multiplication

The number to be multiplied is called the *multiplicand*. The number of times the multiplicand will be multiplied is called the *multiplier*. The answer to a multiplication problem is called the *product*.

Multiplication is performed by entering

the multiplicand and striking the multiplication key ($\times$). The multiplier is then entered, followed by the equals key ($=$). The calculator will automatically multiply and give the product.

Division

The number to be divided is called the *dividend*. The number the dividend will be divided by is called the *divisor*. The answer to a division problem is called the *quotient*.

Division is performed by entering the dividend and striking the division key ($\div$). The divisor is then entered, followed by the equals key ($=$). The calculator will automatically divide and give the quotient.

Correcting Errors

If an error is made while using a calculator, several methods of correction may be used. If an incorrect number has been entered and the addition key or equals key has not yet been struck, strike the clear entry (CE) key one time. This key will clear only the last number that was entered. However, if the clear entry key is depressed more than one time, the entire problem will be cleared on some calculators. If an incorrect number has been entered and the addition key has been struck, strike the minus key one time only. This will automatically subtract the last number added, thus removing it from the total.

HAND-HELD CALCULATORS PERFORMING MATHEMATICAL OPERATIONS ON COMPUTERS

On a computer keypad or a hand-held calculator, addition is performed in much the same way as on a desktop calculator. However, after the + key is depressed, the display usually shows the accumulated total. Therefore, the total key is not found. Some computer programs will not calculate the total until Enter is pressed.

Subtraction is performed differently on many computer keypads and hand-held calculators. The minuend is usually entered, followed by the minus ($-$) key. Then the subtrahend is entered. Pressing either the + key or the = key will display the difference. Some computer programs will not calculate the difference until Enter is pressed.

Multiplication and division are performed the same way on a computer keypad and hand-held calculator as on a desktop calculator. Keep in mind that computers use the * for multiplication and / for division.

SAFETY CONCERNS

Whenever electrical equipment such as a calculator or computer is being operated in a classroom or office, several safety rules apply. These rules protect the operator of the equipment, other persons in the environment, and the equipment itself.

1. Do not unplug equipment by pulling on the electrical cord. Instead, grasp the plug at the outlet and remove it.

2. Do not stretch electrical cords across an aisle where someone might trip over them.

3. Avoid food and beverages near the equipment where a spill might result in an electrical short.

4. Do not attempt to remove the cover of a calculator, computer, or keyboard for any reason while the power is turned on.

5. Do not attempt to repair equipment while it is plugged in.

6. Always turn the power off or unplug equipment when finished using it.

Instructions for Desktop Calculators

Complete each drill using the touch method. Set the decimal selector at the setting indicated in each drill. Compare the answer on the calculator to the answer in the book. If the two are the same, progress to the next problem. It is not necessary to enter 00 in the cents column if the decimal selector is set at 0-F. However, digits other than zeros in the cents column must be entered preceded by a decimal point.

Instructions for Computer Keypads

Complete each drill using the touch method. There is no decimal selector on computer keypads. Set the number of decimal places as directed in the instructions for the computer program. In spreadsheets, for example, use the formatting options to set the number of decimal places. When the drill indicates "F" for floating, leave the computer application in its default format. Compare the answer on the computer monitor to the answer in the book. If the two are the same, progress to the next problem. It is not necessary to enter 00 in the cents column. However, digits other than zeros in the cents column must be entered preceded by a decimal point.

DRILL D-1 Performing addition using the home row keys
Decimal Selector—2

4.00	44.00	444.00	4,444.00	44,444.00
5.00	55.00	555.00	5,555.00	55,555.00
6.00	66.00	666.00	6,666.00	66,666.00
5.00	45.00	455.00	4,455.00	44,556.00
4.00	46.00	466.00	4,466.00	44,565.00
5.00	54.00	544.00	5,544.00	55,446.00
6.00	56.00	566.00	5,566.00	55,664.00
5.00	65.00	655.00	6,655.00	66,554.00
4.00	64.00	644.00	6,644.00	66,555.00
5.00	66.00	654.00	6,545.00	65,465.00
49.00	561.00	5,649.00	56,540.00	565,470.00

DRILL D-2 Performing addition using the 0, 1, 4, and 7 keys
Decimal Selector—2

4.00	11.00	444.00	4,440.00	44,000.00
7.00	44.00	777.00	7,770.00	77,000.00
4.00	74.00	111.00	1,110.00	11,000.00
1.00	71.00	741.00	4,400.00	41,000.00
4.00	70.00	740.00	1,100.00	71,000.00
7.00	10.00	101.00	4,007.00	10,000.00
4.00	14.00	140.00	7,001.00	10,100.00
1.00	17.00	701.00	1,007.00	40,100.00
4.00	40.00	700.00	1,004.00	70,100.00
7.00	77.00	407.00	7,700.00	74,100.00
43.00	428.00	4,862.00	39,539.00	448,400.00

RECYCLING PROBLEM 1-1

Determining how transactions change an accounting equation and preparing a balance sheet

Alston Eubanks is starting Reef Divers, a scuba diving service. Reef Divers uses the accounts shown in the following accounting equation. Use the form given in the *Recycling Problem Working Papers* to complete this problem.

| Trans. No. | Assets | | | = Liabilities | + Owner's Equity |
	Cash +	Supplies +	Prepaid Insurance =	Accts. Pay.— Divers Supply	+ Alston Eubanks, Capital
New Bal. 1.	0 +1,700	0	0	0	0 +1,700
New Bal. 2.	1,700	0	0	0	1,700

Transactions:

1. Received cash from owner as an investment, $1,700.00.
2. Bought supplies on account from Divers Supply, $800.00.
3. Paid cash for insurance, $175.00.
4. Paid cash for supplies, $230.00.
5. Received cash from owner as an investment, $400.00.
6. Paid cash on account to Divers Supply, $500.00.

Instructions:

1. For each transaction, complete the following. Transaction 1 is given as an example.
   a. Analyze the transaction to determine which accounts in the accounting equation are affected.
   b. Write the amount in the appropriate columns, using a plus (+) if the account increases or a minus (−) if the account decreases.
   c. Calculate the new balance for each account in the accounting equation.
   d. Before going on to the next transaction, determine that the accounting equation is still in balance.
2. Using the final balances in the accounting equation, prepare a balance sheet for Reef Divers. Use November 30 of the current year as the date of the balance sheet.

Check Figures: Final New Balances: 1,195; 1,030; 175; 300; 2,100

RECYCLING PROBLEM 2-1

Determining how transactions change an accounting equation and preparing a balance sheet

Alston Eubanks operates a scuba diving business called Reef Divers. Reef Divers uses the accounts shown in the following accounting equation. Use the form given in the *Recycling Problem Working Papers* to complete this problem.

Trans. No.	Cash	+	Accts. Rec.— Club Scuba	+ Supplies +	Prepaid Insurance	=	Accts. Pay.— Divers Supply	+	Alston Eubanks, Capital
			Assets			=	Liabilities	+	Owner's Equity
Beg. Bal.	1,195		—0—	1,030	175		300		2,100
1.	−150								−150 (expense)
New Bal.	1,045		—0—	1,030	175		300		1,950
2.									

Transactions:

1. Paid cash for telephone bill, $150.00.
2. Received cash from owner as an investment, $200.00.
3. Paid cash for rent, $400.00.
4. Received cash from sales, $550.00.
5. Bought supplies on account from Divers Supply, $220.00.
6. Sold services on account to Club Scuba, $300.00.
7. Paid cash for supplies, $300.00.
8. Paid cash for advertising, $550.00.
9. Received cash on account from Club Scuba, $200.00.
10. Paid cash on account to Divers Supply, $300.00.
11. Paid cash for insurance, $175.00.
12. Received cash from sales, $1,900.00.
13. Paid cash to owner for personal use, $1,000.00.

Instructions:

1. For each transaction, complete the following. Transaction 1 is given as an example.
   a. Analyze the transaction to determine which accounts in the accounting equation are affected.
   b. Write the amount in the appropriate columns, using a plus (+) if the account increases or a minus (−) if the account decreases.
   c. For transactions that change owner's equity, write in parentheses a description of the transaction to the right of the amount.
   d. Calculate the new balance for each account in the accounting equation.
   e. Before going on to the next transaction, determine that the accounting equation is still in balance.
2. Using the final balances in the accounting equation, prepare a balance sheet for Reef Divers. Use the date December 31 of the current year.

Check Figures: Final
New Balances: 1,170; 100;
1,550; 350; 220; 2,950

RECYCLING PROBLEM 3-1

Analyzing transactions into debit and credit parts

Harrison Ennis owns a business called Cayman Copies. Cayman Copies uses the following accounts:

Cash

Accounts Receivable—Coral Supply Company

Accounts Receivable—Coconut Inn

Supplies

Prepaid Insurance

Accounts Payable—Palms Paper

Accounts Payable—Pappagallo Company

Harrison Ennis, Capital

Harrison Ennis, Drawing

Sales

Advertising Expense

Miscellaneous Expense

Rent Expense

Repair Expense

Utilities Expense

Instructions:

Use the forms given in the *Recycling Problem Working Papers.*

1. Prepare a T account for each account.
2. Analyze each transaction into its debit and credit parts. Write the debit and credit amounts in the proper T accounts to show how each transaction changes account balances. Write the date of the transaction in parentheses before each amount.

Transactions:

July   1. Received cash from owner as an investment, $6,000.00.

       2. Paid cash for supplies, $120.00.

       4. Paid cash for rent, $400.00.

       4. Received cash from sales, $700.00.

       5. Paid cash for repairs, $20.00.

       8. Sold services on account to Coral Supply Co., $400.00.

       9. Bought supplies on account from Pappagallo Co., $1,000.00.

     10. Paid cash for insurance, $200.00.

     11. Received cash from owner as an investment, $1,800.00.

     11. Received cash from sales, $600.00.

     12. Bought supplies on account from Palms Paper, $100.00.

     13. Received cash on account from Coral Supply Co., $250.00.

     15. Paid cash for miscellaneous expense, $10.00.

     16. Paid cash on account to Pappagallo Co., $100.00.

     22. Paid cash for electric bill (utilities expense), $70.00.

     23. Paid cash for advertising, $60.00.

     25. Sold services on account to Coconut Inn, $440.00.

     26. Paid cash to owner for personal use, $1,200.00.

     30. Received cash on account from Coconut Inn, $200.00.

Check Figures: Cash
account has 6 debits and 9 credits

RECYCLING PROBLEM 4-1

Journalizing transactions

Merilda Bodden owns a service business called Bodden Express, which uses the following accounts:

Cash	Accts. Pay.—Bahling Supplies	Sales	Repair Expense
Supplies	Accts. Pay.—Kirk Company	Advertising Expense	Utilities Expense
Prepaid Insurance	Merilda Bodden, Capital	Miscellaneous Expense	
Accts. Rec.—Leta Scott	Merilda Bodden, Drawing	Rent Expense	

Transactions: Aug. 1. Received cash from owner as an investment, $8,750.00. R1.
2. Paid cash for rent, $200.00. C1.
3. Paid cash for supplies, $600.00. C2.
4. Bought supplies on account from Bahling Supplies, $1,000.00. M1.
5. Paid cash for insurance, $2,250.00. C3.
8. Paid cash on acount to Bahling Supplies, $750.00. C4.
8. Received cash from sales, $375.00. T8.
8. Sold services on account to Leta Scott, $100.00. S1.
9. Paid cash for electric bill, $30.00. C5.
10. Paid cash for miscellaneous expense, $9.00. C6.
10. Received cash from sales, $375.00. T10.
11. Paid cash for repairs, $50.00. C7.
11. Received cash from sales, $425.00. T11.
12. Received cash from sales, $350.00. T12.
15. Paid cash to owner for personal use, $175.00. C8.
15. Received cash from sales, $375.00. T15.
16. Paid cash for supplies, $750.00. C9.
17. Received cash on account from Leta Scott, $100.00. R2.
17. Bought supplies on account from Kirk Company, $375.00. M2.
17. Received cash from sales, $300.00. T17.
18. Received cash from sales, $400.00. T18.
19. Received cash from sales, $375.00. T19.
22. Bought supplies on account from Kirk Company, $40.00. M3.
22. Received cash from sales, $350.00. T22.
23. Paid cash for advertising, $65.00. C10.
23. Sold services on account to Leta Scott, $325.00. S2.
24. Paid cash for telephone bill, $30.00. C11.
24. Received cash from sales, $300.00. T24.
25. Received cash from sales, $275.00. T25.
26. Paid cash for supplies, $35.00. C12.
26. Received cash from sales, $300.00. T26.
29. Received cash on account from Leta Scott, $325.00. R3.
30. Paid cash to owner for personal use, $160.00. C13.
30. Received cash from sales, $400.00. T30.

Instructions:
1. Use page 1 of the journal given in the *Recycling Problem Working Papers*. Journalize the transactions for August 1 through August 16 of the current year. Source documents are abbreviated as follows: check, C; memorandum, M; receipt, R; sales invoice, S; calculator tape, T.
2. Use page 2 of the journal to journalize the transactions for the remainder of August.

Check Figures: Cash
debited 16 times; Cash credited 13 times

RECYCLING PROBLEM 5-1

Journalizing transactions and posting to a general ledger

Janet Porter owns a service business called Porter's Parties. Porter's Parties' general ledger accounts are given in the *Recycling Problem Working Papers*.

Transactions:

Aug. 1. Received cash from owner as an investment, $8,500.00. R1.
  3. Paid cash for rent, $500.00. C1.
  5. Sold services on account to Nicholas Calendo, $250.00. S1.
  6. Received cash from sales, $830.00. T6.
  9. Paid cash for miscellaneous expense, $15.00. C2.
  11. Paid cash for supplies, $230.00. C3.
  13. Bought supplies on account from Jordan Supplies, $700.00. M1.
  13. Received cash from sales, $650.00. T13.
  16. Paid cash for electric bill, $95.00. C4.
  18. Paid cash on account to Jordan Supplies, $400.00. C5.
  20. Paid cash for advertising, $55.00. C6.
  20. Received cash on account from Nicholas Calendo, $150.00. R2.
  25. Paid cash for supplies, $50.00. C7.
  27. Paid cash for supplies, $75.00. C8.
  27. Received cash from sales, $1,200.00. T27.
  30. Paid cash to owner for personal use, $450.00. C9.
  30. Received cash from sales, $780.00. T30.

Instructions:

1. Open an account for Utilities Expense. Use the 3-digit numbering system described in the chapter.
2. Journalize the transactions completed during August of the current year. Use page 1 of a general journal. Source documents are abbreviated as follows: check, C; memorandum, M; receipt, R; sales invoice, S; calculator tape, T.
3. Post from the general journal to the general ledger.
4. Prove cash. The balance on the next unused check stub is $10,240.00.

Check Figures:
Cash debited 6 times;
Cash credited 9 times

RECYCLING PROBLEM 6-1

Reconciling a bank statement; journalizing a bank service charge, a dishonored check, and petty cash transactions

Emil Ibraham owns a business called Fast Print. Selected general ledger accounts are given below. Forms are given in the *Recycling Problem Working Papers*.

110 Cash	140 Prepaid Insurance	535 Repair Expense
115 Petty Cash	320 Emil Ibraham, Drawing	540 Supplies Expense
120 Accts. Rec.—Angus Restaurant	520 Miscellaneous Expense	550 Utilities Expense
130 Supplies	530 Rent Expense	

Instructions:

1. Journalize the following transactions completed during May of the current year. Use page 12 of a journal. Source documents are abbreviated as follows: check, C; memorandum, M.

Transactions:

May 21. Paid cash to establish a petty cash fund, $100.00. C61.

24. Paid cash for repairs, $115.00. C62.

26. Paid cash for supplies, $20.00. C63.

27. Received notice from the bank of a dishonored check from Angus Restaurant, $45.00, plus $20.00 fee; total, $65.00. M22.

28. Paid cash for miscellaneous expense, $24.00. C64.

31. Paid cash to owner for personal use, $200.00. C65.

31. Paid cash to replenish the petty cash fund, $65.00: supplies, $55.00; miscellaneous expense, $10.00. C66.

2. On May 31 of the current year, Fast Print received a bank statement dated May 30. Prepare a bank statement reconciliation. Use May 31 of the current year as the date. The following information is obtained from the May 30 bank statement and from the records of the business.

Bank statement balance	$1,486.00
Bank service charge	25.00
Outstanding deposit, May 31	340.00
Outstanding checks, Nos. 65 and 66	
Checkbook balance on Check Stub No. 67	$1,586.00

3. Continue using the journal and journalize the following transaction.

Transaction:

May 31. Received bank statement showing May bank service charge, $25.00. M23.

RECYCLING PROBLEM 7-1

Completing a work sheet

On February 28 of the current year, Chisholm Hair Care has the following general ledger accounts and balances. The business uses a monthly fiscal period.

	Account Balances	
Account Titles	**Debit**	**Credit**
Cash	$1,609.00	
Petty Cash	300.00	
Accounts Receivable—Margo Angelo	581.00	
Supplies	795.00	
Prepaid Insurance	1,100.00	
Accounts Payable—Virginia Supplies		$ 450.00
Montana Freemantle, Capital		3,550.00
Montana Freemantle, Drawing	300.00	
Income Summary		
Sales		3,000.00
Advertising Expense	525.00	
Insurance Expense		
Miscellaneous Expense	250.00	
Rent Expense	1,100.00	
Supplies Expense		
Utilities Expense	440.00	

Instructions:

1. Prepare the heading and trial balance on the work sheet given in the *Recycling Problem Working Papers*. Total and rule the Trial Balance columns.
2. Analyze the following adjustment information into debit and credit parts. Record the adjustments on the work sheet.

Adjustment Information, February 28	
Supplies inventory	$ 250.00
Value of prepaid insurance	1,000.00

3. Total and rule the Adjustments columns.
4. Extend the up-to-date balances to the Balance Sheet or Income Statement columns.
5. Rule a single line across the Income Statement and Balance Sheet columns. Total each column. Calculate and record the net income or net loss. Label the amount in the Account Title column.
6. Total and rule the Income Statement and Balance Sheet columns.

Check Figures: Net Income, 40.00

RECYCLING PROBLEM 8-1

Preparing financial statements

The following information is obtained from the work sheet of Robbie's Rugcare for the month ended August 31 of the current year. Forms are given in the *Recycling Problem Working Papers*.

	ACCOUNT TITLE	INCOME STATEMENT DEBIT	INCOME STATEMENT CREDIT	BALANCE SHEET DEBIT	BALANCE SHEET CREDIT	
1	Cash			8 7 5 2 00		1
2	Accounts Receivable—Crystal Thompson			2 0 0 00		2
3	Accounts Receivable—Robert Boje			1 7 5 00		3
4	Supplies			4 0 0 00		4
5	Prepaid Insurance			2 2 0 00		5
6	Accounts Payable—Daniel Supplies				4 4 2 00	6
7	Accounts Payable—Irene's Irons				6 7 6 00	7
8	Roberta Greenstein, Capital				7 9 5 1 00	8
9	Roberta Greenstein, Drawing			1 8 0 0 00		9
10	Income Summary					10
11	Sales		5 7 0 7 00			11
12	Advertising Expense	9 0 0 00				12
13	Insurance Expense	2 0 00				13
14	Miscellaneous Expense	2 6 7 00				14
15	Supplies Expense	5 0 0 00				15
16	Utilities Expense	1 5 4 2 00				16
17		3 2 2 9 00	5 7 0 7 00	1 1 5 4 7 00	9 0 6 9 00	17
18	Net Income	2 4 7 8 00			2 4 7 8 00	18
19		5 7 0 7 00	5 7 0 7 00	1 1 5 4 7 00	1 1 5 4 7 00	19
20						20

Instructions:
1. Prepare an income statement for the month ended August 31 of the current year.
2. Calculate and record the component percentages for total expenses and net income. Round percentage calculations to the nearest 0.1%.
3. Prepare a balance sheet for August 31 of the current year.

Check Figures: Total
Liab. and Owner's Eq., 9,747.00

RECYCLING PROBLEM 9-1

Journalizing adjusting and closing entries

The following information is obtained from the work sheet of Robbie's Rugcare for the month ended August 31 of the current year.

	ACCOUNT TITLE	ADJUSTMENTS DEBIT	ADJUSTMENTS CREDIT	INCOME STATEMENT DEBIT	INCOME STATEMENT CREDIT	BALANCE SHEET DEBIT	BALANCE SHEET CREDIT	
1	Cash					8 7 5 2 00		1
2	Accts. Rec.—Crystal Thompson					2 0 0 00		2
3	Accts. Rec.—Robert Boje					1 7 5 00		3
4	Supplies		(a) 5 0 0 00			4 0 0 00		4
5	Prepaid Insurance		(b) 2 0 00			2 2 0 00		5
6	Accts. Pay.—Daniel Supplies						4 4 2 00	6
7	Accts. Pay.—Irene's Irons						6 7 6 00	7
8	Roberta Greenstein, Capital						7 9 5 1 00	8
9	Roberta Greenstein, Drawing					1 8 0 0 00		9
10	Income Summary							10
11	Sales				5 7 0 7 00			11
12	Advertising Expense			9 0 0 00				12
13	Insurance Expense	(b) 2 0 00		2 0 00				13
14	Miscellaneour Expense			2 6 7 00				14
15	Supplies Expense	(a) 5 0 0 00		5 0 0 00				15
16	Utilities Expense			1 5 4 2 00				16
17		5 2 0 00	5 2 0 00	3 2 2 9 00	5 7 0 7 00	1 1 5 4 7 00	9 0 6 9 00	17
18	Net Income			2 4 7 8 00			2 4 7 8 00	18
19				5 7 0 7 00	5 7 0 7 00	1 1 5 4 7 00	1 1 5 4 7 00	19
20								20

Instructions:
1. Use page 16 of the journal given in the *Recycling Problem Working Papers*. Journalize the adjusting entries.
2. Continue to use page 16 of the journal. Journalize the closing entries.

Check Figures: 2 adjusting entries; 4 closing entries

RECYCLING PROBLEM 10-1

Journalizing purchases, cash payments, and other transactions

Judy Daily and Donald Steele, partners, own a bookstore.

Instructions:
Journalize the following transactions completed during September of the current year. Journals are given in the *Recycling Problem Working Papers*. Use page 9 of a purchases journal, page 17 of a cash payments journal, and page 9 of a general journal. Source documents are abbreviated as follows: check, C; memorandum, M; purchase invoice, P.

Transactions:

Sept.
1. Paid cash for monthly rent, $800.00. C405.
2. Purchased merchandise for cash, $200.00. C406.
4. Purchased merchandise on account from Bookmaster, Inc., $900.00. P91.
5. Paid cash for office supplies, $75.00. C407.
7. Bought store supplies on account from Deluxe Display, $240.00. M53.
8. Paid cash on account to National Press, $600.00, covering P89. C408.
11. Purchased merchandise on account from Classic Books, $1,500.00. P92.
11. Paid cash for advertising, $75.00. C409.
12. Paid cash for electric bill, $160.00. C410.
13. Purchased merchandise for cash, $210.00. C411.
14. Bought office supplies on account from Office Source, $125.00. M54.
15. Paid cash for store supplies, $86.00. C412.
15. Judy Daily, partner, withdrew cash for personal use, $1,000.00 C413.
15. Donald Steele, partner, withdrew cash for personal use, $900.00. C414.
18. Paid cash on account to Audio Books, Inc., $475.00, covering P89. C415.
19. Paid cash on account to Bookmaster, Inc., $900.00, covering P91. C416.
21. Judy Daily, partner, withdrew merchandise for personal use, $120.00. M55.
22. Paid cash for advertising, $90.00. C417.
25. Paid cash to replenish the petty cash fund, $210.00: office supplies, $29.00; store supplies, $36.00; advertising, $90.00; miscellaneous, $55.00. C418.
25. Donald Steele, partner, withdrew merchandise for personal use, $100.00. M56.
26. Paid cash for telephone bill, $86.00. C419.
27. Paid cash on account to Deluxe Display, $240.00, covering M53. C420.
29. Purchased merchandise for cash, $220.00. C421.
30. Paid cash to replenish the petty cash fund, $42.30: office supplies, $5.80; store supplies, $7.50; advertising, $18.00; miscellaneous, $11.00. C422.

2. Total the amount columns of cash payments journal page 17. Prove the equality of debits and credits and rule the cash payments journal page 17 to carry the totals forward.
3. Record the totals brought forward from cash payments journal page 17 to line 1 of page 18 of the cash payments journal. Prove the equality of debits and credits again.
4. Journalize the following transactions:

Transactions:

Sept. 30. Judy Daily, partner, withdrew cash for personal use, $1,000.00. C423.
30. Donald Steele, partner, withdrew cash for personal use, $900.00. C424.

5. Total and rule page 9 of the purchases journal.
6. Total the amount columns of cash payments journal page 18. Prove the equality of debits and credits of cash payments journal page 18.
7. Rule page 18 of the cash payments journal.

Check Figures:
Purchases journal total: 2,400.00;
Cash payments journal page 17 totals:
4,154.30; 2,215.00; 6,369.30;
Cash payments journal page 18 totals:
6,054.30; 2,215.00; 8,269.30

RECYCLING PROBLEM 11-1

Journalizing sales and cash receipts transactions; proving and ruling journals

Olga Flores and James Lazarus, partners, own Outdoor Living, a hunting and fishing equipment store.

Sales journal page 17 and cash receipts journal page 18 for Outdoor Living are given in the *Recycling Problem Working Papers*. Balances brought forward are provided on line 1 of each journal.

Instructions:
1. Journalize the following transactions completed during the remainder of August of the current year in the appropriate journal. Sales tax rate is 6%. Source documents are abbreviated as follows: receipt, R; sales invoice, S; cash register tape, T.

Transactions:

Aug. 25. Received cash on account from Timothy Cole, $82.68, covering S69. R100.
25. Sold merchandise on account to Doretha Hunt, $160.00, plus sales tax, $9.60; total, $169.60. S74.
26. Received cash on account from Valerie Seeley, $110.24, covering S70. R101.
26. Recorded cash and credit card sales, $5,372.00, plus sales tax, $322.32; total, $5,694.32. T26.
29. Sold merchandise on account to Anthony Zolte, $230.00, plus sales tax, $13.80; total, $243.80. S75.
31. Recorded cash and credit card sales, $3,581.00, plus sales tax, $214.86; total, $3,795.86. T31.

2. Total and prove the equality of debits and credits for the sales journal.
3. Rule the sales journal.
4. Total and prove the equality of debits and credits for the cash receipts journal.
5. Prove cash. The August 1 cash account balance in the general ledger was $15,425.75. The August 31 cash credit total in the cash payments journal was $25,145.55. On August 31, the balance on the next unused check stub was $19,863.26.
6. Rule the cash receipts journal.

Check Figures: Sales journal totals: 3,830.31; 3,613.50; 216.81; Cash receipts journal totals: 3,009.92; 25,069.00; 1,504.14; 29,583.06

RECYCLING PROBLEM 16-1

Preparing financial statements

Mat's Antiques prepared the following work sheet for the year ended December 31 of the current year. Forms are given in the *Recycling Problem Working Papers*.

Mat's Antiques
Work Sheet
For Year Ended December 31, 20--

	ACCOUNT TITLE	TRIAL BALANCE DEBIT	TRIAL BALANCE CREDIT	ADJUSTMENTS DEBIT	ADJUSTMENTS CREDIT	INCOME STATEMENT DEBIT	INCOME STATEMENT CREDIT	BALANCE SHEET DEBIT	BALANCE SHEET CREDIT	
1	Cash	22300.00						22300.00		1
2	Petty Cash	300.00						300.00		2
3	Accounts Receivable	10270.00						10270.00		3
4	Merchandise Inventory	295780.00			(a)12200.00			283580.00		4
5	Supplies—Office	5890.00			(b)3730.00			2160.00		5
6	Supplies—Store	5610.00			(c)3920.00			1690.00		6
7	Prepaid Insurance	5550.00			(d)3450.00			2100.00		7
8	Accounts Payable		9610.00						9610.00	8
9	Sales Tax Payable		1130.00						1130.00	9
10	Mathew Logan, Capital		135400.00						135400.00	10
11	Mathew Logan, Drawing	18220.00						18220.00		11
12	Jerry Hill, Capital		133270.00						133270.00	12
13	Jerry Hill, Drawing	18320.00						18320.00		13
14	Income Summary			(a)12200.00		12200.00				14
15	Sales		270800.00				270800.00			15
16	Purchases	132440.00				132440.00				16
17	Advertising Expense	6210.00				6210.00				17
18	Credit Card Fee Expense	2660.00				2660.00				18
19	Insurance Expense			(d)3450.00		3450.00				19
20	Miscellaneous Expense	2860.00				2860.00				20
21	Rent Expense	21000.00				21000.00				21
22	Supplies Expense—Office			(b)3730.00		3730.00				22
23	Supplies Expense—Store			(c)3920.00		3920.00				23
24	Utilities Expense	2800.00				2800.00				24
25		550210.00	550210.00	23300.00	23300.00	191270.00	270800.00	358940.00	279410.00	25
26	Net Income					79530.00			79530.00	26
27						270800.00	270800.00	358940.00	358940.00	27
28										28

Instructions:

1. Prepare an income statement. Calculate and record the following component percentages: (a) cost of merchandise sold, (b) gross profit on sales, (c) total expenses, and (d) net income or loss. Round percentage calculations to the nearest 0.1%.
2. Prepare a distribution of net income statement. Net income or loss is to be shared equally.
3. Prepare an owners' equity statement. No additional investments were made.
4. Prepare a balance sheet in report form.

Check Figure: Total Liabilities and Owner's Equity: 322,400.00

RECYCLING PROBLEM 17-1

Journalizing adjusting and closing entries

Use the following partial work sheet of Let's Go Camping for the year ended December 31 of the current year.

	ACCOUNT TITLE	ADJUSTMENTS DEBIT	ADJUSTMENTS CREDIT	INCOME STATEMENT DEBIT	INCOME STATEMENT CREDIT
4	Merchandise Inventory		(a)11 81 0 00		
5	Supplies—Office		(b) 3 01 2 00		
6	Supplies—Store		(c) 3 15 6 00		
7	Prepaid Insurance		(d) 3 09 6 00		
22	Income Summary	(a)11 81 0 00		11 81 0 00	
23	Sales				357 60 0 00
24	Purchases			149 22 0 00	
25	Advertising Expense			5 73 6 00	
26	Credit Card Fee Expense			4 77 6 00	
27	Insurance Expense	(d) 3 09 6 00		3 09 6 00	
28	Miscellaneous Expense			2 56 8 00	
29	Payroll Taxes Expense			7 17 6 00	
30	Rent Expense			15 84 0 00	
31	Salary Expense			70 70 0 00	
32	Supplies Expense—Office	(b) 3 01 2 00		3 01 2 00	
33	Supplies Expense—Store	(c) 3 15 6 00		3 15 6 00	
34	Utilities Expense			3 31 0 00	
35		21 07 4 00	21 07 4 00	280 40 0 00	357 60 0 00
36	Net Income			77 20 0 00	
37				357 60 0 00	357 60 0 00
38					

Instructions:

1. Use page 25 of the general journal given in the *Recycling Problem Working Papers*. Journalize the adjusting entries using information from the partial work sheet.
2. Continue using page 25 of the journal. Journalize the closing entries using information from the work sheet. The distribution of net income statement shows equal distribution of earnings. The partners' drawing accounts show the following debit balances in the work sheet's Balance Sheet Debit column: Tom Hill, Drawing, $22,170.00; Vern Teel, Drawing, $22,680.00.

Check Figures:
4 adjusting entries; 5 closing entries

RECYCLING PROBLEM 18-1

Journalizing and posting purchases and cash payment transactions

The general ledger and accounts payable ledger accounts of Central Heating Supply are given in the *Recycling Problem Working Papers*. The balances are recorded as of July 1 of the current year. Use the following account titles.

PARTIAL GENERAL LEDGER	ACCOUNTS PAYABLE LEDGER
1105 Cash	210 Carson Company
1110 Petty Cash	220 Delmar, Inc.
1140 Supplies	230 Garrison Supply
2115 Accounts Payable	240 Macon Wire Company
5105 Purchases	250 Sanders Company
5110 Purchases Discount	
5115 Purchases Returns and Allowances	
6105 Advertising Expense	
6110 Cash Short and Over	
6135 Miscellaneous Expense	
6145 Rent Expense	

Instructions:

1. Journalize the following transactions affecting purchases and cash payments completed during July of the current year. Use page 7 of a purchases journal, page 11 of a cash payments journal, and page 7 of a general journal.

Transactions:

July 1. Paid cash for rent, $600.00. C461.
   3. Purchased merchandise on account from Delmar, Inc., $3,250.00. P215.
   4. Paid cash on account to Carson Company covering P210 for $1,364.00, less 2% discount. C462.
   5. Bought supplies on account from Garrison Supply, $210.00. M235.
   9. Purchased merchandise on account from Carson Company, $1,056.00. P216.
   9. Paid cash on account to Sanders Company covering P211 for $2,480.00, less 2% discount. C463.
   10. Paid cash for supplies, $536.00. C464.
   12. Purchased merchandise on account from Macon Wire Company, $362.00. P217.
   14. Paid cash on account to Carson Company, covering P216, less 2% discount. C465.
   Posting. Post the items that are to be posted individually. Post from the journals in the following order: purchases, general, cash payments. Some transactions will not be in order by date in the accounts.
   16. Returned merchandise to Delmar, Inc., $549.00, from P215. DM47.
   18. Paid cash to Jackson Company for merchandise with a list price of $192.25. Jackson offers its customers a 60% trade discount. C466.
   21. Purchased merchandise on account from Garrison Supply, $378.00. P218.
   22. Paid cash on account to Delmar, Inc., $2,701.00, covering P215, no discount. C467.
   23. Paid cash for miscellaneous expense, $90.00. C468.
   24. Bought supplies on account from Sanders Company, $650.00. M242.
   25. Returned merchandise to Macon Wire Company, $80.00, from P217. DM48.
   29. Purchased merchandise on account from Carson Company, $700.00. P220.
   31. Paid cash to replenish the petty cash fund: supplies, $26.40; advertising, $41.70; miscellaneous, $14.80; cash short, $0.60. C469.
   Posting. Post the items that are to be posted individually.
2. Total and rule the purchases journal. Post the total.
3. Prove and rule the cash payments journal. Post the totals of the special columns.
4. Prepare a schedule of accounts payable. Compare the schedule total with the balance of the accounts payable account in the general ledger. The total and balance should be the same.

Check Figures:
Purchases journal total: 5,746.00;
Cash payments journal totals: 1,386.40;
7,601.00; 98.00; 8,889.40;
Total Accounts Payable: 5,848.00

RECYCLING PROBLEM 19-1

Journalizing and posting sales transactions

The general ledger and accounts receivable accounts for Kellogg Supply are given in the *Recycling Problem Working Papers*. The balances are recorded as of March 1 of the current year. Use the following account titles.

PARTIAL GENERAL LEDGER		ACCOUNTS RECEIVABLE LEDGER	
Account No.	**Account Title**	**Customer No.**	**Customer Name**
1105	Cash	110	Sandy Acker
1125	Accounts Receivable	120	Clark, Inc.
1130	Time Drafts Receivable	130	Clayton Company
2140	Sales Tax Payable	140	John Maxwell
4105	Sales	150	Emily Parsons
4110	Sales Discount	160	Reston Company
4115	Sales Returns and Allowances	170	Sawyer Supply
		180	Valley High School
		190	Walsh Associates

Instructions:

1. Journalize the following transactions affecting sales and cash receipts completed during March of the current year. Use page 3 of a sales journal, a general journal, and a cash receipts journal. Kellogg Supply offers terms of 2/10, n/30. The sales tax rate is 8%. Source documents are abbreviated as follows: credit memorandum, CM; memorandum, M; receipt, R; sales invoice, S; cash register tape, T; time draft, TD.

Transactions:

Mar. 1. Sold merchandise on account to Sandy Acker, $725.00, plus sales tax. S63.
    2. Granted credit to John Maxwell for merchandise returned, $60.00, plus sales tax. CM21.
    3. Received a 30-day time draft from Alicia Alcon for international sale of merchandise, $4,300.00. TD10.
    4. Received cash on account from Clayton Company, $444.53, covering S59 for $453.60 ($420.00 plus sales tax, $33.60), less discount and sales tax. R47.
    5. Received cash on account from Reston Company, $555.66, covering S60 for $567.00 ($525.00 plus sales tax, $42.00), less discount and less sales tax. R48.
    5. Recorded cash and credit card sales, $2,735.00, plus sales tax, $218.80; total, $2,953.80. T5.
    7. Sold merchandise on account to Sawyer Supply, $840.00, plus sales tax. S64.
    9. Recorded international cash sale, $6,500.00. M12.
  12. Received cash on account from Sandy Acker, $783.00, covering S63; no discount. R49.
  12. Granted credit to Emily Parsons for damaged merchandise, $128.00, plus sales tax, from S61. CM22.
  12. Recorded cash and credit card sales, $2,534.00, plus sales tax, $202.72; total, $2,736.72. T12.
  14. Received cash for the value of Time Draft No. 7, $8,500.00. R50.
  15. Discovered that a sale on account to Clayton Company on February 16, S52, was incorrectly charged to the account of Clark, Inc., $352.00. M9.
    Posting. Post the items that are to be posted individually. Post from the journals in this order: sales journal, general journal, and cash receipts journal.
  16. Sold merchandise on account to Clark, Inc., $243.75, plus sales tax. S65.
  18. Received cash on account from Sawyer Supply, $907.20, covering S64; no discount. R51.
  19. Recorded cash and credit card sales, $2,184.00, plus sales tax, $174.72; total, $2,358.72. T19.
  22. Granted credit to Walsh Associates for damaged merchandise, $26.00, plus sales tax, from S59. CM23.
  23. Received cash for the value of Time Draft No. 8, $8,000.00. R52.
  24. Sold merchandise on account to Valley High School, $645.50, no sales tax. S66.
  25. Granted credit to Clark, Inc., for merchandise returned, $25.50, plus sales tax. CM24.
  26. Recorded cash and credit card sales, $2,526.00, plus sales tax, $202.08; total, $2,728.08. T26.
  30. Received cash on account from Emily Parsons, $125.00, covering the unpaid portion of S61; no discount. R53.
  31. Received a 30-day time draft from Fernando Cortez for international sale of merchandise, $6,000.00. TD11.
    Posting. Post the items that are to be posted individually.

(continued on next page)

2. Prove the sales journal.
3. Post the totals of the special columns of the sales journal.
4. Prove and rule the cash receipts journal.
5. Post the totals of the special columns of the cash receipts journal.
6. Prepare a schedule of accounts receivable as of March 31 of the current year. Compare the schedule total with the balance of the accounts receivable account in the general ledger. The total and balance should be the same.

RECYCLING PROBLEM 20-1

Recording entries for uncollectible accounts

The accounts receivable and general ledger accounts for Fincher Industries are given in the *Recycling Problem Working Papers*. The following transactions relating to uncollectible accounts receivable occurred during the final quarter of the current fiscal year.

Instructions:

1. Journalize the transactions completed during October using page 10 of a general journal. Post the transactions to the customer accounts and general ledger accounts.

Transactions:

Oct. 6. Wrote off Chittenden Corporation's past-due account as uncollectible, $284.75. M216.
      19. Wrote off Foster Corporation's past-due account as uncollectible, $574.10. M221.

2. Journalize the transactions completed during November using page 11 of a general journal and page 11 of a cash receipts journal. Prove the cash receipts journal. Post the transactions to the customer accounts and general ledger accounts.

Transactions:

Nov. 5. Wrote off Agnew Company's past-due account as uncollectible, $804.24. M236.
      12. Received cash in full payment of Chittenden Corporation's account, previously written off as uncollectible, $284.75. M241 and R616.
      17. Received cash in full payment of Dionne, Inc.'s account, previously written off as uncollectible, $468.30. M243 and R627.

3. Journalize the transactions for December. Use page 12 of a general journal and page 12 of a cash receipts journal. Prove the cash receipts journal. Post the transactions to the customer accounts and general ledger accounts.

Transactions:

Dec. 4. Wrote off Grant Company's past-due account as uncollectible, $705.18. M257.
      10. Received cash in full payment of Agnew Company's account, previously written off as uncollectible, $804.24. M259 and R702.
      21. Received cash in full payment of Foster Corporation's account, previously written off as uncollectible, $574.10. M265 and R729.

4. Journalize the December 31 adjusting entry for estimated uncollectible accounts expense for the year. Use page 13 of the general journal. Uncollectible accounts expense is estimated as 1.2% of total sales on account. Total sales on account for the year were $987,660.00. Post the transaction to the general ledger accounts.

RECYCLING PROBLEM 21-1

Recording transactions for plant assets

Diamond Clothing records plant assets in two accounts: Store Equipment, Account No. 1215, and Office Equipment, Account No. 1205. Store equipment is depreciated using the straight-line method. Office equipment is depreciated using the double declining-balance method. Journals and plant asset records are given in the *Recycling Problem Working Papers*.

Instructions:

1. Record the following transactions completed during 20X1 on page 1 of a cash payments journal.

Transactions:

Jan. 3. Purchased a color printer: cost, $900.00; estimated salvaged value, $100.00; estimated useful life, 4 years; plant asset No. 642; serial number, ZE532N34. C168.

Feb. 26. Paid property tax on plant assets assessed at $620,000.00. The tax rate is 1.4%. C216.

Apr. 3. Purchased a store display: cost, $3,000.00; estimated salvage value, $500.00; estimated useful life, 5 years; plant asset No. 643; serial number, 754NFE. C275.

2. Complete Section 1 of a plant asset record for each new plant asset.
3. Prepare a depreciation table for each new plant asset.
4. Complete Section 3 of the plant asset record for 20X1-20X4.
5. Record the following transactions completed during 20X5. Use page 2 of a cash receipts journal and page 2 of a general journal.

Transactions:

Jan. 3. Received cash for sale of a color printer, plant asset No. 642, $60.00. R7.

June 29. Received cash for sale of a store display, plant asset No. 643, $950.00. M69 and R171.

Dec. 31. Recorded the adjusting entry for depreciation expense—store equipment. Total 20X5 depreciation expense of store equipment was $17,765.00.

6. Complete the plant asset records for each plant asset sold during 20X5.

Check Figure: Gain on plant asset sold June 29: 75.00

RECYCLING PROBLEM 22-1

Determining the cost of inventory using the fifo, lifo, and weighted-average inventory costing methods

Stevens Company made the following purchases of a part during the fiscal year. There are 32 units in ending inventory. Forms for costing inventory are given in the *Recycling Problem Working Papers*.

Purchase Date	Quantity	Unit Price
January 1, beginning inventory	3	$12.30
January 3, purchases	20	13.00
March 29, purchases	20	13.20
August 15, purchases	15	13.25
November 13, purchases	15	13.45

Instructions:

1. Calculate the cost of ending inventory using the fifo, lifo, and weighted-average methods.
2. Which of the inventory costing methods resulted in the highest cost of merchandise sold?

RECYCLING PROBLEM 23-1

Journalizing notes payable and notes receivable transactions

The following transactions related to notes payable and notes receivable were completed by Miles Company during April of the current year. Journals are provided in the *Recycling Problem Working Papers*.

Transactions:

Apr. 5. Signed a 90-day, 10% note for $30,000.00 with First National Bank. R34.

9. Accepted a 90-day, 15% note from Phillip Majure for an extension of time on his account, $650.00. NR18.

12. Received cash for the maturity value of a 60-day, 18% note for $900.00. R67.

16. Accepted a 60-day, 14% note from Avery Harris for an extension of time on her account, $2,450.00. NR19.

19. Received cash for the maturity value of a 60-day, 18% note for $500.00. R74.

20. Signed a 90-day, 15% note with Rossman Supply for an extension of time on this account payable, $2,500.00. M49.

22. Patrick Isamen dishonored his 90-day, 15% note, for $3,000.00. M53.

27. Signed a 120-day, 12% note, for $20,000.00 with First Commerce Bank. R84.

29. Received cash for the maturity value of a 90-day, 18% note for $1,800.00. R89.

Instructions:

1. Journalize each transaction using page 3 of a general journal and page 6 of a cash receipts journal. Source documents are abbreviated as follows: check, C; receipt, R; memorandum, M; note receivable, NR.

2. Determine the maturity date and maturity value of each note signed by Miles Company.

3. Journalize the following transactions on page 10 of a cash payments journal. Use the maturity dates and maturity values calculated in the previous step.

Transactions:

Paid cash for the maturity value of the $30,000.00 note dated April 5. C452.

Paid cash for the maturity value of the $2,500.00 note dated April 20. C489.

Paid cash for the maturity value of the $20,000.00 note dated April 27. C672.

Check Figures:
Maturity Values: April 5—$30,750.00;
April 20—$2,593.75;
April 27—$20,800.00

RECYCLING PROBLEM 24-1

Journalizing and posting entries for accrued interest revenue and expense

The accounting forms for Rucker Company are given in the *Recycling Problem Working Papers*. The balances are recorded as of December 31 of the current year before adjusting entries.

Rucker Company completed the following transactions related to notes receivable and notes payable during the current year and the following year. The first two transactions have already been journalized and posted. One note receivable and one note payable are the only notes on hand at the end of the fiscal period. Source documents are abbreviated as follows: receipt, R; check, C; note receivable, NR.

Transactions:
20X1

Nov. 9. Accepted a 90-day, 18% note from Kayla Nelson for an extension of time on her account, $800.00. NR18.

Dec. 14. Signed a 120-day, 12% note, $4,800.00 with First National Bank. R364.

20X2

Feb. 7. Received cash for the maturity value of NR18. R132.

Apr. 13. Paid cash for the maturity value of the First National Bank note. C342.

Instructions:
1. Plan the adjustments on a work sheet.
2. Journalize and post the adjusting entries for accrued interest income and accrued interest expense on December 31. Use page 15 of a general journal.
3. Journalize and post the closing entries for interest income and interest expense. Continue to use page 15 of a general journal.
4. Journalize and post the reversing entries for accrued interest income and accrued interest expense. Use page 16 of a general journal.
5. Journalize the receipt of cash for the maturity value of NR18. Use page 13 of a cash receipts journal. Post the amounts in the General columns of the cash receipts journal.
6. Journalize the cash payment for the maturity value of the note payable. Use page 18 of a cash payments journal. Post the amounts in the General columns of the cash payments journal.

Check Figures:
Interest Income Feb. 7, 20X2, balance: 15.20 cr.;
Interest Expense Apr. 13, 20X2, balance: 164.80 dr.

RECYCLING PROBLEM 25-1

Journalizing dividends and preparing a work sheet for a corporation

Accounting forms are given in the *Recycling Problem Working Papers*. Dugan Corporation completed the following transactions during December of the current year and January of the next year.

Transactions:

Dec. 15. The board of directors declared a dividend of $0.20 per share; capital stock issued is 80,000 shares. M232.

Jan. 15. Paid cash for dividend declared December 15. C798.

Instructions:

1. Use page 12 of a general journal. Journalize the dividend declared on December 15.
2. Use page 18 of a cash payments journal. Journalize payment of the dividend on January 15.
3. Prepare Dugan Corporation's work sheet for the current year ended December 31. Record the adjustments on the work sheet using the following information. Do not total the Adjustments columns.

Adjustment Information, December 31

Accrued interest income	$ 52.50
Uncollectible accounts expense estimated as 1.0% of sales on account.	
Sales on account for year, $978,000.00.	
Merchandise inventory	209,326.60
Supplies inventory	413.50
Value of prepaid insurance	3,200.00
Annual depreciation expense—office equipment	5,335.00
Annual depreciation expense—store equipment	4,210.00
Accrued interest expense	400.00

4. Extend all amounts except Federal Income Tax Expense to the appropriate Income Statement and Balance Sheet columns. Do not total the columns.
5. On the form provided in the *Recycling Problem Working Papers*, total the work sheet's Income Statement columns. Calculate the difference between the debit and credit totals. This difference becomes the net income before federal income tax expense.
6. Using the tax table on page 649, calculate the federal income tax expense and record the income tax adjustment on the work sheet. Complete the work sheet.

Check Figures:
Jan. 15 debit to Dividends Payable:
16,000.00;
Dec. 31 Net Income after Fed. Inc. Tax:
200,154.03

RECYCLING PROBLEM 26-1

Preparing financial statements and end-of-fiscal-period entries for a corporation

Use the work sheet provided in the *Recycling Problem Working Papers* for Dugan Corporation to prepare the financial statements and end-of-fiscal-period entries for the corporation for the current year.

Instructions:

1. Prepare an income statement. Calculate and record the following component percentages. (a) cost of merchandise sold; (b) gross profit on operations; (c) total operating expenses; (d) income from operations; (e) net addition or deduction resulting from other revenue and expenses; and (f) net income before federal income tax. Round percentage calculations to the nearest 0.1%.
2. Analyze the corporation's income statement by determining if component percentages are within acceptable levels. If any component percentage is not within an acceptable level, suggest steps that the company should take. The corporation considers the following component percentages acceptable.

Cost of merchandise sold	Not more than 64.0%
Gross profit on operations	Not less than 36.0%
Total operating expenses	Not more than 20.0%
Income from operations	Not less than 16.0%
Net deduction from other revenue and expenses	Not more than 1.0%
Net income before federal income tax	Not less than 15.0%

3. Prepare a statement of stockholders' equity. Use the following additional information.

January 1 balance of capital stock account	$80,000.00
(80,000 shares issued for $1.00 per share)	
Shares issued during the year	None

4. Prepare a balance sheet.
5. Calculate the corporation's (a) working capital and (b) current ratio. Determine if these items are within acceptable levels. The corporation considers the following levels acceptable.

Working capital	Not less than $200,000.00
Current ratio	Between 3.0 to 1 and 4.0 to 1

6. Journalize the adjusting entries using page 15 of a general journal.
7. Journalize the closing entries using page 16 of a general journal.
8. Journalize the reversing entries using page 17 of a general journal.

Check Figure:
Total Liabilities and Stockholders' Equity:
358,792.80

Chapter 1, Page 8

1. Planning, recording, analyzing, and interpreting financial information.

2. Answers will vary but should involve businesses that perform activities for a fee.

3. A business owned by one person.

4. Assets = Liabilities + Owner's Equity.

Chapter 1, Page 12

1. The right side must be increased.

2. If one account is increased, another account on the same side of the equation must be decreased by the same amount.

3. Buying items and paying for them at a future date.

Chapter 1, Page 15

1. Assets, liabilities, and owner's equity.

2. Assets.

3. Liabilities and owner's equity.

4. Find the errors before completing any more work.

Chapter 2, Page 29

1. Increased.

2. Increased

3. Decreased.

Chapter 2, Page 31

1. The name of the business, the name of the report, and the date of the report.

2. Assets.

3. Liabilities and owner's equity.

Chapter 3, Page 44

Assets = Liabilities + Owner's Equity

1.

2. (1) Account balances increase on the normal balance side of an account. (2) Account balances decrease on the side opposite the normal balance side of an account.

Chapter 3, Page 50

1. (1) Which accounts are affected? (2) How is each account classified? (3) How is each classification changed? (4) How is each amount entered in the accounts?

2. Supplies and Cash.

Chapter 3, Page 56

1. Cash and Sales.

2. Accounts Receivable and Sales.

3. Owner's drawing account and Cash.

4. Credit.

5. Debit.

Chapter 4, Page 71

1. By date.

2. Source documents are one way to verify the accuracy of a specific journal entry.

3. Date, debit, credit, and source document.

Chapter 4, Page 75

1. Prepaid Insurance.

2. Supplies.

3. Accounts Payable.

4. Cash.

Chapter 4, Page 81

1. Cash.

2. Sales.

3. Sales.

4. C.

5. R.

Chapter 4, Page 85

1. When there is insufficient space to record any more entries.

2. Draw neat lines through all parts of the incorrect entry. Journalize the entry correctly on the next blank lines.

3. Draw neat lines through all incorrect parts of the entry. Record the correct items on the same lines as the incorrect items, directly above the canceled parts.

Chapter 5, Page 100

1. The first digit indicates in which general ledger division the account is located. The second and third digits indicate the location of the account within that division.

2. (1) Write the account title in the heading. (2) Write the account number in the heading.

Chapter 5, Page 105

1. (1) Write the date in the Date column of the account. (2) Write the journal page number in the Post. Ref. column of the account. (3) Write the amount in the Debit or Credit column. (4) Calculate and write the new account balance in the Balance Debit or Balance Credit column. (5) Write the account number in the Post. Ref. column of the journal.

2. Whenever the credits in an account exceed the debits, the balance is a credit. Whenever the debits in an account exceed the credits, the balance is a debit.

Chapter 5, page 111

1. The cash balance as shown in the checkbook and the cash balance in the cash account.

2. A journal entry made to correct an error in the ledger.

3. To show the increase in this expense account.

4. To show the decrease in this expense account.

Chapter 6, Page 124

1. Blank endorsement, special endorsement, and restrictive endorsement.

2. (1) Write the amount of the check after the dollar sign at the top of the stub. (2) Write the date of the check on the Date line. (3) Write to whom the check is to be paid on the To line. (4) Record the purpose of the check on the For line. (5) Write the amount of the check after the words *Amt. This Check*. (6) Calculate the new checking balance and record it in the amount column on the last line of the stub.

3. (1) Write the date. (2) Write to whom the check is to be paid following the words *Pay to the order of*. (3) Write the amount in figures following the dollar sign. (4) Write the amount in words on the line with the word *Dollars*. (5) Write the purpose of the check on the line labeled For. (6) Sign the check.

Chapter 6, Page 129

1. (1) A service charge may not have been recorded in the depositor's business records. (2) Outstanding deposits may be recorded in the depositor's records but not on a bank statement. (3) Outstanding checks may be recorded in the depositor's records but not on a bank statement. (4) A depositor may have made a math or recording error.

2. An outstanding check.

Chapter 6, Page 134

1. (1) The check appears to be altered. (2) The signature on the check does not match the signature on the signature card. (3) The amounts written in figures and in words do not agree. (4) The check is postdated. (5) The person who wrote the check has stopped payment on it. (6) The account of the person who wrote the check has insufficient funds to pay the check.

2. Cash.

3. Cash.

Chapter 6, Page 138

1. For making small cash payments.

2. The check issued to replenish petty cash is a credit to Cash and does not affect Petty Cash.

Chapter 7, Page 152

1. Name of the business, name of report, and date of report.

2. All general ledger accounts are listed in the Trial Balance columns of a work sheet, even if some accounts do not have balances.

Chapter 7, Page 158

1. An expense should be reported in the same fiscal period that it is used to produce revenue.

2. (1) What is the balance of the account? (2) What should the balance be for this account? (3) What must be done to correct the account balance? (4) What adjusment is made?

Chapter 7, Page 163

1. Asset, liability, and owner's equity accounts.

2. Revenue and expense accounts.

3. Income Statement Debit and Balance Sheet Credit columns.

4. Income Statement Credit and Balance Sheet Debit Columns.

Chapter 7, Page 167

1. Subtract the smaller total from the larger total to find the difference.

2. The difference between two column totals can be divided evenly by 9.

3. A slide.

Chapter 8, Page 180

1. Heading, revenue, expenses, and net income or net loss.

2. Total Expenses *divided by* Total Sales *equals* Total Expenses Component Percentage.

3. Net Income *divided by* Total Sales *equals* Net Income Component Percentage.

Chapter 8, Page 185

1. Heading, assets, liabilities, and owner's equity.

2. Capital Account Balance *plus* Net Income *minus* Drawing Account Balance *equals* Current Capital.

Chapter 9, Page 196

1. To update general ledger accounts.

2. Adjustments column of the work sheet.

3. Supplies Expense and Insurance Expense.

Chapter 9, Page 203

1. Beginning balances.

2. Changes in the owner's capital for a single fiscal period.

3. (1) An entry to close income statement accounts with credit balances. (2) An entry to close income statement accounts with debit balances. (3) An entry to record net income or net loss and close the income summary account. (4) An entry to close the owner's drawing account.

Chapter 9, Page 209

1. To assure a reader that a balance has not been omitted.

2. Only those with balances (permanent accounts).

3. Because they are closed and have zero balances.

Chapter 10, Page 228

1. Purchases of merchandise on account.

2. Frequently occurring transactions.

3. Because the same two accounts are always affected by purchase on account transactions.

4. Time is saved because using special amount columns eliminates writing an account title in the Account Title column.

Chapter 10, Page 233

1. Cash payment transactions that do not occur often.

2. A business purchases merchandise to sell but buys supplies for use in the business. Supplies are not intended for sale.

3. Cash is decreased by a credit.

Chapter 10, Page 239

1. The titles of the accounts for which the petty cash fund was used.

2. Withdrawals are normally recorded in separate accounts so that the total amounts are easily determined for each accounting period.

3. (1) Rule a single line across all amount columns. (2) Write the date in the Date column. (3) Write *Totals* in the Account Title column. (4) Write each column total below the single line. (5) Rule a double line across all amount columns.

Chapter 10, Page 243

1. General journal.

2. To note that the invoice is for store supplies and not for purchases, ensuring that no mistake is made.

3. Because the single credit amount is posted to two accounts.

4. After each general journal entry is recorded.

5. The withdrawal is of merchandise and not cash.

Chapter 11, Page 258

1. A merchandising business sells merchandise; a service business sells services.

2. As a percentage of sales.

3. The amount of sales tax collected is a business liability until paid to the government.

4. Accounts Receivable.

Chapter 11, Page 264

1. Cash is debited, and Accounts Receivable is credited.

2. A check mark.

3. Cash on hand at the beginning of the month, *plus* total cash received during the month, *less* total cash paid during the month, *equals* cash balance on hand at the end of the month. Cash is proved if the balance on the next unused check stub is the same as the cash proof.

Chapter 12, Page 277

1. Accounts for vendors from whom items are purchased or bought on account.

2. The balance of a controlling account equals the total of all account balances in its related subsidiary ledger.

3. Credit Balance.

Chapter 12, Page 282

1. Accounts Payable Debit column.

2. Vendor accounts.

Chapter 12, Page 286

1. Customer accounts.

2. The customer accounts listed in the Account Debited column.

Chapter 12, Page 290

1. Accounts Receivable Credit column.

2. All customer accounts that have balances.

Chapter 12, Page 295

1. Amounts in the Debit and Credit columns.

2. (1) Write the date in the Date column of the account. (2) Write the journal page number in the Post. Ref. column of the account. (3) Write the amount in the Debit or Credit column of the account. (4) Calculate and write the new account balance in the Balance Debit or Balance Credit column of the account. (5) Write the general ledger account number in the Post. Ref. column of the general journal.

Chapter 12, Page 302

1. Each special amount column.

2. (1) Sales journal, (2) purchases journal, (3) general journal, (4) cash receipts journal, (5) cash payments journal.

Chapter 13, Page 315

1. The total amount earned by all employees for a pay period.

2. $3\frac{1}{2}$ hours.

3. Overtime earnings × the overtime rate.

4. $440.00.

Chapter 13, Page 321

1. Form W-4, Employee's Withholding Allowance Certificate.

2. Employee marital status and number of withholding allowances.

3. Both the employee and the employer.

Chapter 13, Page 326

1. The payroll register summarizes the payroll for one pay period and shows total earnings, payroll withholdings, and net pay of all employees.

2. By subtracting total deductions from total earnings.

3. Because a business must send a quarterly report to federal and state governments showing employee taxable earnings and taxes withheld from employee earnings.

Chapter 13, Page 329

1. To help protect and control payroll payments.

2. The payroll register.

3. Individual checks are not written and do not have to be distributed.

Chapter 14, Page 343

1. Salary Expense.

2. Employee Income Tax Payable.

3. Social Security Tax Payable.

4. Medicare Tax Payable.

Chapter 14, Page 348

1. Social security: 6.5% of earnings up to a maximum of $65,400.00 in each calendar year; Medicare: 1.5% of total employee earnings; federal unemployment: 0.8% of the first $7,000.00 earned by each employee; state unemployment: 5.4% on the first $7,000.00 earned by each employee.

2. The first $7,000.00.

Chapter 14, Page 353

1. By January 31.

2. Federal income tax, social security tax, and Medicare tax.

Chapter 14, Page 359

1. By the 15th day of the following month.

2. For paying payroll taxes and for paying federal unemployment tax.

Chapter 15, Page 379

1. In the same order they appear in the general ledger.

2. Merchandise Inventory and Income Summary.

Chapter 15, Page 385

1. Supplies—Office and Supplies Expense—Office.

2. Prepaid Insurance and Insurance Expense.

Chapter 15, Page 392

1. Income Statement Debit or Credit column.

2. When the Income Statement Debit column total (costs and expenses) is larger than the Credit column total (revenue).

3. Balance Sheet Debit.

4. Trial balance amounts after adjustments are extended to the Adjusted Trial Balance columns, and the Adjusted Trial Balance columns are proved before extending amounts to the Income Statement and Balance Sheet columns.

Chapter 16, Page 404

1. The cost of merchandise sold section.

2. Beginning merchandise inventory, *plus* purchases, *equals* total cost of merchandise available for sale, *less* ending merchandise inventory, *equals* cost of merchandise sold.

3. By comparing it with the amount calculated on the work sheet.

Chapter 16, Page 409

1. (1) Cost of merchandise sold, (2) gross profit on sales, (3) total expenses, and (4) net income.

2. By making comparisons with prior fiscal periods as well as with industry standards that are published by industry organizations.

3. Net loss.

Chapter 16, Page 415

1. Each partner's share of net income or loss.

2. (1) Beginning capital, (2) additional investments, and (3) each partner's withdrawal of assets.

3. The January 1 capital, *plus* the net increase in capital, *equals* the December 31 capital.

Chapter 16, Page 420

1. A business's financial condition on a specific date.

2. In account form or report form.

3. The Balance Sheet columns of a work sheet and the owner's equity statement.

4. A schedule of accounts payable and a schedule of accounts receivable.

Chapter 17, Page 433

1. Insurance Expense and Income Summary.

2. Because the explanation "Adjusting Entries" is recorded in the Account Title column to explain all of the adjusting entries that follow.

3. Adjusting entry for merchandising inventory.

Chapter 17, Page 438

1. Income Statement and Balance Sheet columns of the work sheet and the distribution of net income statement.

2. Income Summary.

Chapter 17, Page 442

1. The distribution of net income statement and the Balance Sheet columns of the work sheet.

2. An amount equal to its balance is recorded on the side opposite the balance.

Chapter 17, Page 447

1. General ledger accounts with balances.

2. To prove the equality of debits and credits in the general ledger.

3. In the same order as they appear in the general ledger.

Chapter 18, Page 465

1. A corporation can own property, incur liabilities, enter into contracts in its own name, and sell ownership in itself.

2. A corporation has separate capital accounts for the stock issued and for the earnings kept in the business.

3. The debit to Purchases increases the total of purchases during the year. The credit to Accounts Payable increases the current balance of this liability.

Chapter 18, Page 469

1. To encourage early payment

2. Two ten means 2% of the invoice amount may be deducted if the invoice is paid within 10 days of the invoice date. Net thirty means that the total invoice amount must be paid within 30 days.

3. Accounts Payable is debited, Purchases Discount is credited, and Cash is credited.

Chapter 18, Page 474

1. The cash short and over account is closed to Income Summary.

2. Each amount in the General columns is posted individually to the general ledger account named in the Account Title Column.

Chapter 18, Page 479

1. A business can track the amount of purchases returns and allowances in a fiscal period if a separate account is used.

2. A purchases return is credit allowed for the purchase price of returned merchandise. A purchases allowance is credit allowed for part of the purchase price of merchandise that is not returned.

3. The transaction can be recorded immediately without waiting for written confirmation from the vendor.

Chapter 19, Page 495

1. The state government.

2. So that each customer account will show an up-to-date balance.

Chapter 19, Page 500

1. To encourage early payment.

2. Cash, Sales Discount, and Sales Tax Payable are debited; Accounts Receivable is credited.

Chapter 19, Page 505

1. Sales Returns and Allowances and Sales Tax Payable are debited; Accounts Receivable is credited.

2. Sales journal, purchases journal, general journal, cash receipts journal, and cash payments journal.

Chapter 19, Page 511

1. (1) Settlement of disputes is more difficult; (2) transactions take more time to complete; (3) the risk of uncollected amounts is increased; (4) unstable political conditions may affect the ability to receive payments.

2. (1) A receipt signed by the authorized agent of a transportation company for merchandise received and (2) a contract for the delivery of the merchandise.

3. A sight draft is payable on sight when the holder presents it for payment. A time draft is payable at a fixed or determinable future time after it is accepted.

4. To assure receipt of payment for sales.

5. A draft is generally paid by a bank and a trade acceptance by the buyer.

Chapter 20, Page 532

1. The loss is considered a regular expense of doing business. Revenue was earned when the sale was made. Failing to collect an account does not cancel the sale.

2. At the end of a fiscal period.

3. (1) Reports a balance sheet amount for Accounts Receivable that reflects the amount the business expects to collect in the future. (2) Recognizes the expense of uncollectible accounts in the same period in which the related revenue is recorded.

4. It reduces its related asset account, Accounts Receivable.

5. The difference between the balance of Accounts Receivable and its contra account, Allowance for Uncollectible Accounts.

Chapter 20, Page 538

1. The balance of the customer account is an *actual* uncollectible amount and no longer an *estimate* of an uncollectible amount.

2. The book value is the same because the same amount is deducted from the accounts receivable and the allowance accounts.

3. To show an accurate credit history.

Chapter 21, Page 550

1. Current assets and plant assets.

2. Office Equipment is debited; Cash is credited.

3. Land and anything attached to the land.

4. Tax authorities referred to as assessors.

Chapter 21, Page 554

1. *Matching Expenses with Revenue.*

2. Original cost; estimated salvage value; estimated useful life.

3. Because of land's permanent nature. Land can be used indefinitely.

Chapter 21, Page 558

1. Plant asset record.

2. The balance of the asset account is not changed by an adjusting entry for depreciation expense.

Chapter 21, Page 563

1. Disposal date, disposal method, and disposal amount.

2. Partial year's depreciation.

3. Cash received less the book value of the asset sold.

4. Other Expenses.

Chapter 21, Page 567

1. Depreciation rate.

2. Double declining-balance method.

3. It declines.

4. Its estimated salvage value.

Chapter 22, Page 579

1. Successful business must have merchandise available for sale that customers want. A business needs controls that assist managers in maintaining a merchandise inventory of sufficient quantity, variety, and price.

2. (1) Excess inventory requires that a business spend money for expensive store and warehouses space. (2) Excess inventory uses capital that could be invested in other assets to earn a profit for the business. (3) Excess inventory requires that a business spend money for expenses, such as taxes and insurance premiums, that increase with the cost of the merchandise inventory. (4) Excess inventory may become obsolete and unsalable.

3. At the end of a fiscal period.

4. A business frequently establishes its fiscal period to end when inventory normally is at a minimum because it takes less time to count a smaller inventory.

5. A customary practice is to take a periodic inventory at least once a fiscal period. The periodic inventory is then compared with the perpetual inventory records.

Chapter 22, Page 584

1. The most recent invoices for purchases are used in recording prices for each item on the inventory record.

2. The most recent costs of merchandise should be charged against current revenue.

3. Lifo.

4. Using the same inventory costing method for all fiscal periods provides financial statements that can be compared with other fiscal period statements. If a business changes inventory cost methods, part of the difference in gross profit and net income may be caused by the change in methods.

Chapter 22, Page 587

1. By using the gross profit method of estimating inventory.

2. Actual net sales and net purchases amounts; the beginning inventory amount; and the gross profit percentage.

3. The beginning inventory for the month is the same as the ending inventory from the previous month.

Chapter 23, Page 599

1. Sometimes a business receives more cash from sales than is needed to pay for pur-

chases and expenses. When this occurs, a business may deposit the extra cash in a bank or other financial institution for a short period. At other times, the receipt of cash from sales does not occur at the same time and in sufficient amounts to pay for needed purchases and expenses. When this occurs, a business needs to borrow additional cash or make arrangements with its vendors to delay payment for a period of time.

2. A note can be useful in a court of law as written evidence of a debt.

3. Ten cents will be paid for the use of each dollar borrowed for a full year.

4. Multiply the principal times the interest rate times the time stated as a fraction of a year.

Chapter 23, Page 604

1. Because notes payable generally are paid within one year.

2. Accounts Payable and the vendor are debited. Notes Payable is credited.

Chapter 23, Page 608

1. A note receivable does not pay the amount the customer owes. Therefore, the amount of the asset does not change at the time the note is signed. The form of the asset does change from an account receivable to a note receivable. However, the asset will remain classified as a current asset.

2. Other Revenue.

3. Accounts Receivable and the customer account are each debited for the principal of the note and the interest. Notes Receivable is credited for the principal of the note. Interest Income is credited for the interest.

4. Because the interest has been earned.

Chapter 24, Page 622

1. *Realization of Revenue.*

2. To avoid the inconvenience of determining how much, if any, of each cash receipt is for interest income earned and accrued during the previous year and how much is earned in the current year.

Chapter 24, Page 628

1. So that the income statement will report all expenses for the period even though some of the expenses have not yet been paid. Also, so that the balance sheet will report all liabilities, including the accrued expenses payable.

2. Interest Payable is debited; Interest Expense is credited.

Chapter 25, Page 641

1. (1) Different accounts are used to record owners' equity. (2) Different procedures are used to distribute income to owners. (3) Corporations calculate and pay federal income tax.

2. One capital stock account.

3. Retained Earnings.

4. When a corporation's board of directors declares a dividend, the liability for the dividend must be recorded in the accounts.

Chapter 25, Page 647

1. If ending merchandise inventory is greater than beginning merchandise inventory.

2. If ending merchandise inventory is less than the beginning merchandise inventory.

Chapter 25, Page 654

1. Any additional tax owed that was not paid in quarterly installments must be paid when the final return is sent.

2. Because you must first determine the net income before federal income tax expense.

Chapter 26, Page 667

1. (1) Owners' equity for all owners is reported as a single amount rather than for each owner. (2) Owners' equity is reported in two categories: (a) capital contributed by the owners and (b) capital earned by the corporation.

2. Sales, cost of merchandise sold, and operating expenses are used to determine income from operations. Other revenue and other expenses, such as interest income, interest expense, and gains or losses on plant assets, are not normal business activities. Therefore, they are not included in calculating income from operations and are reported separately.

3. Each component percentage shows the percentage that each item is of net sales.

Chapter 26, Page 670

1. The changes in a corporation's ownership for a fiscal period.

2. Capital stock and retained earnings.

3. In the Capital Stock general ledger account.

4. In the Balance Sheet Credit column of a work sheet.

5. As a dividend.

6. In the Balance Sheet Debit column of a work sheet.

Chapter 26, Page 676

1. Current and plant assets.

2. (1) The balance of asset account, (2) the balance of the asset's contra account, and (3) book value.

3. Mortgage payable.

4. From the statement of stockholders' equity.

5. The amount of total current assets less total current liabilities.

6. The current ratio permits a business to compare itself to its industry or to provide a convenient relative measure from year to year.

Chapter 26, Page 683

1. Federal income tax expense.

2. Closing entry for the dividends account.

3. Retained earnings.

A

Account a record summarizing all the information pertaining to a single item in the accounting equation. (p. 9)

Account balance the amount in an account. (p. 9)

Account number the number assigned to an account. (p. 97)

Account title the name given to an account. (p. 9)

Accounting planning, recording, analyzing, and interpreting financial information. (p. 4)

Accounting cycle the series of accounting activities included in recording financial information for a fiscal period. (p. 208)

Accounting equation an equation showing the relationship among assets, liabilities, and owner's equity. (p. 7)

Accounting period see *fiscal period.*

Accounting records organized summaries of a business's financial activities. (p. 4)

Accounting system a planned process for providing financial information that will be useful to management. (p. 4)

Accounts payable ledger a subsidiary ledger containing only accounts for vendors from whom items are purchased or bought on account. (p. 272)

Accounts receivable ledger a subsidiary ledger containing only accounts for charge customers. (p. 272)

Accrued expenses expenses incurred in one fiscal period but not paid until a later fiscal period. (p. 623)

Accrued interest expense interest incurred but not yet paid. (p. 623)

Accrued interest income interest earned but not yet received. (p. 618)

Accrued revenue revenue earned in one fiscal period but not received until a later fiscal period. (p. 616)

Accumulated depreciation the total amount of depreciation expense that has been recorded since the purchase of a plant asset. (p. 553)

Adjusting entries journal entries recorded to update general ledger accounts at the end of a fiscal period. (p. 192)

Adjustments changes recorded on a work sheet to update general ledger accounts at the end of a fiscal period. (p. 154)

Allowance method of recording losses from uncollectible accounts crediting the estimated value of uncollectible accounts to a contra account. (p. 528)

Assessed value the value of an asset determined by tax authorities for the purpose of calculating taxes (p. 549)

Asset anything of value that is owned. (p. 7)

B

Bad debts see *uncollectible accounts.*

Balance sheet a financial statement that reports assets, liabilities, and owner's equity on a specific date. (p. 13)

Bank statement a report of deposits, withdrawals, and bank balances sent to a depositor by a bank. (p. 125)

Bill of exchange see *draft.*

Bill of lading a receipt signed by the authorized agent of a transportation company for merchandise received that also serves as a contract for the delivery of the merchandise. (p. 507)

Blank endorsement an endorsement consisting only of the endorser's signature. (p. 121)

Board of directors a group of persons elected by the stockholders to manage a corporation. (p. 639)

Book inventory see *perpetual inventory.*

Book value the difference between an asset's account balance and its related contra account balance. (p. 528)

Book value of a plant asset the original cost of a plant asset minus accumulated depreciation. (p. 553)

Book value of accounts receivable the difference between the balance of Accounts Receivable and its contra account, Allowance for Uncollectible Accounts. (p. 528)

C

Capital the account used to summarize the owner's equity in a business. (p. 9)

Capital stock total shares of ownership in a corporation. (p. 462)

Cash discount a deduction from the invoice amount, allowed by a vendor to encourage early payment. (p. 467)

Cash over a petty cash on hand amount that is more than a recorded amount. (p. 470)

Cash payments journal a special journal used to record only cash payment transactions. (p. 229)

Cash receipts journal a special journal used to record only cash receipt transactions. (p. 259)

Cash sale a sale in which cash is received for the total amount of the sale at the time of the transaction. (p. 259)

Cash short a petty cash on hand amount that is less than a recorded amount. (p. 470)

Charge sale see *sale on account.*

Chart of accounts a list of accounts used by a business. (p. 45)

Check a business form ordering a bank to pay cash from a bank account. (p. 67)

Checking account a bank account from which payments can be ordered by a depositor. (p. 120)

Closing entries journal entries used to prepare temporary accounts for a new fiscal period. (p. 197)

Commercial invoice a statement prepared by the seller of merchandise addressed to the buyer, showing a detailed listing and description of merchandise sold, including prices and terms. (p. 507)

Component percentage the percentage relationship between one financial statement item and the total that includes that item. (p. 178)

Contra account an account that reduces a related account on a financial statement. (p. 467)

Contract of sale a document that details all the terms agreed to by seller and buyer for a sales transaction. (p. 507)

Controlling account an account in a general ledger that summarizes all accounts in a subsidiary ledger. (p. 272)

Corporation an organization with the legal rights of a person and which may be owned by many persons. (p. 462)

Correcting entry a journal entry made to correct an error in the ledger. (p. 109)

Cost of goods sold see *cost of merchandise sold.*

Cost of merchandise the price a business pays for goods it purchases to sell. (p. 223)

Cost of merchandise sold the total original price of all merchandise sold during a fiscal period. (p. 400)

Credit an amount recorded on the right side of a T account. (p. 42)

Credit card sale a sale in which a credit card is used for the total amount of the sale at the time of the transaction. (p. 259)

Credit memorandum a form prepared by the vendor showing the amount deducted for returns and allowances. (p. 501)

Creditor a person or organization to whom a liability is owed. (p. 596)

Current assets cash and other assets expected to be exchanged for cash or consumed within a year. (p. 546)

Current liabilities liabilities due within a short time, usually within a year. (p. 600)

Current ratio a ratio that shows the numeric relationship of current assets to current liabilities. (p. 675)

Customer a person or business to whom merchandise or services are sold. (p. 252)

D

Date of a note the day a note is signed. (p. 596)

Debit an amount recorded on the left side of a T account. (p. 42)

Debit card a bank card that, when making purchases, automatically deducts the amount of the purchase from the checking account of the cardholder. (p. 133)

Debit memorandum a form prepared by the customer showing the price deduction taken by the customer for returns and allowances. (p. 475)

Declaring a dividend action by a board of directors to distribute corporate earnings to stockholders. (p. 639)

Declining-balance method of depreciation multiplying the book value by a constant depreciation rate at the end of each fiscal period. (p. 564)

Depreciation expense the portion of a plant asset's cost that is transferred to an expense account in each fiscal period during a plant asset's useful life. (p. 551)

Dishonored check a check that a bank refuses to pay. (p. 130)

Dishonored note a note that is not paid when due. (p. 607)

Distribution of net income statement a partnership financial statement showing net income or loss distribution to partners. (p. 410)

Dividends earnings distributed to stockholders. (p. 638)

Double-entry accounting the recording of debit and credit parts of a transaction. (p. 66)

Doubtful accounts see *uncollectible accounts.*

Draft a written, signed, and dated order from one party ordering another party, usually a bank, to pay money to a third party. (p. 507)

E

Electronic funds transfer a computerized cash payments system that uses electronic impulses to transfer funds. (p. 132)

Employee earnings record a business form used to record details affecting payments made to an employee. (p. 324)

Endorsement a signature or stamp on the back of a check transferring ownership. (p. 121)

Endorsement in full see *special endorsement.*

Entry information for each transaction recorded in a journal. (p. 66)

Equities financial rights to the assets of a business. (p. 7)

Estimated salvage value the amount an owner expects to receive when a plant asset is removed from use (p. 551)

Exhibit see *supporting schedule.*

Expense a decrease in owner's equity resulting from the operation of a business. (p. 27)

Exports goods or services shipped out of a seller's home country to a foreign country. (p. 506)

F

Face amount see *principal of a note.*

Federal unemployment tax a federal tax used for state and federal administrative expenses of the unemployment program. (p. 346)

Fifo see *first-in, first-out inventory costing method.*

File maintenance the procedure for arranging accounts in a general ledger, assigning account numbers, and keeping records current. (p. 98)

First-in, first-out inventory costing method using the price of merchandise purchased first to calculate the cost of merchandise sold first. (p. 580)

Fiscal period the length of time for which a business summarizes and reports financial information. (p. 150)

G

Gain on plant assets revenue that results when a plant asset is sold for more than book value. (p. 561)

General amount column a journal amount column that is not headed with an account title. (p. 229)

General journal a journal with two amount columns in which all kinds of entries can be recorded. (p. 66)

General ledger a ledger that contains all accounts needed to prepare financial statements. (p. 97)

Gross earnings see *total earnings*.

Gross pay see *total earnings*.

Gross profit method of estimating inventory estimating inventory by using the previous year's percentage of gross profit on operations. (p. 585)

Gross profit on sales the revenue remaining after cost of merchandise sold has been deducted. (p. 402)

I

Imports goods or services bought from a foreign country and brought into a buyer's home country. (p. 506)

Income statement a financial statement showing the revenue and expenses for a fiscal period. (p. 160)

Interest an amount paid for the use of money for a period of time. (p. 597)

Interest expense the interest accrued on money borrowed. (p. 601)

Interest income the interest earned on money loaned. (p. 606)

Interest rate of a note the percentage of the principal that is paid for use of the money. (p. 596)

Inventory the amount of goods on hand. (p. 376)

Inventory record a form used during a periodic inventory to record information about each item of merchandise on hand. (p. 577)

Invoice a form describing the goods or services sold, the quantity, and the price. (p. 67)

J

Journal a form for recording transactions in chronological order. (p. 64)

Journalizing recording transactions in a journal. (p. 64)

L

Last-in, first-out inventory costing method using the price of merchandise purchased last to calculate the cost of merchandise sold first. (p. 581)

Ledger a group of accounts. (p. 97)

Letter of credit a letter issued by a bank guaranteeing that a named individual or business will be paid a specified amount, provided stated conditions are met. (p. 507)

Liability an amount owed by a business (p. 7)

Lifo see *last-in, first-out inventory costing method*.

List price a business's printed or catalog price. (p. 466)

Long-term liabilities liabilities owed for more than a year. (p. 672)

Loss on plant assets the loss that results when a plant asset is sold for less than book value. (p. 562)

M

Maker of a note the person or business who signs a note and thus promises to make payment. (p. 596)

Markup the amount added to the cost of merchandise to establish the selling price. (p. 223)

Maturity date of a note the date a note is due. (p. 596)

Maturity value the amount that is due on the maturity date of a note. (p. 597)

Medicare tax a federal tax paid for hospital insurance. (p. 320)

Memorandum a form on which a brief message is written describing a transaction. (p. 68)

Merchandise goods that a merchandising business purchases to sell. (p. 222)

Merchandise inventory the amount of goods on hand for sale to customers. (p. 376)

Merchandising business a business that purchases and sells goods. (p. 222)

N

Net income the difference between total revenue and total expenses when total revenue is greater. (p. 161)

Net loss the difference between total revenue and total expenses when total expenses is greater. (p. 162)

Net pay the total earnings paid to an employee after payroll taxes and other deductions. (p. 323)

Net purchases total purchases less purchases discount and purchases returns and allowances. (p. 665)

Net sales total sales less sales discount and sales returns and allowances. (p. 665)

Nominal account see *temporary accounts*.

Normal balance the side of the account that is increased. (p. 42)

Note see *notes payable*.

Notes payable promissory notes signed by a business and given to a creditor. (p. 596)

Notes receivable promissory notes that a business accepts from customers. (p. 605)

Number of a note the number assigned to identify a specific note. (p. 596)

O

Opening an account writing an account title and number on the heading of an account. (p. 99)

Owner's equity the amount remaining after the value of all liabilities is subtracted from the value of all assets. (p. 7)

Owners' equity statement a financial statement that summarizes the changes in owners' equity during a fiscal period. (p. 412)

P

Par value a value assigned to a share of stock and printed on the stock certificate. (p. 668)

Partner each member of a partnership. (p. 220)

Partnership a business in which two or more persons combine their assets and skills. (p. 220)

Pay period the period covered by a salary payment. (p. 310)

Payee of a note the person or business to whom the amount of a note is payable. (p. 596)

Payroll the total amount earned by all employees for a pay period. (p. 310)

Payroll register a business form used to record payroll information. (p. 322)

Payroll taxes taxes based on the payroll of a business. (p. 316)

Periodic inventory a merchandise inventory determined by counting, weighing, or measuring items of merchandise on hand. (p. 576)

Permanent accounts accounts used to accumulate information from one fiscal period to the next. (p. 197)

Perpetual inventory a merchandise inventory determined by keeping a continuous record of increases, decreases, and balance on hand. (p. 576)

Personal property all property not classified as real property. (p. 549)

Petty cash an amount of cash kept on hand and used for making small payments. (p. 135)

Petty cash slip a form showing proof of a petty cash payment. (p. 136)

Physical inventory see *periodic inventory.*

Plant asset record an accounting form on which a business records information about each plant asset. (p. 555)

Plant assets assets that will be used for a number of years in the operation of a business. (p. 546)

Post-closing trial balance a trial balance prepared after the closing entries are posted. (p. 207)

Postdated check a check with a future date on it. (p. 122)

Posting transferring information from a journal entry to a ledger account. (p. 101)

Principal of a note the original amount of a note; sometimes referred to as face amount of a note. (p. 596)

Promissory note a written and signed promise to pay a sum of money at a specified time. (p. 596)

Proprietorship a business owned by one person. (p. 6)

Proving cash determining that the amount of cash agrees with the balance of the cash account in the accounting records. (p. 109)

Purchase invoice an invoice used as a source document for recording a purchase on account transaction. (p. 225)

Purchases allowance credit allowed for part of the purchase price of merchandise that is not returned, resulting in a decrease in the customer's accounts payable. (p. 475)

Purchases discount a cash discount on purchases taken by a customer. (p. 467)

Purchases journal a special journal used to record only purchases of merchandise on account. (p. 224)

Purchases return credit allowed for the purchase price of returned merchandise, resulting in a decrease in the customer's accounts payable. (p. 475)

R

Ratio a comparison between two numbers showing how many times one number exceeds the other. (p. 675)

Real accounts see *permanent accounts.*

Real estate see *real property.*

Real property land and anything attached to the land. (p. 549)

Receipt a business form giving written acknowledgement for cash received. (p. 68)

Residual value see *estimated salvage value.*

Restrictive endorsement an endorsement restricting further transfer of a check's ownership. (p. 121)

Retail merchandising business a merchandising business that sells to those who use or consume the goods. (p. 222)

Retained earnings an amount earned by a corporation and not yet distributed to stockholders. (p. 638)

Revenue an increase in owner's equity resulting from the operation of a business. (p. 26)

Reversing entry an entry made at the beginning of one fiscal period to reverse an adjusting entry made in the previous fiscal period. (p. 620)

S

Salary the money paid for employee services. (p. 310)

Sale on account a sale for which cash will be received at a later date. (p. 26)

Sales allowance credit allowed a customer for part of the sales price of merchandise that is not returned, resulting in a decrease in the vendor's accounts receivable. (p. 501)

Sales discount a cash discount on sales. (p. 496)

Sales invoice an invoice used as a source document for recording a sale on account. (p. 67)

Sales journal a special journal used to record only sales of merchandise on account. (p. 255)

Sales return credit allowed a customer for the sales price of returned merchandise, resulting in a decrease in the vendor's accounts receivable. (p. 501)

Sales slip see *sales invoice*.

Sales tax a tax on a sale of merchandise or services. (p. 252)

Salvage value see *estimated salvage value*.

Schedule of accounts payable a listing of vendor accounts, account balances, and total amount due all vendors. (p. 281)

Schedule of accounts receivable a listing of customer accounts, account balances, and total amount due from all customers. (p. 289)

Scrap value see *estimated salvage value*.

Service business a business that performs an activity for a fee. (p. 6)

Share of stock each unit of ownership in a corporation. (p. 462)

Sight draft a draft payable on sight when the holder presents it for payment. (p. 507)

Social security tax a federal tax paid for old-age, survivors, and disability insurance. (p. 320)

Sole proprietorship see *proprietorship*.

Source document a business paper from which information is obtained for a journal entry. (p. 66)

Special amount column a journal amount column headed with an account title. (p. 224)

Special endorsement an endorsement indicating a new owner of a check. (p. 121)

Special journal a journal used to record only one kind of transaction. (p. 223)

State unemployment tax a state tax used to pay benefits to unemployed workers. (p. 346)

Statement of stockholders' equity a financial statement that shows changes in a corporation's ownership for a fiscal period. (p. 668)

Stock ledger a file of stock records for all merchandise on hand. (p. 578)

Stock record a form used to show the kind of merchandise, quantity received, quantity sold, and balance on hand. (p. 578)

Stockholder an owner or one of more shares of a corporation. (p. 638)

Straight-line method of depreciation charging an equal amount of depreciation expense for a plant asset in each year of useful life. (p. 552)

Subsidiary ledger a ledger that is summarized in a single general ledger account. (p. 272)

Supplementary report see *supporting schedule*.

Supporting schedule a report prepared to give details about an item on a principal financial statement. (p. 419)

T

T account an accounting device used to analyze transactions. (p. 42)

Tax base the maximum amount of earnings on which a tax is calculated. (p. 320)

Temporary accounts accounts used to accumulate information until it is transferred to the owner's capital account. (p. 197)

Terms of sale an agreement between a buyer and a seller about payment for merchandise. (p. 225)

Glossary

Time draft a draft that is payable at a fixed or determinable future time after it is accepted. (p. 509)

Time of a note the days, months, or years from the date of signing until a note is to be paid. (p. 596)

Total earnings the total pay due for a pay period before deductions. (p. 314)

Trade acceptance a form signed by a buyer at the time of a sale of merchandise in which the buyer promises to pay the seller a specified sum of money, usually at a stated time in the future. (p. 510)

Trade discount a reduction in the list price granted to customers. (p. 466)

Transaction a business activity that changes assets, liabilities, or owner's equity. (p. 9)

Trial balance a proof of the equality of debits and credits in a general ledger. (p. 151)

U

Uncollectible accounts accounts receivable that cannot be collected. (p. 526)

V

Vendor a business from which merchandise is purchased or supplies or other assets are bought. (p. 223)

W

Weighted-average inventory costing method using the average cost of beginning inventory plus merchandise purchased during a fiscal period to calculate the cost of merchandise sold. (p. 582)

Wholesale merchandising business a business that buys and resells merchandise to retail merchandising businesses. (p. 222)

Withdrawals assets taken out of a business for the owner's personal use. (p. 28)

Withholding allowance a deduction from total earnings for each person legally supported by a taxpayer, including the employee. (p. 317)

Work sheet a columnar accounting form used to summarize the general ledger information needed to prepare financial statements. (p. 150)

Working capital the amount of total current assets less total current liabilities. (p. 675)

Writing off an account canceling the balance of a customer account because the customer does not pay. (p. 533)

A

Account
accounts payable, 224, 231, 250
asset, 76–77
balance sheet, 3
cash, 10–11, 78, 99, 101
chart of, 3, 45, 97
checking, 120–124
closing entries for, 678–679
contra, 467
with credit balance, 678
with debit balance, 679
defined, 9
form, 94, 96
general ledger. *See* General ledger account
income statement (closing entries for), 199–200
income summary, 198. *See also* Income summary account
increases and decreases in, 43
on. *See* On account
opening in general ledger, 99
owner's drawing, 202
owner's equity, 51–56
permanent, 197
posting to wrong, 165
reopening written off, 535–536
revenue, sales, 76
sales tax payable, 252
T. *See* T account
temporary, 197
transactions' affect on, 11, 45–50
writing off, 533

Accountant. *See also* Accounting at Work; Accounting in Your Career; Careers

Account balance, 9, 42

Account form, 94, 96

Accounting
for accrued revenue and expenses, 616–635
in ancient civilizations, 102
careers in. *See* Accounting in Your Career; Accounting at Work; Careers

defined, 4
double-entry, 66, 77
history and, 480
for inventory, 574–593
legal issues. *See* Legal Issues in Accounting
for merchandising business, 218–689
for notes and interest, 594–615
for partnership, 218–457
for performing artist, 77
for plant assets and depreciation, 546–573
for proprietorship, 1–217
for service business, 1–217
standard practices in, 84
for uncorrectable accounts receivable, 526–545

Accounting cycle, 95
for corporation, 682
defined, 208
manual vs. automated, 173
for merchandising business, 446, 682
for partnership, 446
for service business, 208
steps in, 208
See also Accounting period cycle

Accounting equation, 6–8
analyzing, 40
balance sheet and, 30–31, 182
business activities and change in, 9–12
cash payments and, 10
defined, 7
transactions and, 26–29, 48

Accounting estimates, 539

Accounting information, 172

Accounting period cycle, 150, 159, 174, 192, 208, 374, 445, 642, 662, 665, 671. *See also* Accounting cycle

Accounting procedures
for corporation, 458–689
for partnership, 218–457
for proprietorship, 1–217

Accounting records, 4

Accounting system
in ancient China, 54
defined, 4
design of, 393

Accounting at Work
Aguirre, Pamela, 468
Chuang, John, 227
Cousins, Glenda, 384
Crawford, James W., 627
Stanhoff, Tracy, 529
Stanton, Daryl, 162
Velasquez, Arthur R., 603
Witherspoon, Mary, 74

Accounting in Your Career
adding a department, 41
business loans, 595
business opportunity, 25
business taxes, 637
cash payments, 221, 461
company benefits, 311
competitive secrets, 547
computerized system, 193
credit problems, 527
credit terms, 491
employee costs, 339
financial reporting, 175
financial statements, 429
growing the business, 253
inventory, 575
job interview, 5
journalizing, 65
keeping your job, 273
managing cash and checking account, 119
new accounting system, 663
notes payable spreadsheet, 617
posting, 95
restaurant partnership, 399
work sheets, 149, 373

Account number
automated accounting, 63
defined, 97
three-digit, 97–98

Accounts payable
account, 224, 231, 250
as A/P, 49
new accounts, 275
schedule of, 281

Accounts payable ledger, 272
completed, 280

forms, 275
posting to, 274–277
posting from cash payments journal to, 278, 472
posting credit entry from general journal to, 279
posting from purchases journal to, 276, 464
proving, 281

Accounts receivable, 254, 261
account, 77
automated accounting, 270–271
book value of, 528
posting entries for collecting written-off, 537
schedule of, 289, 504
uncollectible, 526–545, 533–538

Accounts receivable ledger, 272
completed, 288
forms, 284
posting to, 283–286
posting from cash receipts journal to, 287, 498
posting from sales journal to, 285, 493
proving, 289
unused account, 284

Account title, 9, 72, 97

Accrued expenses, 623–628
automated accounting, 634–635
reversing entry for, 620

Accrued interest expense
adjusting entry for, 624
defined, 623
reversing entry for, 625

Accrued interest income, 618, 620

Accrued revenue, 616, 618–622
automated accounting, 634–635
reversing entry for, 620

Accumulated depreciation, 553

Accuracy, importance of, 293

Adequate disclosure, 174, 192, 398, 546, 574, 616, 624, 665

Adjusting entries
for accrued interest expense, 623–624

for accrued interest income, 618–619
automated accounting, 215, 634, 688
for corporation, 677
defined, 192
for depreciation expense, 557, 646
federal income tax expense, 648, 650
interest expense, 646
interest income, 643
for merchandise inventory, 377–378, 431, 644
for partnership, 428–433
for prepaid insurance, 195, 383–384, 432, 645
recording, 194–196, 430–433
for supplies, 155, 194, 381–382, 432, 645
for uncollectible accounts expense, 530–531, 643
on work sheet, 157, 376, 381–385, 431, 642
See also Adjustment

Adjustment, 154. *See also* Adjusting entries

Advising bank, 428

Africa
abacus use, 299
accountancy in, 237
accounting in ancient, 102

Aguirre, Pamela, 468

Allowance
method of recording losses from uncollectible accounts, 528
purchases, 475

Alternative fiscal years, 421

American Business Women's Association (ABWA), 74

Annual report, 168, 486, 629

Applied Communication
accounting decisions, 172
accounting procedures documentation, 658
annual report, 486
career research, 91
entrepreneur, 62

essay, 687
fax memorandum, 115
financial statements, 189
graph of sales growth, 613
interview, 591
letter about damaged goods, 308, 519
letter of complaint, 249
letter explaining depreciation, 572
letter of first-notice, 396
local issues, 142
memorandum about uncollectible account, 542
opinion memo, 632
price table, 269
productivity analysis, 335
public speaking, 454
report, 21, 425
resume, 37
tax research, 365
World Wide Web, 214

Asia Minor, accounting in ancient, 102

Assessed value, 549

Asset
account, 76, 78, 154
acquisition, 548
assessed value, 549
on balance sheet, 13, 183, 671
categories 546
current, 546
defined, 7
plant, 546
record, 555

ATM card, 340

Auditing, 210, 655

Automated Accounting
adjusting and closing entries for accrued revenues and expenses, 634–635
adjusting and closing entries for proprietorships, 215
adjustments in, 160, 381
calculating notes and interest using planning tools, 614–615
cash control systems, 142–143
computer operation basics, 22–23

computer safety tips, 22
correction of errors, 309
for depreciation, 573
end-of-fiscal-period work for corporation, 688–689
end-of-fiscal-period work for partnership, 455
financial statements, 190, 426–427
general ledger accounting, 116–117
graphs, 397
inventory systems, 592–593
language and skills for, 38–39
loan planner, 660–661
manual accounting cycle vs. automated accounting cycle, 173
mouse and keyboard operations, 23
payroll accounting, 336–337
payroll taxes and journal entries, 366–367
planning tools for notes and interest, 614–615
purchases and cash payment entries using special journals, 250–251, 487
recording transactions, 92–93
sales and cash receipts using special journals, 270–271, 520
software database, 63
uncollectible accounts and write-offs, 544–545

Automated Accounting 7.0 software, 38–39

B

Babylonia
abacus use, 299
banking in, 102

Bad debt, 526. *See also* Uncollectible accounts

Balance
account, 42
trial, 151. *See also* Trial balance

Balance sheet, 181, 416–420

accrued interest expense adjustment on, 624
analyzing, 675
assets section, 182, 671
automated accounting, 190, 426–427
for corporation, 671–676
defined, 13
extending account balances on work sheet, 159
heading, 181
information on work sheet, 181–185, 416
liabilities section, 182, 672
for merchandising business, 417
owner's equity section, 183–184
preparing, 14, 30, 671–676
reporting changed accounting equation on, 30–31
reporting financial information on, 13–15
sections of, 13
stockholders' equity section, 673
supporting schedules for, 419

Banking
branch manager, 384
international transactions, 428
payroll account, 327
reconciliation, 125–130
service charge, 127–128

Bank statement, 125–126

Batching process, 223

Bill of lading, 507

Blank endorsement, 121

Board of directors, 639

Book value
of accounts receivable, 528
defined, 528
of plant asset, 553, 559, 561–562

Borrowing, 594

Business entity, 9, 639
corporation, 462. *See also* Corporation
partnership, 220. *See also* Partnership
proprietorship, 6. *See also* Proprietorship

Business ethics, 7. *See also* Professional Business Ethics

Business expenses, ethics and, 665

Business forms, 265

Business plan, 431

Business transaction. *See* Transaction

Business year
natural, 421
See also Calendar year; Fiscal year; Year

Buying supplies
on account, 73
for cash, 230

C

Calculator tape, 68, 76

Calendar year, 168, 198. *See also* Business year; Year

Canceled check, 128

Capital
defined, 9
account, partners', 412
stock, 462, 668

Careers
accounting clerk, 25, 41, 65, 273
accounting department assistant, 149, 617
accounting manager, 663
administrative assistant, 5, 119, 149
banking, 384
bookkeeper, 95
certified public accountant, 627
chief executive officer, 227, 468
credit manager, 527
financial analyst, 617
gas balancing accountant, 74
internal auditor, 461
internship, 162
inventory specialist, 575
job interview, 5
junior accountant in accounting firm, 373

office clerk, 5
office manager, 175, 253
research about, 91
resume, 37, 99
senior accountant, 547
senior financial accountant, 162
See also Accounting at Work;
    Accounting in Your Career

Cash
business use of, 118
buying supplies for, 230
depositing, 120
for expenses, 27, 78
for insurance, 47, 72
from owner as investment, 45,
    69
to owner for personal use, 55,
    57, 80
paid on account, 28, 54, 74,
    76–81
paid for supplies, 10, 46, 70
paying, 10
petty, 135–138
proving, 109, 263
purchasing merchandise for,
    230
receiving, 9
from sales, 26, 51, 76
sales of merchandise for, 259
systems to control, 118–144

Cash controls, 118–144

Cash discount, 467

Cash flows, statement of, 684

Cash payments
on account, 231, 467–468
of expense, 232
journalizing using cash
    payments journal, 229
to replenish petty cash, 234,
    471
untangling, 221

Cash payments journal
automated accounting, 250
carrying totals forward, 236
defined, 229
end-of-month activities, 238
journalizing cash papyments
    using, 229

posting to accounts payable
    ledger from, 278
posting from general amount
    column to general ledger,
    292
posting separate amounts from,
    472
posting total of special amount
    columns to general ledger,
    300–301, 473
recording purchases transactions
    using, 466
starting new page, 237

Cash purchases, journalizing cash
    payments for, 466

Cash receipts
on account, 261, 496–497
journalizing from time drafts,
    510
journalizing using cash receipts
    journal, 259–264
journalizing using special jour-
    nals, 252–271
recording using cash receipts
    journal, 496–500

Cash receipts journal, 259
automated accounting,
    270–271, 520–521
defined, 259
journalizing cash receipts using,
    259–264
posting to accounts receivable
    ledger from, 287, 498
posting to general ledger from,
    499
posting totals of special amount
    columns to general ledger,
    298
proving, 262
recording cash receipts using,
    496–500
ruling, 262
totaling, 262

Cash sale, 259

Cash withdrawals, by partners,
    235

Certified public accountant (CPA),
    139

Chart of accounts, 97
in African accountancy, 237
automated accounting, 63,
    116–117
as COA, 49
defined, 45
designing, 112
Encore Music, 3
Omni Import, 219
preparing, 96–100
Winning Edge, 459

Charts, automated accounting,
    397

Check, 67, 78
canceled, 128
completed, 122
defined, 67
dishonored, 130–131
payroll, 328
postdated, 122
total net pay, 327
voided, 123

Checking account, 120–124

Check stub
completed, 122
recording bank service charge
    on, 127
recording deposit on, 120
recording dishonored check on,
    130

Chief financial officer (CFO), 242

China
abacus use, 299
accounting in ancient, 54
business day in, 281
feng shui philosophy, 182

Chronological record, 66

Chuang, John, 227

Closing entries, 197–203
for accounts with credit balance,
    678
for accounts with debit balance,
    679
for accrued expenses, 625
for accrued revenue, 620
automated accounting, 215,
    634, 689

Interim financial statements, 186

Internal control, categories of, 303

Internal Revenue Service (IRS)
Electronic Federal Tax Payment system (EFTPS), 354
Form 8109, 354–355, 357
Form 940, 357
Form 941, 350–351
Form W-2, 349
Form W-3, 352
Form W-4, 317
partnership returns to, 414
proprietorship rules, 57
reporting requirements, 168
responsibilities of, 360
tax rate table, 649
withholding funds for, 330
withholding tables, 318–319

International business
work day, 281
transactions, 428
See also Global Perspective

International Chamber of Commerce, 506

International quality standards, 352

International sales, 506
of goods, 428
processing, 507
journalizing, 508

Inventory, 376
accounting for, 574–593
estimating, 585–587
most efficient quantity of, 576
periodic method, 448, 576
perpetual method, 448, 576
record, 577
See also Merchandise inventory

Inventory costing method
comparing, 583
first-in, first-out, 580
last-in, first-out, 581
weighted-average, 582

Investment, cash from owner as, 45, 69

Invoice, 67
commercial, 507

defined, 67
memorandum attached to, 240
purchase, 225
sales, 255

IRS. *See* Internal Revenue Service

J

Job interview, 5

Journal
cash receipts, 259
defined, 64
entry, 69. *See also* Entries; Journal entry
page. *See also* Journal page, purchases; Purchases journal
posting to general ledger from, 291–295
special, 223
special columns, 231
starting new page, 82–85
transactions in automated accounting, 309
using, 66
See also General journal

Journal entry, 69
in automated accounting, 309
to record correcting entry, 110
See also Entry

Journalizing
accepting note for extension of time on account receivable, 605
bank service charge, 128
buying supplies on account, 241
cash payment on account, 231, 467–468
cash payment for cash purchases, 466
cash payment for expense, 78, 232
cash payment for insurance, 72
cash payment for maturity value of note payable, 601
cash payment to replenish petty cash, 137, 234
cash payment to replenish petty cash fund, 471

cash payment using cash payments journal, 229–233
cash receipts on account, 79, 261, 497
cash receipts from time drafts, 510
cash receipts using cash receipts journal, 259–264
cash receipts for maturity value of note receivable, 606
cash receipts from note payable, 600
cash receipts from owner as investment, 69
cash receipts from sales, 76
cash for supplies, 70
cash withdrawals by partners, 235
closing entry for accounts with credit balance, 678
closing entry for dividends, 680
closing entry for net income to retained earnings, 680
correcting entry, 110, 503
debit card transaction, 133
defined, 64
depreciation expense, 555–558
dishonored check, 131
dishonored note receivable, 607
electronic funds transfer, 132
employee income tax payment, 356
employer payroll taxes, 347
entry to replenish petty cash, 137
federal unemployment tax payment, 358
international sale, 508
Medicare tax payment, 356
merchandise withdrawals by partners, 242
payment of dividends, 640
payroll payment, 342
purchase of merchandise on account, 226
purchases on account, 463
purchases returns and allowances, 476
purchases using purchases journal, 222–228
reversing entries, 681

sale on account, 254–258, 492
sales returns and allowances, 502
services sold on account, 77
signing note payable for extension of time, 602
social security tax payment, 356
standards for, 65
supplies bought on account, 73
time drafts, 509
transactions affecting owner's equity, 76–81
uncollectible account receivable, 533

Journal page, 82
with posting completed, 104
proving, 257

L

Last-in, first-out inventory costing method, 581

Law
ethics and, 7
See also Legal Issues in Accounting

Leases, 568

Ledger
automated accounting software, 63
defined, 97
stock, 578
subsidiary, 272

Legal Issues in Accounting
dissolving a corporation, 566
dissolving a partnership, 316
dissolving a proprietorship, 80
forming a corporation, 536
forming a proprietorship, 80
forming a partnership, 254
limited liability partnership (LLP), 372
piercing the corporate veil, 478
See also Law, ethics and

Lending, 594

Letter of credit, 428, 507, 510

Liabilities
on balance sheet, 13, 183, 672
current, 600, 672
defined, 7
long-term, 672

Lifo. *See* Last-in, first-out (lifo) inventory costing method, 580

Limited liability
of corporation, 536
partnership (LLP), 372

List price, 466

Loan
choosing, 595
Small Business Administration, 51

Loan Planner (Automated Accounting), 660–661

Long-term liabilities, 672

Loss
net, 179
on plant assets, 562
recording from uncollectible accounts, 528

M

Manual accounting
automated accounting vs., 38–39
cycle, 173

Markup, 223

Matching expenses with revenue, 154–156, 176, 194, 197, 381, 434–436, 443, 528–529, 529, 564, 581–582, 582, 616, 623

Maturity date of promissory note, 598

Maturity value, 597
of note payable, 601
of note receivable, 606

Medicare tax, 320, 330, 344, 354, 356

Memorandum, 68
attached to invoice, 240
for buying supplies on account, 240
for correcting entry, 109
faxing, 115
objective evidence, 73

Merchandise
cost of, 223, 583
defined, 222
purchasing, 223
sales on account, 254
sales for cash, 259
withdrawals by partners, 242

Merchandise inventory, 376
account, 250
adjusting entry for, 431, 644
adjustment, 377–378
cost of, 580–584
importance of, 574
quantity of, 576–579
See also Inventory

Merchandising business
accounting cycle for, 446, 682
automated accounting for, 487–488
balance sheet for, 417–418
corporation as, 458–689
defined, 222
income statement for, 400–404
partnership as, 218–457
retail, 222
wholesale, 222
work sheet for, 372–397

Metric system, 157

Mexico, international sales to, 507

Multicultural awareness. *See* Cultural Diversity

N

National Association of Black Accountants, 13

Natural business year, 168, 421

CHAPTER 14
p. 338: © Bruce Forster/Tony Stone Images; p. 339: © Greg Grosse/Location courtesy of Quality Central Hotel & Suites, Cincinnati, Ohio; p. 344: © John Elk/Stock, Boston; p. 346: © R. A. Clevenger/Westlight; p. 355: © Richard Pasley/Stock, Boston; p. 357: © R. Ian Lloyd/Westlight

CHAPTER 15
p. 373: © Greg Grosse/Location courtesy of St. Xavier High School, Cincinnati, Ohio; p. 376: © Lawrence Migdale/Stock, Boston; p. 377: Photo courtesy of Pier 1 Imports; p. 383: © John Eastcott/Yva Momatiuk/Photo Researchers; p. 384: © Fred M. Middendorf; p. 387: © Mark Adams/Westlight

CHAPTER 16
p. 399: © Ian O'Leary/Tony Stone Images; p. 406: © Bob Daemmrich/Stock, Boston; p. 408: The Nature Company; p. 414: The Nature Company

CHAPTER 17
p. 429: © Tom McCarthy/PhotoEdit; p. 431: The Bombay Company; p. 437: Photo courtesy of Pier 1 Imports; p. 441: Photo courtesy of Pier 1 Imports

CHAPTER 18
p. 461: Photo courtesy of Maxis, a wholly owned subsidiary of Electronic Arts; p. 462: © Greg Grosse

CHAPTER 19
p. 491: © Greg Grosse/Location courtesy of Ohio Valley Audio—East, Cincinnati, Ohio; p. 496: 1998 Trek Bicycle Corporation; p. 498: Photo courtesy of Golfsmith International, Inc.; p. 519: Tubbs Snowshoes, Stowe, VT, 800-882-2748

CHAPTER 20
p. 527: © Geoff Tompkinson/SPL/Photo Researchers; p. 542: Courtesy of K2 Snowboards

CHAPTER 21
p. 547: © Quest/SPL/Photo Researchers; p. 572: Black Diamond Equipment, Ltd.

CHAPTER 22
p. 575: © Greg Grosse/Location courtesy of King Arthur's Court Toys, Cincinnati, Ohio; p. 583: Black Diamond Equipment, Ltd.

CHAPTER 23
p. 595: © David Parker/SPL/Photo Researchers; p. 596: Black Diamond Equipment, Ltd.

CHAPTER 24
p. 617: © Greg Grosse/Location courtesy of Mariemont Theatre, Cincinnati, Ohio; p. 619: Photo courtesy of Rollerblade, Inc.; p. 633: O'Brien International, Inc.

CHAPTER 25
p. 637: © Billy E. Barnes/PhotoEdit; p. 638: Rossignol Ski Company, Inc.; p. 640: MIKASA SPORTS U.S.A.; p. 642: O'Brien International, Inc.

CHAPTER 26
p. 663: © Greg Grosse; p. 672: Black Diamond Equipment, Ltd.; p. 677: Black Diamond Equipment, Ltd.